New York City

2006

Selection *of* 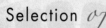 Restaurants

and Hotels

Manufacture française des pneumatiques Michelin

Société en commandite par actions au capital de 304 000 000 EUR
Place des Carmes-Déchaux – 63 Clermont-Ferrand (France)
R.C.S. Clermont-Fd B 855 200 507

© Michelin et Cie, Propriétaires-éditeurs
Dépôt légal Novembre 2005 – ISBN 2-06-711555-3

Made in: Canada

Typesetting: Nord Compo (France)
Printed in Canada: Quebecor World Inc.
Bounded in: Multi-Reliure S.F. Inc. (Canada)

Published in 2005

Please send your comments at:

Travel Publications

Michelin North America, Inc.
Travel Publications
One Parkway South
Greenville, SC 29615
TEL.: 1-800-423-0485
FAX: 1-800-378-7471
www.michelintravel.com
michelin.guides@us.michelin.com

A letter *from* Edouard MICHELIN *to* **our readers**

I am thrilled to launch our first Michelin Guide for North America. Our teams have made every effort to produce a selection that does full justice to the rich diversity of the New York City restaurant and hotel scene.

For its debut in North America, the Michelin Guide provides a comprehensive selection and rating, in all categories of comfort and prices.

As part of our meticulous and highly confidential evaluation process, Michelin inspectors – American and European – conducted anonymous visits to New York City restaurants and hotels. The Michelin inspectors are the eyes and ears of the customers, and thus their anonymity is key to ensure that they receive the same treatment as any other guest.

The decision to award a star is a collective one, based on the consensus of all inspectors who have visited a particular establishment.

Our company's two founders, Edouard and André Michelin, published the first Michelin Guide in 1900, to provide motorists with practical information about where they could service and repair their cars and find quality accommodations or a good meal. The star-rating system for outstanding restaurants was introduced in 1926.

I sincerely hope that the Michelin Guide New York City 2006 will become your favorite guide to the restaurants and hotels of the Big Apple. On behalf of all our Michelin employees, let me wish you the very best enjoyment in your New York hotel and dining experiences.

E. Michelin

Table of Contents

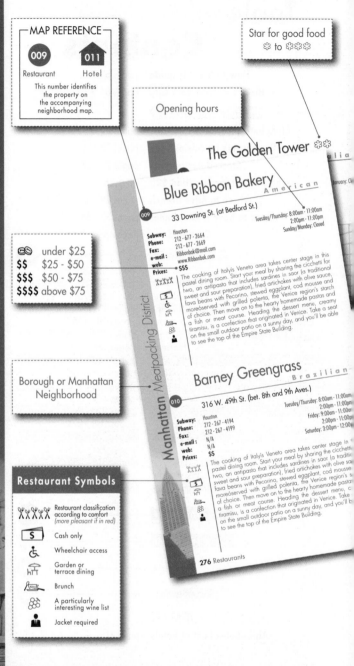

MAP REFERENCE

009 Restaurant

011 Hotel

This number identifies the property on the accompanying neighborhood map.

Star for good food
✼ to ✼✼✼

Opening hours

Borough or Manhattan Neighborhood

Restaurant Symbols

𝕏𝕏𝕏𝕏𝕏 Restaurant classification according to comfort *(more pleasant if in red)*

⑤ Cash only

♿ Wheelchair access

🍽 Garden or terrace dining

🥂 Brunch

🍷 A particularly interesting wine list

👔 Jacket required

The Golden Tower ✼✼

Italia

Blue Ribbon Bakery

American

009

33 Downing St. (at Bedford St.)

Tuesday/Thursday: 8:00am - 11:00am
2:00pm - 11:00pm
Sunday/Monday: Closed

Subway:	Houston
Phone:	212 - 677 - 2664
Fax:	212 - 677 - 2669
e-mail:	Ribbonbak@mail.com
web:	www.Ribbonbak.com
Prices:	$$$

𝕏𝕏𝕏𝕏
⑤
♿
🍽
🥂
👔

The cooking of Italyis Veneto area takes center stage in this pastel dining room. Start your meal by sharing the cicchetti for two, an antipasto that includes sardines in saor (a traditional sweet and sour preparation), fried artichokes with olive sauce, fava beans with Pecorino, stewed eggplant, cod mousse and moreöserved with grilled polenta, the Venice region's starch of choice. Then move on to the hearty homemade pastas and a fish or meat course. Heading the dessert menu, creamy tiramisu, is a confection that originated in Venice. Take a seat on the small outdoor patio on a sunny day, and you'll be able to see the top of the Empire State Building.

Barney Greengrass

Brazilian

010

316 W. 49th St. (bet. 8th and 9th Aves.)

Tuesday/Thursday: 8:00am - 11:00am
2:00pm - 11:00pm
Friday: 9:00am - 11:00pm
2:00pm - 11:00pm
Saturday: 3:00pm - 12:00am

Subway:	Houston
Phone:	212 - 267 - 4194
Fax:	212 - 267 - 4199
e-mail :	N/A
web:	N/A
Prices:	$$

𝕏𝕏𝕏𝕏
⑤
🥂
👔

The cooking of Italyis Veneto area takes center stage in pastel dining room. Start your meal by sharing the cicchetti two, an antipasto that includes sardines in saor (a traditio sweet and sour preparation), fried artichokes with olive sa fava beans with Pecorino, stewed eggplant, cod mousse moreöserved with grilled polenta, the Venice region's s of choice. Then move on to the hearty homemade pastas a fish or meat course. Heading the dessert menu, c tiramisu, is a confection that originated in Venice. Take on the small outdoor patio on a sunny day, and you'll b to see the top of the Empire State Building.

276 Restaurants

Manhattan Meatpacking District

💰	under $25
$$	$25 - $50
$$$	$50 - $75
$$$$	above $75

How to use *this* Guide

Min - Max prices
plus 13.375% taxes and $3.50 per night for occupation tax and unit fee

Louisiana Hotel

220 Sunset Ave. (E.41th St.)

Subway:	Houston	
Phone:	212 - 677 - 2664	April: Closed
Fax:	212 - 677 - 2664	
e-mail :	Blueribbonbakery@hotmail.com	
web:	www.blueribbon.us	
Prices:	rooms $235 - $368 - Suites $950	

185 rooms

Only a short walk away from Lincoln Center and Central Park, this early 20th-century structure was recently renovated and updated with early 21st-century accommodations. Flat-screen plasma TVs and Italian black-marble bathrooms will appeal to the cool in you, while the Frette robes and the complimentary Belgian chocolates left on your pillow at turndown will make you feel appropriately pampered. Nightly piano music in the lobby makes a nice prelude to a refreshing sleep in feather beds adorned with 310-thread-count Italian cotton linens. Rooms on the top three floors boast balconies and afford views of the Hudson River or the trees of Central Park. If your room doesn't have a view, take the elevator to the landscaped balcony on the 16th floor; this pleasant space is equipped with Adirondack chairs for relaxing. All this, and a 24-hour business center, too.

Manhattan Chelsea

Hotels **389**

Hotel Symbols

🏨🏨	Hotel classification according to comfort (more pleasant if in red)
185 rooms	Number of rooms and suites
♿	Wheelchair access
🏋	Exercise room
Spa	Spa
🏊	Swimming pool
🛋	Equipped conference room

A brief history *of*
New York City

From sushi to steak frites—and everything in between—New York jams a staggering world of food into about 320 square miles. With more than 17,300 eating establishments to feed its eight million residents (at last count), there's a restaurant on nearly every corner. Besides being a food-lover's paradise, the most populous city in the US is a global melting pot, a cultural magnet, an economic powerhouse. It's not for nothing that New Yorkers have a reputation for being swaggering and brash. Theirs is one great city.

It's also a relatively young one. European settlement began in earnest here in 1625, when the Dutch East India Company established the Nieuw Amsterdam trading post at the southern tip of Manhattan Island. That name, which comes from an Algonquian term meaning "island of hills," suggests that the natives ventured farther than the colonists, who for the better part of 200 years remained on flat land near the shore, behind a defensive wall (today's Wall Street).

The transfer of authority from Dutch to British hands in 1664—and the new name, after the Duke of York—was hardly earth-shattering for early New Yorkers, most of whom had little allegiance to either crown. They were here to make money.

Manhattan, as it turns out, was perfectly suited to global trade, thanks to the snug arrangement of other landmasses (today's Staten Island, New Jersey and Brooklyn) around its harbor. As port activity grew, so did friction with the British system of "taxation without representation," the bulk of which fell on importers and exporters. When war broke out, the British took over the city almost immediately, and occupied it until independence.

After briefly serving as US capital, New York established the commercial links and financial institutions that led the new nation into the Industrial Age. In 1792 brokers met under a buttonwood tree at Wall and Williams streets and founded the forerunner to the New York Stock Exchange, then based largely on handshakes. Around the turn of the century

© Martha Cooper

Manhattan's gridiron plan was laid out, and the exploding population spread northward into what was then mostly pastureland.

Then came the 363-mile-long Erie Canal, which in 1825 linked the city with the Great Lakes. Shipping costs to and from Buffalo dropped 90 percent virtually overnight, and New York became the nation's preeminent port and shipbuilding capital. The city's leading businessmen leveraged this advantage skillfully, investing their profits in new building projects, which were carried out by a steady supply of cheap labor. New York's population doubled every 20 years, fed by waves of European immigrants, who would help build the city not just with their hands but with their ideas.

These immigrants, who clustered in little enclaves around the city, contributed something else to New York's culture. From foreign lands they brought their own foodways and family recipes, which melted into the multicultural stew that is New York City. With an ever-growing influx of people from around the globe, New York maintains the ethnic diversity that still defines its restaurant scene today.

In the second half of the 20C, the city solidified its international position in industry, commerce and finance, and its skyline, newly bristling with skyscrapers, reflected that prosperity. To this day, the dynamic metropolis attracts plucky types who are looking to succeed in New York's proving ground (as the words to Frank Sinatra's famous song attest: "If I can make it here, I can make it anywhere . . ."

Of course, restaurateurs and chefs number among those risk-takers who have worked up an appetite for the Big Apple. Whether their ventures are hole-in-the-wall red-sauce joints in Little Italy, Lower East Side Kosher delis, or Uptown culinary palaces ruled by renowned chefs they all revel equally in one thing: they're all part of the dizzying dining world in New York City, the reigning U.S. capital of great cuisine.

Where to **eat**

Alphabetical list *of* Restaurants

Where To Eat

Where To Eat

Alphabetical List Of Restaurants

Restaurants *by*
Cuisine type

Where To Eat

American

American Grill	413	Henry's End	395
Bar Americain	244	Joe Allen	264
Bayard's	74	Métrazur	216
Bayou	148	New Leaf Café	374
Beacon	245	Nicole's	190
Boathouse Central Park	332	Orsay	350
Brasserie	196	Sarabeth's	265
Bridge Café	76	Sardi's	256
Bryant Park Grill	247	The Four Seasons	184
Carol's Cafe	412	The Odeon	311
DuMont	392	The Parsonage	412
Good Enough to Eat	369	21 Club	260
Harlem Grill	148	Water's Edge	403

Asian

Cendrillon	286	Spice Market	169
China Grill	248	Tao	193
Momofuku Noodle Bar	68		

Austrian

Café Sabarsky	344	Wallsé	116
Danube	298		

Belgian

Café de Bruxelles	133

Brazilian

Caviar and Banana	94	Malagueta	406
Circus	333	Zebú Grill	355

Chinese

Dim Sum Go Go	50	Oriental Garden	48
Fuleen Seafood	51	Peking Duck House	49
Golden Unicorn	48	Phoenix Garden	274
Great N.Y. Noodletown	51	Ping's Seafood	49
Mandarin Court	52	Shanghai Pavilion	352
Mr Chow	204	Shun Lee Palace	208
New Wonton Garden	52	66	312

Contemporary

Contemporary Asian (see also Asian)

Contemporary French *(see also French)*

Contemporary Japanese *(see also Japanese)*

Contemporary Mexican *(see also Mexican)*

Contemporary Thai *(see also Thai)*

Cuban

Deli

Egyptian

European

French

Marseille	253	Quatorze Bis	341
Paradou	171	Quercy	397
Park Bistro	104	Raoul's	290
Pastis	172	René Pujol	256
Payard	350	718 - Seven One Eight	407
Petrossian	240	Tournesol	409
Picholine	360		

Fusion

| Asia de Cuba | 271 | Public | 289 |
| Chubo | 161 | Stanton Social | 160 |

Gastro-Pub

| PJ Clarke's | 217 | Spotted Pig | 118 |

Greek

Avra Estiatorio	195	Periyali	98
Eliá	393	Snack	291
Estiatorio Milos	237	Taverna Kyclades	408
Ithaka	337	Trata Estiatorio	342
Molyvos	254		

Hawaiian

| Roy's New York | 74 | | |

Indian

Banjara	61	Pongal	351
Bombay Talkie	42	Sapphire	367
Däwat	199	Shaan of India	242
Dévi	95	Surya	131
Diwan	214	Tamarind	91
Jackson Diner	405	Vatan	105
Khyber Grill	215		

Italian

Abboccato	243	Barbalùc	332
Acappella	306	Barbetta	234
Acqua Pazza	244	Basta Pasta	92
Aleo	100	Becco	245
Al Di Lá	390	Bellini	195
Ama	284	Beppe	101
Ápizz	161	Bice	185
Areo	388	Bottega del Vino	186
Aroma Kitchen		Bread Tribeca	313
and Wine Bar	132	Bricco	247
Babbo	110	Bruno	197

Japanese

Korean

Latin American

Malaysian

Mediterranean

Mexican

Alamo	193	Mexicana Mama	140
Dos Caminos	102	Rocking Horse Cafe	44
Itzocan	63	Rosa Mexicano	367
Maz Mezcal	348	Zarela	219

Middle Eastern

Mamlouk	67

Moroccan

Café Mogador	61	Park Terrace Bistro	374

Persian

Persepolis	351

Russian

Firebird	238

Scandinavian

Aquavit	194

Seafood

Aquagrill	280	Mary's Fish Camp	139
Atlantic Grill	330	Oceana	180
BLT Fish	80	Ocean Grill	363
Blue Fin	246	Pearl Oyster Bar	141
Fresh	310	Shaffer City	99
Grand Central Oyster Bar	214	The Mermaid Inn	67
Jack's Luxury Oyster Bar	63	The Pearl Room	389
Le Bernardin	224	The Sea Grill	257
Lure Fishbar	280	The Water Club	270
Manhattan Ocean Club	239	Tropica	211

Southern

Ida Mae	251

Southwestern

Mesa Grill	97

Spanish

Alcala	194	La Paella	65
Bolo	94	Picasso	206
Casa Mono	101	Pipa	104
El Cid	170	Sevilla	130
El Faro	134	Suba	160

Steakhouse

Thai

Turkish

Vegetarian

Venezuelan

Vietnamese

Restaurants By Cuisine Type

Starred Restaurants

Within the selection we offer you, some restaurants deserve to be highlighted for their particularly good cuisine. When giving one, two or three Michelin stars, there are a number of things that we judge, including the quality of the ingredients, the technical skill and flair that goes into their preparation, the blend and clarity of flavors, and the balance of the menu. Just as important is the ability to produce excellent cooking time and again. We make as many visits as we need, so that our readers can be sure of quality and consistency.

A two- or three-star restaurant has to offer something very special in its cuisine; a real element of creativity, originality or "personality" that sets it apart from the rest. Three stars – our highest award – are given to the very best restaurants, where the whole dining experience is superb.

Cuisine in any style, modern or traditional, may be eligible for a star. Because we apply the same independent standards everywhere, the awards have become benchmarks of reliability and excellence in over 20 European countries, particularly in France, where we have awarded stars for almost 80 years, and where the phrase "Now that's real three-star quality!" has entered into the language.

The awarding of a star is based solely on the quality of the cuisine.

❀ ❀ ❀

Exceptional cuisine, worth a special journey

One always eats here extremely well, often superbly. Distinctive dishes precisely executed, using superlative ingredients.

		page
Alain Ducasse	XxXxX	222
Jean Georges	XxxX	358
Le Bernardin	XxXxX	224
Per Se	XxXxX	226

✿✿
Excellent cuisine, worth a detour

Skillfully and carefully crafted dishes of outstanding quality.

✿
A very good restaurant in its category

A place offering cuisine prepared to a consistently high standard.

Starred Restaurants

Where to eat *for* less than $25

Where To Eat

Where *to* **have brunch**

Where To Have Brunch

Where To Eat

Where To Have Brunch

© Jeff Greenberg/NYC & Company NYC, Inc.

Where To Have Brunch

Where to have *a*
late dinner

Restaurants taking last orders after 11:30pm at least four nights a week

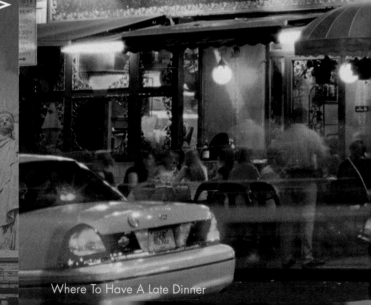

Where To Have A Late Dinner

© Jeff Greenberg/NYC & Company NYC, Inc.

Where To Have A Late Dinner

Where To Eat

About
Chelsea

enter of New York's art world and gay community, Chelsea is situated west of Avenue of the Americas (Sixth Avenue) between 14th and 30th streets. It's a place of stark contrasts—busy commercial avenues intersect quiet residential side streets, and tiny neighborhood cafes abut gargantuan dance clubs. You'll find restaurants in this eclectic neighborhood cater to a wide range of tastes, from French bistros and old-fashioned Spanish places to sushi bars and authentic Mexican eateries. Be sure to check out **Chelsea Market** *(75 Ninth Ave., between 15th & 16th Sts.; 212-243-6005; www.chelseamarket.com)*. This 1898 Nabisco factory (where the Oreo cookie was first made, in 1912) was reopened in 1997 as an urban food market. Interspersed with stores selling flowers, meats, cheeses and other gourmet essentials are cafes, bakeries, and several soup-and-sandwich shops.

A Bit of History – Chelsea got its name in 1750, when British army captain Thomas Clarke bought a farm here (bounded by 21st and 24th streets, Eighth Avenue and the Hudson River) and named it after his London neighborhood. In 1813 the property passed to Clarke's grandson **Clement Clarke Moore**, a scholar and literary figure best known for writing *A Visit from St. Nicholas* (aka *The Night before Christmas*). In the 1820s Moore helped shape the development of the district by setting aside land for park-like squares, giving the neighborhood a distinctly English feel, even as its population increasingly hailed from Germany, Italy, Scotland and Ireland. He also specified that residences had to be set back from the street behind spacious front yards. The Hudson River

© Martha Cooper

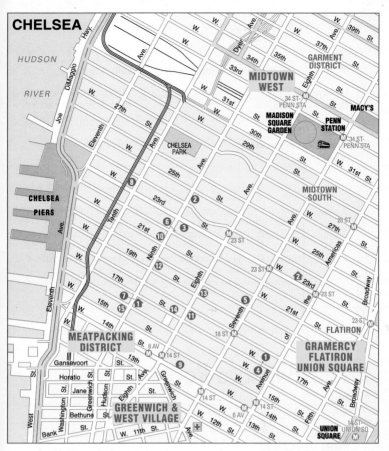

Railroad opened along 11th Avenue in 1851, spawning slaughterhouses, breweries and tenements. From about 1905 to 1915, several motion-picture studios operated here. Dock activity along the Hudson River began to decline in the 1960s, opening up warehouses and industrial spaces for new uses. Slowly artists moved in, and town houses began to be refurbished.

Chelsea's Gallery Scene – More than 100 world-class **galleries** now occupy garages and lofts on the district's western flank (concentrated between 20th and 30th streets, west of 10th Avenue), offering museum-quality exhibitions alongside up-and-coming group shows. Be sure to pick up a **Gallery Guide**, which contains a fold-out map locating all the galleries in the area. The guide also lists opening receptions, a fun way to drink in the scene. On 20th, 21st, and 22nd streets, a lovely **historic district** preserves Clement Clarke Moore's vision of elegant city living in some of Chelsea's loveliest brownstones. While you're in the neighborhood, check out the ever-evolving waterfront area, home to the mammoth Chelsea Piers recreation complex and the Hudson River Greenway.

Amuse

Contemporary

001

108 W. 18th St. (bet. Sixth & Seventh Aves.)

Subway:	18 St	Monday - Thursday noon - 11pm
Phone:	212-929-9755	Friday - Saturday noon - midnight
Fax:	212-989-2203	Closed Sunday
e-mail:	N/A	
Web:	www.amusenyc.com	
Prices:	$$	

Surrounded by furniture stores and home décor shops, Amuse fits right in with the neighborhood's avant-garde ambience. Refined, contemporary décor incorporates warm earth tones and a ceiling skylight. Creatively conceived and artfully presented items on the regularly changing menu span the United States for inspiration. And in keeping with its name (which derives from the French term *amuse-bouche*, a bite-size appetizer served before the meal to spark the appetite), Amuse organizes its menu into a variety of small plates. Check out the attractive wine cellar, which is prominently featured behind a large, lighted window on the lower level.

Biltmore Room

Contemporary

002

290 Eighth Ave. (bet. 24th & 25th Sts.)

Subway:	23 St	Monday - Sunday 5pm - 11pm
Phone:	212-807-0111	
Fax:	212-807-0074	
e-mail:	chrismedeiros@thebiltmoreroom.com	
Web:	www.thebiltmoreroom.com	
Prices:	$$$	

Splendid surroundings of Carrera and rose marble, sparkling chandeliers, and Art Deco furnishings make for an elegant soirée at the Biltmore Room (hard to believe this space once held a speakeasy!). While the decorative elements are Old World—they were salvaged from the 1913 Biltmore Hotel, which stood near Grand Central Terminal—the ever-changing menu is contemporary. Complicated and eclectic preparations incorporate influences from as far away as Asia and North Africa (think Algerian spiced roast rack of lamb with dried fig couscous and tomato-eggplant chutney). The crowd tends to be old money or terminally hip, both attracted to a place that features a private cell-phone booth.

Chelsea Bistro

003

358 W. 23rd St. (bet. Eighth & Ninth Aves.)

Subway:	23 St
Phone:	212-727-2026
Fax:	212-727-2180
e-mail:	chelseabistro@optonline.net
Web:	www.chelseabistro.com
Prices:	$$

Monday - Sunday 5pm - 11pm
Closed major holidays & Monday in summer

❌❌ The bright red façade of Chelsea Bistro stands out amid the other storefronts on this block, beckoning diners inside. An intimate atmosphere created by velvet curtains, tapestry-pattern banquettes, a brick fireplace and candlelight set the mood for a romantic evening. Cuisine sticks to French favorites like roasted free-range chicken, grilled pork chops with silky mashed potatoes, and classic desserts such as tarte Tatin, crème brûlée, and profiteroles blanketed with warm chocolate sauce. To accompany your meal, you can choose among some 250 wines; the list concentrates on French and American vintages. The glass-roofed Garden Terrace Room brings the outdoors in (without the cold!) year-round.

Da Umberto

004

107 W. 17th St. (bet. Sixth & Seventh Aves.)

Subway:	14 St
Phone:	212-989-0303
Fax:	212-989-6703
e-mail:	N/A
Web:	N/A
Prices:	$$

Monday - Saturday noon - 3pm
& 5:30pm - 11pm
Closed Sunday

❌❌ You're likely to hear as much Italian as English spoken at Da Umberto—certainly a good clue to the authenticity of the cuisine. The chic dining room fills nightly with a crowd of regulars, but whether you're a frequent diner here or not, you'll be greeted warmly. Northern Italian specialties—house-made pastas, hearty risottos, grilled fish, and the veal chop with a fresh-rosemary and cognac sauce—are complemented by a long list of daily specials to further tantalize your palate. Knowledgeable servers cater to the smartly dressed clientele, efficiently checking back on a regular basis to make sure everyone is happy.

Le Zie 2000

005

172 Seventh Ave. (bet. 20th & 21st Sts.)

Subway:	23 St	Monday - Sunday noon - 11:30pm
Phone:	212-206-8686	
Fax:	212-924-9984	
e-mail:	info@lezie.com	
Web:	www.lezie.com	
Prices:	$$	

The cooking of Italy's Veneto area takes center stage in this pastel dining room. Start your meal by sharing the cicchetti for two, an antipasto that includes sardines in saor (a traditional sweet and sour preparation), fried artichokes with olive sauce, fava beans with Pecorino, stewed eggplant, cod mousse and more—served with grilled polenta, the Venice region's starch of choice. Then move on to the hearty homemade pastas and a fish or meat course. Heading the dessert menu is creamy tiramisu, a confection that originated in Venice. Take a seat on the small outdoor patio on a sunny day, and you'll be able to see the top of the Empire State Building.

Magnifico

006

200 Ninth Ave. (bet. 22nd & 23rd Sts.)

Subway:	23 St	Monday - Saturday 5pm - 11pm
Phone:	212-633-8033	Closed Sunday
Fax:	N/A	
e-mail:	magnificorestaurant@yahoo.com	
Web:	www.magnificorestaurant.com	
Prices:	$$	

The name says it all. Inside Magnifico's bright yellow façade you'll find a cream-toned dining room where attentive service and savory regional Italian fare keep locals coming back for more. Venetian glass sconces illuminate the space, which serves as a gallery where New York City artists can display their work (yes, the paintings are available for purchase). Here the gnocchi and pastas are made fresh every day and a list of daily specials complements the generous menu. Signature dishes include pappardelle with rabbit ragu, and beet gnocchi with goat cheese and arugula. And they make their own creamy gelato for dessert. Be sure to consider the serious selection of Italian wines.

Manhattan Chelsea

Matsuri

007

363 W. 16th St. (bet. Eighth & Ninth Aves.)

Subway:	14 St	Sunday - Wednesday 6pm - midnight
Phone:	212-243-6400	Thursday - Saturday 6pm - 1am
Fax:	212-242-1188	
e-mail:	N/A	
Web:	www.themaritimehotel.com	
Prices:	$$	

ΨΨ Matsuri is a place to soak up the scene, and what a scene it is! True to its name ("festival" in Japanese), Matsuri exudes a party atmosphere, especially in the evening. Housed in a cavernous space underneath the Maritime Hotel *(see hotel listings)*, the restaurant is the domain of chef Tadashi Ono, whose commitment to using the freshest ingredients requires him to have fish flown in daily from Japan. In the multilevel dining room, large Japanese lanterns hang like bright moons from the dark vaulted ceiling. And the stars are here, too, in a galaxy of celebs and supermodels who frequent the place. Be sure to try a few of the 200 different types of sake, including Matsuri's own house brew.

The Red Cat

Contemporary

008

227 Tenth Ave. (bet. 23rd & 24th Sts.)

Subway:	23 St	Monday - Thursday 5:30pm - 11pm
Phone:	212-242-1122	Friday - Saturday 5:30pm - midnight
Fax:	212-242-1390	Sunday 5pm - 10pm
e-mail:	N/A	
Web:	www.theredcat.com	
Prices:	$$	

ΨΨ Tired of schlepping around Chelsea's art galleries? The Red Cat makes a good place for a break—and a good meal. Chef Jimmy Bradley and his partner Danny Adams have a clear winner in their first New York venture (since founding The Red Cat in 1999, they've opened Mermaid Inn, Harrison and Pace). With its wood-paneled walls, red-and-white color scheme, and modern art, the dining room has a New England-meets-the-big-city feel. While the vibe may be cool and casual, the service is warm and efficient. Bradley, who grew up in Rhode Island, selects top-quality ingredients for dishes such as sautéed Chatham cod with spring vegetable risotto, and pan-roasted organic chicken with grilled escarole.

Manhattan Chelsea

Bistro Cassis

French

009

243 W. 14th St. (bet. Seventh & Eighth Aves.)

Subway:	14 St	Monday - Sunday noon - 3pm
Phone:	212-871-6020	& 5pm - 11pm
Fax:	212-871-6022	
e-mail:	N/A	
Web:	www.bistrocassisnyc.com	
Prices:	$$	

A relative newcomer to the Chelsea scene, Bistro Cassis has been regaling diners with authentic French bistro fare since it opened in late 2003. The interior looks like you'd expect: red banquettes, mosaic-tiled floor, tin ceiling, and walls hung with vintage posters. The menu doesn't hold many surprises either, but it does include a good choice of bistro dishes made with high-quality ingredients—four different preparations of mussels, steak tartare, skate with white wine and caper sauce, magret de canard (their duck breast is finished with a touch of cassis). And speaking of classics, the list of daily *plats du jour* is where you'll find the likes of cassoulet, coq au vin and bouillabaisse.

Bombay Talkie

Indian

010

189 9th Ave. (W. 21st & 22nd Sts.)

Subway:	23 St	Monday - Thursday 11am - 11pm
Phone:	212-242-1900	Friday - Saturday 10am - midnight
Fax:	212-242-6366	Sunday 10am - 11pm
e-mail:	N/A	
Web:	N/A	
Prices:		

Street food from India steals the spotlight at this Chelsea restaurant, opened in early 2005. Owner Sunitha Ramaiah named Bombay Talkie after the 1970 film that inspired her, and Thomas Juul-Hansen designed the dining space accordingly with painted murals of Indian movie stars, and an LCD flat screen running Bollywood films in the downstairs bar. Styled as an Indian teahouse, Bombay Talkie divides its menu into sections dubbed "Street Bites," "Dinner by the Roadside" and "Curbside Condiments." Regional dishes range from Kathi rolls and dosas to pork vindaloo. Don't skip dessert here; the delicate flavors of Mariebelle cardamom ganache or carrot Halwa will satisfy most any sweet tooth.

Gascogne

011

158 Eighth Ave. (bet. 17th & 18th Sts.)

Subway:	14 St
Phone:	212-675-6564
Fax:	212-627-3018
e-mail:	jennifer@nyct.net
Web:	www.gascognenyc.com
Prices:	$$

Monday - Sunday noon - 3pm
& 5:30pm - midnight

A jewel in the heart of Chelsea, Gascogne sparkles with its cuisine, which celebrates rustic fare from the southwest of France. Fine cassoulet, foie gras, and veal kidneys flamed with Armagnac are examples of the carefully prepared dishes here. In cold weather, ask for a table by the window overlooking the charming, flower-filled garden; in summer you can dine outside in this pleasant, shady space. In true French fashion, the bar stocks a good selection of fine aged Armagnac for after-dinner sipping. If you're on a budget, go for the prix-fixe pre-theater menu *(cash only)*, which is offered all evening on Monday.

Omai

012

158 Ninth Ave. (bet. 19th & 20th Sts.)

Subway:	23 St
Phone:	212-633-0550
Fax:	212-633-0575
e-mail:	N/A
Web:	www.omainyc.com
Prices:	$$

Monday - Sunday 5:30pm - 10:30pm
Closed Thanksgiving & Christmas Day

Don't look for a sign to identify this little restaurant in the heart of Chelsea—there isn't one. Once you find the place, though (look for the pots of bamboo outside), you'll step into a space tastefully underdecorated with exposed-brick walls and Southeast Asian accents. Vietnamese dishes here manage to be creative while staying true to their roots. Omai's takes on entrées such as roasted duck, jumbo shrimp and sautéed chicken are perfumed with tamarind, curry and coconut, and lemongrass. Want something lighter? The menu offers options from spring rolls to rice and vegetables, to noodle dishes. Hint: avoid the middle row of tables if you don't want to be jostled while you eat.

Rocking Horse

Mexican

013

182 Eighth Ave. (bet. 19th & 20th Sts.)

Subway:	8 Av - 14 St	Monday - Sunday 11am - 11pm
Phone:	212-463-9511	
Fax:	212-243-3245	
e-mail:	rockinghorsecafe@aol.com	
Web:	N/A	
Prices:	$$	

Vivid wall colors—orange, red, green—make a fitting canvas on which to present the cafe's vibrant regional Mexican dishes. Niman Ranch pork, free-range chicken and fresh vegetables provide the filling for supple burritos, quesadillas and enchiladas at lunch, while the likes of black tiger prawns with caramelized papaya and poblano chiles, and chiltepe-chile-glazed tuna take the stage at dinner. As an appetizer, the house-made guacamole is flavorful and lightly spiced, served with warm corn tortilla chips. Save room for the oh-so-rich tres leches cake, topped with sliced bananas and banana cream. If it's warm out, snag a patio table and take in the street scene while you sip a Margarita.

Sueños

Contemporary Mexican

014

311 W. 17th St. (bet. Eighth & Ninth Aves.)

Subway:	14 St	Sunday - Wednesday 5pm - 11pm
Phone:	212-243-1333	Thursday - Saturday 5pm - midnight
Fax:	212-243-3377	
e-mail:	info@suenosnyc.com	
Web:	www.suenosnyc.com	
Prices:	$$	

Sueños ("dreams" in Spanish) is a literal dream come true for chef/owner Sue Torres. Formerly of Rocking Horse Cafe, also in Chelsea, Torres supervises the operation of the kitchen and the dining room at her new restaurant, which opened in 2003. There's nothing timid about this place; from the brightly painted magenta and orange brick walls to the bold, chile tasting menu, Sueños celebrates the best of Mexico. Dining spaces center on a glass-enclosed patio, complete with a fountain and flowers. Bring the kids and come Monday, Tuesday or Wednesday night for the Make Your Own Taco menu. And check out the *cocinera* in the corner of the dining room, cooking fresh tortillas on a cast-iron comal.

202

Contemporary

75 Ninth Ave. (bet. 15th & 16th Sts.)

Subway:	14 St
Phone:	646-638-1173
Fax:	646-638-2188
e-mail:	N/A
Web:	N/A
Prices:	$$

Monday - Friday 11:30am - 10pm
Saturday 10am - 10pm
Sunday 10am - 6pm

New to Chelsea Market, 202 gives shoppers in the Nicole Farhi boutique a respite from difficult fashion decisions. Does that dress really make you look fat? Who cares? Grab a table—there's virtually no separation between the shop and the restaurant—and order a tuna burger with guacamole. By the time you finish your chocolate pot de crème, you'll wonder why you were stressing out over such a silly thing. Little sister to Nicole's in Midtown, 202 offers a classy, bistro vibe and smart service sans the attitude. Freshly baked pastries fill the large counter and daily specials are noted on the blackboard. Brunch fare is available here every day of the week.

Manhattan Chelsea

About
Chinatown

Sprawling Chinatown is a veritable city within a city. Narrow streets at its core feel utterly unlike the rest of New York City. Densely packed markets stock everything from lychee to lipstick, while more than 200 restaurants serve up 20 distinct Asian cuisines. Especially crowded on weekends, the area marked by pagoda-roofed buildings and Buddhist temples bursts its seams at **Chinese New Year** (first full moon after January 19), when dragons dance down the streets accompanied by costumed revelers and fireworks.

Just Visiting – The first Chinese came to New York in the 1870s from the California goldfields or from jobs building the transcontinental railroad in the western U.S. Most were men who, unlike other immigrants, had no intention of staying—they simply wanted to make their fortunes and return to a comfortable life in China. By the 1880s, New York's Chinese community numbered about 10,000 people. In 1882, the Chinese Exclusion Act was passed to stop further immigration, and growth came to a standstill. Unable to earn passage back to China, many "temporary" residents stayed. In part because single men continued to make up the majority of the population, the neighborhood took on a rough-and-tumble character in the late 19th and early 20th centuries. Opium dens, brothels and gambling parlors sprang up, as did social clubs called tongs.

© Martha Cooper

Here to Stay – Following the 1943 repeal of the Chinese Exclusion Act, a new influx of immigrants arrived in New York from Taiwan and Hong Kong, as well as from mainland China. Garment factories, Chinese laundries, shops and restaurants appeared in the quarter, which has inexorably spread out from its dense heart into neighboring Little Italy and the Lower East Side.

Today Manhattan's Chinatown now holds the largest Chinese immigrant community outside Asia. The hub of the neighborhood lies in the

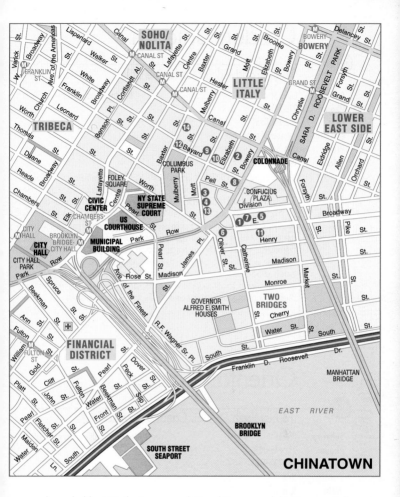

area bounded by Worth, Baxter, and Canal Streets and the Bowery. Pell, Doyers, and Bayard streets—the most atmospheric in the district—are so narrow that they're almost always in the shade. Mulberry and Mott streets are lined with shops piled high with displays of bamboo plants, tea sets, silk dresses, Chinese lanterns, fans, and the like. Browse the food markets here for exotic products from duck eggs to Durian fruit, then check out Mott Street when you get hungry; many of the quarter's best restaurants are located here. Be sure to experience **dim sum**, a multicourse meal of small snacks (buns, pastries, dumplings and more) served on rolling carts.

Golden Unicorn

Chinese

001

18 E. Broadway (at Catherine St.)

Subway:	Canal St
Phone:	212-941-0911
Fax:	212-941-0951
e-mail:	peteyau@hotmail.com
Web:	N/A
Prices:	

Monday - Sunday 10am - 10:30pm

You'll enter the Golden Unicorn through a commercial building in a quiet part of Chinatown. Take the elevator to either the second or third floor (both offer the same menu and décor, highlighted by fanciful golden unicorns romping across the back wall) and you're in for a dim sum treat at lunch. The street may be quiet, but inside, the restaurant is animated day and night. Family-size tables in the large rooms leave just enough space for the waitstaff to wheel carts of delectable dim sum past each diner. Choose from an assortment of shrimp dumplings, rice rolls with roast pork, won tons, and much more. At dinner, there's a menu of Cantonese and Hong Kong dishes.

Oriental Garden

Chinese

002

14 Elizabeth St. (bet. Canal & Bayard Sts.)

Subway:	Canal St
Phone:	212-619-0085
Fax:	212-732-9409
e-mail:	N/A
Web:	N/A
Prices:	

Monday - Sunday 9:30am - 10:30pm

You'll know what the food focus is here as soon as you walk in the door. On either side of the entrance, two aquarium tanks swim with live fish and lobsters, awaiting your order (okay, they may not be anticipating it quite so fondly, since they're the ones that will soon be on the plate!). If you're not a fish lover, don't worry, there are plenty of other dishes on the menu; in fact, there's an extensive selection of classic Chinese fare. The walls of the tidy, single dining room are lined with framed Chinese ideograms, the service is attentive, and the place is always hopping. Just be sure to bring cash; Oriental Garden doesn't accept credit cards for bills under $60.

Peking Duck House

003

28 Mott St. (bet. Chatham Sq. & Pell St.)

Subway:	Canal St
Phone:	212-227-1810
Fax:	212-227-1920
e-mail:	pekingduck@verizon.net
Web:	www.pekingduckhousenyc.com
Prices:	🍴🍴

Sunday - Thursday 11:30am - 10:30pm
Friday - Saturday 11:30am - 11:30pm

XX

Round up a few friends and go for the specialty of the house—you guessed it: Peking duck—at this Chinatown establishment. The slow-roasted duck comes out juicy inside with pleasingly crispy skin, and it's a surefire crowd pleaser (the dish, which consists of a whole duck, is only prepared for groups of two or more). In ceremonial fashion, the bird is sliced tableside by the chef and served with house-made pancakes, scallions, cucumbers and a dark, sweet sauce, sparked by piquant notes of ginger. Don't care for duck? There's a full menu of other selections, from Szechuan prawns to crispy sea bass to "volcano" steak, strips of filet mignon flamed with Grand Marnier.

Ping's Seafood

004

22 Mott St. (bet. Pell St. & Chatham Sq.)

Subway:	Canal St
Phone:	212-602-9988
Fax:	212-602-9992
e-mail:	N/A
Web:	www.chinatownweb.com/pings
Prices:	🍴🍴

Monday - Thursday 10am - midnight
Friday - Saturday 9am - 2am
Sunday 9am - midnight

XX

Discreet Asian décor highlights this bustling, comfortable, well-lit place—complete with white tablecloths—in the middle of Chinatown. The menu, as overseen by chef/owner Chuen Ping Hui, concentrates on Hong Kong-style dishes, characterized by their light sauces and simple preparations—especially, but not limited to, seafood. There's little doubt of the freshness of the latter here; a stack of fish tanks near the entrance swim with the day's catch. If you're seeking something on the exotic side, consider the braised sea cucumber, stir-fried pork stomach and dried squid, or cuttlefish and conch in XO sauce (a Hong Kong invention made with red chiles, dried fish, salt-cured ham and garlic).

Manhattan *Chinatown*

Sunrise 27

Chinese

005

27 Division St. (bet. Catherine & Market Sts.)

Subway:	Canal St
Phone:	212-219-8498
Fax:	212-219-8055
e-mail:	N/A
Web:	N/A
Prices:	🍜

Monday - Sunday 9am - midnight

Large windows face the street at Sunrise 27, beckoning diners into the understated restaurant, where golden dragons sprawl across a red-velvet screen at the back of the room. At lunch, you have your choice of the regular menu or the cart of dim sum that is circulated around the room. For dinner, you'll be hard-pressed to decide among the pages of offerings, which include casseroles filled with the likes of fresh frog with ginger and scallions, or sliced eel. Several chicken dishes (salt-baked or crispy fried) are offered as half or whole portions, catering to a variety of appetites. The pleasant waitstaff is well-organized, so there always seems to be a waiter handy when you need something.

Dim Sum Go Go

Chinese

006

5 E. Broadway (at Chatham Sq.)

Subway:	Canal St
Phone:	212-732-0797
Fax:	212-964-3149
e-mail:	N/A
Web:	N/A
Prices:	🍜

Monday - Sunday 10am - 10:30pm

Despite the name, you won't find dancers in white go-go boots here. Nor will you find a place that strictly features take-out. What you will find is a bright, sophisticated restaurant decorated with sleek metal chairs and red voile lining the ceiling. Attentive servers can offer good advice about navigating your way through the sizable dim sum menu, which is served à la carte, not on a cart, as in many dim sum establishments. The brainchild of food writer Colette Rossant and Hong Kong chef Guy Liu, Dim Sum Go Go serves dim sum all day—even at dinner. These little jewels come bundled in rainbow-colored wrappers on bamboo steamers. Go for the dim sum platter if you want a well-priced sampling.

Fuleen Seafood

007

11 Division St. (bet. Catherine & Market Sts.)

Subway:	Canal St
Phone:	212-941-6888
Fax:	N/A
e-mail:	N/A
Web:	www.chinatownweb.com/fuleen
Prices:	💰

Monday - Sunday 11am - 4am

If you fancy Chinese food, you won't dig up a better lunch special in Chinatown—or perhaps in all of Manhattan—than the $4.95 lunch deal at Fuleen Seafood. Less than $5 here buys your choice of an entrée, and they throw in rice and soup on the house. It seems unbelievable, but the locals who crowd the large, round tables here know where to go for a good, and filling, meal for an incredibly low price. The long list of main courses offers something for everyone: seafood, shellfish, chicken, beef, pork, and vegetable dishes. And the lunch special is offered daily from 11am to 3pm.

Great N.Y. Noodletown

Chinese

008

28 Bowery (at Bayard St.)

Subway:	Canal St
Phone:	212-349-0923
Fax:	N/A
e-mail:	N/A
Web:	N/A
Prices:	💰

Monday - Sunday 9am - 4am

If you're looking for fancy décor, keep on walking. But if it's tasty, inexpensive Chinese food you seek, stop right here. Great N.Y. Noodletown is a casual place, to say the least—the menu is displayed under the pane of glass that tops the tables; they only take cash; and you pay the cashier before you leave. Of course, noodles dominate the menu here; you can get them pan-fried, Cantonese-style, or in Hong Kong-style lo mein. There's also a choice of salt-baked dishes and barbecued meats; check out the samples hanging in the restaurant's window. Best reason to come here? The dependably good food at this Chinatown noodle joint is an outstanding value for the money.

Mandarin Court

Chinese

009

61 Mott St. (bet. Canal & Bayard Sts.)

Subway:	Canal St
Phone:	212-608-3838
Fax:	212-226-6110
e-mail:	N/A
Web:	N/A
Prices:	⊗

Monday - Sunday 8am - 11pm

Dim sum is not just for weekend brunch anymore. At Mandarin Court, dim sum is served every day from 8am to 3:30pm. The presentation here is traditional; the waiters roll carts full of dumplings, buns, wontons, and other savories past your table so you can take your pick. There's even sweet dim sum for dessert (think egg custard, almond- or coconut-flavored gelatin, sesame ball). If you're really hungry, try one of the regular entrées, which include steaming bowls of broth full of noodles, vegetables, meat or seafood. The dining room may not look like much, but folks don't come here for the décor, they come for good Hong Kong-style food at very reasonable prices.

New Wonton Garden

Chinese

010

56 Mott St. (bet. Canal & Bayard Sts.)

Subway:	Canal St
Phone:	212-966-4886
Fax:	N/A
e-mail:	N/A
Web:	N/A
Prices:	⊗

Monday - Sunday 24 hours

Hard chairs and benches here may not lend themselves to lingering, but copious quantities of well-prepared Cantonese cuisine will most likely convince you to stay. This style of regional Chinese cooking emphasizes fresh seasonal ingredients, in prepared-to-order dishes. Typically, Cantonese-style preparations are quick-fried or stewed to preserve their freshness; homemade noodles, for example, are stewed as in lo mein or pan-fried as in chow mein, both overflowing with roast duck, sweet and sour pork, beef, chicken, shrimp or vegetables, depending on your taste. If you've never tried them, the steamed Cantonese roast pork buns are a favorite dim sum dish.

The Nice Restaurant

011

35 E. Broadway (bet. Catherine & Market Sts.)

Subway: Canal St
Phone: 212-406-9776
Fax: 212-571-6827
e-mail: N/A
Web: N/A
Prices: 🍝

Monday - Sunday 9:30am - 10:30pm

Locals flock to the second-floor dining room (especially on weekends) at Nice for the Cantonese-style dim sum, a traditional meal composed of snack-size bites. Take a seat in the large, bright dining room, decorated by a red-velvet wall hanging on which golden dragons hold sway. Then settle back and wait for the carts carrying steamer baskets filled with stuffed buns, dumplings and barbecued meats to parade past your table. You can choose among a seemingly never-ending array of meats, fish and sweets; the waiters will keep circulating with the trolleys until you indicate that you've had enough. There's also a buffet featuring noodle and rice dishes.

Pongsri Thai

012

106 Bayard St. (at Baxter St.)

Subway: Canal St
Phone: 212-349-3132
Fax: N/A
e-mail: N/A
Web: www.pongsri.com
Prices: 🍝

Monday - Sunday 11:30am - 11:30pm
Closed Thanksgiving Day

Tired of Chinese food? Try Pongsri Thai (aka Thailand Restaurant, per the sign out front), for a taste of the traditional cuisine of Thailand with its hot, sour, sweet and tangy elements. Seafood shines here, and the extensive menu cites choices from spicy fried whole fish to steamed mussels. For vegetarians, there's a wide selection of curries (six different types), almost all made solely with vegetables, as well as noodle dishes like pad Thai. While the Chinatown location is the original (it's been here for 35 years), there are two additional outposts in Manhattan: in the Theater District at 244 West 48th Street, and in Gramercy Park at 311 Second Avenue.

Sweet-n-Tart Restaurant

Chinese

013

20 Mott St. (bet. Mosco & Worth Sts.)

Subway:	Canal St	Monday - Friday 11am - midnight
Phone:	212-964-0380	Saturday - Sunday 10am - midnight
Fax:	212-571-7697	
e-mail:	N/A	
Web:	www.sweetntart.com	
Prices:	◌	

Not feeling up to snuff? A visit to Sweet-n-Tart might just be good for what ails you. Opened in 1995 by Spencer Chan, the restaurant adheres to the concept of tong shui, revolving around hot-sweet desserts and teas with healing qualities—think of it as chicken soup for the Chinese soul. Some of the ingredients are pretty far out, so come prepared to experiment. Such tonics as milk and ginger juice (a headache cure), and double-boiled pear with almond (to banish a cough) are complemented by a menu of more mainstream small plates and appetizers. Will frog ovaries really keep your skin from wrinkling? Who knows, but it sure makes a good story—and it's a lot cheaper than plastic surgery!

Thai So'n

Vietnamese

014

89 Baxter St. (bet. Canal & Bayard Sts.)

Subway:	Canal St	Monday - Sunday 10:30am - 10:30pm
Phone:	212-732-2822	
Fax:	N/A	
e-mail:	N/A	
Web:	N/A	
Prices:	◌	

Set on a busy street in Chinatown, Thai So'n is known in the neighborhood for serving high-quality Vietnamese fare at low prices. The place has a simple, dining-hall-like atmosphere, improved by the photographs of the Asian countryside on the walls; comfort is minimal, but that's not why folks come here. They come for the contrasting flavors and textures that form the basis of the cuisine, which incorporates fresh vegetables, fiery peppers and herbs like basil, coriander, mint and lemongrass, along with a minimal amount of oil. If it's cold out, try a steaming bowl of Pho (beef broth full of rice noodles and your choice of other ingredients) to chase away the chill.

One day you'll tell your grandkids about flat tires.

Imagine never again being stranded on the side of the road with a flat tire. Michelin® PAX System™ combines a revolutionary anchoring system with a run-flat system that allows you to drive up to 125 miles at 55 mph with a flat tire. It's one step closer to a future that could include airless tires and other innovations that will change the way the world moves. Visit michelinman.com to see the future of tire technology.

MICHELIN
A better way forward

About the
East Village

The neighborhood bounded by 14th and Houston streets, and Bowery and the East River is the center of alternative culture in New York—rock concerts, poetry readings, and Off-Off Broadway theater productions take place here nightly. Not only does the East Village have a highly developed cafe culture; it's also one of the best places in the city to shop for used books and records and vintage clothes. In general the East Village caters to a very young crowd—almost all the cafes, bars and boutiques attract patrons in their twenties and thirties who, if they're not living on a limited budget, like to pretend they are.

A Bit of History – In 1651 **Peter Stuyvesant**, the Dutch-born director-general of the New Netherland colony, purchased the land bounded by today's 17th Street, 5th Street, 4th Avenue, and the East River from the Indians for use as a farm. After surrendering to the English in 1664, Stuyvesant withdrew from public affairs and moved to his manor house on present-day Stuyvesant Street.

Briefly in the early 1800s, the district west of Second Avenue boasted fashionable town houses, home to a social elite that included **John Jacob Astor**, the fur-trade and real-estate magnate who helped develop the surrounding neighborhood starting in 1825, and railroad tycoon **"Commodore" Cornelius Vanderbilt**. The working-class neighborhoods farther east were home to Polish, Ukrainian and German immigrants until the early 20C. The term "East Village" was coined in the early 1960s to distinguish the neighborhood from the rest of the Lower East Side. The glory days of the East Village were the 1980s, when rock bands like the

© Martha Cooper

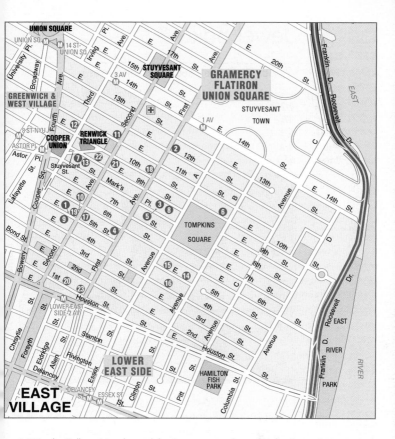

B-52's, the Talking Heads, and the Ramones made names for themselves at the legendary club **CBGB & OMFUG** (a.k.a. Country, Bluegrass, Blues and Other Music for Uplifting Gourmandizers).

A Taste of East Village – The East Village today contains vestiges of almost all chapters of its history. Laid out in 1834, ten-acre **Tompkins Square Park**, sits roughly at the center of the village. Its 150-year-old elms, flowers and fountains, make the park one of downtown Manhattan's most attractive public spaces. Most of the village's side streets are lined by 19th-century brownstones, spiffed-up tenements, and lush trees. **St. Mark's Place** is the most densely commercial street in the East Village, drawing hordes of students and hippies to its sushi bars, jewelry and sunglass stalls, record stores and head shops. **Second Avenue** is really the district's spine. Here you'll find an astounding variety of ethnic eateries—Italian, Russian, Korean, Thai, Jewish and Mexican among them. Sixth Street between First and Second avenues is known as **Little India** for the many super-cheap Indian and Bangladeshi restaurants that line the block.

Jewel Bako ✿

J a p a n e s e

239 E. 5th St. (bet. Second & Third Aves.)

Subway:	Lower East Side - 2 Av	Monday - Saturday 6:30pm - 10:30pm
Phone:	212-979-1012	Closed Sunday
Fax:	N/A	
e-mail:	N/A	
Web:	N/A	
Prices:	$$$	

Jewel Bako/Swee Phuah

Jewel Bako—the name means "jewel box"—is the flagship of husband-and-wife-restaurateur-team Jack and Grace Lamb. And a jewel box it is, with its tables strewn beneath a pair of striking back-lit bamboo arches. Beyond the bamboo tunnel, hidden behind a mirrored wall, lies the little sushi bar, also fashioned of bamboo strips. Each piece of sushi is a gem here, including rare varieties like Japanes spotted sardine, needlefish and live octopus flown in from the Tsukiji Market in Tokyo. To brighten the taste even further, wasabi is grated fresh at the table, where polished river stones make a pretty rest for chopsticks.

Known for their warm welcome, the Lambs manage to divide their time between their four restaurants (the other three are Jack's Luxury Oyster Bar, Jewel Bako Makimono, and the newest, Grace Kalbi Bar, located right next door to Jewel Bako.

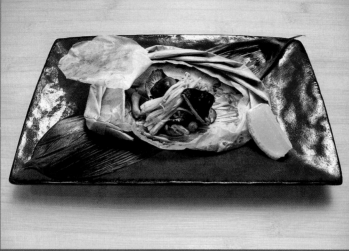

Yuzu and Sake-Steamed Mushrooms en Papillote

Serves 4

- 4 shitake mushrooms
- 28 shimeji mushrooms
- 2 bunches enoki mushrooms
- 4 Tbsp. sake
- 1 tsp. yuzu zest
- 2 tsp. butter
- sea salt and freshly ground black pepper to taste
- 4 sheets parchment paper

Method

Fold parchment paper in half and cut out four large heart shapes. Unfold and place one quarter of the mushroom mixture on one side of the paper heart. Sprinkle mushrooms with 1 teaspoon sake, ¼ teaspoon yuzu zest, salt and pepper, and then add ½ teaspoon of butter on top. Fold paper over the mushrooms and seal edges with a series of overlapping folds around the curve. Repeat three times. Bake packages in a 450°F degree oven for 13 minutes, or until the paper has puffed. Serve immediately.

Hearth

Mediterranean

002

403 E. 12th St. (at First Ave.)

Subway:	1 Av
Phone:	646-602-1300
Fax:	646-602-0552
e-mail:	N/A
Web:	www.restauranthearth.com
Prices:	$$

Monday - Thursday 6pm - 10pm
Friday - Saturday 6pm - 11pm
Sunday 6pm - 10pm

A relative newcomer to the East Village restaurant scene, Hearth opened in late 2003. The joint venture by chef Marco Canora and partner Paul Grieco emphasizes Mediterranean-inspired cuisine (the chef's family has roots in Tuscany) on its seasonal menu. You can watch signature dishes, such as rabbit ballotine, red-wine-braised octopus with celery root, cabbage stuffed with veal sweetbreads, and steamed black bass with saffron risotto, being prepared in the open kitchen. The apple cider doughnuts, served with apple compote and maple cream, will help stave away the chill of a crisp fall or winter night. In addition to the generous menu, the chef offers a five-course tasting menu nightly.

I Coppi

Italian

003

432 E. 9th St. (bet. First Ave. & Ave. A)

Subway:	1 Av
Phone:	212-254-2263
Fax:	212-254-2069
e-mail:	icoppi@nyc.rr.com
Web:	www.icoppinyc.com
Prices:	$$

Monday - Thursday 5pm - 11pm
Friday 5pm - 11:30pm
Saturday 11:30am - 3pm & 5pm - 11:30pm
Sunday 11:30am - 3pm & 5pm - 11pm

From the farmhouse ambience to the menu conceived by Alberta Innocenti, who grew up amid the olive orchards of Pistoia, it's all about Tuscany at I Coppi. Restaurant owners John Brennan and his wife, Lorella Innocenti (her mother is the one who donated her family recipes), bring the Tuscan hills to the East Village in a room accented with Italian ceramics and a mural of the Tuscan countryside. In back, the enclosed winter garden provides a leafy oasis year-round. The kitchen turns out crispy thin-crust pizzas from the wood-burning oven, along with an ambitious number of other dishes, balanced between pastas, meat and fish. Be sure to check out the award-winning selection of Italian wines.

Banjara

Indian

97 First Ave. (at 6th St.)

Subway:	Lower East Side - 2 Av	Monday - Sunday noon - midnight
Phone:	212-477-5956	
Fax:	212-533-2676	
e-mail:	info@banjaranyc.com	
Web:	www.banjaranyc.com	
Prices:	$$	

Named for the Banjara gypsy tribes of Eastern India, this restaurant stands out at the corner of two busy streets, among the numerous other Indian eateries that mark the neighborhood. Banjara isn't flashy; the dining room is tastefully decorated with fresh flowers on each table and rich-hued Indian tapestries gracing the back wall of the bar area, creating an exotic ambience to match the origin of the cuisine. Authentic regional dishes fill the menu here, from clay-oven-fired tandooris to dumpakht, a traditional stew that is sealed in its cooking vessel under a dome of pastry (think of it as the aromatic Indian version of a pot pie).

Café Mogador

Moroccan

101 St. Mark's Pl. (bet. First Ave. & Ave. A)

Subway:	1 Av	Monday - Friday 11:30am - 11pm
Phone:	212-677-2226	Saturday - Sunday 5pm - 11pm
Fax:	212-533-2159	
e-mail:	N/A	
Web:	www.cafemogador.com	
Prices:	☜☜	

In the heart of the bohemian East Village, Café Mogador adds a North African note to the neighborhood's ethnic restaurant mix. Moorish lanterns, jars of spices, and black-and-white photographs of Morocco lend an exotic air to this little café, where prices are approachable and service is cheerful and attentive. Couscous, Morocco's national dish, is interpreted here with an array of veggies (turnips, carrots, cabbage, zucchini and pumpkin) and topped with chickpeas, onions and raisins. Traditional bastilla fills layers of crispy filo with shredded chicken, eggs, almonds and cinnamon. For good measure, the menu throws in hints of the Mediterranean with choices like hummus and charmoulla.

Manhattan East Village

Gnocco

006

337 E. 10th St. (bet. Aves. A & B)

Subway:	1 Av	Monday - Friday 4pm - midnight
Phone:	212-677-1913	Saturday - Sunday noon - midnight
Fax:	212-477-7610	
e-mail:	info@gnocco.com	
Web:	www.gnocco.com	
Prices:	$$	

Gnocco's light-filled front room, with its brick walls and paintings of huge Georgia O'Keeffe-style flowers, overlooks Tompkins Square Park from the floor-to-ceiling windows. Don't leave without sampling the signature gnocco, crispy deep-fried pillows of dough served with thin slices of prosciutto di Parma and coppa ham. Well-executed homemade pastas, including the more familiar gnocchi, make a fitting first course; then there's a small selection of meat and fish dishes. If you don't have room for dessert, the almond cookie accompanied by a glass of vin santo makes a light ending to the meal. The shady back terrace, with its vine-covered walls, is a great place to sit in nice weather.

Hasaki

007

210 E. 9th St. (bet. Second & Third Aves.)

Subway:	Astor Pl	Monday - Tuesday 5:30pm - 11:30pm
Phone:	212-473-3327	Wednesday - Friday noon - 3pm
Fax:	212-260-0036	& 5:30pm - 11:30pm
e-mail:	N/A	Saturday - Sunday 1pm - 4pm
Web:	www.hasakinyc.com	& 5:30pm - 11:30pm
Prices:		

On weekends, you'll recognize this sushi restaurant by the line that snakes out the door onto the sidewalk. Hasaki doesn't take reservations, but that doesn't seem to deter the devotees of this small, often-crowded place. The lively sushi bar is where the action is; belly up and see what all the fuss is about. Sashimi (buttery yellowtail, eel, King crab, tuna, not to mention the daily list of specials) is carefully presented and served with soba noodles, a bowl of rice, and the requisite wasabi and aromatic pickled ginger. Aside from sashimi and sushi, the menu offers tempura, chicken teriyaki and grilled salmon, among other cooked selections—all at prices that won't break the budget.

Itzocan

008

438 E. 9th St. (bet. First Ave. & Ave. A)

Subway:	1 Av
Phone:	212-677-5856
Fax:	N/A
e-mail:	bellozeroomega@aol.com
Web:	N/A
Prices:	⊗⊗

Monday - Sunday noon - midnight

This little hole in the wall near Tompkins Square Park packs a big punch for its tiny size. Inside there are seats for less than 20 people, but the authentic Mexican food at inexpensive prices (dinner entrées range from $10 to $15) more than make up for the cramped quarters. Start your meal with the wonderfully fresh house-made guacamole, which has just the right amount of heat. For lunch you'll find an assortment of burritos and quesadillas. At dinner the choices ratchet up a notch (flank steak in chile pasilla, semolina epazote dumplings with roasted poblano peppers) and include several specials. Save room for the moist chocolate molé cake—accented with a hint of chile pepper.

Jack's Luxury Oyster Bar

009

246 E. 5th St. (bet. Second & Third Aves.)

Subway:	Lower East Side - 2 Av
Phone:	212-673-0338
Fax:	N/A
e-mail:	N/A
Web:	N/A
Prices:	$$$

Monday - Saturday 6pm - 10:30pm
Closed Sunday

Owners Jack and Grace Lamb tucked this little restaurant into the first two floors of their East Village townhouse. Like the dining spaces, the menu is small, tending toward fresh seafood—including several preparations of oysters, of course. The chef celebrates her native state of Louisiana with such ingredients as crayfish and Louisiana red snapper, and the knowledgeable staff is well versed in which wines go best with which dishes. The short dessert menu changes regularly, depending on the whim of the pastry chef (if it's on the menu, try the baba au rhum cake, served warm with fluffy whipped cream). The nightly tasting menu is available only by reservation in the upstairs dining room.

Manhattan East Village

Jewel Bako Makimono

J a p a n e s e

010

101 Second Ave. (bet. 5th & 6th Sts.)

Subway:	Lower East Side - 2 Av	Monday - Saturday 6pm - 10pm
Phone:	212-253-7848	Closed Sunday
Fax:	N/A	
e-mail:	N/A	
Web:	N/A	
Prices:	$$	

✗ Little sister to Jewel Bako around the corner on Fifth Street, Jewel Bako Makimono is the least expensive address of Jack Lamb's four restaurants (which include Jack's Luxury Oyster Bar). This tiny gem of a sushi place seats 18 people in its two narrow rows of blond wood tables. Separated from the main room by a bamboo screen, the eight-seat sushi bar is the place to sit and sample artisan sake to drink with some 50 varieties of fish. No matter where you sit, you'll be treated to cheerful service and fresh-from-the-ocean sushi and sashimi such as big-eye tuna, salmon, yellowtail, freshwater eel and Spanish mackerel. *Reservations not accepted.*

Koi

J a p a n e s e

011

175 Second Ave. (at 11th St.)

Subway:	3 Av	Monday - Saturday 5:30pm - midnight
Phone:	212-777-5266	Sunday 5pm - 11pm
Fax:	212-777-0911	
e-mail:	daigooman@hotmail.com	
Web:	www.koisushinyc.com	
Prices:	$$	

✗ This new sushi restaurant named for the common carp, a symbol of prosperity and happiness in Japan, has recently changed ownership and décor since its former incarnation as Iso. But that hasn't affected its popularity. The young staff attends to a crowd that includes the NYU set (the university is nearby). Take your place at the seven-seat sushi bar if you want to watch the show; the sushi chefs, who for years were protégés of Iso, prepare their orders with an amazing sleight of hand. Here you'll find some lesser-known varieties of fish—bluefin tuna, needlefish, sea urchin—some of which are flown in directly from Japan. It's not inexpensive, but the quality stands up to the price.

Lan

Contemporary Japanese

56 Third Ave. (bet. 10th & 11th Sts.)

Subway:	3 Av	Sunday - Thursday 5:30pm - 11:30pm
Phone:	212-254-1959	Friday - Saturday 5:30pm - midnight
Fax:	212-477-5561	
e-mail:	N/A	
Web:	www.lan-nyc.com	
Prices:	$$	

Behind its red awning, Lan reveals a candelit haven of small white-cloth-covered tables and exposed brick accented by orange-painted walls. Sure, they serve the normal menu of sushi, sashimi and rolls, but Lan also features entrées such as broiled black cod marinated in Saikyo miso sauce—which change according to the season. Appetizers, such as Kobe beef tongue stewed with miso and red wine, and steamed Chilean sea bass with simmered lotus roots, are especially creative. Try the hot pots for two; they come with everything you need to cook your meal at the table. Shabu shabu (thin slices of prime ribeye with assorted market vegetables and dipping sauces) is a favorite.

La Paella

Spanish

214 E. 9th St. (bet. Second & Third Aves.)

Subway:	Astor Pl	Monday 5pm - 11pm
Phone:	212-598-4321	Tuesday - Sunday noon - 11pm
Fax:	N/A	
e-mail:	lapaellaon9th@yahoo.com	
Web:	N/A	
Prices:	$$	

La Paella is a good place to come with friends, so you can sample an even wider array of the well-prepared vegetable, meat and seafood tapas. Decorated to resemble an Old World Iberian inn, with gold-toned walls, wrought-iron accents, and wooden ceiling beams draped with dried flowers, the dark dining space can get crowded—and loud—in the evening (all the better atmosphere for a party). The specialty is—of course!—paella, and they serve several types of the traditional Spanish dish, including a vegetarian and an all-seafood preparation, as well as a Basque version, made with chorizo, chicken, shellfish and squid atop a bed of saffron rice. Keep the party going with a pitcher of fruity sangria.

Manhattan *East Village*

Lavagna

Italian

014

545 E. 5th St. (bet. Aves. A & B)

Subway:	Lower East Side - 2 Av	Monday - Thursday 6pm - 11pm
Phone:	212-979-1005	Friday - Saturday 6pm - midnight
Fax:	212-253-0666	Sunday 5pm - 11pm
e-mail:	info@lavangnanyc.com	Closed Thanksgiving Day
Web:	www.lavagnanyc.com	& Christmas Day
Prices:	$$	

Who says you should quit while you're ahead? Sami Kader didn't, and East Villagers are glad of it. After successfully launching Le Tableau, just down the street, Kader decided to try his version of an Italian trattoria. It seems he has the magic touch—at least judging from the crowds that pack the place on weekends. Lavagna's atmosphere is cozy and laid-back; any diner here is treated like a friend. The menu may be short, but it's supplemented with a host of daily specials. Cuisine is refined and innovative, in dishes such as rigatoni with sweet fennel, spicy sausage, peas and tomato cream; or roast pork chop with braised cabbage and butternut squash in vin santo sauce.

Le Tableau

French

015

511 5th St. (bet. Aves. A & B)

Subway:	Lower East Side - 2 Av	Monday - Sunday 5:30pm - 11:30pm
Phone:	212-260-1333	
Fax:	212-979-1729	
e-mail:	m0211m0@yahoo.com	
Web:	www.letableaunyc.com	
Prices:	$$	

This modern bistro, with its vivid orange walls, enjoys a good reputation in the neighborhood—and rightly so. The cuisine at Le Tableau boasts excellent quality at a reasonable price. Creative brasserie fare includes seasonal offerings such as pomegranate-glazed duck and Berkshire pork loin with yam and walnut gnocchi gratin. Priced at less than $30, the three-course, prix-fixe menu is the best deal (offered before 7pm Tuesday to Saturday, and all night Sunday and Monday); there's also a five-course chef's tasting menu, which includes wines if you so desire. If you order à la carte, be sure to save room for the likes of almond cake with apricot coulis, and Valrhona chocolate truffle cake.

Mamlouk

Middle Eastern

211 E. 4th St. (bet. Aves. A & B)

Subway:	Lower East Side - 2 Av	Tuesday - Sunday 7pm - 11pm
Phone:	212-529-3477	Closed Monday
Fax:	N/A	
e-mail:	N/A	
Web:	N/A	
Prices:	$$	

For an authentic and thoroughly delightful Middle Eastern meal, head to Mamlouk. Inside, you'll be enveloped in an exotic ambience, furnished with copper-topped tables and wide cushioned seats, with antique jewelry framed on the walls. In this cozy atmosphere, hosted by the charming Iraqi owner, you have only to settle back and savor the multicourse, prix-fixe meal (there is no menu). The feast begins with an assortment of pickles, crudités and fresh-baked pita. Next, a selection of hot and cold mezzes (lebneh, baba ganoush, hummus) come to the table. These are followed by several entrées, and, finally, dessert. After your meal, try a hookah, filled with your choice of flavored smokes.

The Mermaid Inn

Seafood

96 Second Ave. (bet. 5th & 6th Sts.)

Subway:	Astor Pl	Monday - Saturday 5:30pm - midnight
Phone:	212-674-5870	Sunday 5pm - 10pm
Fax:	N/A	
e-mail:	N/A	
Web:	www.themermaidnyc.com	
Prices:	$$	

With its rough-hewn wood columns, exposed brick walls and dark wainscoting, The Mermaid Inn does a good imitation of a New England fish shack. This is no side-of-the-road joint, though. The stylish, casual eatery offers only seafood, so carnivores need not apply. Instead of hot dogs, you'll find "cod dogs" on the menu—crispy, breaded strips of codfish served with coleslaw and lemon-caper remoulade. If you have an incurable sweet tooth, be forewarned: they don't do dessert here. Instead, you'll automatically receive a complimentary demitasse of creamy chocolate or butterscotch pudding to put the finishing touches on your meal.

Manhattan East Village

Momofuku Noodle Bar

A s i a n

018

163 First Ave. (bet. 10th & 11th Sts.)

Subway:	1 Av	Sunday - Thursday noon - 11pm
Phone:	212-475-7899	Friday - Saturday noon - midnight
Fax:	212-504-7967	Closed major holidays
e-mail:	eatmomofuku@gmail.com	
Web:	www.eatmomofuku.com	
Prices:	⊜	

A recent addition to the East Village dining scene, Momofuku is a peach of a restaurant—which is appropriate since its name means "lucky peach" in Japanese. There are no tables here; diners sit, as they do in noodle bars in Japan, on high stools at long, communal counters. It's a great way to make new friends, slurping noodles elbow-to-elbow and watching the chefs' sleight of hand behind the blond-wood bar. Owner David Chang, a former line cook at Craft, fashioned Momofuku's menu with Asian street food in mind. Ramen noodles share the menu with small dishes; try the steamed pork dumplings filled with Iowa Berkshire black pork, an ingredient that figures prominently in this restaurant.

Mosto

I t a l i a n

019

87 Second Ave. (at 5th St.)

Subway:	Astor Pl	Monday - Saturday 5:30pm - midnight
Phone:	212-228-9912	Sunday 4pm - midnight
Fax:	N/A	
e-mail:	mostonyc@aol.com	
Web:	www.mostoosteria.com	
Prices:	$$	

Named for the juice that results when grapes are first crushed in the wine press, Mosto sticks to what it's good at: offering excellent Italian fare at very approachable prices, with wines to match. The informal dining space, decked out with tropical plants, caters to couples with its intimate candlelit aura, and to groups—or single diners—with its communal table. Loud rock music enlivens the crowded bar scene. On the menu, you can count on abundant portions of pasta (spinach gnocchi, spaghetti with clam sauce, pappardelle with lamb ragu), and a short list of entrées, from grilled pork loin to homestyle chicken cutlet. Expect the service to be pleasant and helpful.

Prune

Contemporary

54 E. 1st St. (bet. First & Second Aves.)

Subway:	Lower East Side - 2 Av	Monday - Thursday 6pm - 11pm
Phone:	212-677-6221	Friday 6pm - midnight
Fax:	212-677-6982	Saturday 10am - 3:30pm
e-mail:	N/A	& 6pm - midnight
Web:	www.prunerestaurant.com	Sunday 10am - 3:30pm & 5pm - 10pm
Prices:	$$	Closed July 1 - 14

This shoe box-size bistro began in 1999 as Gabrielle Hamilton's modest vision of a neighborhood restaurant. While it hasn't grown in size since then, it has grown well beyond the East Village in popularity. Despite its cramped quarters, Hamilton's recipe for a home-style eatery, has been wildly successful. At Prune she combines vintage bistro décor with a small menu of comfort food—the kind of meals you'd cook for friends in your home. The menu is not broken down by category (appetizers, entrées), so if you just want a plate of veggies, that's just fine. Signature dishes include the whole grilled fish, fried sweetbreads, and the fluffy Dutch-style pancake at the acclaimed weekend brunch.

Second Avenue Deli

Deli

156 Second Ave. (at 10th St.)

Subway:	3 Av	Sunday - Thursday 7am - midnight
Phone:	212-677-0606	Friday - Saturday 7am - 3am
Fax:	212-353-1836	
e-mail:	2ndavedeli@2ndavedeli.com	
Web:	www.2ndavedeli.com	
Prices:	⊜	

The Lebewohl family's Kosher deli has stood on this corner for decades, and New Yorkers still fill the cramped booths here for house-cured corned beef and tongue, triple-decker pastrami sandwiches, chopped liver, and chicken and matzoh-ball soup like only a Jewish mother can make. They're in good company: the roster of celebrities who have dined here over the years is impressive; check out the photos of the famous that hang on the walls while you wait for your meal. With such hearty portions, it's doubtful that you'll have room for dessert, but if you do, sweets run the gamut from cheesecake to rugalach to good, old-fashioned Jello. Of course, the deli also does a brisk take-out business.

Manhattan East Village

Soba-Ya

Japanese

022

229 E. 9th St. (bet. First & Second Aves.)

Subway:	Astor Pl	Monday - Sunday noon - 4pm
Phone:	212-533-6966	& 5:30pm - 10:30pm
Fax:	212-260-0036	
e-mail:	akean@earthlink.net	
Web:	www.sobayany.com	
Prices:		

Students from nearby NYU favor this place for its Zen-like minimalist ambience and its hearty and inexpensive noodle dishes. Soba (Japanese buckwheat noodles) are made on the premises and are ladled into steaming bowls of hot broth (along with an array of additional ingredients ranging from shrimp tempura to meat and vegetables), or are served cold with your choice of ingredients heaped on top. You can substitute the chewier udon, or wheat noodles (which some say taste more like traditional pasta), if you prefer. There's also a good selection of Japanese beer and sake to complement your meal.

Tasting Room

Contemporary

023

72 E. 1st St. (bet. First & Second Aves.)

Subway:	Lower East Side - 2 Av	Tuesday - Saturday 5:30pm - 11pm
Phone:	212-358-7831	Closed January 1 - 9
Fax:	212-358-8432	
e-mail:	thetastingroom@msn.com	
Web:	www.thetastingroomnyc.com	
Prices:	$$	

Diners at the Tasting Room can create their own meal combinations from among the dishes sized as "tastes" (appetizer portions) or "shares" (akin to a reasonably sized entrée). In fact, the teeny dining room invites sharing, since you'll be elbow-to-elbow with your neighbor. The chef takes inspiration from fresh market fare; dishes on the changing menu feature the likes of Maine diver scallops, heirloom tomatoes, brook trout and local wild matsutake mushrooms. Of special note here is the well-chosen selection of American wines, citing more than 350 different labels, within a wide price range. While you eat, check out the monthly changing exhibits of local art that line the walls.

**We've packed your weekend
in this convenient carrying case.**

A long weekend doesn't have to be short on activities. From spas to kid stuff, outdoor fun to nightlife, the Michelin® Must Sees have something for everyone to see and do. To learn more, visit michelintravel.com.

A better way forward

About the
Financial District

Widely considered the financial center of the world, the southern tip of Manhattan isn't as buttoned-up as you might expect. Its ample, U-shaped waterfront, lined with appealing parks, draws hordes of visitors to enjoy views of New York Harbor and catch ferries to Staten Island and the Statue of Liberty. Cradled within are the narrow, twisting streets laid out by New York's first Dutch settlers in the 17th century; developers left the curvy street plan largely intact when they built their gargantuan office towers. Gaze up and you'll feel as though you're at the bottom of a deep well, with only tiny patches of sky visible among the tight clusters of looming skyscrapers.

A Bit of History – The area now known as the Financial District was the birthplace of New York in 1625. Trade flourished here under the Dutch West India Company, and the settlement of Nieuw Amsterdam grew quickly. In 1653 the colonists built a wall of wooden planks between the Hudson and East rivers to protect the settlers from Indian attack. Later dismantled by the British, who took over the colony in 1664, the wall is remembered today on **Wall Street**, which traces the original length (less than one mile) of the fortress.

© Martha Cooper

Legend has it that in 1792 a group of 24 brokers met beneath a buttonwood tree at the corner of Wall and Williams streets, and founded the stock exchange. The New York Stock Exchange wasn't formally organized, however, until 1817. Inside the classical façade of the Exchange today, you'll find one of the most technically sophisticated financial operations on the globe.

A Neighborhood Reborn – Two of the Financial District's most famous landmarks, the **World Trade Center** towers, were destroyed in the terrorist attack on September 11, 2001, which left some 2,800 people dead. After that tragic event, the Financial District—indeed,

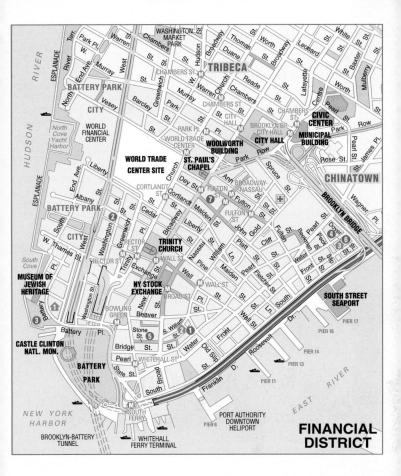

the entire city—understandably saw a downturn in commerce. But in the months that followed, businesses rebounded and restaurateurs put their faith—and their money—back into the area by opening new establishments. Fears that the neighborhood's spirit would always be clouded by that day have, happily, turned out to be unfounded. Today in the Financial District, camera-wielding tourists rub shoulders with briefcase-toting bankers on and around Wall Street, and Battery Park, under the watchful eye of Lady Liberty, teems with cyclists, runners, artists and souvenir-peddlers. Restaurants here cater to power-lunchers during the day, and to business travelers at dinnertime.

Bayard's

American

001

1 Hanover Sq. (bet. Pearl & Stone Sts.)

Subway:	Wall St	Monday - Thursday 5:30pm - 10pm
Phone:	212-514-9454	Friday - Saturday 5:30pm - 10:30pm
Fax:	212-514-9443	Closed Sunday
e-mail:	N/A	
Web:	www.bayards.com	
Prices:	$$$	

Facing charming Hanover Square, Bayard's restaurant occupies the beautifully renovated Hanover Bank building, erected in 1853. This landmark Italian Renaissance-style structure has gone from a private residence to the New York Cotton Exchange to a private club (the India House) for overseas merchants (ask for a copy of the complete history while you're there). The décor reflects the building's past with maritime artifacts, ships' models and figureheads, and nautical paintings—all discovered during the structure's renovation. In this warm and elegant atmosphere, you'll dine on fine American cuisine, equally balanced between meat and seafood. And don't miss the extensive wine list.

Roy's New York

Hawaiian

002

130 Washington St. (bet. Albany & Carlisle Sts.)

Subway:	World Trade Center	Monday - Friday 11:30am - 10pm
Phone:	212-266-6262	Saturday 5:30pm - 10pm
Fax:	212-266-6269	Closed Sunday
e-mail:	N/A	
Web:	www.roysnewyork.com	
Prices:	$$	

Inside the Marriott Financial Center hotel you'll find something unexpected: Hawaiian cuisine. Tokyo-born chef Roy Yamaguchi's sizable empire of eateries began when he opened the first Roy's in Honolulu in 1998. There are now 30 of the chef's eponymous establishments around the world. An open kitchen forms the focal point of the colorful, contemporary dining room. If you want a front-row seat, grab a spot at the counter where chefs intent on their art add a pinch of coconut powder here, a dollop of mango sauce there. It's all about fusing bold Asian spices with fresh Hawaiian seafood, as in roasted macadamia-nut-crusted mahi-mahi with lobster-butter sauce, a Roy's classic.

Gigino at Wagner Park

Italian

20 Battery Pl. (in Wagner Park)

Subway:	Bowling Green	Monday - Sunday 11:30am - 11pm
Phone:	212-528-2228	
Fax:	212-528-1756	
e-mail:	gigino@earthlink.net	
Web:	www.gigino-wagnerpark.com	
Prices:	**$$**	

Sleek sister to the rustic Gigino Trattoria in TriBeCa, this Wagner Park restaurant sits at the tip of Manhattan island, between Battery Park's Pier A and the Museum of Jewish Heritage. From its delightful outdoor terrace, you can take in the splendid view of Liberty Island, Ellis Island and New York Harbor. (As you'd expect, reservations are highly recommended in the warmer months.) If it's not nice enough to sit outside, the small, contemporary dining room offers plenty of large windows for enjoying harbor views. Chef's specialties include grilled octopus with black beans, homemade chicken sausage and Gigino's gnocchi with chicken, butter and sage.

MarkJoseph

Steakhouse

261 Water St. (bet. Peck Slip & Dover St.)

Subway:	Fulton St	Monday - Thursday 11:30am - 10pm
Phone:	212-277-0020	Friday 11:30am - 11pm
Fax:	212-277-0022	Saturday 5pm - 11pm
e-mail:	N/A	Closed Sunday
Web:	www.markjosephsteakhouse.com	
Prices:	**$$$**	

Nestled in the shadow of the Brooklyn Bridge in the South Street Seaport Historic District, MarkJoseph's caters to financiers, Wall Street wunderkinds and tourists with deep pockets. The cozy dining room is a notch above the standard steakhouse design, with art-glass vases and pastoral photographs of the wine country adding sleek notes. At lunch, regulars devour hefty half-pound burgers (there's even a turkey variety); at dinnertime, Prime dry-aged porterhouse takes the stage, with a choice of salads and sides that includes several steamed vegetables. And what better to wash your steak down with than one of the selections on the generous wine list of red wines?

Manhattan Financial District

Nebraska Beef

Steakhouse

005

15 Stone St. (bet. Broad & Whitehall Sts.)

Subway:	Bowling Green	Monday - Friday noon - 10pm
Phone:	212-952-0620	Closed Saturday - Sunday
Fax:	N/A	
e-mail:	N/A	
Web:	N/A	
Prices:	**$$**	

XX

You could easily walk down Stone Street without noticing the discreet red façade of this little restaurant, three blocks away from the clamor of the New York Stock Exchange. But the unpretentious place, with its long bar area opening into a dark, wood-paneled dining room, is worth seeking out for its quiet and comfortable setting and its high-quality, grain-fed Nebraska beef, cooked to your liking. As far as beef goes, there are no surprises on the menu here (a whopping 32-ounce prime rib-eye that goes by "The Steak!" on the menu is the signature dish). On the other end of the spectrum, the list of sushi adds unusual fare for a steakhouse.

Bridge Cafe

American

006

279 Water St. (at Dover St.)

Subway:	Fulton St	Sunday - Monday 11:45am - 10pm
Phone:	212-227-3344	Tuesday - Thursday 11:45am - 11pm
Fax:	212-619-2368	Friday 11:45am - midnight
e-mail:	bridgecafechef@aol.com	Saturday 4:45pm - midnight
Web:	www.bridgecafe.citysearch.com	
Prices:	**$$**	

Not many establishments in New York City can claim as colorful a history as this one. Billing itself as "New York's oldest drinking establishment," the business opened in 1794 as a grocery in a two-and-a-half-story wooden structure on the bank of the East River. Over the years, the building has housed a restaurant, a saloon, a boardinghouse and a brothel before it became the Bridge Cafe in 1979. The current 1920s structure stands on the corner of Water and Dover streets, at the foot of the Brooklyn Bridge. In this simple and cozy atmosphere, embellished by paintings of the bridge, you'll find good food at a reasonable price. Go Sunday for the popular Bridge Brunch.

Les Halles Downtown

007

15 John St. (bet. Broadway & Nassau St.)

Subway:	World Trade Center	Monday - Sunday 11:30am - midnight
Phone:	212-285-8585	Closed major holidays
Fax:	212-791-3280	
e-mail:	N/A	
Web:	www.leshalles.net	
Prices:	$$	

One of the first new restaurants to open in Lower Manhattan after September 11, 2001, Les Halles is located less than two blocks from the World Trade Center site. This brasserie is the sister to Les Halles on Park Avenue near Madison Square; both are run by chef Anthony Bourdain. Like its sister, Les Halles Downtown offers the same menu of tasty authentic French fare. If you're in town in July, head over to the restaurant for the Les Halles Liberty Festival and Bastille Day celebration that takes place from July 4 to 14. During this time, the brasserie features a special menu, and the festivities culminate in a free block party—including the annual Waiters Race—on Bastille Day.

Manhattan Financial District

About **Gramercy, Flatiron & Union Square**

The retail district that stretches from 14th to 30th Streets between the East River and Avenue of the Americas (Sixth Avenue) contains a concentration of fine restaurants with names you'll no doubt recognize. Large 19th-century and early-20th-century buildings line Broadway, and Fifth and Sixth avenues. Originally built as department stores, many of them now house national chains selling clothing or furniture.

Gramercy Park – New York City's only private park anchors this tranquil neighborhood known for its lovely brownstones and good cafes and restaurants. The area was laid out in 1831 by developer Samuel B. Ruggles, who drained an old marsh (Gramercy is a corruption of a Dutch phrase meaning "little crooked swamp") to build an exclusive residential enclave. Enclosed by an eight-foot-high cast-iron fence, to which only local residents have keys, the green rectangle of **Gramercy Park** consists of formal gardens, paths, benches and trees.

A few blocks northwest of Gramercy Park, lovely six-acre **Madison Square** has been transformed in the past five years into one of downtown's most inviting public spaces. From the 1870s to 1925, a succession of entertainment venues stood on the north end of the square, including the first two (of four) arenas called Madison Square Garden.

Union Square – On the south edge of the district, this pleasant park is crisscrossed with tree-lined paths. The park, so-named because it marked the union of Broadway and the Bowery, was created in 1831; by the mid-19th century it formed the gated focal point of an elegant residential district. In the early 20th century Union Square became a popular place for

© Martha Cooper

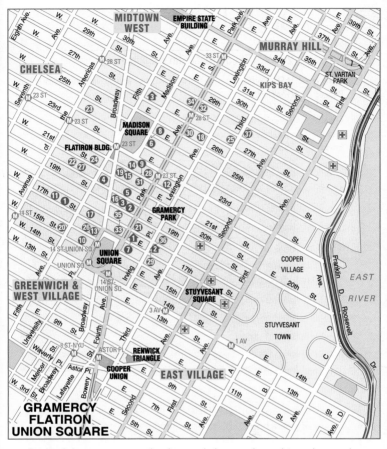

rallies and demonstrations; today the tiered plaza on the park's southern end still serves as a stage for protesters, who share space with street performers.

Every Monday, Wednesday, Friday and Saturday year-round, **Union Square Greenmarket** hosts farmers, bakers, flower growers, ranchers and artisanal-food makers from all over New York, Pennsylvania and New Jersey. Neighborhood chefs and residents flock here to forage for the freshest meats, cheeses and vegetables to incorporate into their menus.

Flatiron District – This moniker refers to the area around the **Flatiron Building** (Daniel Burnham, 1902). Even if you've never been to New York City, you've likely seen this building before—it's a popular backdrop in television shows and movies. Viewed from the north side (the side that faces Madison Square Park), the structure looks like an iron—hence the name—the acute angle of its façade formed by Broadway and Fifth Avenue. Though it's only 6 feet wide on this sharp corner, the building rises 22 stories straight up from the sidewalk.

BLT Fish ✿

001

21 W. 17th St. (bet. Fifth & Sixth Aves.)

Subway:	14 St - Union Sq	Monday - Thursday 5:30pm - 11pm
Phone:	212-691-8888	Friday - Saturday 5:30pm - 11:30pm
Fax:	212-255-5180	Closed Sunday
e-mail:	reservations@bltfish.com	
Web:	www.bltfish.com	
Prices:	$$$	

BLT Fish

Much-lauded chef Laurent Tourondel turns his sights to the sea at BLT Fish. After establishing his successful steakhouse, BLT Steak, in Midtown, Tourondel decided to change from turf to surf. His fine-dining seafood restaurant occupies the third floor of this Flatiron District town house, while New England-style BLT Fish Shack *(open for lunch & dinner; no reservations)* sits on the ground floor.

The refined setting upstairs boasts walnut wood tables, suede-covered walls, and—coolest of all—a retractable glass roof that opens to starry skies on warm, clear nights. Exceptionally fresh fish swim away with the awards here. Whole fish and shellfish, brushed with olive oil and grilled, are available by the pound; or you can order the less expensive fish filets. Side dishes come separately in cute little cast-iron pans. And in case you've got a meat-lover in your midst, Tourondel always lists one seasonal "Not Fish" dish on the menu.

BLT Fish/Quentin Bacon

Grilled Sardine Crostini

Serves 6

Tomato Vinaigrette

¼ cup + 1 Tbsp. olive oil
6 tomatoes, chopped
1 sprig of thyme
1 Tbsp. sugar
½ tsp. Tabasco sauce
2 Tbsp. sherry vinegar
½ medium yellow onion, diced
¼ tsp. sea salt and freshly ground black pepper

Heat ¼ cup of the olive oil in a pot over medium-high heat. Add the onion and sauté until translucent, about 4 minutes. Add tomato, thyme and sugar, and stir. Cover and cook 1-3 minutes or until the tomatoes begin to break apart. Remove the pot from the heat and transfer mixture to the bowl of a food processor fitted with the metal blade. Process to a fine purée. Press mixture through a fine-mesh strainer set over a bowl. Discard solids. Add Tabasco, sherry vinegar, salt and pepper, and allow to cool. Cover and refrigerate for at least 3 hours.

Tomato Salad

2 cups mixed tricolor cherry tomatoes, halved
½ cup extra virgin olive oil
2 Tbsp. Thai basil, julienned
2 Tbsp. red onion, julienned
2 Tbsp. sherry vinegar
2 Tbsp. ginger juice
Sea salt and freshly ground black pepper to taste

Whisk together the oil, vinegar and ginger juice. Toss the tomatoes, onions and basil with the vinaigrette and season to taste with salt and pepper.

Garnish

18 sardine fillets, deboned
¼ cup seeded, diced tomato
6 slices of cooked bacon
6 thin slices of grilled country bread (½-inch thick)
18 Thai basil leaves
Sea salt and freshly ground black pepper to taste

Brush the sardines with oil, sprinkle with salt and pepper and grill until cooked through, approximately one minute per side. Generously spoon half of vinaigrette on bottom of each plate. Place grilled bread on the vinaigrette, top with evenly divided tomato salad, 3 sardine filets, 3 leaves of basil and a strip of bacon. Drizzle remaining vinaigrette on top.

Craft ✤

Contemporary

43 E. 19th St. (bet. Broadway & Park Ave. South)

Subway:	14 St - Union Sq
Phone:	212-780-0880
Fax:	212-780-0580
e-mail:	N/A
Web:	www.craftrestaurant.com
Prices:	$$$

Sunday - Thursday 5:30pm - 10pm
Friday - Saturday 5:30pm - 11pm

XXX

Craft/Bill Bettencourt

Ever go out to eat with one of those people who wants to change everything about his order ("I'd like the salad, but hold the tomatoes, and put the dressing on the side")? Now you can take your pickiest friends to this smart, contemporary restaurant with its huge, glassed-in wine cellar, and they can tailor their meals to their own tastes. At Craft, chef/owner Tom Colicchio (also of Gramercy Tavern) offers a choice of basic products—fish and shellfish, charcuterie, roasted meat, salad, vegetables— to be combined however you desire (dessert works the same way).

Colicchio believes that cooking is first a craft; he presents ultra-fresh artisanal ingredients, prepares them simply, and lets the unadulterated taste of each do its own talking. At the end of a meal here, one thing will be clear: Colicchio's daring restaurant raises the craft of cooking to an art form.

Manhattan Gramercy, Flatiron & Union Square

Pan-roasted Striped Bass

Serves 4

2 Tbsp. peanut oil

4 one-inch thick, center-cut striped bass filets (about 6 oz. each), skin-on

¼ cup unsalted butter

4 sprigs fresh thyme

Kosher salt and freshly ground black pepper

Method

Heat the oil in a large skillet over medium heat. Generously sprinkle the bass filets with Kosher salt and pepper. Once oil is very hot, add to the skillet skin-side down. Reduce the heat and cook the filets until the skins crisp, about 3 minutes. Turn the filets and gently brown the other side, about 3 minutes more. Add the butter and thyme to the pan.

Continue cooking the filets, turning fish over once or twice so they brown evenly, and basting with the lightly browning butter. Cook until the fish is opaque, about 4 minutes more. Place fish on plates and spoon browned butter over top. Garnish each plate with a sprig of thyme from the pan.

Gramercy Tavern ✿

Contemporary

42 E. 20th St. (bet. Broadway & Park Ave. South)

Subway:	14 St - Union Sq	Monday - Thursday noon - 2pm
Phone:	212-477-0777	& 5:30pm - 10pm
Fax:	212-477-1160	Friday noon - 2pm & 5:30pm - 11pm
e-mail:	info@gramercytavern.com	Saturday 5:30pm - 11pm
Web:	www.gramercytavern.com	Sunday 5:30pm - 10pm
Prices:	$$$$	

Gramercy Tavern/Paul Walsh

The word "tavern" conjures up images of a cozy, wood-paneled room, tankards of ale and convivial conversation. That country-inn ambience is what Tom Colicchio and Danny Meyer were going for when they opened Gramercy Tavern in 1994. They must have done something right, since their restaurant still ranks highly among many New Yorkers.

At Gramercy Tavern, you'll have a choice of two different dining spaces. In the back of the restaurant, the formal, main dining room kicks the tavern concept up a notch with its wood-beamed ceiling, velvet draperies and fine artwork. Here, Colicchio's seasonal tasting menus spotlight the best products of the market, masterfully prepared in creative combinations such as roasted cod with brussel sprouts, potatoes boulanger and apple cider. In front, the flower-bedecked tavern room captures the essence of hospitality with its casual, all-day menu.

Gramercy Tavern/Paul Walsh

Rustic Braised Rabbit

Serves 4

1 3½ lb. rabbit
8 oz. whole shallots, peeled
4 oz. whole garlic cloves, peeled
2 Tbsp. tomato paste
1 sprig fresh rosemary
1 quart chicken stock
4 oz. Picholine or Niçoise olives
4 oz. sweet Italian sausage, crumbled
4 oz. tomato, finely diced
salt and pepper to taste
¼ cup olive oil

Method

Cut the rabbit into pieces (legs into four, loin into two, saddle into two). In a heavy-bottomed pot, heat the oil over medium heat. Season the rabbit generously with salt and pepper and brown in the oil. Do this in small batches so the pot is not overcrowded. Set browned pieces aside on a plate. When the rabbit is all lightly browned, add shallots and garlic to an empty pot.

After five minutes, add tomato paste, rosemary, sherry vinegar and chicken stock. Then add the rabbit back into the pot and correct seasoning as desired. Cover the pot with a lid and simmer until the meat is tender when pressed with a fork (1½-2 hours). Add sausage, olives and tomato, and cook for 2-3 minutes more, or until sausage is cooked through.

Fleur de Sel ✿

Contemporary French

5 E. 20th St. (bet. Broadway & Fifth Ave.)

Subway: 23 St
Phone: 212-460-9100
Fax: 212-460-8319
e-mail: contact@fleurdeselnyc.com
Web: www.fleurdeselnyc.com
Prices: $$$

Monday - Saturday noon - 2pm
& 5:30pm - 10:30pm
Sunday noon - 2pm & 5pm - 9pm

Fleur de Sel/Xenia B. Buxo

There are many reasons to dine in this charming French restaurant, whose name ("flower of the salt" in French) refers to a prized type of pure salt hand-harvested on France's Brittany coast. Foremost among them is the delectable, original cuisine prepared by chef/owner Cyril Renaud. His winning concept at Fleur de Sel is to distill the essence of seasonal ingredients and highlight dishes of his native Brittany with daily tasting menus for both lunch and dinner (the three-course lunch menu is a particularly good deal).

Renaud's talent shines in dishes like sea scallops with sunchokes and sweet and sour honey gastrique, or sugarcane and coffee-marinated pork chop with sweet potato purée. Weighted toward French varietals, the wine list offers more than 1,000 selections. The sophisticated dining room is embellished with the chef's original watercolors of—what else?—food.

Fleur de Sel/Xenia B. Buxo

Brittany Caramelized Apple Crêpe

Serves 4

Crêpe Batter

½ quart milk
9 oz. flour
1 oz. sugar
1½ oz. melted unsalted butter

4 eggs
½ oz. fleur de sel

Method

Pour flour in a bowl and make a small in-dentation in the center of the flour mound. One by one, start adding the eggs, stirring gently, without scraping or forcing in any of the flour. As you stir the eggs, they should coat the flour and gradually incorporate the flour into the egg mixture. Once the batter starts to become very thick, add a very small amount of milk and continue to stir. Repeat this process until all of the milk has been used. Lightly season with salt and sugar in a 1:2 ratio of salt to sugar. Strain the batter through a fine chinois into a bowl and then beat in the melted butter. Place in a refrigerator to cool.

To Assemble Crêpes

2 Granny Smith apples, peeled, cored and cut in ¼-inch slices
12 oz. crêpe batter
1 oz. unsalted butter, divided into 8 pats
2 oz. sugar
Whipped cream, ice cream or Devonshire cream, as desired

For each serving, in an 8-inch nonstick pan, combine 1/8 oz. of butter and 3 apple slices. When the butter starts to change color, flip the apple slices and add 3 oz. crêpe batter. Cook crêpe until the batter has set and then flip. Add another 1/8 oz. butter and coat the crêpe with ½ oz. sugar. Flip again. Rotate the pan in a circular motion over the heat to allow the butter and sugar to melt evenly and cara-melize. Flip again and serve immediately. Repeat procedure and quantities for each crêpe. Top with cream, if desired.

Veritas ✿

Contemporary

43 E. 20th St. (bet. Broadway & Park Ave. South)

Subway: 14 St - Union Sq
Phone: 212-353-3700
Fax: 212-353-1632
e-mail: info@veritas-nyc.com
Web: www.veritas-nyc.com
Prices: $$$$

Monday - Saturday 5:30pm - 10:15pm
Sunday 5pm - 9:30pm
Closed major holidays

Veritas/©Emily Cantrell

In vino veritas. There is truth in wine, and the truth is that Veritas spells paradise for oenophiles. Some 100,000 bottles of wine cool their heels in the restaurant's temperature-controlled cellar. It may take you a while to read through the voluminous wine list—or, rather, tome, of 3,000 labels from around the globe. No need to feel overwhelmed, though; the sommelier is always on hand in the stylish dining room to help you narrow down your choices.

While wine may steal the spotlight here, be sure you don't ignore the food. Perfectly prepared creative American dishes, such as braised short ribs with parsnip purée, wild striped bass with hedgehog mushrooms, and roasted organic chicken with mascarpone polenta, are presented in a three-course, fixed-price menu. Sure, it's expensive, but that's the price you pay for bacchanalian pleasures.

Veritas/©Emily Cantrell

Braised Short Ribs

Serves 4

2 bottles of red wine (Dolcetto)
4 lbs. beef short ribs, cleaned
4 plum tomatoes, seeded, peeled and diced
1 cup diced onion
1 cup diced carrot
1 cup diced celery
1 head of garlic
½ lb. fresh Porcini mushrooms, sliced
½ cup butter
¼ cup canola oil
2 sprigs each of fresh rosemary, thyme and sage
¼ cup minced chives
Salt and freshly ground pepper
Potato purée or soft polenta

Method

Preheat oven to 350°F. In a heavy-bottomed sauce pan, heat canola oil. Generously season short ribs with salt and pepper and sear them until golden. Remove ribs and put them in a casserole dish. Add tomatoes and garlic to saucepan and cook until soft. Add wine and bring to a boil. Pour over ribs and add herbs. Cover casserole with foil and place in oven for 2 ½ hours.

Remove ribs from casserole and set aside. Strain juices from casserole through fine chinois. Return ribs to casserole and pour juices back on top.

Melt 3 Tbsp. butter in sauté pan over medium heat. Add onion, carrot and celery and sauté until tender and pale, about ten minutes. Add to ribs in casserole. Return sauté pan to heat and melt remaining butter. Once hot, add mushrooms and sauté until tender and golden, again about ten minutes. Taste and adjust seasoning. Add to ribs.

Sprinkle chives over casserole and serve with potato purée or soft polenta.

Manhattan Gramercy, Flatiron & Union Square

Eleven Madison Park

Contemporary

006

11 Madison Ave. (at 24th St.)

Subway:	23 St	Monday - Thursday 11:30am - 2pm
Phone:	212-889-0905	& 5:30pm - 10:30pm
Fax:	212-889-0918	Friday - Saturday 11:30am - 2pm
e-mail:	N/A	& 5:30pm - 11pm
Web:	www.elevenmadisonpark.com	Sunday 11:30am - 2pm
Prices:	$$$	& 5:30pm - 10pm

XXX
&
🛏

The address of this comfortable, cavernous restaurant, located in the Art Deco MetLife Insurance tower across from Madison Square, is no secret; the name says it all. The restaurant boasts a splendid 1930s-style dining room, distinguished by its 30-foot-high ceiling, stylish chandeliers, sprawling fresh flower arrangements, and huge windows with views of the square and the Flatiron Building. An enterprise by Danny Meyer and the Union Square Hospitality Group, this tony establishment owes its French-inspired American fare to chef/partner Kerry Heffernan, who serves up such specialties as gougères, sautéed skate wing "Grenobloise," and seared loin and almond-crusted shank of lamb with Basquaise peppers.

Olives

Mediterranean

007

201 Park Ave. South (at 17th St.)

Subway:	14 St - Union Sq	Monday - Friday noon - 2:30pm
Phone:	212-353-8345	& 6pm - 10:30pm (Friday 11pm)
Fax:	212-353-9592	Saturday 10:45am - 2:15pm
e-mail:	contact@toddenglish.com	& 6pm - 11pm
Web:	www.toddenglish.com	Sunday 10:45am - 2:15pm
Prices:	$$$	& 6pm - 10:30pm

XXX
&
🛏
🛏

Chef Todd English burst onto the New York City dining scene in 2000 when he opened this outpost of Olives, his popular Boston restaurant, on the first floor of the W Hotel. A link in the chain of English's 13 eateries (Olives is now in six cities, including Tokyo), Olives on Union Square packs 'em in seven nights a week. The draw? A trendy, elegant setting, a chic crowd in the lounge, and English's innovative Mediterranean cuisine. Handmade tortelli of butternut squash, oven-roasted branzino with curried lobster vinaigrette, and pistachio-crusted lamb loin represent the offerings here. Can't get enough of Olives? Purchase a copy of English's cookbook *The Olives Table* at the reception desk.

Tabla

008

11 Madison Ave. (at 25th St.)

Subway:	23 St	Monday - Friday noon - 2pm
Phone:	212-889-0667	& 5:30pm - 10:30pm
Fax:	212-889-3865	Saturday 5:30pm - 10:30pm
e-mail:	twilson@tablany.com	Sunday 5:30pm - 10pm
Web:	www.tablany.com	
Prices:	$$	

XXX
&

A member of Union Square Hospitality Group, Tabla faces Madison Square, next door to Eleven Madison Park (another of Danny Meyer's restaurants). At Tabla you have two dining options. On the first floor, boisterous Bread Bar at Tabla features a short menu of home-style regional Indian fare at reasonable prices. If you're in the mood for a more upscale dining experience, climb the suspended staircase to the second floor and have a seat in Tabla's sensuous, Art Deco dining room. There, chef Floyd Cardoz, a native of Bombay, skillfully fuses contemporary American cuisine with spicy Indian accents (as in baby lamb with garam masala jus, or crab cakes with papadum and tamarind chutney) on his daily changing menu.

Tamarind

009

41-43 E. 22nd St. (bet. Broadway & Park Ave. South)

Subway:	23 St	Sunday - Thursday 11:30am - 3pm
Phone:	212-674-7400	& 5:30pm - 11:30pm
Fax:	212-674-4449	Friday - Saturday 11:30am - 3pm
e-mail:	N/A	& 5:30pm - midnight
Web:	www.tamarinde22.com	
Prices:	$$	

XXX
&

Unlike the sweet-and-sour tropical fruit for which it's named, Tamarind hits no sour notes. Instead, the restaurant achieves a pleasing harmony between its restrained and sophisticated décor (no goddess statues here) and its regional Indian cuisine. Cowbells hang in alcoves in the sparkling, white dining room; a large, wrought-iron wall hanging from a maharaja's palace graces the wall at the front of the restaurant. Inside the glassed-in kitchen, a serious brigade of cooks busies itself preparing piquant dishes from Goa, Punjab, Madras and Calcutta. A good, balanced wine list and a staff of smiling, attentive servers add the final crescendo to this epicurean aria.

Manhattan Gramercy, Flatiron & Union Square

Tocqueville

Contemporary

010

15 E. 15th St. (bet. Fifth Ave. & Union Sq.)

Subway:	14 St - Union Sq
Phone:	212-647-1515
Fax:	212-647-7148
e-mail:	tocqueville15@aol.com
Web:	www.tocquevillerestaurant.com
Prices:	$$

Monday - Saturday 11:45am - 2pm
& 5:30pm - 10:30pm
Sunday 5pm - 10pm

XXX
&
⅋

Named for Alexis de Tocqueville, this restaurant takes its cues from the 19th-century French writer. While de Tocqueville's 1835 book, *Democracy in America*, gave a Frenchman's view of the American political system, Tocqueville, the restaurant, puts an American spin on French dishes. Husband-and-wife chef team Jo-Ann Makovitzky and Brazilian-born Marco Moreira rule the roost here. Jo-Ann put together the 200-label wine list, which features selections from boutique wineries and little-known wine regions around the world. In fall 2005, the restaurant plans to move from the elegant dining space they've occupied since 2000 down the street to 1 East 15th Street (at Fifth Avenue).

Basta Pasta

Italian

011

37 W. 17th St. (bet. Fifth & Sixth Aves.)

Subway:	14 St - Union Sq
Phone:	212-366-0888
Fax:	212-366-0402
e-mail:	N/A
Web:	www.bastapastanyc.com
Prices:	$$

Monday - Friday noon - 2:30pm
& 6pm - 11pm
Saturday 6pm - 11pm
Sunday 5pm - 10pm

XX
Talk about East meets West—how about an Italian restaurant from Tokyo? Basta Pasta was founded in Tokyo in 1985 and modeled after the TV show *Iron Chef*. The idea here is that cooking is theater; indeed, you'll feel like part of the show as you walk through the open kitchen to get to your table. Settle in and enjoy the performance, as a team of Asian chefs plate up the likes of spaghetti with flying fish roe and black squid-ink tagliolini with impeccable precision. As an additional feast for the eyes, a changing gallery of artwork hangs on the walls of the modern dining room. This is delicious dinner theater—and you don't even have to call ahead for tickets (but reservations are recommended).

BLT Prime

Steakhouse

012

111 E. 22nd St. (bet. Park & Lexington Aves.)

Subway:	23 St	Monday - Thursday 11:45am - 2:30pm
Phone:	212-995-8500	& 5:30pm - 11pm
Fax:	212-460-5881	Friday 11:45am - 2:30pm
e-mail:	info@bltprime.com	& 5:30pm - 11:30pm
Web:	www.bltrestaurants.com	Saturday 5:30pm - 11:30pm
Prices:	$$$$	Sunday 5pm - 10pm

Chef Laurent Tourondel had a busy year in 2005. His newest venture, BLT Prime, opened in June, hot on the heels of BLT Fish (launched in January). Tourondel outfitted the space formerly occupied by Union Pacific restaurant in elegant neutral tones ranging from beige to sepia. Under the vaulted glass ceiling, a large blackboard reiterates the menu, which is divided into sections by product, with an obvious emphasis on meat—beef, veal, lamb and poultry. Fish lovers are not forgotten, though; a short selection of fish and shellfish rounds out the list. All dishes are realized by a talented cooking team, and diners are free to choose their own sauces and sides.

Blue Water Grill

Contemporary

013

31 Union Square West (at 16th St.)

Subway:	14 St - Union Sq	Monday - Thursday 11:30am - 4pm
Phone:	212-675-9500	& 5pm - midnight
Fax:	212-675-1899	Friday -Saturday 11:30am - 4pm
e-mail:	N/A	& 5pm - 1am
Web:	www.brguestrestaurants.com	Sunday 10:30am - 4pm
Prices:	$$	& 5pm - midnight

Overlooking Union Square, the 1903 Bank of the Metropolis building still welcomes moneyed clients, only now they must be hungry, too. Today, the building's soaring ceilings, decorative moldings, floor-to-ceiling windows and white-marble walls enclose the main dining room of the Blue Water Grill. There's another reason to come here besides seeing the lovely interior of the former bank. Fresh seafood, from Maryland crab cakes to live Maine lobster, will vie with the décor for your attention. And don't ignore the sushi and maki rolls, or the raw-bar offerings, which include a good selection of oysters. Live jazz plays every night in the downstairs lounge, and there's a jazz brunch on Sunday.

Bolo

Spanish

014

23 E. 22nd St. (bet. Broadway & Park Ave. South)

Subway:	23 St	Monday - Thursday noon - 2:30pm
Phone:	212-228-2200	& 5:30pm - 10pm
Fax:	212-228-2239	Friday noon - 2:30pm & 5:30pm - 11pm
e-mail:	N/A	Saturday 5:30pm - 11pm
Web:	www.bolorestaurant.com	Sunday 5:30pm - 10pm
Prices:	$$$	Closed Christmas Day

Bolo is brought to you by chef Bobby Flay ("Bo") and restaurateur Lawrence Kretchmer ("Lo"), of Mesa Grill fame. Although the spirit is Spanish, it's not traditional; the cooking here reflects Flay's modernized version of Spanish cuisine. A long wood bar lines one side of the comfortable dining room; tables nestle up to a cranberry-red wall on the other. Whether you choose an entrée such as grilled chicken stuffed with Serrano ham and Manchego cheese, or one of the tempting tapas dishes, you'll find that the food isn't inexpensive here. To partially make up for the prices, the portions are copious, so you won't go away lighter, even though your wallet will.

Caviar & Banana

Brazilian

015

12 E. 22nd St. (bet. Broadway & Park Ave. South)

Subway:	23 St	Monday - Thursday 5pm - 10pm
Phone:	212-353-0500	Friday - Saturday 5pm - 11pm
Fax:	212-353-0025	Sunday noon - 6pm
e-mail:	N/A	Closed major holidays
Web:	www.chinagrillmanagement.com	
Prices:	$$$	

Remember the NBC reality-TV series *The Restaurant*? Well, Rocco DiSpirito's ill-fated, eponymous eatery gave way to this new enterprise by ubiquitous New York City restaurateur Jeffrey Chodorow in late 2004. The name refers to the odd-sounding amuse-bouche invented by the restaurant's chef, Claude Troigros (yes, of the Troigros family): tapioca "caviar" served with crispy plaintain chips. The space has been refurbished with blue walls and patchwork banquettes, and for entertainment, lively Brazilian music plays in the background while a small screen shows footage of Claude Troigros in Brazil. As for food and drink, churrascos come with five different sauces, and the caipirinhas flow freely.

Craftbar

Contemporary

900 Broadway (bet. 19th & 20th Sts.)

Subway:	14 St - Union Sq	Sunday - Monday noon - 2:30pm
Phone:	212-461-4300	& 5:30pm - 10pm
Fax:	212-598-1859	Tuesday - Saturday noon - 2:30pm
e-mail:	N/A	& 5:30pm - 11pm
Web:	N/A	
Prices:	SS	

In April 2005, Craftbar, the seductive annex to Tom Colicchio's Craft restaurant, moved to bigger digs around the corner. At Craft's casual cousin, you can sample Colicchio's food at a lower price point. The cuisine, realized by a talented cooking team, successfully blends contemporary American style with undeniably French flair. The menu changes every day so customers can enjoy the fresh flavors of select seasonal products (think cured hamachi with fresh chamomile and pickled ramps followed by Niman Ranch pork loin with braised smoked bacon and fiddlehead ferns). Here, as at Craft, you'll find a large wine list, with many selections by the glass.

Dévi

Indian

8 E. 18th St. (bet. Broadway & Fifth Ave.)

Subway:	14 St - Union Sq	Monday - Saturday noon - 2:30pm
Phone:	212-691-1300	& 5:30pm - 11pm
Fax:	212-691-1695	Sunday 5:30pm - 11pm
e-mail:	chef@suvir.com	
Web:	www.devinyc.com	
Prices:	SS	

It's no wonder that the dining-room décor at Dévi seems fit for a goddess, since the Hindu mother goddess inspired the restaurant's name. Once you step inside, you'll be struck by the heavenly interior, which blends elements from both Indian homes and temples. In this sumptuous setting, gauzy jewel-tone fabrics swathe the walls; banquettes covered in a patchwork of brown, yellow and orange provide cozy seating; and clusters of colored lanterns hang from the red ceiling. Cookbook author Survir Saran and Tandoori master Hemant Mathur, who opened the 75-seat restaurant in fall 2004, preside over the kitchen and put a new spin on traditional Indian fare.

Manhattan Gramercy, Flatiron & Union Square

I Trulli

Italian

018

122 E. 27th St. (bet. Park Ave. South & Lexington Ave.)

Subway:	28 St	Monday - Thursday noon - 3pm
Phone:	212-481-7372	& 5:30pm - 10pm
Fax:	212-481-5785	Friday noon - 3pm & 5pm - 10:30pm
e-mail:	N/A	Saturday 5pm - 10:30pm
Web:	www.itrulli.com	Sunday 5pm - 10pm
Prices:	$$	Closed major holidays

Located near Madison Square, the family of establishments that falls under the I Trulli umbrella includes something for almost everyone. Next door to the restaurant is a wine bar called Enoteca I Trulli, and, across the street, you'll find Vino, which sells Italian wines and spirits. I Trulli features the cuisine of Puglia, the owner's native region; the restaurant even has its own label of olive oil, harvested and bottled in Italy. The dining room's rustic fireplace, open kitchen and wood-burning oven evoke the Italian countryside. In the warm seasons, you can dine on the covered terrace out back. Prices of both the food and wine are quite reasonable—the lunch menu is an exceptional value.

Komegashi

Contemporary Japanese

019

928 Broadway (bet. 21st & 22nd Sts.)

Subway:	23 St	Monday - Sunday 11:30am - 11:30pm
Phone:	212-475-3000	
Fax:	212-475-3207	
e-mail:	info@komegashi.com	
Web:	www.komegashi.com	
Prices:	$$	

Take an experienced Japanese chef assisted by a solid Nippon team, add traditional Japanese recipes interpreted using classic French techniques, blend it into a large, trendy setting, shake with professionalism, and voila!—you get Komegashi. «Reconstruction cuisine» is how the restaurant describes itself, a novel concept, to be sure, but a delicious one nonetheless. Tofu blancmange, terrine of foie gras with teriyaki chicken, steak-frites rolls, and a variety of grilled meat and vegetable skewers are just a sampling of the unusual offerings here. Save room for confections like banana chiboust, served with rum ice cream and citrus-chocolate sauce.

Mesa Grill

020

Southwestern

102 Fifth Ave. (bet. 15th & 16th Sts.)

Subway:	14 St - Union Sq	Monday - Friday noon - 2:30pm
Phone:	212-807-7400	& 5:30pm - 10:30pm
Fax:	212-989-0034	Saturday 11:30am - 3pm
e-mail:	sb@mesagrill.com	& 5:30pm - 11pm
Web:	www.mesagrill.com	Sunday 11:30am - 3pm
Prices:	$$$	& 5:30pm - 10:30pm

Between his three shows on the Food Network, his four cookbooks, and his three restaurants (Mesa Grill and Bolo in NYC, and Mesa Grill in Las Vegas), celebrity chef Bobby Flay is hard to miss. A graduate of the French Culinary Institute, Flay gravitated not to foie gras and truffles, but to products native to the Americas: corn, chiles, black beans, avocados. While you wouldn't choose Mesa Grill, with its boisterous, brightly colored dining room, for a quiet evening out, you would choose it for kicked-up Southwestern cuisine like zesty shrimp and roasted-garlic corn tamales, sizzling sixteen-spice chicken, and a margarita list that includes more than 25 different tequilas.

Park Avalon

021

Contemporary

225 Park Ave. South (bet. 18th & 19th Sts.)

Subway:	14 St - Union Sq	Monday 11:30am - 11:30pm
Phone:	212-533-2500	Tuesday - Saturday 11:30am - 12:30am
Fax:	212-533-2661	Sunday 10:30am - 4pm
e-mail:	N/A	& 5pm - 11:30pm
Web:	www.brguestrestaurants.com	
Prices:	$$	

A member of the B.R. Guest Restaurant Group, Park Avalon brings a sleek sophistication to the restaurant scene around Union Square. The high-ceilinged dining room is part contemporary-chic, part 1930s New York supper club. Huge mirrors amplify the attractive space, decorated with tile-covered square columns, shelves of bottles neatly lined up behind the bar, and a chapel-like counter of lighted candles. Asian accents pepper American fare such as wasabi-crusted big-eye tuna, and Maryland crab cakes with mango chutney and mizuna greens. On Sunday, the popular brunch stars a menu of egg and pancake dishes, along with live jazz—and even a complimentary mimosa.

Periyali

Greek

022

35 W. 20th St. (bet. Fifth & Sixth Aves.)

Subway:	23 St	Monday - Thursday noon - 3pm
Phone:	212-463-7890	& 5:30pm - 11pm
Fax:	212-924-9403	Friday noon - 3pm & 5:30pm - 11:30pm
e-mail:	info@periyali.com	Saturday 5:30pm - 11:30pm
Web:	www.periyali.com	Closed Sunday & major holidays
Prices:	$$	

If it's a break from the city's hustle and bustle you're looking for, you'll find it here. With its white-plaster walls and wood-beamed ceiling—draped, sail-like, with white fabric—Periyali suggests the rustic ambience of islands in the Aegean. As you'd expect of a restaurant whose name means "seashore" in Greek, the cuisine focuses on the sunny cuisine of the Greek islands. Entrées range from traditional moussaka to salmon baked in phyllo with spinach and feta. The dining space, divided into four small rooms, makes a great place to have an intimate rendezvous or to discuss business over a good bottle of Greek wine. Service is attentive and professional.

Sapa

Vietnamese

023

43 W. 24th St. (bet. Fifth & Sixth Aves.)

Subway:	23 St	Monday - Wednesday 5:30pm - 11:30pm
Phone:	212-929-1800	Thursday - Saturday 5:30pm - 1:30am
Fax:	212-929-7070	Sunday 11am - 4pm
e-mail:	info@sapanyc.com	& 5:30pm - 10:30pm
Web:	www.sapanyc.com	
Prices:	$$$	

Since Sapa opened in fall 2004, throngs of beautiful people clad in the latest prêt-à-porter designs have filled this restaurant on the border of Chelsea and Gramercy. Why all the buzz? A festive atmosphere; a seductive, contemporary setting designed by AvroKo with Asian wire lanterns, French garden urns and exotic woods; and an amazing culinary alchemy that expertly marries Vietnamese and French cuisine. If it sounds schizophrenic, it doesn't taste that way. Named for a North Vietnamese village built by the French in the 1920s, Sapa brines chicken in oolong tea, brushes roasted duck breast with red curry-pineapple glaze, and steams mussels and clams in lemongrass-coconut broth.

Shaffer City

024

5 W. 21st St. (bet. Fifth & Sixth Aves.)

Subway:	23 St	Monday - Saturday noon - 11pm
Phone:	212-255-9827	Closed Sunday, Christmas Day
Fax:	212-414-1621	& New Year's Day
e-mail:	ajshef@aol.com	
Web:	www.shaffercity.com	
Prices:	$$$	

Owner Jay Shaffer personally welcomes oyster lovers to his charming restaurant, located two blocks from the Flatiron Building. In the dining room, with its exposed brick and tile walls, maritime artifacts, and models and paintings of antique ships, you could just as easily be in someone's seaside house on the Atlantic Ocean. Oysters take center stage here; the extensive list, from the Atlantic and the Pacific, offers informative explanations about the distinctive qualities of each. But don't overlook the fish dishes, such as braised cod served atop Maine peekytoe crabmeat and tomato risotto, and shellfish slow-cooked in truffled corn and lobster velouté. And expect service with a smile.

Turkish Kitchen

025

386 Third Ave. (bet. 27th & 28th Sts.)

Subway:	28 St	Monday - Thursday noon - 3pm
Phone:	212-679-6633	& 5:30pm - 11pm
Fax:	212-679-1830	Friday noon - 3pm & 5pm - 11:30pm
e-mail:	info@turkishkitchenny.com	Saturday 5pm - 11:30pm
Web:	www.turkishkitchenny.com	Sunday 5pm - 10:30pm
Prices:		

You'll see red when you step inside the Turkish Kitchen's windowed façade on Third Avenue—red walls, that is. The inside of the first-floor dining room is all painted bright red, with a dark ceiling. The decoration is minimal, but effective; wall shelves and alcoves are filled with copper urns and fresh orchids. At night, the place glows in the candlelight of blue-glass votives that hang on the walls. When you taste the food here, you'll be reminded of Turkey's proximity to Greece; lamb, eggplant, yogurt and feta cheese all figure prominently on the menu. For both lunch and dinner, the 3-course, prix-fixe menu is a terrific deal; be sure to try a glass of Turkish wine.

Union Square Cafe

Italian

026

21 E. 16th St. (bet. Union Sq. & Fifth Ave.)

Subway:	14 St - Union Sq	Monday - Thursday noon - 2:15pm
Phone:	212-243-4020	& 5:30pm - 9:45pm
Fax:	212-627-2673	Friday - Saturday noon - 2:15pm
e-mail:	info@unionsquarecafe.com	& 5:30pm - 10:45pm
Web:	www.unionsquarecafe.com	Sunday 5:30pm - 9:45pm
Prices:	$$$	Closed major holidays

A young entrepreneur named Danny Meyer opened this cafe in 1985 as the first restaurant on Union Square. Three years later, executive chef/partner Michael Romano came on board, and he's been here ever since. You probably know the rest of the story; this popular place still packs in crowds of locals and tourists most every night. Given Union Square Cafe's comfortable bistro décor, winning service and Italian-inspired cooking, it's not hard to see why. The menu offers a selection of entrées as well as daily and weekly specials (osso buco, for instance, is only served on Sunday). If you're planning a special occasion here, be sure to call for reservations at least two weeks in advance.

Aleo

Italian

027

7 W. 20th St. (bet. Fifth & Sixth Aves.)

Subway:	14 St - Union Sq	Monday - Friday noon - 11pm
Phone:	212-691-8136	Saturday 3pm - midnight
Fax:	212-691-8286	Sunday 3pm - 10pm
e-mail:	aleorestaurant@yahoo.com	
Web:	www.aleorestaurant.com	
Prices:	$$	

The name of this simple Italian restaurant honors the owner's parents: A for his mother, Antoinette, and Leo for his father, Leonardo. In the modest dining room, soberly decorated with black-and-white photos of Italy, Aleo proposes a nice choice of antipasti, pastas and entrées. Unmistakable Mediterranean accents appear in many of the dishes, such as chicken breast marinated in chermoula, and squid stuffed with feta cheese and spinach. Prices are attractively reasonable; don't miss the two-course, fixed-price menu served at lunch—it's a real bargain. Out back, the cute little walled patio garden provides a quiet respite no matter the season—in winter the space is covered and heated.

Beppe

Italian

45 E. 22nd St. (bet. Broadway & Park Ave. South)

Subway:	23 St	Monday - Thursday noon - 2:30pm
Phone:	212-982-8422	& 5:30pm - 10:30pm
Fax:	212-982-6616	Friday noon - 2:30pm
e-mail:	info@beppenyc.com	& 5:30pm - 11:30pm
Web:	www.beppenyc.com	Saturday 5:30pm - 11:30pm
Prices:	SS	Closed Sunday

Cesare Casella followed in his parents' footsteps (they owned a little trattoria outside the Tuscan town of Lucca), traveling from Tuscany to New York City to make a name for himself. Now Casella is the chef and owner of Beppe, which he named for his grandfather. Located a half-block from the Flatiron Building, Beppe is a modest place, with an intentionally aged-looking décor made warm and cozy by a working fireplace in winter. The designer-clad clientele doesn't seem to mind paying uptown prices for food that reflects the best of each season. Casella is committed to offering homemade prosciutto, salami and sausage, and Italian varieties of produce organically grown in upstate New York.

Casa Mono

Spanish

52 Irving Pl. (at 17th St.)

Subway:	14 St - Union Sq	Monday - Sunday noon - midnight
Phone:	212-253-2773	Closed Thanksgiving Day
Fax:	212-253-5318	& Christmas Day
e-mail:	barjamon@yahoo.com	
Web:	N/A	
Prices:	SS	

Brought to you by the winning restaurant duo of Joseph Bastianich and chef Mario Batali, Casa Mono opened in fall 2003. A lively crowd has been filling up the tiny, rustic dining room ever since. They come to sample Spanish wines and sherries and to nibble small plates of mussels with chorizo, Serrano ham, tripe with chickpeas, and crema catalana—served here with fried laurel leaves—created by chef/owner Andy Nusser, an alumnus of Batali ventures Babbo and Pó. If you can't get into Casa Mono, try its baby sister, Bar Jamón (Spanish for "ham bar") next door; there you can nosh on bocadillos (Spanish sandwiches) washed down with a glass of Rioja.

Manhattan Gramercy, Flatiron & Union Square

Dos Caminos

030

373 Park Ave. South (bet. 26th & 27th Sts.)

Subway:	28 St	Sunday - Monday 11:30am - 11pm
Phone:	212-294-1000	Tuesday - Thursday 11:30am - midnight
Fax:	212-294-1090	Friday - Saturday 11:30am - 12:30am
e-mail:	N/A	
Web:	www.brguestrestaurants.com	
Prices:	$$	

If you've never tasted good tequila, here's your chance. The bar at Dos Caminos offers 100 different types of the alcohol made by distilling the fermented juice of the agave plant. Don't taste too many, though, or you won't be able to appreciate the restaurant's vibrant 250-seat dining space, colored in bright pink, orange and brown, and dimly lit by a group of hand-carved wood light fixtures dangling from the ceiling. And you don't want to dull your taste buds before sampling the piquant Mexican cuisine, beginning with the guacamole, prepared tableside. From tomatillos to tortillas, the dishes recall the different regions of Mexico. Drop by Sunday for the salsa brunch—salsa music, that is.

Kitchen22

Contemporary

031

36 E. 22nd St. (bet. Broadway & Park Ave. South)

Subway:	23 St	Monday - Thursday 5pm - 10:30pm
Phone:	212-228-4399	Friday - Saturday 5:30pm - 11pm
Fax:	212-228-4612	Closed Sunday
e-mail:	info@charliepalmer.com	
Web:	www.charliepalmer.com	
Prices:	⊜	

Residents of Gramercy Park can count themselves lucky to have Kitchen22 as their neighborhood restaurant. This is the kind of casual, contemporary place you'll want to come back to often—and with prices this moderate, you'll be able to do just that. Be prepared to stand in line, though; this member of Charlie Palmer's restaurant group doesn't take reservations. While you wait, you can claim a spot at the bar and brush up on your geography by studying the unique globe light fixtures. Once your table is ready, you can make your selection from the three-course, fixed-price menu, offering a short but creative choice of updated American cuisine.

Manhattan Gramercy, Flatiron & Union Square

Les Halles

F r e n c h

411 Park Ave. South (bet. 28th & 29th Sts.)

Subway:	28 St
Phone:	212-679-4111
Fax:	212-779-0679
e-mail:	N/A
Web:	www.leshalles.net
Prices:	$$

Monday - Sunday 8am - midnight

This brasserie (with its sister location in the Financial District) serves as home base for Anthony Bourdain, culinary bad boy and author of the restaurant exposé, *Kitchen Confidential*. A graduate of the Culinary Institute of America, Bourdain presides over the kitchen here, turning out classic bistro fare in a typically bustling Belle Époque atmosphere. Named for the famous French market, Les Halles is designed with dark wood moldings, a stamped-tin ceiling, and antique light fixtures. To re-create dishes like choucroute garnie, steak au poivre, and coq au vin at home, you can buy Bourdain's *Les Halles Cookbook*; then again, it's much easier to just make a reservation at Les Halles.

Lucy

L a t i n   A m e r i c a n

35 E. 18th St. (bet. Broadway & Park Ave. South)

Subway:	14 St - Union Sq
Phone:	212-475-5829
Fax:	212-598-3020
e-mail:	N/A
Web:	www.abchome.com
Prices:	$$

Monday - Thursday noon - 3:30pm
& 6pm - 11pm
Friday noon - 3:30pm
& 5:30pm - midnight
Saturday 5:30pm - midnight
Sunday 5:30pm - 11pm

Fortunately for hungry shoppers, the sprawling ABC Home & Carpet store contains two restaurants, Lucy and Pipa. The former showcases Latin dishes in a hacienda-style room with a wood-beamed ceiling, terra-cotta tiles, and white walls embellished by images of sunny Mexico. The cuisine of Mexico, Cuba and South America provide inspiration for empanadas, ceviches, enchiladas and entrées such as shell steak a la Catalina and lobster paella, while the wine list focuses on Spanish labels. Don't have time to eat? Take a break at the brightly colored bar, where you can enjoy the lively Latin music and sip the likes of a Kafir lime and mango mojito or a passion capirinha.

Manhattan Gramercy, Flatiron & Union Square

Park Bistro

034

414 Park Ave. South (bet. 28th & 29th Sts.)

Subway:	28 St	Monday - Sunday noon - 3pm
Phone:	212-689-1360	& 5pm - 10:30pm
Fax:	212-689-6437	
e-mail:	parkbistronyc@aol.com	
Web:	N/A	
Prices:	$$	

A black-and-white portrait of actress Simone Signoret welcomes you at the entrance of this French bistro, opened in 1989. Step inside and you're immersed in 1920s Paris: photographs of the City of Light by Robert Doisneau decorate the ivory-colored wall, French singers croon in the background, and red banquettes and bistro chairs cozy up to white linen and paper-topped tables in the recently refurbished room. For lunch and dinner, the fixed-price menu (served before 7pm) is a real bargain. A la carte selections showcase French classics (escargots, quiche, duck confit, coq au vin), and the short wine list offers a good but inexpensive selection of wines from France.

Pipa

035

38 E. 19th St. (bet. Broadway & Park Ave. South)

Subway:	14 St - Union Sq	Monday - Thursday noon - 3pm
Phone:	212-677-2233	& 6pm - 11pm
Fax:	212-598-3020	Friday noon - 3pm & 5:30pm - midnight
e-mail:	N/A	Saturday 5:30pm - midnight
Web:	N/A	Sunday 5:30pm - 10pm
Prices:	$$	

You can access Pipa directly from 19th Street, but it's much more fun to enter the restaurant by perusing your way to the back of the ABC Home & Carpet store (at 888 Broadway). You're sure to work up an appetite browsing the seven floors of furnishings, fabrics, handicrafts, tableware and knickknacks. When you're ready for a bite to eat, Pipa offers a variety of tapas as well as sandwiches and salads for lunch; for dinner, the menu adds Catalan flatbreads, paellas and a short list of entrées. There's an interesting selection of Spanish wines, too. While you're eating, you can pick out a chandelier from the eclectic collection that hangs overhead (they're all for sale in the store).

Pure Food and Wine

036

54 Irving Pl. (bet. 17th & 18th Sts.)

Subway:	14 St - Union Sq	Monday - Saturday 5:30pm - 11pm
Phone:	212-477-1010	Sunday 5:30pm - 10pm
Fax:	212-477-6916	
e-mail:	purefoodandwine@yahoo.com	
Web:	www.purefoodandwine.com	
Prices:	$$	

Carnivores beware: this restaurant's name means what it says. A disciple of the raw food movement—no, it's not just another food fad—Pure Food and Wine serves only raw vegetarian dishes. If you're a first-timer here, the waiters will explain that to preserve vitamins, enzymes, minerals and flavors in the food, nothing is heated above 118°F. Spicy Thai lettuce wraps with tamarind chile sauce, and zucchini and golden tomato lasagne with basil-pistachio pesto don't just taste good, they're good for you. Just ask chef/owner Matthew Kenney, who uses only the freshest organic products he can find. In warm weather, the quiet garden terrace makes a great place to commune with nature while you eat.

Vatan

037

409 Third Ave. (bet. 28th & 29th Sts.)

Subway:	28 St	Tuesday - Thursday 5:30pm - 9pm
Phone:	212-689-5666	Friday - Sunday 5:30pm - 10:15pm
Fax:	N/A	Closed Monday
e-mail:	N/A	
Web:	www.vatanny.com	
Prices:		

When you step inside Vatan, you'll instantly be transported to a Gujarati village on the Arabian Sea in western India. Portraits of Ganesh, the god of wisdom, and of Annapurnadevi, the goddess of prosperity, welcome you at the end of a bamboo-lined corridor. Keep going, and you'll find yourself in a setting of huts, banyan trees, wisteria vines, and a whimsical mural of the Indian countryside. Take your shoes off and have a seat at one of the low tables. There's no need for decision making here. The fixed-price, all-you-can-eat menu comprises a 20-course repast of regional Indian specialties—all strictly vegetarian—served by waitresses dressed in bright sarongs.

Manhattan Gramercy, Flatiron & Union Square

About Greenwich & the West Village

Manhattan Greenwich & the West Village

Centering on Washington Square, New York's historic bohemia lies between Houston and 14th streets, from Bowery west to the Hudson River. Known as the **West Village**, this neighborhood holds within it several distinct areas. The prettiest and oldest of these is **Greenwich Village**, which spreads west from Washington Square and nearby New York University to the vicinity of Hudson Street, where the village originated. Lined with trees and Federal and Greek Revival row houses, this beguiling tangle of narrow streets is ideal for wandering. As for eating, this area contains a high concentration of fine restaurants, offering cuisines from around the globe.

A Bit of History – Prior to settlement, the area now occupied by Greenwich Village was covered with woods and streams and sheltered an Algonquian Indian settlement. In 1696 British colonists founded a hamlet here, called Greenwich after the city in England.

What is now the West Village was originally a marshland and a favorite hunting ground of the early colonists. The site on which Washington Square now stands was purchased by the city in 1788 for use as a potter's field and public gallows. In 1826 the square was designated as a military parade ground, and a fashionable residential enclave grew up around it. Irish, Italian and Chinese immigrants, as well as free blacks, came to the area in the late 19th century, driving the "old money" uptown and creating an ethnically diverse new bohemia. The early 1900s saw intellectuals, social reformers, artists and radicals pour into Greenwich Village, making the neighborhood the nexus of the American avant-garde.

© Cucina Stagionale/NYC & Company, Inc.

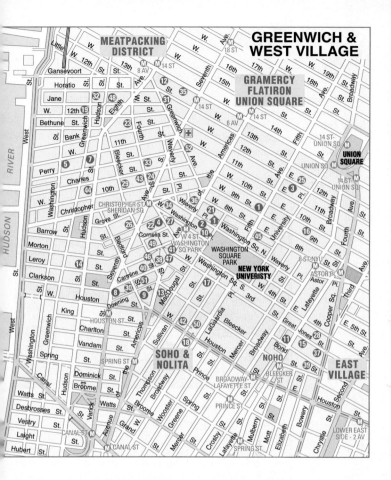

The heart of historic **Greenwich Village** is bounded by *(clockwise from north)* Christopher Street, Seventh Avenue South, St. Luke's Place and Hudson Street, inside of which is a skewed layout of crooked streets lined with town houses and old trees. The commercial spine of Greenwich Village, **Bleecker Street** grows increasingly upscale as it nears the Meatpacking District. The stretch of **Hudson Street** between Christopher and Bank streets is lined with restaurants and cafes.

The area anchored by **Washington Square** is largely defined by the presence of **New York University**, founded in 1831 by Albert Gallatin, secretary of the Treasury under Thomas Jefferson. One of the largest private universities in the country, NYU has an undergraduate population of 40,000. The blocks south of the square are filled with student hangouts.

Cru ✤

Contemporary

001

24 Fifth Ave. (at W. 9th St.)

Subway:	8 St - NYU	Monday - Saturday 5:30pm - 11pm
Phone:	212-529-1700	Closed Sunday
Fax:	212-529-6300	
e-mail:	robert@cru-nyc.com	
Web:	www.cru-nyc.com	
Prices:	$$$$	

As its name suggests, Cru spotlights fine wines in its Greenwich Village dining room. The wine "list" here is more of a book—a 222-page book, to be exact—and ranks as one of the best in New York City. Some 3,500 selections span the globe and include some truly exceptional premier cru bottles; nearly a third of the roster is devoted to burgundies. And since you'll need something to eat while you're enjoying your wine, Cru offers chef Shea Gallante's innovative seasonal tasting menus, which often include her signature homemade pastas. Fish dishes here, such as day boat snowy grouper and Columbia River sturgeon, particularly sparkle.

All this wonderful food and wine is served by an attentive waitstaff in a smart Art Deco setting of lustrous woods, black-leather banquettes, soft lighting, and muted tones. The casual bar area up front serves small plates and doesn't require reservations.

Cru/Thomas Schauer

Ravioli with Pecorino, Snap Peas and Parsley

Serves 4

Pasta Dough

17 oz. durum flour 3 whole eggs
2 egg yolks 3 oz. water
1 tsp. salt 1 Tbsp. olive oil

Filling

½ cup grated Pecorino Romano
½ cup Italian parsley
¼ cup grated Asiago Vecchio
1 oz. grated Tartufello (black truffle Pecorino)
2 oz. Ricotta Romano
1 oz. grated Parmesan
salt and pepper to taste

Sauce

1 cup chicken stock 1 sprig fresh marjoram
1 Tbsp. butter 1 Tbsp. olive oil
1 tsp. grated Parmesan
salt and pepper to taste

Garnish

1 tsp. walnut oil
freshly grated parmesan cheese to taste

Method

Combine the ingredients for the pasta dough and mix either by hand or in a mixer until blended. Let mixture rest for 2 hours. After this, roll dough out by hand into thin sheets or pass through a pasta machine. Ideally, you should have 6-by-12-inch sheets.

In a pot of salted water, blanch the parsley for ten seconds and then shock it in ice water. When it has cooled, drain and squeeze all the water out of it; purée it in the blender.

Mix all ingredients for the filling and pass mixture through a fine sieve.

Lay out one sheet of pasta and, using a spoon, place piles of filling about the size you want the ravioli to be. Dot filling with parsley purée and cover with another layer of filling. Cover with another pasta sheet and form your ravioli making sure there are no air bubbles around the filling. Cut around the formed ravioli. Repeat until all the filling is used.

In a large sauté pan, combine all the ingredients for the sauce over a low flame. Stir to combine.

Bring a large pot of salted water to a boil. Gently place the ravioli in the boiling water, and when they float to the top, carefully remove the ravioli; drain and place in sauté pan with the sauce. Toss the ravioli and divide between four bowls. Garnish with a few drops of walnut oil and Parmesan.

Babbo ☆

Italian

110 Waverly Pl. (bet. Sixth Ave. & MacDougal St.)

Subway: W 4 St - Wash Sq Pk
Phone: 212-777-0303
Fax: 212-777-3365
e-mail: N/A
Web: www.babbonyc.com
Prices: $$$

Monday - Saturday 5:30pm - 11:30pm
Sunday 5pm - 11pm

Babbo/Christopher Hirsheimer

It's not for nothing that Babbo's celebrity chef/owner is known to Food Network groupies as "Molto" Mario. With an empire of New York City restaurants, including Lupa, Esca and Otto, three TV shows, and five cookbooks, Mario Batali is indeed "extremely" Mario. It's amazing that this ponytailed chef, who spent three years cooking in a little village in Italy, finds time to cook at his flagship restaurant, but luckily for diners, he does.

Local seasonal ingredients, fresh from the Union Square Greenmarket (organic and heirloom produce), made in house (cured meats), or imported from Italy (Parmigiano Reggiano, balsamic vinegar, prosciutto San Daniele) make for memorable meals at this boisterous, always-crowded osteria (hint: reserve a table—well in advance—in the quieter second-floor dining room). To pair with the rustic cuisine, the excellent wine list contains only Italian varietals.

Two-Minute Calamari

Serves 4

1 Tbsp. Kosher salt
1 cup Israeli couscous
¼ cup extra virgin olive oil
2 Tbsp. pine nuts
2 Tbsp. currants
1 Tbsp. hot red pepper flakes
¼ cup caperberries
2 cups basic tomato sauce
1 ½ pounds cleaned calamari tubes, cut into ¼-inch rounds, tentacles halved
¼ tsp. kosher salt
¼ tsp. freshly ground pepper
3 scallions, thinly sliced

Bring 3 quarts of water to a boil and add 1 Tbsp. of salt. Set up a bowl of ice water nearby. Cook the couscous in the boiling water for 2 minutes, then drain and immediately plunge it into the ice bath. Once cooled, drain the couscous and set it aside on a plate to dry.

In a 12- or 14-inch sauté pan, heat the oil until just smoking. Add the pine nuts, currants, and red pepper flakes, and sauté until the nuts are just golden brown, about 2 minutes. Add the caperberries, tomato sauce and couscous and bring to a boil. Add the calamari to the pan, stir to mix, and simmer for about 2 minutes, or until the calamari is just cooked and opaque. Season with the salt and pepper, pour into a large warm bowl, sprinkle with scallions and serve immediately.

Gotham Bar and Grill ❀

Contemporary

12 E. 12th St. (bet. Fifth Ave. & University Pl.)

Subway:	14 St - Union Sq	Monday - Thursday noon - 2:15pm
Phone:	212-620-4020	& 5:30pm - 10pm
Fax:	212-627-7810	Friday noon - 2:15pm & 5:30pm - 11pm
e-mail:	gothamgm@aol.com	Saturday 5pm - 11pm
Web:	www.gothambarandgrill.com	Sunday 5pm - 10pm
Prices:	$$$	

Manhattan Greenwich & the West Village

Gotham Bar & Grill

French-trained chef Alfred Portale, who has presided over Gotham Bar and Grill's kitchen since the restaurant opened in 1984, is as well known for being a defining force in New American cuisine as he is for his towering food designs. In the restaurant's high-ceilinged room with its fabric-swathed light fixtures, the chef offers a monthly changing menu of dishes prized for their clean, intense flavors and the high quality of their ingredients.

Portale eschews the heavier French dishes for fresh vegetables and herbs. Add to this careful service that strives to anticipate diners' needs, and you have a surefire recipe for success. Don't have time for dinner? Go for the three-course lunch, served weekdays all year long. It's accompanied by a special wine list that gives you the option of ordering a wine flight of three glasses, a half bottle, or a full bottle, all for the same low price.

Gotham Bar & Grill

Lobster with Cabbage

Serves 4

Sauce

6 lobsters (1 ¼ pounds each) tails and claws removed and reserved, bodies split in half
1 medium Spanish onion, chopped
1 large carrot, chopped
2 celery stalks, chopped
2 heads garlic, split in half
6 plum tomatoes, chopped
2 tablespoons black peppercorns
2 bay leaves
½ bunch parsley
6 sprigs fresh thyme
1 ½ cups white wine
3 cups chicken stock
¼ cup heavy cream
1 cup unsalted butter
¼ tsp. cayenne pepper
salt and ground pepper
¼ cup canola oil

Heat oil in a large stock pot over medium heat. Add lobster bodies and brown for 20 minutes. Add tomatoes and cook for 4 minutes. Add onions, carrots, celery, garlic, parsley, bay leaves, thyme and pepper, and cook for 2-3 minutes. Add wine and reduce by three-quarters. Add stock and bring to a boil; reduce heat and simmer 1 hour. Press entire mixture through a fine sieve, to yield about 4 cups. Return stock to pot over high heat and boil until reduced by half. Add cream and bring to a boil. Remove from heat and whisk in the butter. Season with cayenne, salt and pepper, and set aside.

Cabbage

1 medium head savoy cabbage
12 medium fingerling potatoes
16 garlic cloves, separated but not peeled
2 Tbsp. extra virgin olive oil
Salt and freshly ground pepper

Blanch cabbage in boiling salted water for 3 to 4 minutes. Drain and reserve. Cook the potatoes in salted water until tender, then drain. In a baking dish, combine garlic, extra virgin olive oil, salt, and pepper. Cover with foil and place in a 350°F oven for 25 minutes. Set aside.

Lobster

Split the lobster tails in half, and season with salt and pepper. In 2 large sauté pans, heat oil over medium heat. Add the tails, flesh side down, along with claws and potatoes. Brown for 2-3 minutes and turn. Add roasted garlic cloves and place in a 350°F oven for 2-3 minutes more, until the lobsters are just cooked through and potatoes brown. In a sauté pan, reheat cabbage in half-cup of reserved sauce and a ½ cup of water. Arrange potato, cabbage, lobster and garlic cloves on a plate and spoon reserved sauce over top.

Annisa ✿

13 Barrow St. (bet. Seventh Ave. S. & W. 4th St.)

Subway:	W 4 St - Wash Sq Pk	Monday - Saturday 5:30pm - 10:30pm
Phone:	212-741-6699	Sunday 5:30pm - 9:30pm
Fax:	N/A	
e-mail:	N/A	
Web:	www.annisarestaurant.com	
Prices:	$$$	

✗ ✗

Annisa

A serene vibe enfolds you inside this West Village wonder, whose name is Arabic for "women." Indeed, there is much that is feminine about Annisa, starting with the two owners, chef Anita Lo and sommelier Jennifer Scism. Then there's the minimalist décor, softened by a flowing white curtain that lines one wall. Well-spaced, white-cloth-draped tables and curving coral-colored banquettes fill the dining room. Another tribute to the feminine is the wine list; most of its 90 labels are either made by female vintners and/or made at vineyards with female proprietors.

The chef's inventive, seasonally changing menu is American at heart, but Lo's Asian roots reveal themselves regularly in dishes such as miso-marinated sable with crispy silken tofu. Don't be put off by some of the obscure ingredients—konnyaku, for example—on the menu; the knowledgeable staff will happily answer any questions.

Miso Marinated Sable with Crispy Silken Tofu

Marinade

3 Tbsp. mirin   3 Tbsp. sake
1 tsp. yuzu juice
3 scallions, white part only, julienned
½ cup saikyo miso (sweet white miso)

Bring the sake and mirin to a boil. Remove from heat and allow to come to room temperature. Once cool, combine with miso, scallions and yuzu. Coat fish liberally on both sides with marinade in a non-reactive dish or container. Cover and allow to cure in the refrigerator two to three days.

Dashi

5 cups water   ½ cup bonito flakes
1 four-inch square of kombu, rinsed

Place the kombu and water into a pot and bring to a boil. Turn off heat and add the bonito flakes. Allow to steep for 20 minutes, then strain through a fine cheesecloth. Set aside both broth and drained kombu.

Broth

1 quart dashi   ¼ cup soy
¼ cup mirin (or to taste), boiled for ten minutes
2 Tbsp. yuzu (or to taste)

To make the broth, season the dashi to taste with the mirin, soy and yuzu. Taste and adjust seasoning.

Garnish

reserved kombu, from dashi, cut into strips
1 oz. dashi   1/2 oz. soy sauce
1/2 oz. mirin   1/2 oz. sugar

Bring dashi to a boil. Add kombu, soy, mirin and sugar. Reduce heat and simmer until mixture coats the back of a spoon, about 7-10 minutes.

To Plate

4 six-ounce sable filets, skin on
4 scallions, julienned
6 Tbsp. red tobikko
1 pkg. silken Japanese tofu, cut into 4 slices
1 cup cornstarch combined with ¼ tsp. salt & pepper

Preheat broiler to 500°F. Wipe excess marinade from the fish and place skin side up in a shallow heatproof container filled with a half-inch of water. Place under a preheated broiler and cook until caramelized but not burned, then finish cooking in a 500°F oven. Dredge the tofu squares in the seasoned cornstarch and deep-fry until crisp. Drain on a clean paper towel. Scatter a dozen or so strips of kombu in a heated bowl, along with a heaping tablespoon of tobbiko and a large pinch of scallion. Add 6 ounces of the hot broth and place the tofu square in the center. Top with the fish and serve immediately.

Wallsé ✦

344 W. 11th St. (at Washington St.)

Subway:	Christopher St - Sheridan Sq	Monday - Friday 5:30pm - 11:30pm
Phone:	212-352-2300	Saturday 11am - 3pm
Fax:	212-645-7127	& 5:30pm - 11:30pm
e-mail:	contact@wallse.com	Sunday 11am - 3pm
Web:	www.wallse.com	& 5:30pm - 10:30pm
Prices:	**$$$**	

Wallse

You don't see too many Austrian restaurants in New York, and this one is a keeper. Chef Kurt Gutenbrunner, who was born in the 16th-century Austrian town of Wallsé, brings his talents to the West Village. His sophisticated Austrian cuisine is served in one of two elegant dining rooms, decorated with original 20C German and Austrian art from the Neue Galerie on the Upper East Side (Gutenbrunner also oversees the Galerie's Café Sabarsky).

The ambitious menu showcases traditional dishes (Weiner Schnitzel, Viennese Weisswurst, spätzle with braised rabbit) as well as more updated fare (cod strudel with wild mushrooms, crispy pork belly with Riesling sauerkraut and fingerling potatoes), all of which are beautifully presented and rely on seasonal market produce. The attentive staff can provide good advice about any of the labels on the restaurant's refined list of Austrian wines.

Waltie/Philip Friedman

Halibut with Cucumber, Dill and Chanterelles

Serves 4

4 filets of halibut
2 yellow onions, diced
1 bunch dill, snipped
1 cup + 2 Tbsp. olive oil
2 cucumbers
1 lb. chanterelles, sliced
½ cup canola oil
½ cup Wondra flour
3 Tbsp. shallots, minced
2 Tbsp. thyme leaves
2 Tbsp. butter
2 Tbsp. lemon juice
1 Tbsp. salt
1 Tbsp. freshly ground black pepper

Method

Preheat oven to 375 F. In a shallow baking dish, toss 3 Tbsp. oil with the onions. Cover with foil and bake until onions are soft, approximately 30 minutes. Cool for ten minutes and purée in blender.

Blend olive oil and dill until smooth. Chill until ready to use.

Seed and dice 1 cucumber (reserve seeds and do not peel). Peel and coarsely chop the other cucumber. Blend this cucumber, along with the saved seeds, until smooth. Strain through a fine sieve.

Place a sauté pan over medium heat and add 3 T. Canola oil. Add chanterelles. Sauté until most of the liquid has evaporated. Add 1 Tbsp. shallots, 1 Tbsp. thyme, salt and pepper. Toss and set pan aside.

Combine diced cucumber, 8 Tbsp. cucumber water, 8 Tbsp. onion purée, ¼ tsp. salt and ¼ tsp. pepper in a small sauce pan.

Heat an ovenproof sauté pan over medium heat and add remaining oil. Season the halibut with salt and pepper and sprinkle with flour. Place halibut in the pan. When it is golden brown, turn the fish and place the pan in the oven for 3-4 minutes. While the halibut is cooking, heat the cucumber mixture. Add to it ¼ cup of the dill oil and the lemon juice. Taste, and add salt and pepper if necessary.

Reheat the chanterelles. Remove the halibut from the oven and return it to the stove over medium heat. Add to halibut remaining butter, shallots and thyme and allow to cook 1 minute more, until butter has melted. Divide cucumbers among 4 warm bowls, place filets on top and cover with chanterelles. Drizzle juices from both sauté pans over top.

Spotted Pig ✿

314 W. 11th St. (at Greenwich St.)

Subway: Christopher St - Sheridan Sq
Phone: 212-620-0393
Fax: 212-366-1616
e-mail: info@thespottedpig.com
Web: www.thespottedpig.com
Prices: $$

Monday - Friday noon - 3pm
& 5:30pm - 2am
Saturday - Sunday 11am - 3pm
& 5:30pm - 2am

The Spotted Pig

The gastropub craze has hit Greenwich Village, in the form of The Spotted Pig. Okay, so it's not the most appetizing name for a restaurant, but taste the food before you jump to conclusions. This casual little place just oozes character: brown butcher paper covers the small wood tables; farm animals form the design motif; and members of the young, friendly staff all sport Spotted Pig T-shirts.

Chef/partner April Bloomfield, an alum of London's River Café and Chez Panisse in Berkeley, California, interprets top-quality pub food with an Italian flair. The menu does list standards such as calf's liver and onions, and pan-fired veal kidneys, but read on. There's also octopus salad with celery hearts, and sheep's-milk ricotta gnudi (similar to gnocchi, but made with ricotta cheese) with crispy sage leaves and brown butter—hardly your ploughman's lunch.

Manhattan Greenwich & the West Village

Radish Salad

Serves 4

4 bunches of mixed radishes

4 oz. Parmesan, shaved using a peeler

1 small bunch fresh basil, washed and torn into pieces

4 oz. radish sprouts

2 oz. extra virgin olive oil

Juice of 1 large lemon

1/2 tsp. dried red chile flakes

Maldon sea salt

freshly ground black pepper

Method

Wash and trim radishes. Cut into quarters or halves, so they are evenly sized. Place the slices in a medium-size bowl. Add Parmesan, basil, sprouts, chiles, olive oil and lemon juice. Stir until well mixed and season generously with salt and pepper.

Then lightly squeeze all the ingredients together with your hand until it looks well combined. Taste seasoning and transfer the salad to a platter. Serve immediately.

Mas

Contemporary

008

39 Downing St. (bet. Bedford St. & Seventh Ave. S.)

Subway:	W 4 St - Wash Sq Pk	Monday - Saturday 6pm - 4am
Phone:	212-255-1790	Closed Sunday
Fax:	212-255-0279	
e-mail:	N/A	
Web:	N/A	
Prices:	$$$	

Think French country farmhouse, and you've got Mas, literally (mas refers to the farmhouses of Provence) and figuratively. Amid barn wood and aged beams, blue-suede banquettes, antique flatware, and contemporary furnishings, you'll find yourself ensconced in a rustic-chic ambience. Swiss-born chef Galen Zamarra (formerly of Bouley Bakery in TriBeCa) revels in putting new spins on classic preparations, as in rainbow trout stuffed with wild ramps. Add to this an intriguing wine list and some of the best service in the city and you have a recipe for success. And if you're looking for a place to have a late—as in really late—dinner, Mas stays open until 4am.

AOC Bedford

Mediterranean

009

14 Bedford St. (bet. Downing & Houston Sts.)

Subway:	Houston St	Tuesday - Thursday 5:30pm - 11pm
Phone:	212-414-4764	Friday - Saturday 5:30pm - 11:30pm
Fax:	212-414-4765	Sunday 5:30pm - 11pm
e-mail:	N/A	Closed Monday
Web:	www.aocbedford.com	
Prices:	$$$	

The acronym for the French phrase *appellation d'origine controlée* may seem like a high-falutin' name for a restaurant, but in this case it fits right into the quirky Greenwich Village neighborhood. AOC refers to the French system of designating regional foods and wines, and it symbolizes the restaurant's commitment to using the finest imported and domestic ingredients available. Cuisine centers on French, Spanish and Italian dishes, using items such as fleur de sel from France, Modena vinegar from Italy and manchego cheese from Spain. It's a great place to take a date, with its rustic beamed ceiling and tableside preparations for two, such as the suckling pig and the crêpes Suzettes.

Blue Hill

010

75 Washington Pl. (bet. Sixth Ave. & Washington Sq Pk)

Subway:	W 4 St - Washington Sq Pk	Monday - Saturday 5:30pm - 11pm
Phone:	212-539-1776	Sunday 5:30pm - 10pm
Fax:	212-539-0959	Closed major holidays
e-mail:	info@bluehillnyc.com	
Web:	www.bluehillnyc.com	
Prices:	$$$	

It's not every restaurant that can draw on its own farm for meat and organic vegetables, but luckily for Greenwich Villagers, Blue Hill is one of them. Opened in 2000 by Dan, David and Laureen Barber, Blue Hill occupies a lovely town house near Washington Square Park. Entrées include Berkshire pork, poached duck, pastured chicken and grass-fed lamb, all raised at the family's farm north of the city in the Hudson River Valley. And there's a well-chosen list of international boutique wines to complement the dishes. If you happen to be up that way, stop by Blue Hill at Stone Barns in Pocantico Hills. This working farm also features a restaurant and an educational center.

Bond Street

011

6 Bond St. (bet. Broadway & Lafayette St.)

Subway:	Bleecker St	Tuesday - Saturday 6pm - midnight
Phone:	212-777-2500	Sunday - Monday 6pm - 11pm
Fax:	212-777-6530	
e-mail:	bondstreetrestaurant@hotmail.com	
Web:	N/A	
Prices:	$$$	

You'll want to dress to impress at this stylish NoHo sushi bar—can New Yorkers ever have enough of these?—where the trendy crowd doesn't seem at all concerned about the prices. Sure, they're high—the prices, that is—but the quality of the food stands up to them. Bond Street's ambitious menu lists a wide array of sophisticated sushi, sashimi, rolls and tempura, all well executed and elegantly presented on the plate. Set in a historic brownstone, the restaurant stretches over three levels: the ground-floor bar/lounge, the main dining room and its lively sushi bar on the second floor, and a third-floor dining space, which includes two tatami rooms.

Crispo

Italian

012

240 W. 14th St. (bet. Seventh & Eighth Aves.)

Subway:	14 St - 8 Av	Monday - Thursday 5pm - 11:30pm
Phone:	212-229-1818	Friday - Saturday 5pm - midnight
Fax:	212-229-9979	Sunday 4pm - 11pm
e-mail:	N/A	
Web:	N/A	
Prices:	$$	

Frank Crispo reigns over the kitchen in his eponymous West Village eatery, recognizable by the black wrought-iron fence that encloses its entrance. Crispo, who cut his teeth in Gotham trattorias like La Cote Basque and Zeppole, presents his culinary artwork against a cozy canvas of rough-hewn brick walls, soft lighting, close-spaced tables, and pine flooring. A do-not-miss starter is the fragrant, air-cured prosciutto di San Daniele, from the Friuli region of Italy in the northeast corner of the country. Its delicate, sweet taste is accented by a variety of Italian cheeses, fruit and vegetables. On weekends, expect a long wait for a table if you don't have a reservation.

Da Silvano

Italian

013

260 Sixth Ave. (bet. Bleecker & Houston Sts.)

Subway:	W 4 St - Wash Sq Pk	Monday - Thursday noon - 11:30pm
Phone:	212-982-2343	Friday - Saturday noon - midnight
Fax:	212-982-2254	Sunday noon - 11pm
e-mail:	info@dasilvano.com	
Web:	www.dasilvano.com	
Prices:	$$$	

Think Tuscany. That's the type of simple, rustic food and companionable atmosphere you'll find at Silvano Marchetto's Greenwich Village eatery. Think movie stars. Since he opened in 1975, Marchetto's been pleasing the palates of a good number of film stars. The menu focuses mainly, but not exclusively, on Tuscan dishes (osso buco Milanese, served atop risotto and garnished with gremolata, is a house specialty), and the wine list includes a good selection of Italian labels. If you're lucky, you might be able to snag one of the popular sidewalk tables out front, for some great people watching.

EN Japanese Brasserie

014

435 Hudson St. (at Leroy St.)

Subway:	Christopher St - Sheridan Sq	Monday - Wednesday noon - 2:30pm
Phone:	212-647-9196	& 5:30pm - midnight
Fax:	212-647-7550	Thursday - Friday noon - 2:30pm
e-mail:	info@enjb.com	& 5:30pm - 1am
Web:	www.enjb.com	Saturday 5:30pm - 1am
Prices:	$$$	Closed Sunday

Japanese pub fare? Sure, why not? EN styles itself as a Japanese brasserie, its industrial, high-ceilinged dining space decked out in dark woods, glass and stone and embellished with an eye-catching carved-wood screen. Brainchild of Japanese restaurateurs/siblings Reika and Bunkei Yo, EN centers on an open kitchen, where the chef and his team craft their own tofu and yuba (the delicate skin that forms when soy milk is heated). A house specialty, yuba appears in dishes such as yuba sashimi, and crispy yuba cheese roll stuffed with eel. Tofu, made fresh each night, is available at 90-minute intervals throughout the evening. Chef's features change monthly, as does the list of special sakes.

Five Points

015

31 Great Jones St. (bet. Lafayette St. & Bowery)

Subway:	Bleecker St	Monday - Friday noon - 3pm
Phone:	212-253-5700	& 6pm - midnight
Fax:	N/A	Saturday 11:30am - 3pm
e-mail:	N/A	& 5pm - midnight
Web:	www.fivepointsrestaurant.com	Sunday 11:30am - 3pm & 6pm - 10pm
Prices:	$$	

Setting the tone for this NoHo eatery, a little stream courses through a hollowed-out oak log that runs the length of the room. Beneath the vaulted ceiling spreads a soft palette of neutrals and natural woods. Here, chef Marc Meyer creates consistently good seasonal American cuisine with Mediterranean flair (think fava bean hummus, and cornmeal-crusted skate with Sardinian couscous). Many of the dishes—Arctic char, pizzettes, wild King salmon—are roasted in the wood oven in the open kitchen. Locals come for the Sunday brunch, which features the likes of lemon-ricotta pancakes, dulce de leche French toast, spinach and goat-cheese frittata, and buttermilk fried chicken.

Manhattan Greenwich & the West Village

Il Cantinori

016

32 E. 10th St. (bet. Broadway & University Pl.)

Subway:	8 St - NYU	Monday - Thursday noon - 2:30pm
Phone:	212-673-6044	& 5:30pm - 11:30pm
Fax:	212-353-0534	Friday noon - 2:30pm
e-mail:	N/A	& 5:30pm - midnight
Web:	www.il-cantinori.com	Saturday 5:30pm - midnight
Prices:	$$$	Sunday 5:30pm - 11pm

Andy Warhol was a regular at this elegant, off-the-beaten-track restaurant, from the time it opened in 1983. It's not unusual to see other familiar faces here; Il Cantinori has its fair share of celebrity diners. They, like the not-so-famous patrons, come as much for the food as for the intimate dining room, its tables set with fresh roses, and outdoor seats shaded by the red-and-green-striped awning. The meal starts with a loaf of crusty country bread, complete with fruity olive oil for dipping. Then comes the hard part: narrowing down your choices among the hearty pastas, meat dishes and few fish selections. Like the food, the wine list gravitates toward varietals from Tuscany.

Il Mulino

017

86 W. 3rd St. (bet. Sullivan & Thompson Sts.)

Subway:	W 4 St - Wash Sq Pk	Monday - Friday noon - 2:30pm
Phone:	212-673-3783	& 5pm - 11pm
Fax:	212-673-9875	Saturday 5pm - 11pm
e-mail:	N/A	Closed Sunday
Web:	www.ilmulinonewyork.com	
Prices:	$$$$	

Mouth-watering displays of Italian wines, olive oils, fruits and vegetables tantalize you as you enter the small, dimly lit dining room at this Italian institution (opened in 1981) in the heart of Greenwich Village. Reservations are hard to come by; a cadre of regulars packs the place night after night (lunch reservations are easier to snag). The cuisine here centers on the bold, garlicky flavors of the Abruzzi region, where the owners, Fernando and Gino Masci, were born. Veal is a specialty (there are at least 10 veal dishes on the menu), but you'll find pastas, chicken and a few beef and fish selections, too. Expect black-tie service, big portions and prices to match.

Jane

018

Contemporary

100 W. Houston St. (bet. La Guardia Pl. & Thompson St.)

Subway:	Houston St	Monday - Thursday 11:30am - 5pm
Phone:	212-254-7000	& 5:30pm - 11:30pm
Fax:	212-777-9034	Friday - Saturday 11:30am - 5pm
e-mail:	N/A	& 5:30pm - midnight
Web:	www.janerestaurant.com	Sunday 11am - 4pm & 5pm - 11pm
Prices:	$$	

This is no plain Jane. The brainchild of managing partner Jeff Lefcourt and chef/partner Glenn Harris, Jane strives to present approachable and inventive New American fare in Greenwich Village near SoHo shopping. Chef Harris cherishes his relationships with area farmers, growers and fishermen, and it's on their products that he bases his menu. The large, airy dining room can get pretty noisy, but don't let that distract you from the roster of dishes that are well-balanced between fish and meat—with a homemade pasta or two thrown in for good measure. To accompany your dessert, you can choose among the good selection of port, brandy and cognac—as well as a nice list of herbal teas.

Jarnac

019

Contemporary French

328 W. 12th St. (at Greenwich St.)

Subway:	14 St - 8 Av	Tuesday - Thursday 6pm - 10pm
Phone:	212-924-3413	Friday - Saturday 6pm - 11pm
Fax:	212-414-2505	Sunday 6pm - 10pm
e-mail:	info@jarnacny.com	Closed Monday
Web:	www.jarnacny.com	
Prices:	$$	

Naturally, you'd expect to find a good selection of cognacs on this restaurant's menu. Jarnac is named for the city in the Poitou-Charentes region of France that is home to the famed cognac producer Courvoisier. And that's exactly what you will find at Jarnac. Owner Tony Powe honors the town where he grew up by offering a host of cognacs from a handful of different producers. But wait—have something to eat before your digestif. Contemporary French fare is interpreted with an American flair here; the menu changes daily to reflect what's fresh and in season (skate wing, for example, is sautéed and topped by a concassé of green and black olives; in winter, the cassoulet wins raves).

North Square

021

103 Waverly Pl. (on Washington Sq.)

Subway: W 4 St - Wash Sq Pk

Phone: 212-254-1200

Fax: 212-260-1179

e-mail: info@northsquareny.com

Web: www.northsquareny.com

Prices: $$

Monday - Saturday noon - 3:30pm
& 5:30pm - 10:30pm
Sunday noon - 3pm
& 5:30pm - 10:30pm

At North Square, just off the lobby inside the Washington Square Hotel *(see hotel listings)*, Mexican-born chef Yoel Cruz relies on his varied background for inspiration to reinvent American dishes that change with the seasons. Duck confit is wrapped in empanadas with black-bean and chipotle-peanut sauce; capellini is tossed with shrimp, shiitake mushrooms and chorizo; and red snapper is crusted with crispy tortillas and served with roasted corn flan. The smartly styled, casual eatery bills itself as a "New York bistro," its dining room set about by fresh floral arrangements, abstract paintings and comfortable booths—and NYU professors at lunch.

One if by Land, Two if by Sea

022

17 Barrow St. (bet. Seventh Ave. S. & W. 4th St.)

Subway:	Christopher St - Sheridan Sq	Monday - Thursday 5:30pm - 11pm
Phone:	212-228-0822	Friday - Saturday 5:15pm - 11:15pm
Fax:	212-206-7855	Sunday 5:30pm - 10pm
e-mail:	manetta@oneifbyland.com	
Web:	www.oneifbyland.com	
Prices:	$$$	

Despite the name (a reference to the lantern hung in Boston's Old North Church in 1775 to warn the colonists of the approaching British troops), Paul Revere didn't sleep here. This 18th-century carriage house formed part of the Richmond Hill estate, used by George Washington as his Manhattan headquarters during the Revolution. The lovely two-story brick building, with its four fireplaces, candlelit tables, and live piano music, is justly touted as one of the most romantic restaurants in the city. So grab your significant other and take your pick of well-executed American fare (beef Wellington is the house specialty). If you have any important «proposals» to make, this is the place to do it.

The Place

Contemporary

023

310 W. 4th St. (bet. Bank & 12th Sts.)

Subway:	14 St - 8 Av	Monday - Sunday 5:30pm - 11pm
Phone:	212-924-2711	Closed Christmas Day & New Years Day
Fax:	212-929-8213	
e-mail:	N/A	
Web:	www.theplaceny.com	
Prices:	$$	

Looking for a restaurant for that intimate tête-à-tête? This is The Place. With its grotto-like dining space carved into a series of cozy, dimly lit rooms with rough stone walls and a beamed ceiling, this is the place for romance. White-linen-clad tables are brightened by candles and fresh flowers, and the service is obliging and efficient. The food? It's an ever-evolving roster of well-executed American fare, based on fresh market produce. Tender leg of lamb, for example, is roasted to your taste and accompanied by rosemary roasted potatoes and haricots verts; homemade fettucini is tossed with roasted tomatoes, zucchini, fresh thyme and shaved parmesan.

Manhattan Greenwich & the West Village

Sevilla

Spanish

62 Charles St. (at W. 4th St.)

Subway:	Christopher St - Sheridan Sq
Phone:	212-929-3189
Fax:	212-243-9513
e-mail:	N/A
Web:	www.sevillarestaurantandbar.com
Prices:	$$

Sunday - Thursday noon - midnight
Friday - Saturday noon - 1am

XX

There's something to be said for age. Although Sevilla has been a restaurant since 1941, it retains a warm patina, reinforced by the dark woods and brown leatherette booths that dominate the taberna-style interior. The present owner and former chef, Jose Lloves, who hails from Galicia in northern Spain, acquired Sevilla in 1962 and has been running it ever since (his brother and two sons now partner with him). Tradition reigns here, starting with the waitstaff (many of whom have worked here for years), and continuing with the menu, which offers a slice of Spain in its authentic paellas, seafood and meat dishes. Ask for a table up front by the windows for a view of lovely Charles Street.

Strip House

Steakhouse

13 E. 12th St. (bet. Fifth Ave. & University Pl.)

Subway:	Union Sq
Phone:	212-328-0000
Fax:	212-337-0233
e-mail:	sdenooijer@theglaziergroup.com
Web:	www.theglaziergroup.com
Prices:	$$$

Monday - Thursday 5pm - 11pm
Friday - Saturday 5pm - 11:30pm
Sunday 5pm - 10pm

XX
&

A seductive name, yes—but don't go peeling your clothes off just yet. The "strip" here refers to steak, although the suggestive logo and the alluring décor, in deep bordello-red with photos of seminude pinup girls on the walls, might lead you to think otherwise. Broiled New York strip is the signature dish, available in single or double cut. Then there are the standard steakhouse offerings: filet mignon, veal chops and rack of Colorado lamb (besides the requisite lobster, the menu lists a few seafood entrées, too). Sides (all à la carte) such as potatoes crisped in goose fat and rich black-truffle creamed spinach are not for the faint of arteries, nor are the huge dessert portions.

Surya

302 Bleecker St. (bet. Grove St. & Seventh Ave.)

Subway:	Christopher St - Sheridan Sq	Monday - Friday noon - 3pm
Phone:	212-807-7770	& 5pm - 11pm
Fax:	212-337-0659	Saturday - Sunday noon - 3pm
e-mail:	N/A	& 5pm - midnight
Web:	www.suryany.com	
Prices:	⊜⊜	

There is much that is sunny about this unassuming little Indian restaurant in the West Village. First, there's the name, which means "sun" in Tamil. Then there's the sleek décor, done in bright tones of orange and red; and the service, which is delivered with a politeness and a warmth that's rare to find. Last, but not least, there's a host of meat and vegetable dishes on the menu, which focuses on the fragrant cuisine of Southern India. Lamb, chicken and shrimp are all prepared tandoori-style, cooked over high heat in a traditional Indian clay oven. No time to site down for lunch? Pick up a box lunch to go from noon until 3pm.

Aki

181 W. 4th St. (bet. Sixth & Seventh Aves.)

Subway:	W 4 St - Wash Sq Pk	Tuesday - Thursday 6pm - 10:45pm
Phone:	212-989-5440	Friday - Saturday 6pm - 11:45pm
Fax:	212-744-4348	Sunday 6pm - 10:45pm
e-mail:	akiw4@aol.com	Closed Monday
Web:	www.members.aol.com/akiw4	Closed December 19 - 26
Prices:	$$	

Talk about fusion cuisine. Besides the traditional sushi and sashimi, you'll find contemporary Japanese takes on dishes from around the world at Aki. A savory millefeuille of crispy wontons is layered with mashed eel, pumpkin and ginger; Jamaican jerk chicken is rolled with shrimp paste and veggies in mango teriyaki sauce; and for dessert, pannacotta is made with soy milk, tapioca and green tea syrup. Chef/owner Shigeaki "Siggy" Nakanishi did a stint as private chef to the Japanese ambassador to the West Indies in Kingston, Jamaica, and his cuisine reflects his Caribbean experience. Go before 7pm for the four-course prix-fixe menu.

Aroma Kitchen and Wine Bar

Italian

028

36 E. 4th St. (bet. Bowery & Lafayette St.)

Subway:	Bleecker St	Tuesday - Sunday 6pm - 1am
Phone:	212-375-0100	Closed Monday
Fax:	212-375-0400	
e-mail:	N/A	
Web:	www.aromanyc.com	
Prices:	$$	

This sliver of a restaurant on a quiet block in Greenwich Village has become a festive local spot, where, in warm weather, doors open onto the street and the party spills onto the sidewalk. Owners Alexandra Degiorgio and Vito Polosa are passionate about good food and wine, and it shows in the house-made pastas, marinated olives and other high-quality ingredients, which are a step up from the usual wine-bar fare. All Italian, the unique wine list contains many varietals rarely found outside Italy—all fairly priced; ask Vito for suggestions about what might pair best with your order. Go early for the "Neighbors Menu," a super bargain that includes three courses and a flight of four wines.

August

European

029

359 Bleecker St. (bet. Charles & 10th Sts.)

Subway:	Christopher St - Sheridan Sq	Monday - Sunday 11:30am - 3:30pm
Phone:	212-929-4774	& 5:30pm - 11:00pm
Fax:	N/A	
e-mail:	andrew.chapman@usa.net	
Web:	www.augustny.com	
Prices:	$$	

Set in a small brick town house on a bustling street in Greenwich Village, August offers a small dining room up front, with an open kitchen and a wood-burning oven. A bright veranda adds more dining space in the back. The restaurant bills its cuisine as "regional European," and indeed the entrées range across the continent from Greek oven-roasted bass and Belgian carbonnade to Grenobloise skate and spaghetti carbonara. Spanish tortillas, German pancakes with roasted apples, and pain perdu (real French toast) number among the offerings for brunch; of course, the classic hamburger is available, too.

Blue Ribbon Bakery

030

33 Downing St. (at Bedford St.)

Subway:	Houston St	Monday - Thursday noon - midnight
Phone:	212-337-0404	Friday noon - 2am
Fax:	N/A	Saturday 11:30am - 2am
e-mail:	N/A	Sunday 11:30am - midnight
Web:	www.blueribbonrestaurants.com	
Prices:	$$	

The story of Blue Ribbon Bakery begins with an oven. Specifically, an abandoned 140-year-old, brick oven that brothers Eric and Bruce Bromberg found in the basement of an old bodega on Downing Street in the West Village. Their discovery sparked an idea for a bakery, and they hired a master craftsman from Italy to rebuild the oven. The same appliance now forms the centerpiece of Blue Ribbon Bakery, opened in 1998. Bread, from challah to country white, baked in this oven stars on sandwiches at lunch and appears warm in a basket at dinner. On the extensive menu you'll find a host of impeccable American fare, from a charcuterie plate to grilled striped bass.

Café de Bruxelles

031

118 Greenwich Ave. (at W. 13th St.)

Subway:	14 St	Monday - Sunday noon - 11:30pm
Phone:	212-206-1830	
Fax:	212-229-1436	
e-mail:	N/A	
Web:	N/A	
Prices:	$$	

Mussels are synonymous with Belgian cuisine, and Café de Bruxelles takes this relationship to heart. You'll know why when you see their menu; it includes an entire section just for mussels—at least ten different preparations. And what would a bowl of mussels be without the cafe's sublime, crispy frites? Of course, there are plenty of other options, from waterzooi to carbonade Flamande; the menu is unabashedly Belgian, without concession to American palates. The atmosphere, too, is pure Belgian bistro, complete with photographs of Brussels, exposed brick walls, and framed ads for Belgian beer—which they offer plenty of, along with a good list of imported brews.

El Faro

Spanish

032

823 Greenwich St. (at Horatio St.)

Subway:	14 St - 8 Av	Tuesday - Thursday noon - 11:30pm
Phone:	212-929-8210	Friday - Saturday 11:30pm - 12:30am
Fax:	212-929-8295	Sunday noon - midnight
e-mail:	labruja@msn.com	Closed Monday
Web:	citysearch.com/nyc/elfaro	Closed Christmas Day
Prices:	$$	& Thanksgiving Day

Located in a part of the West Village once known as "Little Spain" for the influx of Spanish immigrants that flocked here in the 1940s after the Spanish Civil War, El Faro began as a bar and grill in 1927. Its current owners, the Lugris and Perez families, purchased the restaurant in 1959 and have run it ever since. Never mind the aging 1960s-era décor, highlighted by a mural of flamenco dancers that covers the walls of the main dining room; it's the food that stands out here. Paella is a favorite, teeming with seafood and sausages and brought to the table in traditional double-handled dishes. If you crave something light, check out the extensive tapas menu. *Reservations not accepted.*

Extra Virgin

Mediterranean

033

259 W. 4th St. (at Perry St.)

Subway:	Christopher St - Sheridan Sq	Monday - Wednesday 5:30pm - 11pm
Phone:	212-691-9359	Thursday 5:30pm - 11:30pm
Fax:	212-691-4512	Friday 5:30pm - midnight
e-mail:	N/A	Saturday - Sunday 11am - 11pm
Web:	www.extravirginrestaurant.com	
Prices:	$$	

Extra Virgin's name, of course, refers to olive oil, which is used liberally in the Mediterranean-inspired dishes served in this West Village brownstone. Mirrors in the bistro-style dining room create a sense of space, and fresh flowers bring the outdoors in. To add to the aesthetics, the young waitresses are as attentive as they are attractive. Moderate prices mark the menu of simple dishes, where Classics for Two, the restaurant's equivalent of *plats du jour*, change regularly. Be sure to save room for dessert, like the warm chocolate cake topped with caramel ice cream. The place is always packed on Sunday for Extra Virgin's popular brunch.

Flor's Kitchen

034

170 Waverly Pl. (bet. Sixth & Seventh Aves.)

Subway:	W 4 St - Wash Sq Pk	Sunday - Thursday 11am - 11pm
Phone:	212-229-9926	Friday - Saturday 11am - midnight
Fax:	516-992-0574	
e-mail:	N/A	
Web:	www.florskitchen.com	
Prices:	ෛ	

Flor Villazan whips up Venezuelan comfort food using her family's traditional recipes at this little no-frills place. Well, perhaps "whips up" isn't the right term, since all the dishes are made from scratch. That means, of course, no fast food: no canned corn is used to make the griddle-browned *cachapas* (corn pancakes), and the empanadas are shaped by hand each day. Flor's takes pride in the fact that their food is as good for you as it is tasty. Be sure to try freshly squeezed fruit juices like papaya, mango, tamarind and papelón (sugarcane with lemon). East Siders, don't despair; there's another Flor's at 149 First Avenue *(at 9th St.)*.

Gavroche

035

212 W. 14th St. (bet. Seventh & Eighth Aves.)

Subway:	14 St	Monday - Sunday noon - 11pm
Phone:	212-647-8553	Closed major holidays
Fax:	212-647-1862	
e-mail:	camelia@spectrotel.net	
Web:	www.gavroche-ny.com	
Prices:	$$	

Gavroche is one of the few restaurants on this strip that are open for lunch, so when you get the urge for some hearty, home-style cuisine *à la Française*, stop by for a plate of coq au vin or steak frites. These traditional French bistro dishes are available at dinner, too, along with free-range roasted chicken, duck terrine, and braised lamb shanks. Named for the street urchin in *Les Misérables*, Gavroche owes its 2004 opening to manager Camelia Cassin. A French-country ambience pervades the small dining room, its bistro tables covered with blue-and-white-checked linen towels. In back, the garden terrace accommodates additional diners in warm weather.

Gobo

Vegetarian

036

401 Sixth Ave. (bet. Waverly Pl. & W. 8th St.)

Subway:	W 4 St - Wash Sq Pk
Phone:	212-255-3902
Fax:	212-255-0687
e-mail:	robert.gonzales@goborestaurant.com
Web:	www.goborestaurant.com
Prices:	🍝

Monday - Sunday 11am - 11pm

Taste, touch, sight, hearing, smell. Gobo (and its Upper East Side sister at 1426 Third Avenue) caters to the five senses with its refined contemporary décor and innovative vegetarian cuisine. Soft neutrals and honey-colored woods highlight the dining area, simply adorned by wooden bowls and glass containers filled with fresh fruit and vegetables. From quick bites (tea-smoked soy sheets with sautéed mushrooms) to small plates (white bean and cremini-mushroom casserole) to large plates (green-tea noodles with vegan Bolognese sauce), the menu spans the globe for inspiration. The name? It's Japanese for burdock root, long used by herbalists to detoxify the body.

Hedeh

Contemporary Japanese

037

57 Great Jones St. (bet. Bowery & Lafayette Sts.)

Subway:	Broadway - Lafayette St
Phone:	212-473-8458
Fax:	212-473-8509
e-mail:	N/A
Web:	www.hedeh.com
Prices:	$$

Monday - Saturday 5pm - midnight
Closed Sunday & major holidays

This NoHo newcomer, opened in late 2004, takes the nickname of its chef, Hideyuki Nakajima, formerly of Nobu. Located at the border of the East Village, Hedeh is a modest place, its contemporary décor limited to neutral colors, soft lighting and a bamboo screen separating the dining room from the sake bar in front. The bar is worth a stop, though, for its impressive list of cold, hot and unfiltered sakes—not to mention Japanese beers. As for the food, there's an inventive selection of top-quality sushi, maki and sashimi, prepared according to the chef's whim. You'll also find a few crossover dishes inspired by French cuisine (foie gras with balsamic ginger sauce, green-tea crème brûlée).

Home

038

20 Cornelia St. (bet. Bleecker & W. 4th Sts.)

Subway:	W 4 St - Wash Sq Pk	Monday - Friday 11am - 4pm
Phone:	212-243-9579	& 5:30pm - 11pm
Fax:	212-647-9393	Saturday 10:30am - 4pm
e-mail:	homeeats@aol.com	& 5:30pm - 11pm
Web:	www.recipesfromhome.com	Sunday 10:30am - 4pm
Prices:	$$	& 5:30pm - 10pm

The domain of husband-and-wife team Barbara Shinn and chef David Page, Home serves three squares a day, beginning with the likes of baked eggs with New York cheddar and grilled homemade salami for breakfast. Bead-board paneling, pine-plank floors and old family photographs create a homey atmosphere at this quintessential neighborhood restaurant. Supporters of sustainable agriculture, the owners rely on nearby Greenwich Village markets and food shops and local family farms for the kicked-up comfort food on their regularly changing menu; labels from Long Island—including their own vineyard—form the core of the wine list. It seems Dorothy was right all along: "There's no place like Home."

Il Buco

039

47 Bond St. (bet. Bowery & Lafayette St.)

Subway:	Bleecker St	Monday 6pm - midnight
Phone:	212-533-1932	Tuesday - Thursday noon - 4pm
Fax:	212-533-3502	& 6pm - midnight
e-mail:	ilbuco@ilbuco.com	Friday - Saturday noon - 4pm
Web:	www.ilbuco.com	& 6pm - 1am
Prices:	$$	Sunday 5pm - midnight

When independent filmmaker Donna Lennard and her Italian partner Alberto Avalle opened their antique shop in NoHo in 1994, little did they guess that they'd be running a restaurant in that same space several years later. Located on cobblestone Bond Street, Il Buco features the aromatic cuisine of Italy and the Iberian Peninsula in a charming dining room that recalls the Italian countryside, and it's perfect for a romantic tête-à-tête. Vintage pine pieces and undressed wood tables with painted chairs furnish the room, which is decorated with antique kitchen utensils and plenty of fresh flowers. The market-based menu looks to the seasons for inspiration.

Manhattan Greenwich & the West Village

Kirara

J a p a n e s e

33 Carmine St. (bet. Bleecker & Bedford Sts.)

Subway:	W 4 St - Wash Sq Pk	Monday - Friday noon - 11pm
Phone:	212-741-2123	Saturday - Sunday 5pm - 11pm
Fax:	N/A	
e-mail:	N/A	
Web:	N/A	
Prices:	$$	

If you're feeling adventurous at this family-run restaurant, ask about the *omakase*, or tasting menu. In Japanese, omakase means "to put yourself in the chef's hands," so go ahead and trust his judgement regarding what you should eat. You'll be treated to an assortment of the chef's choice of appetizers, followed by a generous platter of sushi and sashimi; it's a great idea for sharing. Of course, you can always order off the à la carte menu as your appetite dictates. Whatever you order, you'll be treated to artfully presented dishes, since chef/owner John Hur is an artist himself. You can admire his Japanese-style paintings, which adorn the walls of the restaurant.

Le Gigot

F r e n c h

18 Cornelia St. (bet. Bleecker & W. 4th Sts.)

Subway:	W 4 St - Wash Sq Pk	Tuesday - Sunday noon - 2:30pm
Phone:	212-627-3737	& 5pm - 11pm
Fax:	212-627-1188	Closed Monday
e-mail:	legigot@verizon.net	
Web:	N/A	
Prices:	$$	

A great place to take a date is how many regulars characterize this cozy little bistro, located on the same block as Pó. Of course, you'd expect to find leg of lamb on the menu (since that's what *le gigot* means in French), and so you will; Senegalese chef Alioune Ndiaye's version is an uncomplicated preparation, served with flageolet beans. The handful of tables may cluster elbow to elbow, but the service is eager and smiling, and the Gallic ambience, complete with French posters, oversize mirrors and varnished woods, invites romance. Fresh, healthy bistro dishes here avoid heavy cream sauces in favor of lighter fare, including several vegetarian selections.

Lupa

Italian

170 Thompson St. (bet. Bleecker & Houston Sts.)

Subway:	W 4 St - Wash Sq Pk	Monday - Friday noon - 3pm
Phone:	212-982-5089	& 5pm - 11:30pm
Fax:	212-982-5490	Saturday - Sunday noon - 2:45pm
e-mail:	N/A	& 4:45pm - 11:30pm
Web:	www.luparestaurant.com	
Prices:	$$	

Brought to you by the team of Mario Batali, Joseph Bastianich, Jason Denton and Mark Ladner (the partnership behind Babbo and Esca), Lupa stands out as a pearl among a string of Italian establishments that line Thompson Street. The restaurant is Roman from its trattoria menu to its name, a reference to the she-wolf in Roman mythology. Offering the best authentic seasonal ingredients at reasonable prices is the philosophy here, and Lupa achieves that goal with its own *salumeria* that features Italian artisan meats and cheeses, and by making fresh pastas and other products—including canned tuna—in-house. There's a generous list of wines from regions throughout Italy to complement your meal.

Mary's Fish Camp

Seafood

64 Charles St. (at 4th St.)

Subway:	Christopher St - Sheridan Sq	Monday - Saturday noon - 3pm
Phone:	646-486-2185	& 6pm - 11pm
Fax:	646-486-6703	Closed Sunday
e-mail:	info@marysfishcamp.com	
Web:	www.marysfishcamp.com	
Prices:	$$	

Mary Redding opened this tiny Florida-style seafood joint in a West Village brownstone in 2000. Her lobster rolls overflow with succulent of meat, slathered in mayonnaise and piled upon a buttered hot-dog bun—they might be messy, but they sure are good! Other selections such as conch chowder and conch fritters recall Key West cuisine, while lobster pot pie and Chatham cod filet pay homage to the maritime bounty of New England. Take a seat at the counter, where you can watch the chefs shucking your oysters with lightning speed. Meat-lovers, however, need not apply; Mary's only serves seafood. *Reservations not accepted.*

Manhattan Greenwich & the West Village

Mexicana Mama

Mexican

044

525 Hudson St. (bet. Charles & W. 10th Sts.)

Subway:	Christopher St - Sheridan Sq	Tuesday - Sunday noon - 11pm
Phone:	212-924-4119	Closed Monday
Fax:	N/A	Closed Christmas Day & Easter Sunday
e-mail:	N/A	
Web:	N/A	
Prices:	☜	

A little restaurant with a big heart, Mexicana Mama kicks up Mexican food from the bland, oversauced fare that's come to be known as "Mexican" to American diners. Here the flavors are as bright as the décor (purple walls, tables painted in primary colors), in such dishes as chicken with mole, and roasted chile relleno served with aromatic green rice that gets its color from the addition of cilantro and poblano chile. Save room for the rich pastel tres leches (otherwise known as three-milks cake). This unpretentious and popular place features good food for a good price—and if you're staying in the neighborhood, they offer takeout and local delivery.

Otto

Italian

045

1 Fifth Ave. (at E. 8th St.)

Subway:	W 4 St - Washington Sq Pk	Monday - Sunday 11:30am - 11:30pm
Phone:	212-995-9559	
Fax:	212-995-9052	
e-mail:	rtarpey@pastaresources.com	
Web:	www.ottopizzeria.com	
Prices:	$$	

Think the cooking of chef Mario Batali is beyond your financial reach? Think again . . . and head for Otto in Greenwich Village. The most affordable of Batali's many Gotham establishments (Babbo and Lupa number among the others), Otto bills itself as an enoteca/pizzeria. The enoteca part refers to the restaurant's remarkable number (700) of Italian wines. And for the pizzeria part, thin-crust pies are cooked on a flat-iron griddle, and are complemented by antipasti and pastas. The restaurant only takes reservations for parties of six or more, so come prepared to wait. For impatient types, Otto now delivers, or you can get your pizza to go, along with a pint or two of house-made gelato.

Palma

046

28 Cornelia St. (bet. Bleecker & W. 4th Sts.)

Subway:	W 4 St - Wash Sq Pk	Monday - Sunday noon - 11pm
Phone:	212-691-2223	
Fax:	212-691-3910	
e-mail:	N/A	
Web:	www.palmanyc.com	
Prices:	$$	

A new addition to a lively Greenwich Village restaurant row, Palma exudes a Mediterranean vibe with its sunflower-yellow façade, rustic wood beams and candlelit dining area. The menu tends toward Sicilian dishes, with an emphasis on fresh, simply prepared seafood (think sautéed swordfish with fresh mint, capers and tomato-olive salad; sea bass grilled with herbs and lemon). And if you're not up for a big meal, half-portions are available. Service is casual and efficient, and moderate prices give this place wide appeal. And now the bad news: Palma has some stiff competition on this street, including the popular Italian bistro, Pó.

Pearl Oyster Bar

047

18 Cornelia St. (bet. Bleecker & W. 4th Sts.)

Subway:	W 4 St - Wash Sq Pk	Monday - Friday noon - 2:30pm
Phone:	212-691-8211	& 6pm - 11pm
Fax:	212-691-8210	Saturday 6pm - 11pm
e-mail:	N/A	Closed Sunday
Web:	www.pearloysterbar.com	
Prices:	$$	

Coastal Maine on Cornelia Street? Maybe. One thing's for sure: you can't get fresher fish for the price in Manhattan than at Pearl Oyster Bar. You may not get it fast, either, since this minnow-sized eatery consists of two long marble counters and a small adjoining room with a sprinkling of bistro tables. Chef/owner Rebecca Charles named the restaurant for her grandmother, in memory of childhood summers spent in Maine. The food is New England through and through: Johnnycakes, creamy clam chowder, and the gargantuan lobster roll—chunks of fresh lobster moistened with mayonnaise and served on a toasted bun. Oh, and don't forget the blueberry crumble pie, another Maine staple, for dessert.

Piccolo Angolo

Italian

048

621 Hudson St. (at Jane St.)

Subway:	14 St	Tuesday - Sunday 3:30pm - 10:30pm
Phone:	212-229-9177	Closed Monday
Fax:	N/A	
e-mail:	N/A	
Web:	N/A	
Prices:	$$	

Sited at the little corner («piccolo angolo» in Italian) of Hudson and Jane streets, this family-run Italian place is constantly packed with a throng of diners willing to wait in line for chef Mario Migliorini's wonderful food. If you're looking for a quiet place, you'd best go elsewhere; Piccolo Angolo is noisy, crowded, and the tables are crunched together like sardines in a can. That said, the house-made pastas are superior, the fresh tomato sauce is redolent with garlic and fragrant with basil, and the toasted garlic bread (there's that garlic again) is terrific dipped in a bit of fruity olive oil. Mario's brother, Renato Migliorini, runs the front of the house with aplomb.

Pó

Italian

049

31 Cornelia St. (bet. Bleecker & W. 4th Sts.)

Subway:	Christopher St - Sheridan Sq	Monday - Tuesday 5:30pm - 11pm
Phone:	212-645-2189	Wednesday - Sunday 11:30am - 2:30pm
Fax:	212-367-9448	& 5:30pm - 11pm
e-mail:	porestaurant@verizon.net	
Web:	www.porestaurant.com	
Prices:	$$	

Tables aren't easy to come by at this popular Greenwich Village establishment. Housed in a former coffeehouse/theater (its founder was an out-of-work dancer who staged short plays and served cake and coffee here), Pó now looks to Culinary Institute of America graduate Lee McGrath for its acclaimed contemporary Italian fare. The ambience in the tiny dining room is convivial, and the waitstaff buoys up the mood with cheerful, attentive service. High-quality food at reasonable prices rules here; the four- and six-course tasting menus are the best deals of all. The short wine list includes a good selection of wines by the glass.

Tomoe Sushi

J a p a n e s e

050

172 Thompson St. (bet. Bleecker & Houston Sts.)

Subway:	W 4 St - Wash Sq Pk	Monday - Tuesday 5pm - 11pm
Phone:	212-777-9346	Wednesday - Saturday 1pm - 3pm
Fax:	N/A	& 5pm - 11pm
e-mail:	N/A	Closed Sunday
Web:	N/A	
Prices:	Ꮞ	

Patience is clearly the virtue to have if you're planning dinner at Tomoe Sushi, where the wait in the evening can range up to an hour or more. Why all the buzz? Diners sure don't come for the spartan décor, which consists of a small sushi bar, bare pine tables and specials scrawled on pieces of paper. They do come, though, for the good-quality fish, which is cut in large hunks for those who don't relish bite-size morsels of sushi and sashimi. Of course, if you're squeamish about sushi, there's cooked seafood, too. You might want to give a second thought to Japanese desserts here; Tomoe's creamy version of cheesecake is scented with green tea and served with a coulis of red fruits.

Yama

J a p a n e s e

051

38-40 Carmine St. (bet. Bedford & Bleecker Sts.)

Subway:	Houston St	Tuesday - Friday noon - 2:15pm
Phone:	212-989-9330	& 5:30pm - 11pm
Fax:	N/A	Saturday - Sunday 5:30pm - 11pm
e-mail:	N/A	Closed Monday
Web:	www.yamarestaurant.com	
Prices:	Ꮞ	

The largest in a chain of three sister sushi restaurants, the Carmine Street location of Yama is the most comfortable—and the only one that takes reservations. In its two rooms, exposed brick walls, blond wood floors, and the tiny sushi bar create a pleasant dining space. As for the food, it's the classic offerings plus tempura, and a few additional seafood entrées. Big portions at moderate prices make this place a good deal; the assortments of sushi for two could easily feed an extra person. In case you were wondering, the other two locations are at 122 E. 17th Street *(at Irving Place)* in Gramercy, and 92 Houston Street *(at Thompson St.)* in SoHo.

Zutto

Japanese

62 Greenwich Ave. (bet. Seventh Ave. S. & W. 11th St.)

Subway:	14 St	Monday - Friday noon - 2:15pm & 5pm
Phone:	212-367-7204	- 10:30pm
Fax:	N/A	Saturday 5pm - 10:30pm
e-mail:	N/A	Closed Sunday
Web:	www.sushizutto.com	
Prices:	✆	

Surrounded by vintage clothing stores and coffee shops, Zutto's second outpost holds sway in a little brick town house in Greenwich Village (the restaurant's original home is at 77 Hudson Street, between Jay & Harrison streets, in TriBeCa). Outside, a fanciful wrought-iron sign announces the restaurant, with its red medallion bearing the name. Inside the light-filled room, the décor invents an Oriental feel with its simple blond wood tables, bamboo shades, and Japanese calligraphy. All the usual fare is reasonably priced here. For dinner, the Bento boxes are available in combinations of sushi or sashimi, tempura or shumai, and your choice of teriyaki.

Michelin® MX™ tires.
The only thing that should
come between you and the road
is excellence.

More luxury car makers choose Michelin® MX™ tires to enhance the performance of their cars. MX tires are as close to perfect as we've ever made. Tires that can handle rain, snow, twisting corners, and steep sloping roads and handle them all for a long, long time. Smoothly, quietly, and as close as you can get to perfectly. For more information, visit michelinman.com/MX.

A better way forward

About
Harlem

This incredibly diverse neighborhood has a split personality. East of Fifth Avenue and north of East 97th Street lies East Harlem, with its distinctive Puerto Rican flavor. Northwest of Fifth Avenue is central Harlem, the most famous African-American community in America. This area is bounded by West 145th Street to the north, 110th Street to the south, Frederick Douglass Boulevard, West 125th Street and the Hudson River to the west, and Fifth Avenue and the Harlem River to the east.

A Bit of History – Dutch governor Peter Stuyvesant established Nieuw Haarlem in northern Manhattan in 1658. The hamlet remained largely rural until the railroad and the elevated trains linked it to the rest of the city in the first half of the 19th century. By the 1890s, Harlem was an affluent residential area. Overbuilding took its toll early in the 20th century, as the real-estate market slumped and landlords rented to working-class black families moving to better living conditions from the West Side.

Harlem's golden era, the **Harlem Renaissance**, lasted from 1919 to 1929. During this period, writers Langston Hughes and Zora Neale Thurston electrified the world with their originality. Nightclubs—including the original Cotton Club—hosted performances by jazz greats Duke Ellington, Count Basie, and Cab Calloway. Everything changed with the Depression. Jobs became scarce and poverty set in. By the 1960s, a climate of violence and crime overran Harlem, forcing many middle-class families to leave.

21st-Century Renaissance – Today, a renaissance of another sort is taking place. Investors are renovating old brownstones; even Bill Clinton chose Harlem for his post-presidential office. West 125th Street, the main thoroughfare, teems

with fast-food joints and chain stores. Tour buses fill with visitors, who come to marvel at the neighborhood's wealth of architectural and cultural treasures, such as the historic **Apollo Theater** (253 W.125th St.)—which still packs in the crowds. And soul food restaurants dish up hearty servings of southern fried chicken, collard greens, black-eyed peas and candied yams.

With so many outsiders swarming the neighborhood, though, residents wonder if Harlem will be able to retain its unique character as an African-American community. Only time will tell.

© Martha Cooper

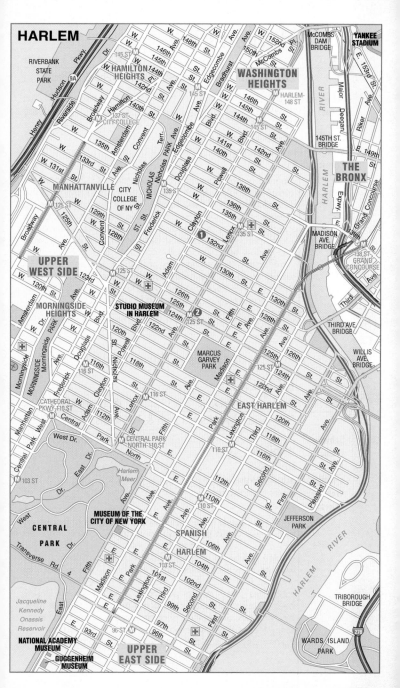

HARLEM

Harlem Grill

American

2247 Adam Clayton Powell Jr. Blvd. (132nd & 133rd Sts.)

001

Subway:	135 St	Monday - Saturday 6pm - 11:30pm
Phone:	212-491-0493	Closed Sunday
Fax:	212-491-0494	
e-mail:	reservations@harlemgrill.com	
Web:	www.harlemgrill.com	
Prices:	**$$**	

Opened at the beginning of 2005, Harlem Grill occupies the former Wells Club, which over the years hosted luminaries like Billie Holliday. In its new incarnation, the restaurant re-creates a supper-club feel with its dim lighting, cool bar, and regular schedule of musical entertainment. Keep going past the bar into the dining room, where an air of sophistication holds sway. The cuisine here successfully combines traditional Southern ingredients with contemporary style (think succulent short ribs served aside creamy grits), and the kitchen demonstrates a light touch that makes Harlem Grill a worthy dining destination, rather than merely an adjunct to a hip music club.

Bayou

American

308 Lenox Ave. (bet. 125th & 126th Sts.)

002

Subway:	125 St	Monday - Sunday 11:30am - 10pm
Phone:	212-426-3800	
Fax:	212-426-0379	
e-mail:	michael@eberstadt.com	
Web:	www.bayouinharlem.com	
Prices:	**$$**	

You don't have to travel all the way down to the real bayou to enjoy zesty Cajun dishes. Just up in Harlem, Bayou restaurant will cure those Louisiana blues with the likes of crawfish étoufée, red beans and rice, and classic jambalaya. You might want to consider sharing an entrée here if you're watching your waistline, though; the food leans heavily toward fried specialties (fried shrimp po' boys, Southern fried chicken, deep-fried catfish) and portions are supersized. Yellow hues, big windows, and framed photographs of Louisiana add to the sunny feel of Bayou's dining room, which is located above a pizza shop. The genial, young staff is eager to please.

Apollo Theater

About
Little Italy

Little Italy, which once ran from Canal Street north to Houston and from Lafayette Street east to the Bowery, may now be more aptly called Micro Italy. Mulberry Street is the main drag in Little Italy, and the tenacious heart of the neighborhood, which is quickly being swallowed up by neighboring Chinatown. The onetime stronghold of Manhattan's Italian-American population has dwindled to a mere corridor—Mulberry Street between Canal and Broome streets—that caters mainly to hungry tourists, though you can still find some authentic delis, bakeries and gelato shops in the neighborhood. Devotees still frequent Mulberry Street for authentic Italian fare, then go over to Ferrara's bakery *(195 Grand St.)* for Italian pastries (cannoli, tiramisu) and a cup of strong espresso.

A Bit of History – Italians have played a powerful role in shaping New York even before there was a city to shape. Italian explorer Giovanni da Verrazzano, working under the auspices of French king Francois I, was the first European to set foot on the island of Manhattan in 1524. Italians didn't cross the Great Pond en masse until the late 1800s, however. Fleeing rural poverty in southern Italy, many initially settled in the notorious Five Points slum, which stood on what is now a corner of Chinatown, but as families got on their feet they moved north to SoHo, Greenwich Village and Little Italy. In 1880, fewer than 20,000 Italians lived in the city; by 1930 that number had risen to more than a million. Many started their own businesses as tailors, barbers, grocers or

© Martha Cooper

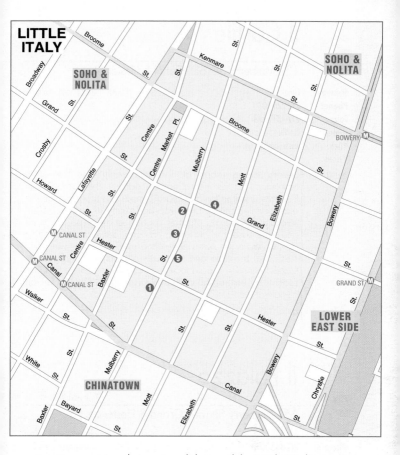

restaurateurs, mixing their native dishes, redolent with Mediterranean ingredients like tomatoes, olive oil and basil, into the melting pot of American cuisine.

Little Italy Today – A visit to Little Italy basically consists of a Mulberry Street stroll. The stretch between Canal and Grand streets is a veritable restaurant row, with white-aproned waiters sweet-talking diners into choosing their linguine over all others. On weekends from May to mid-October, Mulberry Street is closed to vehicular traffic, making Little Italy one big al fresco party—the **Feast of San Gennaro** in mid-September is particularly raucous. Although these days, you can get better Italian food elsewhere in the city, you still can't beat the ambience on Mulberry Street.

Il Cortile

Italian

001

125 Mulberry St. (bet. Canal & Hester Sts.)

Subway:	Canal St	Monday - Sunday noon - midnight
Phone:	212-226-6060	
Fax:	212-431-7283	
e-mail:	ilcortile@aol.com	
Web:	www.ilcortile.com	
Prices:	**$$**	

Several dining rooms at Il Cortile each have their own ambience, but the most pleasant space is the garden room (*il cortile* is Italian for "courtyard"), more like an atrium with its glass-paneled ceiling, brick walls and abundant greenery. Chef Michael DeGeorgio presents a wide array of pastas, meat and seafood dishes, including his Ragu 'del Macellaio, a rich tomato sauce simmered like *nonna* used to make with pork, meatballs, bresaola and sausage—offered only on Sundays. Careful attention is paid to select ingredients such as Bell and Evans chicken, raised in Pennyslvania Dutch Country on an all-natural diet.

Il Palazzo

Italian

002

151 Mulberry St. (bet. Grand & Hester Sts.)

Subway:	Canal St	Sunday - Thursday noon - 11pm
Phone:	212-343-7000	Friday - Saturday noon - midnight
Fax:	212-343-1508	
e-mail:	N/A	
Web:	N/A	
Prices:	**$$**	

Located on Little Italy's main thoroughfare, Il Palazzo dishes up authentic Italian fare to a host of regulars, especially at dinnertime. The main dining room recalls a winter garden with its flowering plants and well-spaced tables, while the menu lists a generous and varied selection of Old World classics (written in Italian with English explanations): veal saltimbocca, chicken Cacciatore, rigatoni alla vodka, linguine with clam sauce, shrimp scampi. If you just can't eat another bite at the end of your meal, you can always skip the sweet course and end your meal with a glass of potent grappa or vintage port instead.

Taormina

003

147 Mulberry St. (bet. Grand & Hester Sts.)

Subway:	Canal St
Phone:	212-219-1007
Fax:	N/A
e-mail:	N/A
Web:	N/A
Prices:	$$

Monday - Sunday noon - 11:30pm

Named for the lovely resort town that towers above the sea on the east coast of Sicily, Taormina remains one of the few culinary strongholds of the slowly disappearing Little Italy neighborhood. The restaurant's classic, contemporary brasserie style showcases light varnished woods and a windowed façade overlooking Mulberry Street. Pastas, like pappardelle with porcini, and linguine del casa (tossed with shellfish, calamari and garlic in a fresh tomato sauce), are homemade and offer a taste of Italy. There's a large and tempting selection of antipasti, and the balanced menu nods to its namesake with a good array of seafood offerings.

Nyonya

004

194 Grand St. (bet. Mott & Mulberry Sts.)

Subway:	Canal St
Phone:	212-334-3669
Fax:	N/A
e-mail:	N/A
Web:	N/A
Prices:	

Sunday - Thursday 11am - 11:30pm
Friday - Saturday 11am - midnight

Now for something completely different: Malaysian food in Little Italy. Okay, so you don't typically go to Little Italy looking for a Malaysian restaurant, but Nyonya is nonetheless worth seeking out for unique dishes at prices that won't blow your budget. A fusion cuisine that resulted from the intermarriage of Chinese and Malaysians in order to strengthen early trade ties between the two countries, Nyonya (a word that refers to the woman in such a hybrid pairing) marries traditional Chinese ingredients with Malay herbs and spices. You're bound to find something you like on the extensive menu, which lists everything from Nyonya seafood rice noodles to curried pork spareribs.

Pellegrino's

005

138 Mulberry St. (bet. Grand & Hester Sts.)

Subway:	Canal St
Phone:	212-226-3177
Fax:	212-343-1508
e-mail:	N/A
Web:	N/A
Prices:	$$

Monday - Sunday noon - 11pm

On a warm summer day, the view from one of Pellegrino's sidewalk tables takes in the heart of Little Italy. You're likely to find a good number of tourists at this restaurant, since the long, narrow dining room is attractive, the umbrella-shaded outdoor tables are inviting, and the service is courteous. Children are welcome here; in fact, Pellegrino's even offers half-portions for those smaller appetites. The food, which stays true to its roots in sunny Italy, includes a balanced selection of pasta, meat and fish. Linguini alla Sinatra, the signature dish named for the beloved crooner, abounds with lobster, shrimp, clams, mushrooms and pine nuts in red sauce.

Colorful storefronts of the Neighborhood

About the
Lower East Side

Despite being one of New York's hippest neighborhoods, the Lower East Side has, for the most part, a refreshing lack of attitude and an astounding amount of local pride. "Come one, come all" has been its message to visitors since the 1880s, when it became the quintessential American melting pot. Though today's immigrants tend to be young artists, musicians and designers, artsy types aren't the only ones working on their craft on the Lower East Side. In recent years the neighborhood has become a breeding ground for new culinary talent, while history lives on in the district's many famous ethnic eateries.

The Governor's Farm – The area now known as the Lower East Side— clockwise from north, is bounded by Houston Street, the East River, Pike Street, and the Bowery—was rural long after the southern tip of Manhattan was developed. Peter Stuyvesant, the last Dutch governor of Nieuw Amsterdam, bought much of the land in 1651 from the Indians. To facilitate transport between his farm, or *bouwerie*, and the urban market, he laid out a straight road now known as the **Bowery**.

Gateway to America – The first mass migration to the Lower East Side occurred with the arrival of Irish immigrants fleeing the Great Hunger of 1845 to 1852. From the 1880s until World War I,

© Martha Cooper

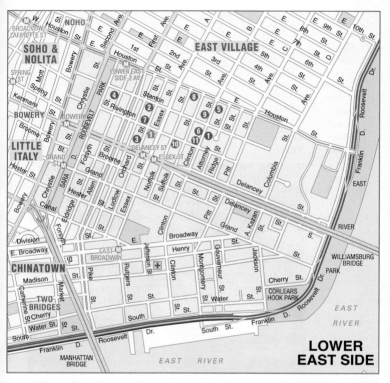

millions of southern and eastern Europeans arrived via Ellis Island and settled in the Lower East Side, where they could meet other recently arrived immigrants. The neighborhood swiftly became the most densely populated in the country.

Eastern European Jews set down some of the strongest roots here, building synagogues and schools, publishing Yiddish newspapers, and opening Kosher delis. The Lower East Side was the original nosher's paradise, and for those in the know, it remains just that.

The Lower East Side Today – Today only 10 percent of Lower East Side residents are Jewish. The southern edge of the district is largely Chinese. Latinos still have a presence, but more prevalent—or at least visible— are the hordes of young Anglos who have transformed the once-gritty neighborhood into a free-spirited urban village. Orchard Street between Canal and Houston streets is the district's spine; to the south it's lined with bargain stores; farther north (around Broome Street) trendy boutiques begin. Stanton and Rivington streets all the way east to Clinton Street are good for galleries, shops and cafes. A carnival atmosphere prevails at night on and around Ludlow Street between Houston and Delancey, where restaurants, bars and clubs stay full until the wee hours.

WD~50 ✿

50 Clinton St. (bet. Rivington & Stanton Sts.)

Subway:	Delancey St
Phone:	212-477-2900
Fax:	212-477-7054
e-mail:	N/A
Web:	www.wd-50.com
Prices:	$$$

Monday - Saturday 6pm - 11:30pm
Sunday 6pm - 10:30pm

XX

&

Manhattan *Lower East Side*

wd-50/Robert Polidori

At WD~50, life, or at least the food part of it, most certainly imitates art. What comes from the kitchen here are avant-garde, meticulously arranged compositions that taste as good as they look. Award-winning chef Wylie Dufresne turns simple plates into works of art by adding, for example, a literal brushstroke of sauce to a curling ribbon of pickled beef tongue. At times it's debatable whether Dufresne, who trained under Jean-Georges Vongerichten (a co-owner of WD~50), is a chef or a mad scientist. His experiments with food are continued by pastry chef Sam Mason, who searches out ingredients not normally associated with dessert—parsnips for cake, miso for ice cream, olives for clafouti.

The dining room boasts custom-designed furnishings and deep tones of blue and brown. And, in case you were wondering, the restaurant's name is composed of the chef's initials and the street number.

Shrimp Noodles with Smoked Yogurt

Serves 4

Chef's Notes

This dish illustrates our work with the enzyme transglutaminase, an enzyme that has a wide range of culinary applications, one of which is restructured muscle food products. In the instance of this dish, the enzyme has been mixed with shrimp meat and allowed to react in the desired shape under refrigerated conditions. Once set, the restructured shrimp is then cooked and portioned. The applications become endless. We have been able to stick scallops together end to end, taken tail pieces from fish and combined them, shaped steaks into desired forms. The ability of this enzyme to react with protein has given us tremendous possibilities.

9 oz. shrimp, peeled and deveined, tails removed
1.62 grams transglutaminase
3 Tbsp. plus 1 tsp. water
salt and cayenne pepper

Blend shrimp, water, salt and pepper to a smooth paste. Dissolve the transglutaminase in 1 Tbsp. plus 2 tsp. of cold water and fold into the shrimp mixture. Place mixture in a pastry bag with a small round tip and pipe into thin noodle shapes onto a Silpat mat on a sheet pan. If you do not have a Silpat, you can use parchment or wax paper. Cover tightly and refrigerate overnight.

Smoked Yogurt Paprika

1 cup yogurt, smoked for 3 minutes
3/4 tsp. sweet paprika
¼ tsp. salt

Mix ingredients together and allow flavors to infuse for one hour.

Prawn Crackers

5 prawn crackers
tomato powder
¼ tsp. salt

Deep-fry crackers until they puff. Crush into small pieces. Drain from oil and dust with tomato powder and salt.

To Serve

6 cups shellfish or other fish stock
2 Tbsp. olive oil

Put stock in a large pot over high heat and bring to a boil. Add olive oil and gently add shrimp noodles. Cook for two minutes and drain. Paint the yogurt onto the plate and top with warm noodles and prawn crackers.

Stanton Social

Fusion

99 Stanton St. (bet. Orchard & Ludlow Sts.)

Subway:	Lower East Side - 2 Av
Phone:	212-995-0099
Fax:	212-995-0083
e-mail:	N/A
Web:	www.thestantonsocial.com
Prices:	$$

Monday - Tuesday 5pm - 2am
Wednesday - Friday 5pm - 3am
Saturday 11:30am - 3pm & 5pm - 3am
Sunday 11:30am - 3pm & 5pm - 2am

Designed by the hip firm of AvroKO, Stanton Social fills a duplex with two floors of fun. The décor here honors the erstwhile haberdashers and seamstress shops of the Lower East Side with elements such as a wall of woven leather, vintage hand mirrors on a wall in the upstairs bar, and wine shelves laid out in a herringbone pattern, inspired by a classic men's jacket. Chris Santos' wildly eclectic menu of small plates zigzags all over the globe, from beef Wellington to Peking duck to chipotle shrimp. Adorable little "sliders," with fillings of lobster, Kobe beef or pulled pork, are served on buttered brioche buns. Don't forget to bring some friends, since sharing is part of the deal.

Suba

Contemporary Spanish

109 Ludlow St. (bet. Delancey & Rivington Sts.)

Subway:	Delancey St
Phone:	212-982-5714
Fax:	212-982-3034
e-mail:	info@subanyc.com
Web:	www.subanyc.com
Prices:	$$$

Sunday - Wednesday 6pm - midnight
Thursday 6pm - 1am
Friday - Saturday 6pm - 4am

Hot, hot, hot. Designed by architect Andre Kikoski, Suba's three sleek dining levels fill a 1909 tenement building from the ground-floor tapas lounge down the twisting steel staircase to the Grotto, where a polished-concrete dining island floats in a rippling pool of water, and farther down still to the brightly painted Skylight Room. Of course, all this high style comes at an equally high price. But it's worth a splurge to sway to the Latin beat while you sip a mojito and sample tapas, ceviche, and entrées such as braised short ribs with glazed fennel in star-anise broth. Come Sunday night to catch a live Flamenco performance *(8pm to 10pm; reservations required)*.

Ápizz

004

217 Eldridge St. (bet. Rivington & Stanton Sts.)

Subway:	Lower East Side - 2 Av	Monday - Saturday 6pm - 11pm
Phone:	212-253-9199	Closed Sunday
Fax:	212-253-6130	
e-mail:	apizz217@verizon.net	
Web:	www.apizz.com	
Prices:	$$	

A huge brick oven froms the focal point of Ápizz (say ah-BEETS), whose name derives from the Neapolitan word for pizza. The restaurant's concept, brought to you by the same duo—John LaFemina and Frank DeCarlo—who run Peasant in SoHo, is simple: "one room, one oven." This means that nearly all the dishes, from baked pastas to wood-roasted whole fish, are fired in the wood-burning oven. Of course, the thin-crust pizzas go without saying. A meal in the dining room here, which blends old and new between the rustic oven, the wood-beamed ceiling and the contemporary table settings, begins with an amuse-bouche of fresh ricotta and warm tomato sauce to eat with crusty country bread.

Chubo

005

6 Clinton St. (bet. Houston & Stanton Sts.)

Subway:	Lower East Side - 2 Av	Sunday - Wednesday 6pm - 11pm
Phone:	212-674-6300	Thursday - Saturday 6pm - 11:30pm
Fax:	212-674-6340	
e-mail:	chubonyc@aol.com	
Web:	www.chubo.com	
Prices:	$$	

East meets West—and points in-between—at Chubo, where the cuisine proves as eclectic as its chef/owner, Claude Chassagne. An American with a French father, a German-American mother, and a Japanese wife, Chassagne can truly claim global influences. So can his edgy cuisine, which borrows from his varied background and results in surprising combinations ("surf and turf" here translates into Indian-spiced mahi-mahi with edamame purée, and shortrib ravioli with sesame-anise salad). So if you're up for something out of the ordinary, drop into Chubo, whose Japanese name means "professional kitchen." Tip: the best deals are the two- and three-course, fixed-price menus.

Cube 63

Contemporary Japanese

006

63 Clinton St. (bet. Rivington & Stanton Sts.)

Subway:	Delancey St	Sunday - Thursday 5pm - midnight
Phone:	212-228-6751	Friday - Saturday 5pm - 1am
Fax:	212-228-6753	
e-mail:	cube63@cube63.com	
Web:	www.cube63.com	
Prices:	$$	

Eclectic sushi is the name of the game at Cube 63. The chef comes up with some pretty far-out combinations, such as the Mexican roll (white fish with jalapeno and spicy sauce) and the Puerto Rico roll (eel tempura and lobster salad with cucumber). You'll need to bring your own bottle if you want an alcoholic beverage at this little sushi joint; they don't have a liquor license yet. Not to worry, though, there's a liquor store just down the street, and the restaurant doesn't charge a corkage fee. The crowd is trendy and the design is sparse and ultra-modern—check out the lime-green spotlights that illuminate the sushi bar.

'inoteca

Italian

007

98 Rivington St. (at Ludlow St.)

Subway:	Delancey St	Monday - Friday noon - 3am
Phone:	212-614-0473	Saturday - Sunday 10am - 3am
Fax:	N/A	
e-mail:	N/A	
Web:	www.inotecanyc.com	
Prices:		

Big sister to 'ino in the West Village, this wine bar caters to the chic, young Lower East Side set. 'Inoteca owes its popularity in part to co-owner Joe Denton, who also has a hand in Lupa and Otto. True to its name (an enoteca is an Italian wine bar), the restaurant offers a superb selection of well-priced Italian wines—some 250 in all—from every region of Italy. Of these, 25 wines are available by the glass. The menu emphasizes small plates and panini (stuffed with the likes of bresaola, fontina and arugula, or roasted vegetables and fresh ricotta). If wine and cheese is your thing, you can choose assortments of 3, 5 or 7 different types of Italian cheeses to sample with your vino.

Petrosino

008

190 Norfolk St. (at Houston St.)

Subway:	Lower East Side - 2 Av	Monday - Sunday 6pm - 11pm
Phone:	212-673-3773	Closed January 1
Fax:	212-673-5286	
e-mail:	N/A	
Web:	www.petrosinonyc.com	
Prices:	$$	

Don't be put off by the bare, back-lit birch branches, bright orange banquettes and the poured-concrete bar. Artsy décor does not necessarily mean mediocre food—at least not at Petrosino. Sure it's a hangout for the hip, but owner Antonio Bellomo and chef Patrick Nuti, are nonetheless serious about their food. Nuti bases his southern Italian dishes on good, fresh products, and supplements the core menu with intriguing specials (venison osso bucco) and scrumptious desserts like the creamy ricotta tart, spiked with fresh-fruit coulis. Riding on Petrosino's success, the same pair recently opened Canapa next door, featuring simpler fare at a lower price—and sharing the same kitchen.

Sachiko's On Clinton

Japanese

009

25 Clinton St. (bet. Houston & Stanton Sts.)

Subway:	Delancey St	Sunday - Wednesday 5:30pm - midnight
Phone:	212-253-2900	Thursday - Saturday 5:30pm - 1am
Fax:	N/A	
e-mail:	N/A	
Web:	www.sachikosonclinton.com	
Prices:	$$	

Opened in November 2004, Sachiko's is a newcomer to the Lower East Side restaurant scene. This little sushi and sake bar, as they bill themselves, is decorated with bright orange walls, blond woods, and an intimate sushi counter where mounds of fresh raw fish are displayed for all to see. The restaurant draws an international clientele for creative sushi, including some made with high-end ingredients such as caviar and lobster. Kushiage is the specialty: beef, chicken or vegetables are threaded on bamboo sticks (*kushi* in Japanese), breaded and deep-fried. Think of kushiage as Japanese kabobs—and be forewarned that they have way more fat calories than sushi.

Manhattan Lower East Side

Schiller's Liquor Bar

European

010

131 Rivington St. (at Norfolk St.)

Subway:	Delancey St	Monday - Friday 11am - 2am
Phone:	212-260-4555	Saturday - Sunday 10am - 2am
Fax:	N/A	
e-mail:	info@schillersny.com	
Web:	www.schillersny.com	
Prices:	$$	

A Lower East Side institution, Schiller's was founded by restaurateur Keith McNally, whose other ventures include Pastis and Balthazar. It's a lively, happening scene, decked out with subway tiles, antique mirrors and bare bistro tables; the noise level ratchets up higher and higher as the night goes on. On the eclectic menu you'll find everything from steak frites to Welsh rarebit to hummus. The wine list is divided into three sections: cheap, decent and good; according to the restaurant, "cheap" is the best. For dessert, don't miss the sticky toffee pudding, a wonderful, creamy confection topped with vanilla ice cream. Brunch is available every day from 11am to 4pm.

71 Clinton Fresh Food

Contemporary

011

71 Clinton St. (bet. Rivington & Stanton Sts.)

Subway:	Delancey St	Sunday - Thursday 6pm - 10:30pm
Phone:	212-614-6960	Friday - Saturday 6pm - 11:30pm
Fax:	212-614-9426	
e-mail:	N/A	
Web:	www.71clintonfreshfood.com	
Prices:	$$	

Beyond the metal-and-glass grid that forms the façade of 71 Clinton, you'll find a tiny contemporary room with a row of close-together tables marching down one side. Of course, this sort of arrangement certainly doesn't invite private conversation, but fans claim it's part of the restaurant's appeal. The constantly changing menu here relies on fresh seasonal ingredients (think striped bass with taleggio ravioli and macerated figs; Sullivan County chicken with baby fennel and chanterelles; salsify "noodles" with butternut squash, smoked-onion jus, watercress and goat cheese). In addition to the à la carte offerings, the chef prepares a five-course tasting menu daily.

Not every atlas comes with
a legend like this.

We put the same quality and reliability into our atlases that we put into
our tires. The innovative design makes for easy navigation, allowing you to
travel with confidence. To learn more, visit michelintravel.com.

About the Meatpacking District

Not so long ago, "trendy" was the last word anyone would ever use to describe the gritty northwest corner of the West Village. Bounded by West 15th, Eighth Avenue, and Horatio Street and the Hudson River, the Meatpacking District has been transformed in recent years into an über-hip shopping, dining and clubbing destination. Where else in the city can you find a wholesale meat company elbow to elbow with an exclusive nightclub?

A Bit of History – In the 1850s, New York was the largest center of beef production in the country; slaughterhouses, meat-packing plants, and storage facilities lined both its east and west sides. As refrigeration technology improved, many of the big meat companies moved their facilities to the Midwest, closer to where the cattle were. In the late 1940s, the slaughtering district on the east side was cleared to make way for the **United Nations**, and later the practice of slaughtering animals was banned from the city altogether. The Meatpacking District was a rather dangerous place until the 1990s; after meat wholesalers would close for the day, drug dealers and prostitutes prowled its moody, cobblestone streets. The booming economy, along with Mayor Rudy Giuliani's heavy-handed crime policy in the early 1990s, cleaned up the neighborhood. Although some meat companies remain in business, the neighborhood's grit is, for the most part, a fashion accessory.

© Martha Cooper

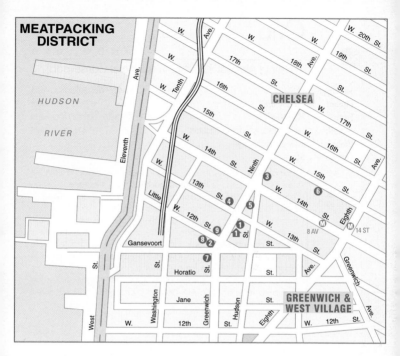

Dining, Dancing and Shopping – Big-name chefs have made inroads into the district recently, opening hard-to-get-into restaurants. All these places are packed to the rafters at night, so try to reserve well in advance.

Famously protean, the **club scene** in New York refuses to be pinned down: once a place is deemed hot, it shuts its doors, only to spring up under some other name in another neighborhood. As a clubbing quarter, the Meatpacking District appears to have some staying power. If you go, dress to impress—the doormen at some of the velvet-rope clubs can be highly selective about who gets in.

The fact that both Stella McCartney and Alexander McQueen both chose to open their first boutiques on West 14th Street between Ninth and Tenth avenues in 2002 says a lot about the sizzle of the Meatpacking District (check out their clothing-as-art at nos. 429 and 417 respectively). And there's much more where they came from. Spend some time window-shopping here, even if you can't afford the haute-couture prices.

Ono

001

18 Ninth Ave. (at 13th St., in the Hotel Gansevoort)

Subway:	14 St	Sunday - Wednesday noon - 3pm
Phone:	212-660-6766	& 5pm - 11pm
Fax:	212-660-6776	Thursday - Saturday noon - 3pm
e-mail:	ono.reservations@chinagrillmgt.com	& 5pm - midnight
Web:	www.chinagrillmgt.com	
Prices:	$$	

It's all about style at Ono. Housed in the Gansevoort Hotel *(see hotel listings)*, Ono is the latest addition to entrepreneur Jeffrey Chodorow's restaurant-management empire. The action begins at the bar, where silk-tunic-clad bartenders mix drinks with names like Blushing Geisha and Blue Yuzu. But the real show centers on the open kitchen, where you can watch the chefs prepare *robatayaki*, meats grilled over an open flame. Here you can choose your ingredients from a bountiful display of Kobe beef and chicken breast, shrimp and scallops, Japanese yams and aged tofu, among other items. And how cool is the edamame "alphabet soup," poured over cubes of tofu carved to form the letters O-N-O?

5 Ninth

002

5 Ninth Ave. (at Little W. 12th St.)

Subway:	14 St - 8 Av	Monday - Sunday 6pm - 2am
Phone:	212-929-9460	
Fax:	212-929-4428	
e-mail:	Rick@5ninth.com	
Web:	www.5ninth.com	
Prices:	$$$	

One of the Meatpacking District's hottest tables, 5 Ninth courts the cognoscenti with its unmarked entrance. Three levels divide this c.1848 brownstone into a ground-floor bar, a second-floor dining room, and an elegant cocktail lounge on the third floor. The décor can best be described as shabby-chic: an open metal staircase and rough exposed-brick walls suggests the neighborhood's erstwhile seediness, while flagstone floors and two fireplaces on each level add sleek touches. A chic crowd prefers the communal table in the back garden, which is enclosed by ivy-covered walls. They don't seem to mind paying the high prices when they can dine on such carefully prepared seasonal fare.

Old Homestead

003

56 Ninth Ave. (bet. 14th & 15th Sts.)

Subway:	14 St	Monday - Thursday noon - 10:45pm
Phone:	212-242-9040	Friday noon - 11:45pm
Fax:	N/A	Saturday 1pm - 11:45pm
e-mail:	N/A	Sunday 1pm - 9:45pm
Web:	www.theoldhomesteadsteakhouse.com	Closed major holidays
Prices:	$$$	

XX

This classic steakhouse has stood in the Meatpacking District since 1868, way before it ever became the trendy neighborhood it is today. Old Homestead is a wealthy-guy's-night-out kind of place, with a focus on domestically raised Kobe beef. Remember that old saying about never eating anything bigger than your head? You'll have to ignore it at this steakhouse, where the "Empire Cut" of prime rib weighs in at two pounds, and the four-and-a-half-pound lobsters are fittingly billed as "whale-size." Prices may be high, but the meat is top quality, the service is professional and the elegant dining rooms are papered with photographs of the district in the early 20th century.

Spice Market

004

403 W. 13th St. (at Ninth Ave.)

Subway:	14 St	Sunday - Wednesday noon - 4pm
Phone:	212-675-2322	& 6pm - midnight
Fax:	212-675-4365	Thursday - Saturday noon - 4pm
e-mail:	N/A	& 6pm - 1am
Web:	www.jean-georges.com	
Prices:	$$$	

XX
&
🛉

Another venture by Jean-Georges Vongerichten, Spice Market has fast become a Meatpacking District hot spot. The cuisine concept is inspired by Southeast Asian food, what you might nosh on while roaming marketplace stalls in Thailand or Malaysia. Subtly seasoned dishes (think chicken samosas, red curried duck, pork vindaloo) are placed in the middle of the table, for all to share. Realized by Jacques Garcia, the design concept changes the mood inside this soaring, 12,000-square-foot former warehouse from industrial to brooding and sexy, in deep shades of red, violet and gold. The crowd is strictly A-list, especially in the evenings.

Vento

005

675 Hudson St. (at 14th St.)

Subway:	14 St	Monday - Tuesday noon - 4pm & 5pm - 11pm
Phone:	212-699-2400	Wednesday - Thursday noon - 4pm
Fax:	212-699-2401	& 5pm - midnight
e-mail:	N/A	Friday - Saturday noon - 4pm & 5pm - 1am
Web:	www.brguestrestaurants.com	Sunday 11am - 4pm & 5pm - 11pm
Prices:	$$	

Residing in a triangular brick building located where Ninth Avenue and Hudson Street run into each other at 14th Street, Vento is a more casual incarnation of chef Michael White's SoHo outpost, Fiamma Osteria. White, who designed Vento's menu, is chef and partner here, but it's executive chef Martin Burge who presides over the kitchen along with pastry guru Elizabeth Katz. Wood-fired pizzas, rustic pastas, and whole-roasted fish are a sampling of the fare served in the pie-shaped dining space, which is lined on two sides with full-length windows and widens to a bar in the back. Before you leave, check out the scene in the cool downstairs bar, called Level V.

El Cid

006

322 W. 15th St. (bet. Eighth & Ninth Aves.)

Subway:	14 St	Tuesday - Sunday noon - 3pm
Phone:	212-929-9332	& 5pm - 11pm
Fax:	N/A	
e-mail:	N/A	
Web:	N/A	
Prices:	$$	

This unpretentious little neighborhood eatery may seem out of place in the hip-for-the-moment Meatpacking District, but the truth is, it was here long before the designer boutiques moved in. Hot and cold tapas provide the food focus in the anything-but-trendy setting, adorned simply with Spanish tiles. Count on the Old World staff to offer careful, kind service to eager crowds. And count on the tapas, from baby eels to chicken, to be flavorful and redolent with garlic. Save room for the signature *torrejas*, a Spanish version of French toast (sweet bread dipped in spiced wine and topped with ice cream). Downside: the smell of fried fish clings to your clothing for hours afterward.

Macelleria

007

Italian

48 Gansevoort St. (bet. Greenwich & Washington Sts.)

Subway:	8 Av - 14 St	Monday - Sunday noon - midnight
Phone:	212-741-2555	Closed Thanksgiving Day
Fax:	212-741-0845	& Christmas Day
e-mail:	macelleria@aol.com	
Web:	www.macelleriarestaurant.com	
Prices:	$$	

In keeping with its past incarnation as a meat warehouse, Macelleria (Italian for "butcher shop") decks out its cavernous space with dangling meat hooks and carving tables to suggest its former use. Its lively, informal ambience is part industrial-chic (high ceiling, brick walls, exposed pipes), part sunny Italian tavola. And, as you might guess, steakhouse items play a big role on a short menu otherwise filled by Italian fare—how convenient that the butcher shop is right next door. The food isn't inexpensive, but portions are generous. Downstairs, the stone-walled wine cellar—where Italian vintages predominate—doubles as a private dining room.

Paradou

French

008

8 Little W. 12th St. (bet. Greenwich & Washington Sts.)

Subway:	14 St	Monday - Friday 6pm - midnight
Phone:	212-463-8345	Saturday - Sunday noon - 5pm
Fax:	N/A	& 6pm - midnight
e-mail:	N/A	
Web:	www.paradounyc.com	
Prices:	$$	

Step into Provence through the weathered French-blue doors of Paradou, which recalls a town in the South of France whose name means "paradise." White-washed walls, high ceilings, and tables fashioned out of vintage French wine crates create an airy, country ambience. Like the atmosphere, the food is Mediterranean in spirit; dishes from that sun-washed region share the menu with the likes of chicken grand-mère and Provençal thick-cut pork chops. Skip dessert and go straight for the plate of four truffles, handmade in 32 different flavors that capture the essence of Provence, by chocolatier Joel Durand. In summer, the verdant garden out back makes a hidden oasis for dining. Ah, paradise.

Manhattan *Meatpacking District*

Pastis

French

9 Ninth Ave. (at Little W. 12th St.)

Subway:	14 St	Monday - Sunday 8am - 2am
Phone:	212-929-4844	
Fax:	212-929-5676	
e-mail:	N/A	
Web:	www.pastisny.com	
Prices:	**$$**	

Brought to you by the same folks that gave you Balthazar, Pastis transports diners back to the south of France circa 1960 with its large decorative mirrors, long zinc bar, bistro tables and walls lined with old Pastis ads. The menu includes all the French classics (steak tartare, skate au beurre noir, steak frites, moules frites, pissaladière) as well as some concessions to the American palate—the ubiquitous hamburger. The place is packed more often than not; it seems Pastis, with its lively atmosphere, is quite a fashionable place to be seen. As you might imagine, the cocktail list leans heavily on the restaurant's namesake anise-flavored aperitif, which hails originally from Marseille.

Manhattan Meatpacking District

World
Champion
Valentino
Rossi

Motocross
Champion
Mike
Brown

To Make Tires This Good, You Need Test Riders Who Can Work Weekends

Dakar Rally
Champion
Cyril
Despres

MotoGP
Rider
Nicky
Hayden

Week in and week out, you'll find Michelin motorcycle tires in the winner's circle. But the real winner is you, because what we learn at the track goes into every tire we make.

About
Midtown East

A bustling business district, the swatch of land east of Fifth Avenue—contains some of the city's finest office buildings, from the Art Deco **Chrysler Building** to the modernist **Lever House**, as well as the spectacular Beaux-Arts **Grand Central Terminal**. All the way east, at the river, you'll find the headquarters of the United Nations. Tucked among these landmarks are historic hotels, posh shops galore lining Madison and Fifth avenues, and, last, but far from least, a plethora of fine restaurants to suit every taste and price range.

A Bit of History – The area bounded by Fifth Avenue and the East River, between East 40th and 60th streets, was not always the tony place it is today. In the early 19th century, steam-powered locomotives chugged down Park Avenue all the way to a depot on 23rd Street, bringing with them noise and dirt. Residents complained, and in 1854 an ordinance was passed banning trains south of 42nd Street. That helped pave the way for downtown development, but did nothing to improve the lot of those in Midtown East, whose tenements surrounded a sooty railyard that spread from 42nd to 56th Street.

© Martha Cooper

Underground Railroad – Enter railroad magnate "Commodore" Cornelius Vanderbilt (1794–1877), who opened the first Grand Central depot in 1871 on the present site of the Grand Central Terminal. Shortly thereafter, he began lowering the tracks feeding into it below street level, reducing some of the noise pollution. But smoke was still a big problem, and in 1889 the city demanded that the railroad electrify the trains or leave the city. To finance the electrification process,

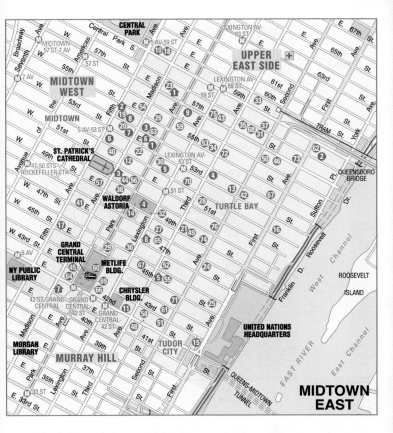

the Vanderbilts sunk the entire railyard fronting the depot below ground and sold the land above it to developers, who soon lined Madison and Park avenues with exclusive apartment buildings. The Grand Central Terminal you see today, a masterpiece of urban architecture, was completed in 1913.

After World War II, many of the original apartment houses along Madison, Park and Lexington avenues in Midtown were replaced by high-rise office towers. Today the area claims an eclectic mixture of old and new. Grand Central Terminal, for instance, accommodates several restaurants on its east and west balconies. Under the East Balcony, **Grand Central Market** teems with gourmet goodies, a butcher, a fishmonger and produce stalls. Beneath the Main Concourse is the sprawling **dining concourse**, a food court featuring locally owned restaurants. Here you'll find the best quick bites in the area, especially on weekends, when lunch spots catering to the office crowd are closed.

Lever House ✿

001

390 Park Ave. (at 53rd St.)

Subway:	Lexington Av - 59 St	Monday - Thursday 11:45am - 2:15pm
Phone:	212-888-2700	& 5:30pm - 11pm
Fax:	212-888-2740	Friday 11:45am - 2:15pm
e-mail:	info@leverhouse.com	& 5:30pm - 11:30pm
Web:	www.leverhouse.com	Saturday 5:30pm - 11:30pm
Prices:	**$$$**	Sunday 5pm - 10pm

XXX

&

Lever House/Roberto D'Addona

If you fancy retro design, make a beeline for this podlike dining room, where almost everything has six sides. Mark Newsen's honeycomb motif grabs the eye here, repeated in everything from the carpet to the light fixtures to the hexagonal cubbyholes that hold the wine bottles. And it's all wrapped in a honey-toned glow, to boot. The rounded corners of the dining room complement the angular tower of green-blue glass and steel that is the Lever House building, designed by Gordon Bunshaft in 1952 as Park Avenue's first glass-clad tower.

The buzz about the food is well deserved. Executive chef Dan Silverman, whose culinary resume includes stints at Chez Panisse, Le Bernardin and Union Square Cafe, knows how to pick excellent ingredients. Tastes of the seasons shine through the straightforward food here, from white tuna tartare to roasted poussin with tarragon jus to grilled côte de boeuf.

Manhattan Midtown East

Shrimp Brochettes

(Spiedini di Scampi)

Serves 4

- 12 large shrimp, heads left on, bodies peeled and deveined
- 12 very thin slices pancetta—preferably pepato (flat peppered pancetta)
- 4 large sprigs of fresh rosemary, all leaves removed and reserved
- 2 Tbsp. olive oil
- ¼ tsp. salt
- ¼ tsp. freshly ground black pepper
- 1 lime, cut in 8 wedges

Method

Wrap each shrimp with a slice of pancetta. Finely chop rosemary leaves removed from sprig. Skewer 3 shrimp on each rosemary branch. Place a sauté pan over medium heat and add olive oil. Sauté skewers, turning occasionally to ensure browning.

When shrimp are almost done, add finely chopped fresh rosemary, salt and pepper, and shake the pan. Remove the brochettes from the pan, arrange on a plate, spoon pan juices over top and serve with lime wedges.

March ✢

Contemporary

405 E. 58th St. (bet. First Ave. & Sutton Place)

Subway:	59 St	Monday - Sunday 5:30pm - 10:30pm
Phone:	212-754-6272	
Fax:	212-838-5108	
e-mail:	marchrestaurant@aol.com	
Web:	www.marchrestaurant.com	
Prices:	$$$	

March/Bartman

Once you enter this attractive town house, through the tiny brick-lined courtyard surrounded by a wrought-iron fence, you'll be immersed in a romantic aura, enhanced by a working fireplace, Limoges china, antique Persian carpets and Lalique vases. You can craft your own meal from the nightly changing selections or put yourself in the creative and capable hands of chef/owner Wayne Nish, whose cuisine highlights New York's diverse culinary heritage.

If you decide on the latter, all you need do is choose how many courses you want (from three to six; wine pairings are available, too). Then sit back and let the chef titillate your taste buds with such combinations as fricasée of seasonal vegetables, spit-roasted rabbit with baby turnips, and milk-fed veal with artichokes and pole beans. From May through October, you can dine alfresco on the rooftop terrace, overlooking Bridgemarket.

Sashimi with Olive Oil and White Soy

Serves 8 as an appetizer

Chef's Notes

The blending of olive oil and soy sauce on the same plate is the perfect embodiment of the multicultural food philosophy prevalent today. This recipe is the purest example I know.

For this dish I use first cold-pressed Ligurian olive oil and imported Japanese soy sauce. Regular soy sauce is fermented from 80% soybeans and 20% wheat. White soy sauce, or shiroshoyu, is made from just the opposite: 80% wheat and 20% soybeans. Niboshi (tiny dried sardines), konbu (dried giant seaweed) and dried shiitake mushrooms are added to the shiroshoyu to produce a more flavorful brew called shirodashi. If shirodashi is not readily available, use a good Japanese whole-bean soy sauce.

Hamachi, or Japanese yellowtail tuna, is an excellent young fish from the mackerel family. They are farmed extensively in the seas off Japan and are also available in the wild. Older and larger specimens not as well suited for sashimi are called Buri in Japanese. I also use Hirame, a flatfish in the flounder family, which is another excellent fish from Japanese waters. Many other fish can be substituted, but I would recommend cold-water varieties over warm-water ones, and be adamant about freshness. Salmon (both aquacultured or wild), fluke, flounder, halibut, bluefin or big-eye tuna, ahi, striped bass or black sea bass are just some of the possible fish you can use for a successful dish.

- 1 lb. fresh sashimi-quality fish such as hirame or hamachi
- 1 cup extra virgin olive oil
- 1 cup shirodashi or regular Japanese soy sauce
- 3 Tbsp. white sesame seeds, not toasted
- 1 oz. fresh chives, finely cut

Method

Slice the fish, straight from the refrigerator, very thinly with a very sharp, thin-bladed knife. Arrange the slices of fish evenly on eight plates. Dress the fish first with the olive oil, then the soy sauce, then the sesame seeds and chives, dividing each ingredient evenly over the fish. Serve immediately.

© Wayne Nish 1991

Oceana ✿

Seafood

55 E. 54th St. (bet. Park & Madison Aves.)

Subway:	5 Av - 53 St	Monday - Friday noon - 2:30pm
Phone:	212-759-5941	& 5:30pm - 10:30pm
Fax:	212-759-6076	Saturday 5:30pm - 10:30pm
e-mail:	N/A	Closed Sunday
Web:	www.oceanarestaurant.com	
Prices:	$$$$	

Oceana/Paul Johnson Photography

Welcome aboard! You'll think you're on the high seas instead of in the East 50s when you step into Oceana. Both the name and the décor suggest a luxury ocean liner, complete with blue-gray leather banquettes and faux windows painted with murals of the glittering sea and passing ships. Culinary Institute of America grad Cornelius Gallagher captains this enterprise, having learned French technique at the Waldorf Astoria. His culinary resume includes time in the kitchens of Lespinasse, Daniel and Bouley, as well as study in France.

At Oceana, Gallagher pairs simple seafood with flavors that spark the natural taste of fresh fish and shellfish; Chatham halibut, for example, might be napped with pork roasting juices, and swordfish served with Armagnac shellfish sauce. For dessert, Oceana's elegant version of sticky toffee pudding can stand up against that of the best British gastro pub.

Chatham Halibut with Carrots and Lentils

Serves 4

Lentils

¾ cup Lentils du Puy
1 tsp. olive oil
3 oz. piece slab bacon, cut in large dice
¼ cup white onion, cut in brunoise
¼ cup celery, cut in brunoise
¼ cup parsnip, peeled and cut in brunoise
1 small bouquet of thyme, rosemary and bay leaf
¼ head of garlic
2 cups pork stock

In a large saucepan, heat the olive oil and the bacon. Cook slowly until the fat is rendered. Add the vegetables and cook until soft. Add the lentils, the herb bouquet, garlic and pork stock. Simmer over very low heat until lentils are tender. Remove the bacon, garlic and bouquet. Set aside and keep warm.

Sauce

4 Tbsp. pork jus
1 Tbsp. minced cornichons
1 Tbsp. minced shallot
2 tsp. cornichon liquid
1 Tbsp. whole-grain mustard
1 Tbsp. chopped parsley

Heat pork jus and add the mustard, cornichons, cornichon liquid, shallots and parsley in a small saucepan. Season to taste.

Carrots

4 organic carrots, peeled and roll-cut
1 cup carrot juice   2 Tbsp. butter, whole
2 Tbsp. acacia honey
1 tsp. cayenne pepper
1 tsp. wasabi oil

Heat carrot juice, honey, cayenne and butter in a sauté pan, whisking until emulsified. Add the carrots and cook until glazed and tender. Finish with wasabi oil and season to taste.

Halibut

four 5 oz. halibut filets
2 Tbsp. grapeseed oil
1 Tbsp. thyme leaves
2 Tbsp. unsalted butter
Salt and freshly ground pepper
1 ramp, (or scallion) minced

Heat the grapeseed oil in a sauté pan. Season the halibut generously with salt and pepper and add it to the pan. When golden, turn fish over and add the butter, thyme and ramp. Baste the fish with pan liquid until tender and cooked. Set aside and keep warm.

To Serve

Lay the carrots in the center of each of 4 dinner bowls. Spoon some sauce around them. Spoon the lentils over the carrots and top with the halibut. Drizzle the juices from the carrots over top, and serve at once.

Vong ✿

Contemporary Thai

200 E. 54th St. (bet. Second & Third Aves.)

Subway:	Lexington Av - 53 St
Phone:	212-486-9592
Fax:	212-980-3745
e-mail:	N/A
Web:	www.jean-georges.com
Prices:	$$$

Monday - Friday noon - 2:30pm
& 5:30pm - 11pm (Friday 11:30pm)
Saturday 5:30pm - 11:30pm
Sunday 5:30pm - 10:30pm

✄✄

♿

Jean-Georges Management

One of the nation's foremost chefs, Jean-Georges Vongerichten has made his mark on American cuisine with a galaxy of restaurants (15 at last count, including satellites in Hong Kong, Shanghai and Paris) and three cookbooks to his credit.

You'll get your first clue about the culinary concept at Vong (which opened in 1992) as you enter the dining room, where bowls of aromatic spices decorate a long table. The Alsatian-born chef fuses Thai flavors—and 150 different herbs and spices—with French technique here. It was a natural evolution for Vongerichten, who started out cooking in France, then spent several years working in Bangkok. It was there he developed an appreciation for Asian foods—particularly, bold spices such as curry, cardamom and coriander. The high-ceilinged dining room recalls the Orient, too, with Thai silks in rich plaids, louvered wooden panels, and tropical plants.

Lobster with Thai Herbs

Serves 4

Lobster

2 1½ lb. Maine lobsters

Put a large pot of water over high heat and bring to a boil. Remove claws and tail from body of lobsters. Cut bodies in half lengthwise, blanch for one minute in boiling water and set aside on a sheet pan. Cook tails for 2 minutes and claws for 4 minutes. Remove meat from shells and set aside, cutting the tail meat in half lengthwise.

Lobster base

1¼ lbs. carrots, julienned
1½ cups white port
1½ golden delicious apples, peeled and julienned
1 stalk lemongrass, smashed
1 Tbsp. triple curry paste
2 lime leaves
2 Tbsp. butter
1¼ tsp. turmeric

In a sauté pan over medium heat, melt butter with curry paste, stirring to combine. After 2 minutes, add carrots and reduce heat to medium low. Sauté carrots until soft, then add lemongrass, lime leaves, and Port. Raise heat to medium-high and reduce liquid by three-quarters. Add apple and turmeric and simmer for 3 minutes. Remove from heat, cool and reserve.

To Serve

1 cup heavy cream
¼ cup lobster base, prepared above
3 Tbsp. unsalted butter
1 medium head bok choy
1½ tsp. grapeseed oil
2 Tbsp. cilantro, chopped
Salt and pepper to taste

Preheat oven to 300°F. Season lobster meat generously with salt pepper and place on a sheet pan with reserved bodies; place in oven. In a saucepan over medium heat, mix lobster base and ½ cup of heavy cream in a sauce pan and slowly bring to a boil. Reduce heat and simmer gently until mixture thickens. Season with salt and pepper. Remove leaves from bok choy, and cut them into 1-inch julienne. Split base and remove the core from bok choy. Quarter the core and place it in oven on a sheet pan with lobster to heat, tossing pan occasionally. Cut stems into ¼-inch julienne. Heat oil in a large sauté pan over medium heat. Add bok choy leaves and stems and sauté until tender. Remove pan from oven. Divide bok choy leaves evenly between four plates. Place the quarter-head of bok choy alongside the leaves and fill with lobster meat. Cover with sauce and garnish with cilantro.

The Four Seasons

American

005

99 E. 52nd St. (bet. Park & Lexington Aves.)

Subway:	51 St	Monday - Friday noon - 2:30pm
Phone:	212-754-9494	& 5pm - 10pm
Fax:	212-754-1077	Saturday 5pm - 11:30pm
e-mail:	N/A	Closed Sunday
Web:	www.fourseasonsrestaurant.com	
Prices:	$$$$	

XXXX

&

The moneyed, the powerful, the terminally chic all frequent the Four Seasons, where they blend right in with the restaurant's sleek opulence. Designed by Mies van der Rohe and Philip Johnson and opened in 1959, the restaurant boasts such opulent appointments as hand-loomed carpets, custom-designed tableware, and original artwork by the likes of Picasso, Joan Miró, and Jackson Pollock. The Pool Room centers on a two-foot-square pool of white marble, while the Grill Room has a comfortable bar for more casual meals. The kitchen puts a contemporary spin on classic dishes (Chateaubriand, Long Island duck, Dover sole), while respecting the intrinsic flavors of the ingredients.

La Grenouille

French

006

3 E. 52nd St. (bet. Fifth & Madison Aves.)

Subway:	5 Av - 53 St	Tuesday - Saturday noon - 2:30pm
Phone:	212-752-1495	& 5:30pm - 11pm
Fax:	212-593-4964	Closed Sunday & Monday
e-mail:	N/A	Closed mid-August - mid-September
Web:	www.la-grenouille.com	
Prices:	$$$$	

XXXX

&

Opened in 1962, La Grenouille manages to remain, all these years later, the Masson family's bastion of high-priced French cuisine in Midtown. Charles and Gisèle Masson founded this establishment; today Charles junior oversees the enterprise his parents started. A high coffered ceiling, silk wall coverings, and stunning arrangements of fresh flowers—a signature of the late Charles Masson the elder—characterize the lovely dining space, which is worthy of a special occasion. Menu selections might include oxtails braised in Burgundy, frogs legs Provençale, or salmon tartare. A prix-fixe theater menu is offered daily from 5:30pm to 6:30pm and from 10pm to 11pm.

Alto

007

520 Madison Ave. (enter E. 53rd St. bet. Fifth & Madison Aves.)

Subway:	5 Av - 53 St	Monday - Thursday noon - 2:30pm
Phone:	212-308-1099	& 5:30pm - 10:30pm
Fax:	212-308-3573	Friday - Saturday noon - 2:30pm
e-mail:	info@altorestaurant.com	& 5pm - 11:30pm
Web:	www.altorestaurant.com	Closed Sunday & major holidays
Prices:	$$$	

Opened in April 2005, Alto is the newest restaurant by chef Scott Conant and his partners from L'Impero. The food takes its inspiration (and the restaurant its name) from the Alto Adige region of northeastern Italy. Since this area is close to Austria, you'll notice the Saxon influence in Alto's cuisine. You'll also notice the large piece of the Berlin Wall that stands just outside the restaurant. Dinner is prix-fixe, although at lunch you have the choice of ordering à la carte. The swanky dining space, with its red velvet chairs and huge windows, includes a floor-to-ceiling wall of wine bottles. The staggering number—7,000—of bottles cited on the wine list is housed in the basement cellar.

Bice

008

7 E. 54th St. (bet. Fifth & Madison Aves.)

Subway:	5 Av - 53 St	Monday - Friday 11:30am - midnight
Phone:	212-688-1999	Saturday noon - midnight
Fax:	212-752-1329	Sunday noon - 11pm
e-mail:	N/A	
Web:	www.bicenewyork.com	
Prices:	$$$	

Opened in 1987, Bice New York forms part of a chain of some 40 Italian restaurants that reaches around the world. Bice was founded in Milan in 1926 by Beatrice ("Bice") Ruggeri. Her sons, Roberto and Remo, later opened additional branches, first in Italy, and in 1987, on East 54th Street in New York City—the first location in North America. The Manhattan outpost owes its oh-so-cool, yet elegant Art Deco custom design to interior designer Adam Tihany, who has done design work for many big-name chefs. Northern Italian fare makes up the menu (veal Milanese, risottos, hearty homemade pastas), and Midtown's chic set dines here on a regular basis.

BLT Steak

Steakhouse

009

106 E. 56th St. (bet. Park & Lexington Aves.)

Subway:	59 St	Monday - Thursday 11:45am - 2:30pm
Phone:	212-752-7470	& 5:30pm - 10:45pm
Fax:	212-752-7420	Friday 11:45am - 2:30pm
e-mail:	info@bltsteak.com	& 5:30pm - 11:15pm
Web:	www.bltrestaurants.com	Saturday 5:30pm - 11:15pm
Prices:	$$$$	Closed Sunday

XXX
&
🎀

Why would a French chef name his restaurant after an American sandwich? He would, if he fancied his restaurant to be a contemporary bistro (B) and his name was Laurent Tourondel (LT). In fact, Bistro Laurent Tourondel is not French bistro at all, but a Frenchman's vision of an American steakhouse. Sleek décor, with its Macassar ebony tables, café-crème-colored banquettes, and sepia-toned photographs of New York, smacks of big-city sophistication. For dinner, naturally aged, corn-fed Certified Angus beef is served with your choice side dish and sauce; there's a wide choice of sauces, from béarnaise to red wine-caper brown butter. And, yes, there are fish selections, too.

Bottega del Vino

Italian

010

7 E. 59th St. (bet. Fifth & Madison Aves.)

Subway:	5 Av - 59 St	Monday - Friday 8am - 11pm
Phone:	212-223-2724	Saturday 9am - midnight
Fax:	212-223-3608	Sunday 10am - 10pm
e-mail:	info@bottegadelvinonyc.com	
Web:	www.bottegadelvinonyc.com	
Prices:	$$$	

XXX
🎀

From Verona comes not two, but one gentleman, Severini Barzan, who opened the New York outpost of his Italian wine bar in November 2004. The words painted on a beam along the restaurant wall sum up his philosophy: *Dio mi guardi da chi non beve vino* ("may God protect me from those who do not drink wine"). Indeed wine steals the show, with bottles displayed on shelf after shelf in the dining room, and a cellar that stocks some 2,800 different labels. Barzan has even designed his own line of hand-blown stemware to highlight the taste of each individual wine. The food hails from the Veneto, too, ranging from panini (available in the cafe) to the signature dish, risotto cooked in Amarone wine.

The Capital Grille

Steakhouse

011

155 E. 42nd St. (bet. Third & Lexington Aves.)

Subway:	Grand Central - 42 St	Monday 11:30am - 3pm & 5pm - 10pm
Phone:	212-953-2000	Tuesday - Friday 11:30am - 3pm
Fax:	212-953-0244	& 5pm - 11pm
e-mail:	N/A	Saturday 5pm - 11pm
Web:	www.thecapitalgrille.com	Sunday 5pm - 10pm
Prices:	$$$	

XXX
&
88

Here's an address that's well located for Midtown business lunchers. Two blocks east of Grand Central Terminal, the clubby Capital Grille occupies the ground floor of the seven-story Trylon Towers, part of the complex that includes the famed Chrysler Building. The Atlanta, Georgia-based chain made its New York debut in summer 2004, and Manhattanites are glad it did. Here you can dine on juicy dry-aged steaks and chops, hand-cut and grilled precisely to your liking, or, if you prefer, there's broiled lobster and a selection of fresh fish. As far as wine goes, the inventory of 400 labels includes a Captain's List of rare vintages to round out your meal.

Fresco by Scotto

Italian

012

34 E. 52nd St. (bet. Park & Madison Aves.)

Subway:	5 Av - 53 St	Monday - Friday 11:30am - 3pm
Phone:	212-935-3434	& 5:30pm 11pm
Fax:	212-935-3436	Saturday 5pm - 11pm
e-mail:	frescobyscotto@earthlink.net	Closed Sunday
Web:	www.frescobyscotto.com	
Prices:	$$$	

XXX
&

You never know what familiar faces you might see at Fresco by Scotto. Known as the "NBC Commissary," this lively Italian restaurant has long attracted media moguls and politicos, whose expense accounts easily accommodate the upscale prices (check out the photographs of *Today Show* newscasters by the staircase). The Scotto family established their restaurant in Midtown in 1993, just a few blocks from Rockefeller Center. Here, Marion Scotto warmly welcomes customers to the bright dining room, which is decorated with sunny scenes of the Italian landscape. Hearty entrées include leg of rabbit braised in red wine, and grilled Italian sausage filled with cheese and parsley.

Manhattan Midtown East

Il Nido

013

Italian

251 E. 53rd St. (bet. Second & Third Aves.)

Subway:	Lexington Av - 53 St	Monday - Saturday noon - 3pm
Phone:	212-753-8450	& 5:30pm - 11pm
Fax:	212-224-0155	Closed Sunday
e-mail:	info@ilnidonyc.com	
Web:	www.ilnidonyc.com	
Prices:	$$$	

XXX   Dark wood wainscoting and beams on white walls give this eatery a Tuscan country charm, while fresh flowers, shaded wall sconces and white linen tablecloths add a note of elegance. Continental-style service becomes theater here, from the effusive greeting from the owner at the door to the show in the center of the dining room, where the staff finishes dishes with dramatic flourish on the gas stoves that are stationed there for all to see. Waiters fuss over diners like mother birds, in keeping with the restaurant's name, which means "the nest." The food is Old World Northern Italian fare like linguine with clam sauce, spaghetti carbonara, and swordfish sautéed with sun-dried tomatoes and capers.

Inagiku

Japanese

014

111 E. 49th St. (bet. Park & Lexington Aves.)

Subway:	51 St	Monday - Friday noon - 2pm
Phone:	212-355-0440	& 5:30pm - 10pm
Fax:	212-888-3735	Saturday - Sunday 5:30pm - 10pm
e-mail:	info@inagiku.com	
Web:	www.inagiku.com	
Prices:	$$$	

XXX   Tucked into a remote corner of the Waldorf-Astoria hotel, Inagiku
    owes its city-slick digs to renowned interior designer Adam Tihany. Traditional and contemporary elements play off each other in the same space here: whimsical representations of rice grains appear in custom-designed wall sconces; the paisley shape of the yin/yang symbol is etched on glass panels; and wooden slats undulate across the ceiling. Like the design, the food also pairs old with new (shark fin on a pool of consommé, squid with nori pasta). Inagiku's version of desserts are flavored with Japanese ingredients such as sweet red beans and green tea; cheesecake and flan are made with tofu.

L'Impero

015

45 Tudor City Pl. (over 42nd St., bet. First & Second Aves.)

Subway:	Grand Central - 42 St	Monday - Thursday noon - 2:30pm
Phone:	212-599-5045	& 5:30pm - 10:30pm
Fax:	212-599-5043	Friday noon - 2:30pm & 5pm - 11:30pm
e-mail:	info@limpero.com	Saturday 5pm - 11:30pm
Web:	www.limpero.com	Closed Sunday & major holidays
Prices:	$$$	

You'll find L'Impero on the ground floor of one of the structures of Tudor City, a complex of 12 Tudor-style apartment buildings completed in 1928. This is the domain of chef Scott Conant, who recently opened another Italian eatery, called Alto (520 Madison Ave.), in Midtown. Conant adheres to Italian culinary tradition by using the best quality artisanal products he can find. This practice pays off in contemporary dishes like rich duck and foie gras agnolotti (all pastas are handmade in house), and roasted Vermont capretto (pasture-raised baby goat). Tables tend to be cramped in the elegant dining room, with its pale gray-green leather chairs and dark fabric banquettes.

Le Perigord

016

405 E. 52nd St. (bet. First Ave. & FDR Dr.)

Subway:	51 St	Monday - Sunday noon - 3pm
Phone:	212-755-6244	& 5pm - 10pm
Fax:	212-486-3906	
e-mail:	N/A	
Web:	www.leperigord.com	
Prices:	$$$	

Just a few short blocks from the United Nations, Le Perigord wraps diners in luxury under its coffered ceiling, amid period chairs covered in willow-green fabric, Limoges china, crystal stemware and fresh flowers in pastel hues. This is a jacket-and-tie kind of place, where waiters in white waistcoats or black tuxedos provide formal service, and the lunch crowd consists largely of diplomats from the nearby U.N. Classic French dishes make up the entrées, from rack of lamb to sole Meunière. For the pièce de résistance, desserts are rolled to your table on a cart; you can count on a mouth-watering selection of homemade seasonal fruit tarts being among the choices.

Morton's

Steakhouse

017

551 Fifth Ave. (at 45th St.)

Subway:	5 Av
Phone:	212-972-3315
Fax:	212-972-0018
e-mail:	cm.mny@mortons.com
Web:	www.mortons.com
Prices:	$$$

Monday - Friday 11:30am - 11pm
Saturday 5pm - 11pm
Sunday 5pm - 10pm

Part of a chain that started in Chicago and now extends across the U.S. and into Canada and the Far East, Morton's reigns as a well-respected chophouse. The Fifth Avenue location lies within easy walking distance from Grand Central Terminal and Times Square. In the often crowded dining space, the soaring ceiling leaves room for a mezzanine overlooking the first floor. Clubby, masculine décor incorporates mahogany paneling, booths lining the wall, and imposing chandeliers. The menu, which is the same in all Morton's locations, centers on USDA Prime aged beef, but also features crab cakes and lobster—all at rather beefy prices. California vintages are the focus of the extensive wine list.

Nicole's

American

018

10 E. 60th St. (bet. Fifth & Madison Aves.)

Subway:	5 Av - 59 St
Phone:	212-223-2288
Fax:	212-233-5112
e-mail:	oscarh@frenchconnection-USA.com
Web:	www.nicolefarhi.com
Prices:	$$

Monday - Saturday noon - 4pm
Closed Sunday

Food follows fashion at Nicole's, the eponymous restaurant located in the basement of Nicole Fahri's Midtown boutique. When you need a break from riffling through the racks of chic men's and women's clothing created by the Britain-based designer, just follow the staircase down to the sleek, 4,000-square-foot restaurant. While you're deciding what to order, you can check out the action in the kitchen, housed in an ice-blue illuminated glass cube. Here, a talented cooking team prepares seasonal dishes with a California spirit. The menu, which changes daily, incorporates premium ingredients from local organic produce to fine imported food items.

Rothmann's

S t e a k h o u s e

019

3 E. 54th St. (bet. Fifth & Madison Aves.)

Subway:	5 Av - 53 St	Monday - Sunday 11:30am - 11pm
Phone:	212-319-5500	
Fax:	212-319-5540	
e-mail:	nyrothmanns@chasrothmanns.com	
Web:	www.rothmannssteakhouse.com	
Prices:	$$$	

It all started in 1907, when Charles and Franziska Rothmann purchased a little cafe in Brooklyn and an inn on Long Island. Now Rothmann's reigns as a Manhattan meat lovers' heaven. Colorado lamb chops, Prime dry-aged porterhouse steaks, roasted pork loin chops, bone-in rib-eyes are all served in a comfortable and upscale atmosphere of rosy carpets, mahogany wood and banquettes covered with soft beige leather. The sommelier can help decipher the extensive wine list; with some 600 different selections from around the globe, you might just need some assistance narrowing down your choices. Don't expect any bargains, though—remember that you're in Midtown.

San Pietro

I t a l i a n

020

18 E. 54th St. (bet. Fifth & Madison Aves.)

Subway:	5 Av - 53 St	Monday - Saturday noon - 3:30pm
Phone:	212-753-9015	& 4pm - 10:45pm
Fax:	212-371-2337	Closed Sunday
e-mail:	N/A	
Web:	www.sanpietro.net	
Prices:	$$$	

At San Pietro, the chef imports more than three-quarters of his ingredients, including cheeses and fish, from southern Italy (a practice, as you'd expect, that comes at a price). Vegetables figure prominently on the generous, seasonally changing menu: fresh fava beans are flavored with pecorino cheese and black truffles, broccoli rape sautéed in olive oil and garlic. Sure, there are pastas and risottos, but the signature dish is Pesce San Pietro, John Dory braised in garlic sauce scented with thyme and served with baked fennel and toasted hazelnuts. Ceramic murals, decorative odes to the owners' native region of Campania, enhance the elegant dining area.

Manhattan *Midtown East*

Smith & Wollensky
Steakhouse

021

797 Third Ave. (at 49th St.)

Subway:	51 St
Phone:	212-753-1530
Fax:	212-751-5446
e-mail:	awong@swrg.com
Web:	www.smithandwollensky.com
Prices:	$$$

Monday - Sunday 11:45am - 2am

XXX
&
🏠
🐜

Part of a well-known chain with locations in 10 other U.S. cities (from Boston to Las Vegas), Smith & Wollensky takes up a corner at the intersection of Third Avenue and 49th Street. The 390-seat New York flagship opened in 1977 and still ranks as one of the city's most celebrated steakhouses. (Oddly enough, the restaurant's name is not related to its owners; founder Alan Stillman picked the two surnames randomly from the phone book.) USDA Prime beef, which is dry-aged on the premises, accounts for Smith & Wollensky's fine reputation. For nightowls, adjoining Wollensky's Grill, the restaurant's separate bar/lounge, serves a less expensive menu of light fare until 2am.

The Steakhouse at Monkey Bar
Steakhouse

022

60 E. 54th St. (bet. Park & Madison Aves.)

Subway:	5 Av - 53 St
Phone:	212-838-2600
Fax:	212-838-9197
e-mail:	dmastrangelo@theglaziergroup.com
Web:	www.theglaziergroup.com
Prices:	$$$

Monday - Friday 11:30am - 2:30pm
& 5:30pm - 11pm
Saturday 5:30pm - 11pm
Closed Sunday

XXX
&

Former haunt of actors Tallulah Bankhead and Marlon Brando, baseball great Joe DiMaggio and playwright Tennessee Williams, the Elysée Hotel's Monkey Bar was the place to be in the 1930s. Today it's still a popular, albeit pricey, watering hole. And while a horde of simians may frolic on the restored hand-painted murals in the 1930s bar, there's no monkeying around when it comes to the food. Order your favorite cut of meat, from New York strip to double-cut lamb T-bone, and settle back to enjoy the scene. You'll feel like you're on the set of an old Hollywood movie, set about by padded walls covered in burgundy fabric, Art Deco chandeliers, and glass panels separating the cushy banquettes.

Tao

A s i a n

42 E. 58th St. (bet. Park & Madison Aves.)

Subway:	59 St	Monday - Tuesday 11:30am - midnight
Phone:	212-888-2288	Wednesday - Friday 11:30am - 1am
Fax:	212-888-4148	Saturday 5pm - 1am
e-mail:	N/A	Sunday 5pm - midnight
Web:	www.taorestaurant.com	
Prices:	$$	

Asia's tastiest dishes star at this former movie theater, built in the 19th century as a stable for the Vanderbilt family. It's hard to imagine catching a flick in this space now, outfitted as it is with a Chinese scroll draped across the ceiling and a 16-foot-high statue of Buddha towering over a reflecting pool in the main dining room. The theater's former balconies now accommodate diners, too—some 300 of them on three levels. The menu spotlights mainly Hong Kong Chinese, Japanese and Thai dishes, from Thai seafood hot pots to Tao lo mein with roast pork. On weekend nights, the scene becomes a real show, as Manhattan's young and restless turn out in droves.

Alamo

M e x i c a n

304 E. 48th St. (bet. First & Second Aves.)

Subway:	51 St	Monday - Friday noon - 11pm
Phone:	212-759-0590	Saturday 5pm - midnight
Fax:	212-759-4619	Closed Sunday
e-mail:	info@thealamorestaurant.com	
Web:	www.thealamorestaurant.com	
Prices:	$$	

Its façade suggesting the real Alamo in Texas, this restaurant reopened in spring 2005, after a hiatus starting in 2002 (the restaurant first opened in 1985). Bright primary colors, red tabletops with fresh roses, and tile floors characterize the dining room. Tasty Mexican specialties ranging from fajitas to chicken mole to paella (a nod to Spain) fill the menu. Don't miss the tequila bar, where the extensive list of spirits is divided into blanca (showcasing the pure spirit of the blue agave), reposado (aged in French oak), or anejo (aged for 1 to 10 years). Across from the bar, note the colorful mural depicting famous Mexican figures from politics and the arts.

Manhattan Midtown East

Alcala

Spanish

342 E. 46th St. (bet. First & Second Aves.)

Subway:	Grand Central - 42 St	Sunday - Thursday noon - 2:30pm
Phone:	212-370-1866	& 5:30pm - 10pm
Fax:	N/A	Friday - Saturday noon - 2:30pm
e-mail:	alcalarestaurant@hotmail.com	& 5:30pm - 11pm
Web:	www.alcalarestaurant.com	
Prices:	**$$**	

In its former incarnation, this restaurant served Basque cuisine as Marichu; now as Alcala, the place has broadened its horizons to include regional fare from across the entire country of Spain. Located just across from the United Nations complex, Alcala serves tapas and other Spanish specialties in its rustic red-brick, wood-beamed dining room. Chef Mariano Aznar comes originally from Barcelona, and more recently from Solera in Midtown. Here, he concentrates on Spanish home-style cooking, using traditional recipes, such as zarzuela, a seafood stew of clams, octopus, scallops, shrimp, mussels, white fish and potatoes. Tapas offerings range from marinated olives to grilled baby lamb chops.

Aquavit

Scandinavian

65 E. 55th St. (bet. Park & Madison Aves.)

Subway:	5 Av - 53 St	Monday - Sunday noon - 2:30pm
Phone:	212-307-7311	& 5:30pm - 10:30pm
Fax:	212-957-9043	
e-mail:	info@aquavit.org	
Web:	www.aquavitrestaurant.com	
Prices:	**$$$**	

Everything about Aquavit is Scandinavian: its design, its cuisine, its chef. Named for the Scandinavian spirit that figures prominently on its beverage menu, Aquavit moved in early 2005 from the West Side to the ground floor of Park Avenue Tower. There's a casual cafe and bar area up front; the more refined contemporary dining room, softened by beige tones and varnished woods, lies beyond. Chef/owner Marcus Samuelsson's take on Scandinavian food is contemporary as well. Born in Ethiopia and raised in Sweden, Samuelsson excels at pairing unexpected textures and flavors. The restaurant even makes its own Aquavit, flavored with everything from horseradish to lingonberries.

Avra Estiatorio

027

141 E. 48th St. (bet. Third & Lexington Aves.)

Subway:	51 St	Monday - Friday noon - midnight
Phone:	212-759-8550	Saturday 11am - midnight
Fax:	212-751-0894	Sunday 11am - 11pm
e-mail:	avra@avrany.com	
Web:	www.avrany.com	
Prices:	**$$**	

This airy taverna-style eatery (operated by the same group that manages Brasserie 8 1/2 and Tao) recalls the Mediterranean with its limestone floors, faux-stone walls, arched doorways and accents of mustard-yellow crockery. Of course, you'll find a host of Greek specialties here such as spanakopita or bifteki souvlaki (grilled skewered ground lamb), but the fish seems to steal the show. Flown in fresh from Europe, or purchased from Manhattan's Fulton Market, fish, including lobster, is simply brushed with olive oil—first-press extra-virgin olive oil—and grilled whole over charcoal. It's priced per pound, so be careful if your eyes tend to be bigger than your stomach.

Bellini

028

208 E. 52nd St. (bet. Second & Third Aves.)

Subway:	51 St	Monday - Thursday noon - 3pm
Phone:	212-308-0830	& 5pm - 10:30pm
Fax:	N/A	Friday noon - 3pm & 5pm - 11pm
e-mail:	N/A	Saturday 5pm - 11pm
Web:	www.bellinirestaurantnyc.com	Closed Sunday & major holidays
Prices:	**$$$**	

Classic and elegant define Bellini's interior design as well as its owner, Donatella Arpaia, daughter of a New York City restaurateur. Think white wainscoting, a coffered ceiling, and baskets of dried flowers adorning the walls; then add blond woods, soothing salmon-toned banquettes, indirect lighting and a white-tile floor, and you've got Bellini. The food? It highlights Neapolitan dishes, with southern Italian ingredients such as fresh buffalo mozzarella, vinegar-cured white anchovies and sweet eggplant. Prices tend a bit toward the expense-account range, and indeed, the restaurant caters to the business crowd—this is Midtown, after all—at lunch.

Manhattan Midtown East

Bobby Van's Steakhouse

S t e a k h o u s e

029

230 Park Ave. (at E. 46th St.)

Subway:	Grand Central - 42 St
Phone:	212-867-5490
Fax:	N/A
e-mail:	infonyc46@bobbyvans.com
Web:	www.bobbyvans.com
Prices:	$$$

Monday - Sunday noon - midnight

Bobby Van's owes its first Manhattan location to Leona Helmsley, who cajoled the owners into opening an outpost here (the original Bobby Van's is in Bridgehampton on Long Island). This is clearly an Atkins-diet paradise, catering to business people on expense accounts. As you'd imagine, it's a clubby, old-boy kind of place, with lots of wood and mirrors in the large dining room. Expect to pay rather dearly for huge portions of meltingly tender beef and well-cooked seafood (lobster is priced by the pound, and you can order the USDA Prime Porterhouse for two, three or four people). The newest Bobby Van's, as of 2003, is at 131 E. 54th Street (between Park and Lexington Avenues) in Midtown.

Brasserie

A m e r i c a n

030

100 E. 53rd St. (bet. Park & Lexington Aves.)

Subway:	Lexington Av - 53 St
Phone:	212-751-4840
Fax:	212-751-8777
e-mail:	N/A
Web:	www.thebrasserieny.com
Prices:	$$

Monday - Friday 7am - 3pm
& 5:30pm - midnight (Friday 1am)
Saturday - Sunday 5:30pm
- 10pm (Saturday 1am)

The original concept of a brasserie as a brewery that provided food for hungry travelers has come a long way to this modern interpretation, reopened and redecorated after a fire in 1995. Today the Brasserie's retro Jetsons-like design uses white-leather chairs and small plastic-topped tables, with pearwood panels lining the ceiling in a sort of wave. Features on the short menu are American, but many are rendered with a timid European touch (steak frites, whole fish with herbes de Provence). Don't make the mistake of coming here for an intimate meal. The noise level is deafening, a fact that is not helped by the positioning of the tables so close together.

Bruno

Italian

240 E. 58th St. (bet. Second & Third Aves.)

Subway:	59 St	Monday - Friday noon - 3pm
Phone:	212-688-4190	& 5pm - 11pm
Fax:	212-688-4342	Saturday 5pm - 1am
e-mail:	N/A	Closed Sunday
Web:	www.brunosnyc.com	
Prices:	$$	

XX

Bruno Selimaj must be doing something right; his eponymous eatery has been around since 1978. A roster of classic Italian dishes fills the menu here, with selections like osso buco Milanese (served with saffron risotto), grilled sea bass (branzino), and ravioli, made in house with a different filling every day. Service is casual in the Art Deco-style dining room, where, as if to inspire diners, a colorful corner mural depicts a crowd of well-dressed revelers. Four nights a week (Wednesday to Saturday from 9pm to 1am), pianist Frederico Noci tickles the ivories for patrons' entertainment in the bar area.

Bull and Bear

Steakhouse

570 Lexington Ave. (at 49th St.)

Subway:	51 St	Monday - Friday noon - 11:30pm
Phone:	212-872-4900	Saturday - Sunday 5pm - 11:30pm
Fax:	212-872-1266	Closed August
e-mail:	bear@hilton.com	
Web:	www.waldorfastoria.com	
Prices:	$$$	

XX
&

Picture an elegant English pub set about with mahogany wood, brass and crystal chandeliers, wine cabinets, cushy banquettes and plenty of mirrors, and you've got the Bull and Bear. Located on the ground floor of the legendary Waldorf Astoria, this bar/restaurant takes its moniker from the bronze bull and bear statues—representing the up and down of the stock market—that lord it over the elegant mahogany bar. The place is popular with bankers and Wall Street types, who come for the dry-aged Prime Angus beef and classy men's-club ambience. Don't try wearing jeans and sneakers here, though; the "elegant casual" dress code forbids them.

Canaletto

Italian

208 E. 60th St. (bet. Second & Third Aves.)

Subway:	Lexington Av - 59 St	Monday - Sunday noon - 3pm
Phone:	212-317-9192	& 5pm - 10pm
Fax:	N/A	
e-mail:	N/A	
Web:	N/A	
Prices:	$$	

✗✗   Attention Bloomingdale's shoppers: this neighborhood Italian spot, a half-block down 60th Street from Bloomie's, makes a great place for a lunch if you're looking to take a break from riffling through the racks. A meal at classy, comfortable Canaletto begins with a plate of Italian salamis and aged Parmesan cheese. Then move on to a pasta such as penne all'arabiatta, cooked al dente with spicy homemade tomato sauce. Entrées are heavy on the meat dishes, although there are several fish offerings as well. You'll find patient, cheerful service here, along with prices that are very reasonable for the neighborhood (at lunch, pasta dishes average $11; dinner entrées top out at $25).

Da Antonio

Italian

157 E. 55th St. (bet. Third & Lexington Aves.)

Subway:	Lexington Av - 53 St	Monday - Saturday noon - 3pm
Phone:	212-588-1545	& 5pm - 11pm
Fax:	212-588-1547	Closed Sunday
e-mail:	daantonio55th@aol.com	
Web:	www.daantonio.com	
Prices:	$$	

✗✗   Owner Antonio Cerra presides over the dining room at his animated restaurant, located a few steps down from the street level. Fresh flowers and oil paintings festoon the space, which is packed with white-clothed tables. From the kitchen come wonderful pastas and well-prepared seafood, poultry and meat dishes, all made with fresh ingredients. Ignore the occasional flaws in the service, which makes up for in sincerity, what it lacks in execution. The bar scene here is a vibrant one, enlivened by nightly entertainment on the piano—you'll hear everything from oldies to jazz to show tunes, depending on who's playing.

Däwat

Indian

210 E. 58th St. (bet. Second & Third Aves.)

Subway:	59 St	Monday - Thursday 11:30am - 3pm
Phone:	212-355-7555	& 5:30pm - 11pm
Fax:	212-355-1735	Friday - Saturday 11:30am - 3pm
e-mail:	dawatny@aol.com	& 5:30pm - 11:30pm
Web:	www.restaurant.com/dawat	Sunday 5pm - 10:30pm
Prices:	$$	

It's not every restaurant whose chef started out as an actor, but that's exactly what Madhur Jaffrey did. The Delhi native came to Däwat by way of the stage in England, and then to America, where she wrote articles about food to help support her family. Those articles led to a series of cookbooks about Indian cuisine, and, well, the rest is history, as they say. With a string of some ten titles to her credit, Jaffrey designed the menu at Däwat, where tandoori, curries and kebabs, as well as a host of vegetarian specialties, are as authentic as they are delicious. Come on, dig in. How can you go wrong at a restaurant whose name means "invitation to feast"?

Django

Mediterranean

480 Lexington Ave. (at 46 St.)

Subway:	Grand Central - 42 St	Monday - Friday 11:30am - 2pm
Phone:	212-871-6600	& 5:30pm - 10:30pm
Fax:	212-871-6163	Saturday 6pm - 10pm
e-mail:	django@msrpgroup.com	Closed Sunday
Web:	www.djangorestaurant.com	
Prices:	$$$	

In the bohemian spirit of jazz guitarist Django Rheinhardt, who wowed Paris audiences in the 1930s with his improvisational riffs, this restaurant embraces the carefree spirit of a gypsy. The eclectic interior, designed by David Rockwell, creates an intimate atmosphere in the upstairs dining area, despite its large size and vaulted ceiling. Here, bright banquettes are backed by cushy pillows, and a Murano glass chandelier lights the room. From the kitchen comes sunny "Riviera cuisine," which can include anything from bouillabaisse to lamb tagine. To get in the mood, start with the house cocktail—the Djangito—a potent blend of Stoli Ohranj, yuzu juice and a dash of Cointreau.

Manhattan Midtown East

Felidia

Italian

037

243 E. 58th St. (bet. Second & Third Aves.)

Subway: Lexington Av - 59 St
Phone: 212-758-1479
Fax: 212-935-7687
e-mail: info@lidiasitaly.com
Web: www.lidiasitaly.com
Prices: $$$

Monday - Friday noon - 2:30pm
& 5pm - 11pm.
Sunday 4pm - 9:45pm

Lidia Bastianich is no stranger to the restaurant business. The empire of this TV personality and cookbook author currently includes eight establishments, four of them in New York City (the other three are: Esca, Becco, Frico Bar), but Felidia remains her flagship. In the bi-level dining room, sunny colors, towering flower arrangements and hardwood wine racks set a refined palette on which to present competent Northern Italian cooking. Whole grilled Mediterranean sea bass, and bitter-chocolate pappardelle with wild boar ragu are just a sampling of what you might find on the seasonal menu. The award-winning wine list cites some 1,400 selections, most of them Italian.

Giambelli 50th

Italian

038

46 E. 50th St. (bet. Park & Madison Aves.)

Subway: 51 St
Phone: 212-688-2760
Fax: 212-751-6290
e-mail: N/A
Web: www.giambelli50.com
Prices: $$$

Monday - Sunday noon - midnight

There's something to be said for consistency, and you can count on Francesco Giambelli for that. Over the years since he opened his Gotham restaurant in 1960, Giambelli has fed mayors and minions, politicos and pundits—and even the Pope, when he visited New York City. The draw? Consistently good, home-style Italian food, cooked to order. Be sure to take a look at the collection of portraits by members of the Bachrach family, who, beginning with Bradford Bachrach, has photographed every American president since Abraham Lincoln in 1868. You'll find the photographs hanging on the walls in both the downstairs and upstairs dining rooms.

Il Menestrello

14 E. 52nd St. (bet. Fifth & Madison Aves.)

Subway:	5 Av - 51 St	Monday - Thursday noon - 11pm
Phone:	212-421-7588	Friday - Saturday noon - midnight
Fax:	212-644-5899	Closed Sunday
e-mail:	N/A	
Web:	N/A	
Prices:	**$$$**	

XX
&

Midtown's corporate crowd favors this bright, comfortable Italian place, conveniently located just off Fifth Avenue, where they broker deals over classic Italian cuisine. The dining room is well-lit and spacious, made seemingly even more so by a wall covered with mirrors. Banquettes line one side of the room, which is decorated with colorful artwork. Il Menestrello gets a lot of regulars, who are well known to the staff. In fact, if your wish is to remain anonymous, be forewarned that the waiters here are skilled at recognizing their patrons, even after just one visit. Authentic pasta, fish and meat dishes please most any palate, and the homemade tiramisu makes a tasty ending to your meal.

Manhattan *Midtown East*

Kurumazushi

Japanese

041

7 E. 47th St. (bet. Fifth & Madison Aves.)

Subway:	47-50 Sts - Rockefeller Ctr	Monday - Saturday 11:30am - 2pm
Phone:	212-317-2802	& 5:30pm - 10pm
Fax:	212-317-2803	Closed Sunday
e-mail:	N/A	Closed major holidays
Web:	N/A	
Prices:	$$$$	

Located on the second floor of a Midtown office building, Kurumazushi offers some of the best sushi in town. The team behind the sushi bar will shout a welcome in Japanese to you as you enter this tiny place. After that, settle in and prepare to be wowed by impeccably fresh toro, yellow tail, Japanese mackerel, bonito, eel and more, all with a remarkably creamy texture. Even the rice here is prepared perfectly. If you sit at the sushi bar, consider asking for a menu, especially if cost is a concern. Otherwise, go for broke (the price of an omakase feast here can add up quickly) and allow the chef to create a wonderful multicourse meal for you.

La Mangeoire

French

042

1008 Second Ave. (bet. 53rd & 54th Sts.)

Subway:	Lexington Av - 53 St	Monday - Friday noon - 2:30pm
Phone:	212-759-7086	& 5:30pm - 10:30pm
Fax:	212-759-6387	Saturday 5:30pm - 11pm
e-mail:	lamangeoire@att.net	Sunday noon - 3pm & 5pm - 9:30pm
Web:	www.lamangeoire.com	Closed Sunday during July & August
Prices:	$$	

The countryside of southern France comes to mind when you enter this sunny restaurant. Copper cookware ornaments the walls, bunches of dried herbs and flowers hang from the beams, and rustic lanterns dangle from the vaulted ceiling. Despite what you see, the cuisine here is not limited to the South of France—though the five-course Flavors of the Côte d'Azur tasting menu does focus on regional dishes from Provence. Entrées (think rabbit legs simmered in mustard, herb-grilled baby lamb chops, sautéed diver scallops) are offered in both small and regular-size portions, so you can tailor your meal size to your appetite. The prix-fixe menu is a deal at lunch or dinner.

Le Colonial

043

149 E. 57th St. (bet. Third & Lexington Aves.)

Subway:	59 St	Monday - Friday noon - 2:30pm
Phone:	212-752-0808	& 5:30pm - 10:30pm
Fax:	212-752-7534	Saturday 5:30pm - 11:30pm
e-mail:	lecolonial@verizon.net	Sunday 5:30pm - 10:30pm
Web:	www.lecolonialnyc.com	Closed major holidays
Prices:	$$$	

New Yorkers can enjoy the tasty cuisine of South Vietnam (where the chef grew up) at Le Colonial. His excellent interpretations of Vietnamese food include Bo Bia, soft vegetable-filled rolls served with a thick, sweet bean sauce; Pho, an aromatic oxtail broth filled with noodles and chunks of beef tenderloin; and Ca Chien Saigon, crisp-seared whole red snapper. The dining room, with its lazy ceiling fans, dark wood furnishings, tropical plants and historic black-and-white photographs, will transport you back to the turn of the 20th century, when Vietnam was a French colony, then known as Indochina.

Maloney & Porcelli

Steakhouse

044

37 E. 50th St. (bet. Park & Madison Aves.)

Subway:	51 St	Monday - Sunday noon - 11:30pm
Phone:	212-750-2233	
Fax:	212-750-2252	
e-mail:	agood@swrg.com	
Web:	www.maloneyandporcelli.com	
Prices:	$$$	

No wonder lawyers frequent this restaurant; it's named after the owner's law firm. Torts are no-doubt discussed in the attractive, bi-level dining room with its varnished woods and copper accents. Whether you have a law degree or not, you'd best bring a big appetite (and a big wallet) to dine on mammoth portions of grilled rib steaks and veal chops here. The signature dish, the much-ordered crackling pork shank, is first deep-fried, then slow-roasted to hold in the juices. The hearty chunk of meat is served with jalapeno-pepper-spiked "firecracker" apple sauce. Side dishes (fresh-cut French fries, creamed spinach, whipped potatoes) come sized for two.

Michael Jordan's
S t e a k h o u s e

045

Grand Central Terminal (corner of Park Ave. & 42nd St.)

Subway:	Grand Central - 42 St	Monday - Friday 11:30am - 2:30pm
Phone:	212-655-2300	& 5pm - 11pm
Fax:	212-271-2324	Saturday 5pm - 11pm
e-mail:	mjordan@theglaziergroup.com	Sunday 5pm - 10pm
Web:	www.theglaziergroup.com	
Prices:	$$$	

XX
&

There's no denying that dining in Grand Central Terminal provides one of the best views in the city—indoor views, anyway. From Michael Jordan's on the west balcony, you can gaze up to see the constellations of the zodiac painted on the soaring vaulted ceiling; its 12-story-height would dwarf even His Airness himself. The menu features typical steakhouse fare; generous servings of Prime dry-aged Angus beef are what you can expect here. Sides are heavy on the carbs (there are only two veggie choices at dinner; at lunch vegetables are combined with a baked potato). Sports fans can catch the game on the 50-inch plasma-screen TV set above the elliptical mahogany bar.

Mr Chow
C h i n e s e

046

324 E. 57th St. (bet. First & Second Aves.)

Subway:	59 St	Monday - Sunday 6pm - 11:30pm
Phone:	212-751-9030	
Fax:	212-644-0352	
e-mail:	N/A	
Web:	www.mrchow.com	
Prices:	$$$	

XX

Michael Chow is nothing if not an interesting guy. Actor, artist, interior designer and restaurateur, Chow did the design for all four of his establishments (two of the others are in Southern California; the fourth is in London). A striking mobile fashioned of red fabric hangs above the bustling and oh-so-hip black and white dining room, where even the waiters have trouble moving between the closely spaced tables. Diners don't seem to mind the cramped quarters, though; Mr. Chow packs in a high-profile crowd night after night. It's not cool to ask for a menu here; it's expected you'll allow your waiter to order for you (though they will grudgingly bring a menu if you insist).

Nanni

047

146 E. 46th St. (bet. Third & Lexington Aves.)

Subway:	Grand Central - 42 St	Monday - Saturday noon - 3pm
Phone:	212-697-4161	& 5pm - 10pm
Fax:	N/A	Closed Sunday
e-mail:	N/A	
Web:	N/A	
Prices:	**$$**	

XX

As you step down into the simple dining room at Nanni's, you'll note that the ceilings are low, the lighting is dim, the walls are painted with murals of Abruzzi. Modest it may be, but local business types know a good thing when they see it. Good quality ingredients, authentic recipes, and smiling service by a mature cadre of waiters (they're all retirees), bring an animated crowd of Midtowners back for more. Homemade pastas are cooked perfectly al dente and served with a salad; veal comes in cutlets, chops or scaloppini; tiramisu is light and freshly made. Top it all off with pleasant, professional service and you'll realize why Nanni's has such a loyal following.

Osteria Laguna

Italian

048

209 E. 42nd St. (bet. Second & Third Aves.)

Subway:	Grand Central - 42 St	Monday - Friday noon - 11pm
Phone:	212-557-0001	Saturday 5pm - 11pm
Fax:	N/A	Sunday 5pm - 10:30pm
e-mail:	N/A	
Web:	www.osteria-laguna.com	
Prices:	**$$**	

XX
&

Convenient to Grand Central Terminal and the United Nations, Osteria Laguna is tucked into the ground floor of a redbrick office building. The dining space is separated into two rooms: a sunny, high-ceilinged front room, lit by large windows and wrought-iron chandeliers; and a more classically decorated and intimate back room, with white-clothed tables and black banquettes lining the walls. Large posters and Palio-style banners add a colorful note. An efficient and courteous waitstaff delivers authentic fare such as homemade pasta, pizza and risotto to your table. Other entrées run the gamut from roasted branzino to veal saltimbocca.

049

Pampano

Contemporary Mexican

209 E. 49th St. (bet. Second & Third Aves.)

Subway:	51 St
Phone:	212-751-4545
Fax:	212-751-0800
e-mail:	pampano_ny@modernmexican.com
Web:	www.modernmexican.com/pampano
Prices:	$$

Monday - Wednesday 11:30am - 3pm
& 5pm - 10pm
Thursday - Friday 11:30am - 3pm
& 5pm - 10:30pm
Saturday 5pm - 10:30pm
Sunday 5pm - 9:30pm

Here's an unlikely marriage: opera star Placido Domingo and Acapulco-born chef Richard Sandoval. It's not a literal marriage, of course, but rather a business partnership; both are co-owners of Pampano. Sandoval, whose restaurant holdings extend to San Francisco, Denver, Las Vegas and Washington, D.C., uses European techniques to interpret the vivid flavors of Mexican cuisine. The airy dining room, with its crisp white walls, sand-colored banquettes, and light pouring in from the loft-style glass ceiling, evokes the sun-bleached beaches of Mexico. Accordingly, fish takes top billing on the menu, and traditional sides include fried plantains and rice and black beans.

050

Picasso

Spanish

303 E. 56th St. (bet. First & Second Aves.)

Subway:	59 St
Phone:	212-759-8767
Fax:	212-759-8801
e-mail:	info@restaurantpicasso.com
Web:	www.restaurantpicasso.com
Prices:	$$

Monday - Friday noon - 11pm
Saturday - Sunday 1pm - 11pm

Posters of toreadors and flamenco dancers on the walls here evoke sunny Spain, as does the range of dishes from paella to tortilla a la Española. There's a varied selection of seafood, meats and poultry on the menu, but if you're not up for a big meal, check out the list of tapas: imported Serrano ham, grilled squid, beef empanadas, and baby eel are just a sampling of the small plates. Then take your pick from the list of full-bodied riojas and other Spanish regional wines. The smiling, efficient waitstaff adds to the warm atmosphere, animated by a lively clientele. So when in New York, do as New Yorkers do: bring some friends and make a night of it.

Pietro's

Italian

051

232 E. 43rd St. (bet. Second & Third Aves.)

Subway:	Grand Central - 42 St	Monday - Saturday noon - 3pm
Phone:	212-682-9760	& 5:30pm - 10:30pm
Fax:	212-682-4379	Closed Sunday & major holidays
e-mail:	N/A	
Web:	www.pietros.com	
Prices:	$$$	

Trendy it's not. Inexpensive? Not with a Midtown address in the shadow of the Chrysler Building. Founded in 1932 by Pietro Donini and his brother Natale, Pietro's is an old-fashioned Italian eatery. The plain dining room sports a patriotic (for Italy) red, green and white color scheme, and the food will certainly be familiar: minestrone, chicken Parmigiana, spaghetti with meatballs, veal Marsala, shrimp scampi, along with steaks and chops. But don't overlook this tried-and-true place; the service is good and preparations are rendered using excellent, fresh ingredients and homemade pasta. Now that's Italian!

Riingo

Contemporary Japanese

052

205 E. 45th St. (bet. Second & Third Aves.)

Subway:	Grand Central - 42 St	Monday - Wednesday noon - 2:30pm
Phone:	212-867-4200	& 5:30pm - 10:30pm
Fax:	212-867-1700	Thursday -Friday noon - 2:30pm
e-mail:	info@riingo.com	& 5:30pm - 11pm
Web:	www.riingo.com	Saturday 5:30pm - 11pm
Prices:	$$	Sunday 11am - 3pm

Derived from the Japanese word for "apple" (as in the Big Apple), Riingo features Scandinavian chef Marcus Samuelsson's interpretation of Japanese and American dishes. The stylish, contemporary restaurant, just off the lobby of the Alex Hotel (see hotel listings), incorporates ebony wood, bamboo floor planks, and thoughtful touches such as custom-made ceramic sake sets. Located in the lounge, an eight-seat sushi bar complements the small (40 seats) downstairs dining room and offers a full range of raw fish and rolls. A Carrera marble staircase leads to the mezzanine. Dishes on the changing menu run the gamut from New York strip steak to rare tuna with black edamame and sea beans.

Manhattan *Midtown East*

Restaurants **207**

Shun Lee Palace

Chinese

053

155 E. 55th St. (bet. Third & Lexington Aves.)

Subway:	Lexington Av - 53 St
Phone:	212-371-8844
Fax:	212-752-1936
e-mail:	N/A
Web:	www.shunleepalace.com
Prices:	$$

Monday - Saturday noon - 11:30pm
Sunday noon - 11pm

What makes Shun Lee Palace special is its décor, revamped by no less than ubiquitous designer Adam Tihany. It's an Oriental fantasy, done with carved-wood partitions, framed contemporary lithographs, and serpentine "rivers" of etched glass shading lights on the ceiling. There are spaces here to fit most any mood, from the lively bar in front, overlooking the street, to the darker back dining room where cozy booths foster intimate conversation. Owner Michael Tong manages this New York institution, which has been a Midtown fixture for more than 30 years. Signature dishes include crispy prawns in XO sauce, sweetbreads with black mushrooms, and whole sea bass braised in hot bean sauce.

Sòlo

Mediterranean Kosher

054

550 Madison Ave. (at 56th St.)

Subway:	5 Av - 53 St
Phone:	212-833-7800
Fax:	212-833-7878
e-mail:	solo@solonyc.com
Web:	www.solonyc.com
Prices:	$$

Monday - Friday 11am - 3pm
& 5pm - 11pm
Sunday 11am - 2pm & 5pm - 11pm
Closed Saturday

Kosher cuisine rises to new heights at Sòlo. A venture by Syrian native Joey Allaham, who founded Prime Grill, this tony restaurant fills space inside the Sony Building's soaring glass-roofed atrium. The restaurant is lit with blue lights at night, echoing the color of the Mediterranean Sea underneath the coffered ceiling. Diners can see the stainless-steel kitchen through a glass partition, where the staff, under the watchful eye of executive chef Hok Chin, prepares the likes of citrus-cured wild King salmon gravlax and salt-baked branzini—all strictly Kosher. The members-only Club Room accommodates 20 for private dinners, who feast on the chef's tasting menu.

Sparks Steak House

055

Steakhouse

210 E. 46th St. (bet. Second & Third Aves.)

Subway:	Grand Central - 42 St
Phone:	212-687-4855
Fax:	212-557-7409
e-mail:	N/A
Web:	www.sparksnyc.com
Prices:	$$$

Monday - Saturday noon - 11pm
Closed Sunday

XX
&
88

Sparks is well equipped to handle crowds—and entourages from the United Nations, a few short blocks away—since the restaurant seats an astounding 687 people in its huge bi-level dining space. There's a masculine, brasserie-type vibe to the place, with its dark woods, glass partitions, and 19th-century landscapes of the Hudson River Valley lining the wainscoted walls. Unlike many New York steakhouses, Sparks doesn't offer a porterhouse, but thick cuts of prime sirloin and filet mignon will surely satisfy your craving for beef (for seafood lovers, lobsters range from 3 to nearly 6 pounds). After dinner, real men retire for a smoke to the humidor at the end of the bar.

Sushi-Ann

056

Japanese

38 E. 51st St. (bet. Park & Madison Aves.)

Subway:	51 St
Phone:	212-755-1780
Fax:	212-755-1788
e-mail:	N/A
Web:	N/A
Prices:	$$

Monday - Sunday noon - 3pm
& 6pm - 11pm

XX
&

Need a sushi break from Fifth Avenue shopping? Located just around the corner from Saks, Sushi-Ann is a refreshingly unpretentious haven with its L-shaped sushi bar and blond varnished-wood tables, all adorned with fresh roses. In a former incarnation, this place next to the New York Palace hotel was part of the Sushisay chain. It's now independent, though the owners of this well-run restaurant haven't changed. Uniformed waiters cater to a casual clientele that includes business types as well as tourists, who all enjoy the excellent quality of the sushi, sashimi and hand rolls served here (Sushi-Ann's menu doesn't list teriyaki or tempura dishes).

Manhattan Midtown East

Sushiden

Japanese

057

19 E. 49th St. (bet. Madison & Fifth Aves.)

Subway:	5 Av - 53 St	Monday - Friday noon - 2:15pm
Phone:	212-758-2700	& 5:30pm - 10pm
Fax:	212-644-2942	Saturday 5pm - 9pm
e-mail:	N/A	Closed Sunday
Web:	www.sushiden.com	
Prices:	$$	

Inside Sushiden's windowed façade you'll find a long sushi bar, behind which several chefs work their magic, carefully preparing raw fish with impressive speed. This is sushi done right. Each piece of fresh fish is sized perfectly over its tiny bed of rice, so the taste of one ingredient doesn't overwhelm the taste of the other (regulars recommend the toro, a fatty and flavorful cut of tuna taken from the fish's belly). This is service done right, too. Young women in kimonos attend to customers in an efficient and pleasant manner. This is a good bet for sushi; and if you're on the West Side; there's a second Sushiden at 123 W. 49th Street.

Sushi Yasuda

Japanese

058

204 E. 43rd St. (bet. Second & Third Aves.)

Subway:	Grand Central - 42 St	Monday - Friday noon - 2:15pm
Phone:	212-972-1001	& 6pm - 10:15pm
Fax:	212-972-1717	Saturday 6pm - 10:15pm
e-mail:	scott@sushiyasuda.com	Closed Sunday
Web:	www.sushiyasuda.com	
Prices:	$$$$	

Discreetly tucked away in the corridor between Grand Central Terminal and the United Nations, Sushi Yasuda appears almost Scandinavian with its blond woods and contemporary style. But look again: the walls, tables, ceiling and floor are all wrapped in solid bamboo planks. Even the sushi bar, the domain of Japanese chef Naomichi Yasuda, is made of unfinished bamboo. Yasuda, whose twenty years of experience include gigs in Tokyo and New York City, is a stickler for purity and simplicity. His raw fish offerings change daily, depending on the freshest products available. Between the deft sushi chefs, the friendly servers and the artfully presented dishes, Sushi Yasuda knows how to please.

Table XII

059

109 E. 56th St. (bet. Park & Lexington Aves.)

Subway:	59 St	Monday - Friday 11:30am - 3:30pm
Phone:	212-750-5656	& 5:30pm - 10:30pm
Fax:	212-750-8050	Saturday 5:30pm - midnight
e-mail:	tableXII@aol.com	Closed Sunday
Web:	www.tableXII.com	
Prices:	SS	

Table XII is restaurateur John Scotto's third restaurant in the same space, once the home of media magnate William Randolph Hearst. The name refers to the table that was reputed to be the best in the house when the place first opened. (There's still a table XII, but now it seats 12 people.) Classical-style comfort abounds in the dramatic, high-ceilinged dining room, decked out with ornate plaster moldings, gilt mirrors, and a marble fireplace. Original lithographs by American artist Alfred Jensen (1903-1981) line the walls. All this makes an elegant setting in which to relish signature dishes such as spaghettini al limone and ravioli ricci di mare (filled with sea urchin and scallops).

Tropica

060

200 Park Ave. (MetLife Building at 45th St.)

Subway:	Grand Central - 42 St	Monday - Friday 11:30am - 3pm
Phone:	212-867-6767	& 5:30pm - 10pm
Fax:	212-949-8266	Closed Saturday & Sunday
e-mail:	press@restaurantassociates.com	
Web:	www.tropicany.com	
Prices:	SS	

Order a rum punch and settle back for an island experience. As the name suggests, tastes of the sunny Caribbean shine through in the cuisine at Tropica. The restaurant is set in the concourse of the 1963 MetLife Building, which towers 59-stories over Grand Central Terminal. Tropica's airy dining room, brightened by skylights, bentwood, cane-back chairs and vases of palm fronds, seamlessly incorporates an open kitchen. Tropical drinks head the cocktail list, and the menu features island notes such as conch chowder, cane sugar-rum barbecued shrimp, and the signature Caribbean-style lobster boil, with sides of blue potato salad and grilled chile corn.

Boi

Vietnamese

061

246 E. 44th St. (bet. Second & Third Aves.)

Subway:	Grand Central - 42 St	Monday - Saturday noon - 3pm
Phone:	212-681-6541	& 5:30pm - 10pm
Fax:	212-681-1563	Closed Sunday
e-mail:	boirestaurant@aol.com	
Web:	www.boi-restaurant.com	
Prices:	$$	

A couple of blocks east of Grand Central Terminal, Boi preserves family recipes that have been passed down to the current chef, Tamie Trans-Le, from her grandmother (known as "Boi"). The color scheme in the long, narrow dining room is red and white, echoing Boi's logo, a silhouette of a woman dressed in a flowing, red traditional Vietnamese gown. At both lunch and dinner you can choose among small and large plates, depending on your appetite. Pastry chef and restaurant partner Bill Yosses puts an Asian spin on the final course with such treats as jackfruit toffee pudding, topped with homemade vanilla ice cream.

Casa La Femme North

Egyptian

062

1076 First Ave. (bet. 58th & 59th Sts.)

Subway:	Lexington Av - 59 St	Sunday - Wednesday 5pm - 1am
Phone:	212-505-0005	Thursday - Saturday 5pm - 4am
Fax:	212-421-8126	
e-mail:	N/A	
Web:	www.oasisgroupny.com	
Prices:	$$	

Now here's a place for a romantic interlude. Gauzy tents provide privacy for the tables lining the walls, creating the perfect setting in which to steal a kiss or make a proposal (be aware that the only dining option available at the tented tables is the prix-fixe menu). Not in the mood for romance? That's okay, you'll still enjoy Casa's exotic feel, with its hanging lanterns, curving banquettes and leafy palm trees. At dinner, a belly dancer shimmies her way around the room—did someone say "Take me to the Casbah?" Tasty North African cuisine, such as tagines served with fluffy homemade couscous, and baked whole fish, will vie with the dancer for your attention.

Cellini

Italian

063

65 E. 54th St. (bet. Park & Madison Aves.)

Subway:	51 St
Phone:	212-751-1555
Fax:	212-753-2848
e-mail:	N/A
Web:	www.cellinirestaurant.com
Prices:	$$

Monday - Sunday noon - 3pm
& 5:30pm - 10:30pm

Rustic and homey, that's Cellini. Indeed, you'll feel like family at this warm and welcoming restaurant, two blocks from the south end of Central Park. The dimly lit dining room is simply decorated with wood wainscoting, and wrought-iron chandeliers and wall sconces. Folk art and crockery plates enliven the otherwise plain walls, while the beamed ceiling is draped with cheery red fabric. Like the décor, the food is not complicated; regional Italian dishes here are interpreted with a careful touch and prepared using high-quality ingredients. Specials might include homemade ravioli, or veal martini, crusted with Parmesan cheese and sautéed in Absolut vodka and dry vermouth.

Cipriani Dolci

Italian

064

Grand Central Terminal (corner of Park Ave. & 42nd St.)

Subway:	Grand Central - 42 St
Phone:	212-973-0999
Fax:	212-973-9666
e-mail:	dolciny@cipriani.com
Web:	www.cipriani.com
Prices:	$$

Monday - Sunday 11am - midnight

You'll find this Italian bistro on the west balcony inside Grand Central Terminal. Its enviable location underneath Grand Central's fantastic vaulted turquoise ceiling affords diners a view of the bustling central court of the restored Beaux-Arts train station. Cipriani Dolci belongs to the family-run Cipriani restaurant group, which encompasses establishments in New York City as well as in Venice, where they began as Harry's Bar. Happy hour is popular here, as is the menu of hearty pastas and grilled fish and meat. Don't leave without sampling the signature Bellini cocktails (made with sparkling wine and peach nectar), a libation invented by Giuseppe Cipriani at Harry's Bar in Venice in 1948.

Diwan

Indian

065

148 E. 48th St. (bet. Third & Lexington Aves.)

Subway:	51 St	Monday - Friday 11:30am - 2:30pm
Phone:	212-593-5425	& 5:30pm - 10:30pm
Fax:	212-593-5732	Saturday 11:30am - 3pm & 5pm - 11pm
e-mail:	diwan94@hotmail.com	Sunday 11:30am - 3pm
Web:	www.diwanrestaurant.com	& 5pm - 10:30pm
Prices:	$$	

The bounteous, inexpensive lunch buffet draws diners here at midday for a rich and varied selection of traditional dishes. Set out in front of the windows looking into the busy kitchen, the buffet is a good way to sample the regional fare of India, from Biryani (a recipe with myriad incarnations, based on Basmati rice) to vegetables spiced by Diwan's own special blend of masala, and curries accompanied by sweet-hot chutneys. At dinner, you can order from the pricier à la carte menu, which bears good explanations of the dishes, if you're not familiar with this type of cuisine. Bread choices run the gamut from lightly leavened nan to roomali, a handkerchief-thin flatbread.

Grand Central Oyster Bar

Seafood

066

Grand Central Terminal (Park Ave. & 42nd St.)

Subway:	Grand Central - 42 St	Monday - Friday 11:30am - 9:30pm
Phone:	212-490-6650	Saturday noon - 9:30pm
Fax:	212-949-5210	Closed Sunday
e-mail:	info@oysterbarny.com	
Web:	www.oysterbarny.com	
Prices:	$$	

Snag a seat at the counter and settle in for a true New York tradition: oysters Rockefeller and clam chowder at the Oyster Bar. Located on the lower level of Grand Central Terminal, the Oyster Bar is a popular place, especially with the business-lunch brigade. The restaurant, which opened in 1913, sports ceiling vaults tiled by 19th-century craftsman Raphael Guastavino—making for a beautiful, but cacophonous, setting. The raw bar menu reads like an ode to the oyster, with dozens of varieties from Long Island's Blue Point to Oregon's Yaquina. If bivalves aren't your thing, there's always the list of the day's fresh catch, but oysters are the clear winners here.

Jubilee

067

347 E. 54th St. (bet. First & Second Aves.)

Subway:	Lexington Av - 53 St	Monday - Friday noon - 3pm
Phone:	212-888-3569	& 5:30pm - 11pm
Fax:	212-755-0614	Saturday 5:30pm - 11pm
e-mail:	jubilee5154@aol.com	Sunday noon - 3pm & 5pm - 10pm
Web:	www.jubileeny.com	Closed Sunday July & August
Prices:	$$	

Your mother was right when she told you never to judge a book by its cover. From the outside, this little building may not look like much, but inside lies a pleasant space with soft lighting, a pressed-tin ceiling and neat rows of tables and banquettes lining the long, narrow room. Prince Edward Island mussels are the signature dish here; they're prepared five different ways, and served Belgian-style with frites, or with a green salad for calorie-counters. Otherwise, the menu has decided French leanings, with such classics as roasted chicken with mashed potatoes, leg of lamb, and escargots. Some dishes have a modern touch, like tuna tartare paired with ginger and guacamole.

Khyber Grill

Indian

068

230 E. 58th St. (bet. Second & Third Aves.)

Subway:	59 St	Monday - Sunday 11:30am - 2:30pm
Phone:	212-339-0090	(Sat 3pm, Sun 4pm)
Fax:	212-339-0071	Sunday - Wednesday 5:30pm - 11pm
e-mail:	info@khybergrill.com	Thursday - Saturday 5:30pm - 11:30pm
Web:	www.khybergrill.com	
Prices:	$$	

Formerly the Bukhara Grill, this spot retains a rustic décor of beamed ceilings, stone tiles lining the walls, and stylish copper light fixtures. Known for their tandoor dishes, the kitchen staff prepares specialities such as the spicy minced-lamb kabobs, coated with herbs and grilled on a skewer in the beehive-shaped tandoor oven. Fish and meat cooked this way are, in essence, smoked in their own juices, which drip from the marinated food onto the glowing charcoals below. Flavorful naan and paratha breads are also baked in the tandoor, where they brown against the hot oven walls. Go at lunch for the bounteous buffet.

Métrazur

American

069

Grand Central Terminal corner of Park Ave. & 42nd St.)

Subway:	Grand Central - 42 St	Monday - Friday 11:30am - 3pm
Phone:	212-687-4600	& 5pm - 10:30pm
Fax:	212-687-5671	Saturday 5pm - 10:30pm
e-mail:	info@charliepalmer.com	Closed Sunday
Web:	www.charliepalmer.com	
Prices:	$$	

Métrazur takes every advantage of its spectacular location on the east balcony of Grand Central Terminal. The sleek design of the restaurant's two large dining rooms plays against the restored opulence of the station's cavernous main concourse. Then there's the name, which refers to a train that once traveled France's Côte d'Azur on its way to Monaco. Indeed, you'll find that flavors of the Mediterranean infuse seasonally changing dishes like tapenade-brushed halibut, and tagliatelle with braised duck, broccoli rape and pressed olives. Owner of Métrazur, famed chef and cookbook author Charlie Palmer opened his first New York venture, Aureole, at the tender age of 28.

Nippon

Japanese

070

155 E. 52nd St. (bet. Third & Lexington Aves.)

Subway:	Lexington Av - 53 St	Monday - Thursday noon - 2:30pm
Phone:	212-758-0226	& 5:30pm - 10pm
Fax:	212-832-2085	Friday noon - 2:30pm
e-mail:	N/A	& 5:30pm - 10:30pm
Web:	www.restaurantnippon.com	Saturday 5:30pm - 10:30pm
Prices:	$$	Closed Sunday

Billing itself as New York's first sushi bar, Nippon was founded in 1963 by Nobuyoshi Kuraoka. It's more modest than many of the new generation of sushi restaurants, but the contemporary décor is pleasant in pastel peach tones with a pale hinoki cypress sushi counter. Of course, there are the usual sushi and sashimi offerings, but with a noteworthy addition here. In season (October to March), Kuraoka features a special menu centered on fugu, a poisonous Japanese puffer fish, which, if not cleaned and prepared correctly, can kill those who consume it—and it's expensive, to boot. Nippon is also known for making their own soba noodles with buckwheat grown on a farm the restaurant owns in Canada.

Palm

Steakhouse

837 Second Ave. (bet. 44th & 45th Sts.)

Subway:	Grand Central - 42 St	Monday noon - 10pm
Phone:	212-687-2953	Tuesday - Friday noon - 11pm
Fax:	212-983-4584	Saturday 5pm - 11pm
e-mail:	kdecicco@thepalm.com	Sunday 5pm - 10pm
Web:	www.thepalm.com	
Prices:	$$$	

In 1926 Italian immigrants Pio Bazzi and John Ganzi opened a restaurant on Second Avenue. They called it Parma, after their native region in Italy, but the name became Americanized to "Palm," and so it remains today. A local institution, The Palm is known for humongous portions of Prime steak. It's crowded and loud; sawdust covers the floors, and caricatures of celebrity diners and cartoons by the likes of Mort Walker (Beetle Bailey) and Carmine Infantino (Batman) line the walls—which are insured for $500,000! Although the Palm has expanded to more than 25 locations across the U.S. (including Palm Too, across the street), you can't beat the timeless aura at the Second Avenue flagship.

PJ Clarke's

Gastro-Pub

915 Third Ave. (at 55th St.)

Subway:	Lexington Av - 53 St	Monday - Sunday 11:30am - 4am
Phone:	212-317-1616	
Fax:	N/A	
e-mail:	info@pjclarkes.com	
Web:	www.pjclarkes.com	
Prices:	෨	

Named for proprietor Patrick Joseph Clarke, who purchased the place in 1904, this saloon remains a slice of old New York, despite its makeover and change of ownership in 2002. The building at the corner of 55th Street itself dates back to 1898 and saw its fair share of bar fights in its feisty heyday. The new owners (who include Yankee owner George Steinbrenner and Philip Scotti of Sarabeth's restaurant) preserved the bar's look and feel, right down to the stained-glass windows and photos on the walls. Pub fare still reigns at the former haunt of Frank Sinatra and Jackie O: big burgers, shepherd's pie, Yankee pot roast, and a large selection of beers on tap with which to wash it down.

Manhattan *Midtown East*

Raffaele

073

1055 First Ave. (bet. 57th & 58th Sts.)

Subway:	Lexington Av - 59 St	Monday - Saturday noon - 11pm
Phone:	212-750-3232	Closed Sunday
Fax:	212-750-0077	
e-mail:	N/A	
Web:	www.raffaele.citysearch.com	
Prices:	$$	

Owner Raffaele Esposito, the restaurant's namesake, greets customers personally here. A former chef at Rome's Grand Hotel, Esposito now manages his own Southern Italian eatery in Midtown. The attractive dining room is done with bright-red walls, a green ceiling and black and white floor tiles. Photographs of Italy line the walls, while small bunches of dried red chiles adorn the white-clothed tables. Traditional Italian dishes fill the menu, along with daily specials (and a frequently changing roster of desserts). If you fall in love with Raffaele's sauce after a meal here, don't despair; you can buy it by the pint before you leave.

Seo

074

249 E. 49th St. (bet. Second & Third Aves.)

Subway:	51 St	Monday - Friday noon - 2:30pm
Phone:	212-355-7722	& 5:30pm - 10:30pm
Fax:	N/A	Saturday - Sunday 5:30pm - 10:30pm
e-mail:	N/A	
Web:	N/A	
Prices:	$$	

Authentic and good Japanese food attracts a Japanese crowd to this sushi restaurant, located, appropriately, a couple of blocks from the Japan Society headquarters (and the adjacent Trump World Tower). It's a small place, with a sushi bar up front, followed by a little, no-frills dining room. While the à la carte list of sushi and sashimi is not extensive, it does provide all the basics. Specials change daily, according to the day's shipment of fresh domestic and imported fish. Out back, beyond the dining room, check out the charming, lantern-lit, open-air garden, planted with bamboo and centering on a traditional Japanese structure with paper walls.

Teodora

075

141 E. 57th St. (bet. Third & Lexington Aves.)

Subway:	Lexington Av - 59 St	Monday - Saturday noon - 11pm
Phone:	212-826-7101	Sunday noon - 10:30pm
Fax:	212-826-7138	
e-mail:	N/A	
Web:	www.teodoranyc.com	
Prices:	$$	

It's a pleasant surprise to discover this dark, cozy restaurant on 57th Street, one of Midtown's busiest commercial thoroughfares. Providing a respite from the hustle and bustle just outside, the long, narrow dining room recalls a typical bistro with its wood bar, Belle Époque-style light fixtures and shelves lined with bottles of wine and carafes of vinegar. Chef Giancarlo Quadalti, who owns this place as well as Celeste on the Upper West Side with his wife, Roberta Ruggini, hails from the Emilia-Romagna area of Italy. Accordingly, the menu emphasizes northern Italian dishes that use staples from his native region, such as Parmigiano Reggiano cheese and balsamic vinegar.

Zarela

076

953 Second Ave. (bet. 50th & 51st Sts.)

Subway:	51 St	Monday - Thursday noon - 3pm
Phone:	212-644-6740	& 5pm - 11pm
Fax:	212-980-1073	Friday noon - 3pm & 5pm - midnight
e-mail:	zarela@zarela.com	Saturday 5pm - midnight
Web:	www.zarela.com	Sunday 5pm - 10pm
Prices:	$$	

Every day's a fiesta in this boisterous bistro, hung with bright paper garlands and flowers, ceremonial masks, puppets and other traditional Mexican artifacts. Zarela Martínez sees to that. The chef opened her restaurant here in 1987, and still draws crowds. As a child growing up in Mexico, Zarela came to think of cooking as a celebration. Accordingly, she courts a carnival ambience with lively Latino music and food that's served family-style for sharing. In the evenings, the place teems with people, who often spill out onto the sidewalk while they wait to dig into regional Mexican dishes such as chicken braised in tequila, and slow-cooked pork shoulder marinated in achiote and sour oranges.

About
Midtown West

When you think of Midtown West, Times Square probably comes to mind. True, brash **Times Square**, at Broadway and 42nd Street, demands your attention with its blazing marquees, but the neighborhood that runs from Fifth Avenue west to the Hudson River is so much more than that. Here you'll also find picturesque **Bryant Park**, the **Empire State Building**, and **Rockefeller Center**, home to NBC studios and the city's famous skating rink. For shoppers, **Macy's** anchors a frenetic shopping hub (on Avenue of the Americas at 34th St.), and **Diamond and Jewelry Way** (W. 47th St., between Fifth & Sixth Aves.) ranks as the world's largest district for diamonds and other precious stones.

MIDTOWN WEST

If it's dining that interests you, look no further. Midtown West holds a dense concentration of eateries, from Restaurant Row (as the block of West 46th Street is popularly known) to the Time Warner Center (on Columbus Circle), home to some of New York's most celebrated new restaurants.

A Bit of History – In the colonial era, this slice of Midtown belonged to the city but was actually the country, as New York's population was concentrated well below Canal Street. By the mid-19th century, the area was covered with brownstone town houses, home to upper-middle-class families who couldn't afford a mansion on Fifth Avenue. Upon the completion of the Sixth Avenue "El" (elevated railway) in 1878, a majority of these residents deemed the quarter too noisy and dirty, and, with their Fifth Avenue neighbors, began moving uptown.

The construction of **Rockefeller Center** between 1930 and 1940 permanently changed the character of the neighborhood. More than 225 buildings, mostly brownstones, were demolished to make room for the original 12 buildings of the complex, and the residential population was dispersed to other parts of the city. But with that loss came significant gain. The center was hailed as an architectural triumph. Rockefeller's insistence that early tenants be affiliated with the television and radio industries soon attracted other media outlets to the district, boosting its worldwide visibility.

The Dividing Line – Although Fifth Avenue officially separates the east and west sides of Manhattan, it is the Avenue of the Americas (still known as Sixth Avenue to locals, though it was officially renamed in 1945) that actually feels like the dividing line. In part, that's because its neighbors are so distinct. One block east, the department stores of **Fifth Avenue** ooze gentility. One block west, the fabled **Theater District** (spreading north from Times Square along Broadway) teems with performance venues and restaurants, the latter touting their pre- and post-theater menus.

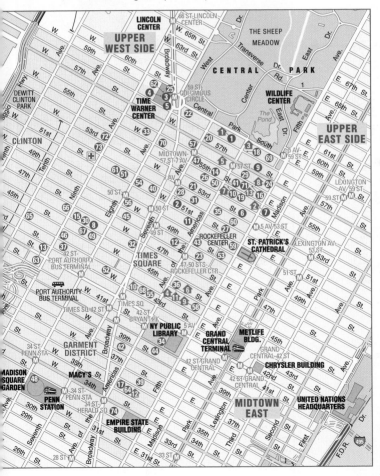

Alain Ducasse ✿✿✿

001

155 W. 58th St. (bet. Sixth & Seventh Aves.)

Subway:	Midtown - 57 St - 7 Av
Phone:	212-265-7300
Fax:	212-265-9300
e-mail:	maitred@alain-ducasse.com
Web:	www.alain-ducasse.com
Prices:	$$$

Monday - Thursday 6:30pm - 9:30pm
Friday - Saturday 5:30pm - 9:30pm
Closed Sunday & major holidays

XXXXX

♿

⎈

Manhattan Midtown West

Alain Ducasse/Mathilde de l'Ecotais

As Alain Ducasse spread his epicurean empire around the globe, it was inevitable that he would hit New York. In 2000 he did, opening his eponymous restaurant at the Essex House Hotel *(see hotel listings)*. As soon as you enter the Grande Salle, you'll be enveloped by Brazilian rosewood paneling, Chinese antiques, and black-granite columns. Vivid gold and red fabrics and a collection of hand-blown glass add to the opulence, and the engaging brigade attends to every detail.

All this would count for nothing, though, without the chef's masterful cooking. Ducasse relies on his own network of U.S. growers for ingredients. Depending on the market, you might dine on milk-fed veal with oven-roasted tomatoes, or line-caught bass in shellfish emulsion. For a special experience, reserve the chef's table in the black-granite-clad "Aquarium," where you can watch the kitchen staff in action.

Crisp and Tender Garden Vegetables

Serves 4

Vegetables

6 baby carrots, washed
6 baby turnips, washed
6 baby yellow beets, washed
2 bulbs baby fennel, washed and
  1 sliced thinly
6 baby zucchini, washed and trimmed
4 asparagus, trimmed
4 scallions, cut on a bias
1 celery stalk
2 cups chicken stock

Peel carrots, turnips and beets and cut 3 of each in small dice. Bring chicken stock to a boil in sauce pan. Blanch cut vegetables in chicken stock until tender, about 2-4 minutes and then drain from stock. Set vegetables aside to cool. Return stock to stove and warm over medium heat; allow to reduce by three-quarters.

Dressing

¼ cup reduced cooking liquid
½ cup extra virgin olive oil
¼ cup lemon juice to taste
¼ tsp. salt and freshly ground pepper

For vinaigrette, whisk together lemon juice, reduced stock, salt and pepper. While whisking, add olive oil in a thin stream until emulsified. Set aside.

Greens

¼ lb. each of arugula, shiso, mizuna and
  tatsoi, washed and dried
2 oz. chervil
12 each of celery leaves and
  chives, minced
12 beet greens, washed, dried and chopped
2 Tbsp. extra virgin olive oil
1 clove garlic, crushed

With a mandoline, shave remaining vegetables as thinly as possible. Submerge in ice water for ten minutes or until crisp. Drain and dry.

In a sauté pan over medium low heat, heat olive oil. Brown garlic and add half the greens and herbs. Season with salt and sauté until lightly wilted, only 2-4 minutes.

To Plate

In a large bowl, toss the shaved vegetables, herbs and greens with the vinaigrette. On four plates, spread a layer of the herbs and greens in a circular mold, followed by a layer of cooked vegetables. Place another layer of herbs and greens as top layer. Remove mold and sprinkle with salt and freshly ground pepper. Serve immediately.

Le Bernardin ✿✿✿

155 W. 51st St. (bet. Sixth & Seventh Aves.)

Subway: 47-50 Sts - Rockefeller Ctr
Phone: 212-554-1515
Fax: 212-554-1100
e-mail: dine@le-bernardin.com
Web: www.le-bernardin.com
Prices: $$$$

Monday - Friday noon - 11pm
Saturday 5pm - 11pm
Closed Sunday & major holidays

XXXXX
♿
₰

Le Bernardin/Shimon & Tammar Photography

In a city where chefs seem to change at the drop of a toque, it's remarkable that Le Bernardin has been under the same ownership since 1986, and that chef Eric Ripert has ruled the kitchen since 1994. Such stability shines through in the effortlessly efficient way that this celebrated restaurant operates. The extensive use of teak in the furnishings and the coffered ceiling gives Le Bernardin its grandeur, and an art collection belonging to owner Maguy Le Coze adds to the opulence.

At lunch, a business clientele tends to rush through their meals; at dinnertime, the ambience is leisurely, with more focus on the food. Divided into sections of "almost raw," "barely touched" and "lightly cooked," the à la carte menu spotlights the bounty of the sea (tasting menus are also available). Sauces here obtain their depth of flavor from ingredients foraged from around the globe.

Hamachi Tandoori

Serves 6

Salad

¼ cup Japanese rice wine vinegar
½ Tbsp. sugar
¼ cup extra virgin olive oil
½ English cucumber, peeled and cut into ¼-inch slices, seeds removed
2 Tbsp. Indian pickled mango pulp
12 cilantro leaves, sliced
1 cup watercress (or any other micro greens)
salt and freshly ground pepper

In a sauté pan, heat the vinegar and sugar just until the sugar dissolves. Add olive oil and cucumbers, toss and remove from heat. Add the pickled mango and a pinch of salt. Let cool and add the cilantro. Let the mixture marinate for 30-45 minutes. Drain liquid from the cucumber mixture and set it aside. Discard the liquid.

Yellowtail

3 four-ounce hamachi filets, fat and skin removed, cut into flat rectangles
¼ cup extra virgin olive oil
1 Tbsp. lemon juice
1 Tbsp. tandoori powder
1 clove garlic, finely minced
1 tsp. Herbes de Provence
salt and freshly ground pepper

In a bowl, combine the olive oil and all other ingredients. Whisk to blend. Place the filets in the bowl with the olive oil mixture and flip over to coat. Place a skillet over medium heat, and sear the hamachi filets gently, approximately 2 minutes on each side, reserving the olive oil mixture. Make sure there is a little color on each side, but do not burn the fish. The fish should be rare in the middle, but not cold. When cooked, remove from pan.

To Serve

Place the cucumber salad in a one-inch ring mold, on the right-hand side of plate. Remove the mold and top the salad with a small bunch of micro greens. Slice the hamachi filet into quarter-inch slices, lengthwise; you should get 10 slices from each filet. Arrange five slices per plate below the salad. Spoon about a tablespoon of sauce over and around the fish, and another tablespoon over the greens. Serve the remainder of the sauce on the side.

Per Se ✿✿✿

003

10 Columbus Circle (in the Time Warner Center)

Subway:	59 St - Columbus Cir	Monday - Thursday 5:30pm - 10pm
Phone:	212-823-9335	Friday - Sunday 11:30am - 1:30pm
Fax:	212-823-9353	& 5:30pm - 10pm
e-mail:	N/A	Closed January 2 - 11
Web:	www.perseny.com	
Prices:	$$$$	

Per Se

Having built his storied reputation at the French Laundry in Napa Valley, California, chef Thomas Keller has blessed New Yorkers with his newest restaurant. Per Se's Adam Tihany design claims its own vibrant personality, characterized, in part, by the fabulous views from its fourth-floor perch in the Time-Warner Center. Precision reigns here, from the choreographed service to the superlative cuisine. The kitchen produces dishes that are as exquisite as they are delicate from a multicourse menu that is perfectly balanced, original, and executed with the highest level of consistency.

With only 16 tables, Per Se plays hard to get with its reservations. They only accept reservations two months in advance, so practice your speed-dialing—and your patience. Getting through on the phone is a challenge, to say the least, but rest assured that a meal at Per Se will far outweigh any frustration.

Foie Gras au Torchon

Serves 4

13 oz. Moulard duck foie gras
2 quarts whole milk
2 tsp. Kosher salt
¼ tsp. white pepper
¼ tsp. sugar
2 quarts water

Method

Rinse the foie gras. Cover with milk and water, and refrigerate overnight. The next day, remove foie gras from milk. Cover with a damp towel and let stand at room temperature for 45 minutes. Remove membranes from the outside of the foie gras. Use your fingers and a knife to remove all veins. Return foie gras to its original shape. Coat foie gras with Kosher salt, white pepper and sugar, and press it into a container in an even layer, one-inch thick. Press plastic wrap against the foie gras to create an airtight environment. Refrigerate for 24 hours.

Using parchment paper, roll foie gras into a log, twisting and squeezing the ends of the parchment paper to help compact the foie gras. Unwrap foie gras, roll in cheesecloth into a tight log. Tie a knot around the cheesecloth; repeat procedure on the other end. Tie three pieces of string around the width of the torchon. Bring water to simmer in a pot. Place torchon in simmering liquid and poach for 90 seconds. Immediately remove the torchon and place it in an ice-water bath to cool just enough to handle. Compress the torchon in a dish towel. Tie the ends of the towel with string and hang the torchon from a shelf in the refrigerator overnight.

To serve, remove towel and cheesecloth. Slice torchon into 6 three-quarter-inch slices, and cut away the darkened exterior. Place a slice on each plate. Sprinkle with sea salt and serve with sliced, grilled bread and diced ripe peaches.

Masa ✿✿

004

10 Columbus Circle (in the Time Warner Center)

Subway:	59 St - Columbus Cir	Monday 6pm - 9pm
Phone:	212-823-9800	Tuesday - Friday noon - 1:30pm
Fax:	212-823-9809	& 6pm - 9pm
e-mail:	info@masanyc.com	Saturday 6pm - 9pm
Web:	www.masanyc.com	Closed Sunday
Prices:	$$$$	& December 24 - January 9

XX

&

Masa/Mikiko Kikuyama

Before you go to Masa, you should know that the price they charge for a meal here will bust any normal budget (the omakase menu will set you back $350). Indeed, many diners make their decision to go or not to go on this point alone (and you will need to decide in advance, since the restaurant doesn't accept walk-ins). What can you expect to get for your money here? Expect the finest sushi you are ever likely to eat.

The memorable dining experience begins with 4 to 5 little appetizers to gently tease the taste buds. Then come 15 to 20 courses of the most exquisite sushi (from squid to sardines, and sea urchin to scallops), all flown in fresh from the market in Japan. There are just 26 seats in the Zen-style room, with 10 of those at the sushi counter. Pick one of the latter if you want to interact with master sushi chef Masa Takayama.

Manhattan Midtown West

Moso/Carolyn Wang

Seki Aji Sashimi Salad

Serves 4

Salad

- 12oz. filet of seki aji (horse mackerel), thinly sliced into strips
- 1 bulb myoga ginger, thinly sliced
- 1oz. peeled ginger, julienned
- 3 bunches hanaho (shiso blossom), plucked from the stalks
- 2 oz. benitade (spicy purple sprouts)
- 2 oz. asatsuki (green onion), chopped
- 4 oz. daikon radish, julienned

Method

Combine all the ingredients for the dressing, and set aside. Assemble the rest of the ingredients into a small tower, creating layers of each ingredient between the fish.

Dressing

- 4 oz. dashi (bonito fish broth)
- 6 oz. soy sauce
- 1 juice of a sudachi (Japanese citrus fruit)

Drizzle dressing over the composed salad and serve.

Café Gray ✿

Contemporary

005

10 Columbus Circle (in the Time Warner Center)

Subway: 59 St - Columbus Cir
Phone: 212-823-6338
Fax: 212-823-6221
e-mail: info@cafegray.com
Web: www.cafegray.com
Prices: $$$

Monday - Saturday 11:30am - 2:15pm
& 5:30pm - 11pm
Closed Sunday

Café Gray

The impersonal vibe of the Time Warner Center disappears as you walk through the book-lined, paneled hallway into the entrancing third-floor world of Café Gray. While the dining room sparkles with its mirrored columns and circular banquettes, its most eye-catching feature is the open kitchen, situated near the window wall and its spectacular park views. The kitchen's location makes you wonder how the chefs concentrate so intently on their job, but concentrate they do.

Chef Gray Kunz's excellent cuisine reflects his global background; he grew up in Singapore and worked in Europe and Asia before settling in New York. Faced with all the offerings on the extensive à la carte menu, you may have trouble deciding between entrées such as sautéed snapper with ramps, green mango, yellow curry and Holy basil, and crisped pork shank and pork belly with sauerkraut and champagne sauce.

Café Gray/ ©Fran Collin

Bouquet of Pencil Asparagus

Serves 4

Mint Sauce

6 oz. yogurt   3 oz. labne
¼ tsp. sugar
1 tsp. honey   1 tsp. lemon juice
6 mint leaves, cut in chiffonade
¼ tsp. salt, black pepper and
   cayenne pepper

Whisk yogurt, labne, honey, lemon juice and mint together. Season with salt, pepper, cayenne and sugar and taste for seasoning.

Pea Sauce

3 oz. white wine   3 oz. white Port
3 oz. chicken stock   1 Tbsp. grapeseed oil
1 small shallot, cut in brunoise
5 oz. frozen peas, defrosted
¼ tsp. salt, black pepper and
   cayenne pepper

Over medium-high heat, reduce the wine and port wine to a syrup. Add chicken stock and remove from heat. In a separate pan, sweat the shallots in oil. Add the liquid and bring to a boil. Remove from heat and chill overnight. Blend the peas with the liquid. Strain through a chinois, add salt and peppers.

Asparagus Bouquet

2 bunches pencil asparagus
1 leek

Bring a pot of salted water to a boil. Blanch asparagus 1-2 minutes; remove from pot and place in a bowl of ice water. Using the same boiling water, blanch the leeks 2-5 minutes and place in bowl of ice water. Cut the leek into 4 strips lengthwise (¼-inch wide). Separate asparagus into 4 bunches and wrap each with a leek strip, tied in a double knot.

Salad

2 Tbsp. tarragon   2 Tbsp. chervil
16 fresh celery leaves 1 cup frisée
½ cup olive oil   ¼ cup lemon juice
16 flat leaf parsley leaves
   1 Tbsp. lemon zest
6 Tbsp. fresh peas, peeled
¼ tsp. salt, black pepper and
   cayenne pepper
3 asparagus, tops removed, sliced thin
½ tsp. freshly ground pink peppercorns

To Serve

Whisk together lemon juice, salt and peppers in a bowl. Add olive oil in a slow stream until emulsified. On a plate, spread 1 Tbsp. of the yogurt sauce into a circle. Combine the pea sauce with the fresh peas, lemon zest and thinly sliced asparagus. Place 1 Tbsp. of pea sauce in the center of mint sauce. Place asparagus bouquet on top and drizzle with half of vinaigrette. Toss the herbs and friseé with remaining vinaigrette and season to taste. Top asparagus bouquet with the salad. Garnish each plate with pink peppercorns and lemon zest.

The Modern ✿

Contemporary

9 W. 53rd St. (bet. Fifth & Sixth Aves.)

Subway:	5 Av - 53 St
Phone:	212-333-1220
Fax:	212-408-6326
e-mail:	N/A
Web:	www.themodernnyc.com
Prices:	$$$

Monday - Thursday noon - 2:15pm
& 5:30pm - 10:30pm
Friday noon - 2:15pm & 5:30pm - 11pm
Saturday 5:30pm - 11pm
Closed Sunday

XXX
&
⅋

The Modern/T. Chouquet

It's not easy to compete with priceless works of art by Giacometti and Picasso, but that's the challenge that chef Gabriel Kreuther faces at The Modern. Operated by Danny Meyer and housed in the boldly renovated Museum of Modern Art, this restaurant overlooks the 31 works displayed in the Abby Aldrich Rockefeller Sculpture Garden. The spare, light-filled dining room fits the atmosphere with its huge window wall, Danish-designed furnishings, and 46-foot-long marble bar. You can order à la carte at lunch; at dinner there's a prix-fixe menu. Either way, you'll relish dishes like foie gras terrine marbled with roasted artichokes, chorizo-crusted cod, and a Napoleon filled with rich layers of lemon cream.

The Dining Room has a separate street entrance, but if you come in this way, prepare to wade through the crowds in the Bar Room, a more informal space with its own identity and menu.

The Modern/Quentin Bacon

Salad of Celeriac, Oysters and Caviar

Serves 4

16 oysters
1 piece medium-size celeriac
8 Tbsp. grapeseed oil
6 Tbsp. chopped chives
3 Tbsp. champagne vinegar
2 Tbsp. crème fraiche
2 Tbsp. mayonnaise
2 oz. caviar (American)
1 Tbsp. almond oil 1 shallot, chopped
1 Tbsp. sour cream 2 Tbsp. lemon juice
4 pieces chervil
Salt and freshly ground pepper to taste

Method
Peel and wash the celeriac. Cut into 1/8-inch cubes. Blanch the celeriac cubes in boiling salted water until they reach a light crunchiness. Shock in ice water; when cold, drain in a colander and dry the cubes with a paper towel. Reserve in the refrigerator.

Shuck oysters and reserve half of them in their juice in the refrigerator. Cut the rest of the oysters in 3 pieces each and put them in a salad bowl over ice. Add 16 Tbsp. of blanched celeriac cubes, 1 oz. caviar, 2 Tbsp. chopped chives, mayonnaise, sour cream, salt, lemon juice, salt and pepper. Mix carefully with a spoon. Make sure that the celeriac cubes are well coated with the dressing. Mold the salad in either 4 rectangular molds (1 1/8" wide by 2 1/8" long by 1½" high), or 4 round ring molds (2" diameter by 1½" high). Press the mixture lightly in the molds and reserve in the refrigerator.

Oyster Glaze

In a bowl, combine crème fraiche, chopped shallots, almond oil, 2 Tbsp. champagne vinegar, salt and pepper. Reserve until needed.

Chive Oil

In a blender, combine the grapeseed oil and remaining chopped chives; blend until smooth. Pass through a coffee filter and reserve liquid.

To Serve
Transfer each salad mold to the center of each of 4 plates. Top it with caviar and oyster glaze (one side caviar, one side oyster glaze). Slowly remove the mold. Remove the whole oysters from their juice, dry them on a paper towel and put 2 oysters on each plate, one on each side. Cover with the oyster glaze, chopped chives, and a line of chive oil. Top the salad with chervil and serve.

Fives

French

007

700 Fifth Ave. (at 55th St., in the Peninsula Hotel)

Subway:	57 St	Monday noon - 2:30pm
Phone:	212-903-3918	Tuesday - Friday noon - 2:30pm
Fax:	212-903-3949	& 5:30pm - 10:30pm
e-mail:	N/A	Saturday 5:30pm - 10:30pm
Web:	www.peninsula.com	Sunday 11:30am - 2:30pm
Prices:	$$$	

XXXX
&
As you sink into the deep leather chairs and surrender to the charms of this effortlessly elegant restaurant on the second floor of the opulent Peninsula Hotel, you'll quickly forget that Fifth Avenue and all its bustle lie just outside. Befitting such graceful surroundings, the chef uses the finest-quality ingredients to produce exquisitely presented dishes with more than a hint of originality. The privacy that the restaurant affords—the waiters are as discreet as they are deft—makes Fives a popular choice at lunchtime for corporate deal-makers. In the evening, the atmosphere turns romantic, making this the perfect place for that intimate tête-à-tête.

Barbetta

Italian

008

321 W. 46th St. (bet. Eighth & Ninth Aves.)

Subway:	50 St	Tuesday - Sunday noon - midnight
Phone:	212-246-9171	Closed Monday
Fax:	212-246-1279	
e-mail:	barbetta100yrs@aol.com	
Web:	www.barbettarestaurant.com	
Prices:	$$$	

XXX
&
In the restaurant business, where longevity is the Holy Grail, Barbetta reigns supreme. In 2006 it will celebrate its 100th birthday, still under the ownership of the Maioglio family who founded it. Step inside the converted 1874 town house, where the ornate dining room boasts Louis XIV-style furnishings and an antique brass and crystal chandelier. Charming, bow-tied waiters proffer rare Old World hospitality here. The seasonal menu, featuring the specialties of Italy's Piemonte region—including some wonderful pastas—lists the date on which a particular dish first made its appearance. Scented by gardenias, oleander and jasmine, the lovely, secluded garden is a coveted spot for summer dining.

Brasserie 8 1/2

009

9 W. 57th St. (bet. Fifth & Sixth Aves.)

Subway:	57 St	Monday - Friday 11:30am - 3pm
Phone:	212-829-0812	& 5:30pm - 11pm
Fax:	212-829-0821	Saturday 5:30pm - 9pm
e-mail:	N/A	Sunday 11:30am - 3pm & 5:30pm - 9pm
Web:	www.brasserie8andahalf.com	Closed major holidays
Prices:	$$$	

Get ready to make a theatrical entrance down the red-carpeted spiral staircase to gain access to the dining room here. At the foot of the stairs, you'll find a circular lounge. A few more steps down, the brasserie is a big, bold, contemporary affair, with a white-tile floor, brown-leather banquettes, and a striking glass mural walling off the kitchen. Well-executed dishes range from truffle-crusted loin of lamb to seared tuna and foie gras. Lunch is particularly busy, but with more than 200 seats, the restaurant copes easily. Service is speedy, ideal for those who need to get back to the office, or to go home to practice their grand entrances.

Brasserie LCB

010

60 W. 55th St. (bet. Fifth & Sixth Aves.)

Subway:	5 Av - 53 St	Monday - Sunday noon - 3pm
Phone:	212-688-6525	& 5pm - 10:30pm
Fax:	212-258-2102	
e-mail:	N/A	
Web:	www.brasserielcb.com	
Prices:	$$	

Formerly La Côte Basque, this Belle Epoque-style brasserie has been reinvented by its venerable chef and owner Jean-Jacques Rachou. In its present incarnation, LCB eschews the pomp and circumstance of La Côte Basque and replaces it with a more casual ambience of black leatherette banquettes, large framed mirrors, tulip-shaped light fixtures, and a mosaic-tile floor. A varied menu respects the regional French *terroir* with specialties such as choucroute Alsacienne, Dover sole meunière, cassoulet with duck confit, and prime steak au poivre. The lunch menu du jour, with a choice of three courses, represents a good balance of quality for price.

Cité

Steakhouse

011

120 W. 51st St. (bet. Sixth & Seventh Aves.)

Subway:	50 St
Phone:	212-956-7100
Fax:	212-956-7157
e-mail:	citenyoffice@swrg.com
Web:	www.citerestaurant.com
Prices:	$$$

Monday - Friday 11:30am - 11:30pm
Saturday - Sunday 5pm - 11:30pm

XXX

&

You don't have to wonder for long why the atmosphere at this steakhouse is always so animated: after 8pm on weeknights (and after 5pm on Sundays), Cité's "wine dinners" are available. For a fixed price, you get your choice of three courses and you can enjoy unlimited wine to go with them—a terrific value any way you look at it. The surroundings themselves are also partly responsible for the diners' purr of satisfaction; the room is done in a striking Art Deco style, and the staff gives the immediate impression that you're in good hands. If it's a lighter menu you crave, the Cité Grill next door offers an informal setting where you can nosh on burgers, sandwiches and salads.

Del Frisco's

Steakhouse

012

1221 Sixth Ave. (at 49th St.)

Subway:	49 St
Phone:	212-575-5129
Fax:	212-575-5491
e-mail:	N/A
Web:	www.delfriscos.com
Prices:	$$$

Monday - Friday 11am - midnight
Saturday 5pm - midnight
Sunday 5pm - 10pm

XXX

&

This sprawling bi-level Midtown steakhouse, with its wraparound floor-to-ceiling windows, exudes a strong aura of corporate muscle. On the ground level of the McGraw Hill Building, Del Frisco's attracts a suited clientele who all look like they know their way around a balance sheet. When the fresh-baked loaf of bread arrives at the table, it's expected that you'll tear into it with your hands (no neat slicing with a knife). Then it's straight to the prime aged, corn-fed steaks from the Midwest, in portions that would make a Texan proud. After delivering your steak, the waiter will remain at your side until you have carved into it and determined that it's cooked to your satisfaction.

Esca

013

402 W. 43rd St. (bet. Ninth & Tenth Aves.)

Subway:	42 St - Port Authority Bus Terminal	Monday noon - 2:30pm
Phone:	212-564-7272	& 5pm - 10:30pm
Fax:	N/A	Tuesday - Saturday noon - 2:30pm
e-mail:	N/A	& 5pm - 11:30pm
Web:	www.esca-nyc.com	Sunday 4:30pm - 10:30pm
Prices:	$$$	

Esca translates as "bait" in Italian, and the fish are indeed biting at this venture headed by chef/partner David Pasternack. Placed in a less crowded part of Midtown, Esca boasts a bright, yellow-toned décor that still looks—five years later—as fresh as the Italian-style seafood that's served here. On the regularly changing menu, raw fish is featured under the heading "crudo," while fish dishes in "secondi" allow the fish to net the starring role without disguising it under a cover of competing flavors. Wine appears prominently displayed in shelves around the room. About ten selections from the all-Italian wine list are available by the quartino (a liter-size carafe).

Estiatorio Milos

014

125 W. 55th St. (bet. Sixth & Seventh Aves.)

Subway:	57 St	Monday - Friday noon - 2:45pm
Phone:	212-245-7400	& 5pm - 11:30pm
Fax:	212-245-4828	Saturday 5pm - 11:30pm
e-mail:	N/A	Sunday 5pm - 10:45pm
Web:	www.milos.ca	
Prices:	$$$	

It's not nice to fool Mother Nature, and at Milos, they don't try. After all, when you use top-quality organic ingredients, you don't need to do much to improve on them. The concept here is simple: you choose your fish (there are a few meat selections, too) from the fresh-from-the-sea array displayed at the counter, decide the weight you want, and specify how you want it to be cooked—charcoal-grilled or baked in sea salt. Soon, it will appear at your table, adorned simply with olive oil and lemon sauce. The cacophonous dining room melds industrial modern with Greek taverna in a setting so bright you'll want to wear shades. Deliriously sweet baklava makes the perfect end to your meal.

Firebird

015

365 W. 46th St. (bet. Eighth & Ninth Aves.)

Subway:	42 St - Port Authority Bus Terminal	Wednesday & Saturday
Phone:	212-586-0244	11:15am - 2:30pm
Fax:	212-957-2983	Tuesday - Saturday 5:15pm - 11:15pm
e-mail:	N/A	Sunday 5:15pm - 8:15pm
Web:	www.firebirdrestaurant.com	Closed Monday
Prices:	$$$	

ȲȲȲ
&

Dramatic décor marks this "pre-Revolutionary" Russian establishment on Restaurant Row (as this block of West 46th Street is popularly known). Drama befits the place, though, standing as it does so near the theater district. The dining room is nearly as intricate as a Fabergé egg, every inch of it set about with Russian art, rare Russian books, plush fabrics and wall sconces dripping with crystals. As you'd expect, the menu lists Russian specialties such as Ukrainian borscht, and an extensive selection of caviar, both local and from the Caspian Sea. The staff, costumed in Cossack garb, provides well-orchestrated formal service—just don't expect the check to come in rubles.

Il Tinello

016

16 W. 56th St. (bet. Fifth & Sixth Aves.)

Subway:	57 St	Monday - Friday Noon - 3pm
Phone:	212-245-4388	& 5pm - 10pm
Fax:	N/A	Saturday 5pm - 10pm
e-mail:	N/A	Closed Sunday & July 1 - 23
Web:	N/A	
Prices:	$$$	

ȲȲȲ
&

In the rush for all things modern and new in the city, it's always refreshing to find a little remnant of old New York, especially when it's tucked away in Midtown. With its long standing (the restaurant opened in 1986) and fierce adherence to tradition, Il Tinello is just that. The extensive menu offers all the classics, and then some; there's even a selection of pizzas (as in carpaccio pizza with truffle oil and arugula). Dressed in immaculate white jackets, the all-male waitstaff services tables with what can only be called old-school polish. The comfortable room boasts an understated elegance, and overall, the place runs as smoothly and reliably as your grandfather's pocket watch.

Keens Steakhouse

017

72 W. 36th St. (bet. Fifth & Sixth Aves.)

Subway:	34 St - Herald Square
Phone:	212-947-3636
Fax:	212-594-6371
e-mail:	bonnie@keens.com
Web:	www.keens.com
Prices:	$$$

Monday - Friday 11:45am - 3pm
& 5pm - 10:30pm
Saturday 5pm - 10:30pm
Sunday 5pm - 9pm

XXX This macho palace of steaks and single-malt Scotch has been around since 1885, the lone survivor of the erstwhile Herald Square Theater District. A palpable sense of history pervades the restaurant, which enforced a strict men-only rule until 1901. That's the year British actress Lillie Langtry challenged Keens' discriminatory policy in court, and won. Look up on the ceiling to see the restaurant's collection of clay smoking pipes, another vestige of its men's-club days. Efficient waiters clad in bow ties serve up hearty steaks and Keens' legendary mutton chops, in portions large enough to satisfy even the most fanatical of Atkins-diet fundamentalists.

Manhattan Ocean Club

018

57 W. 58th St. (bet. Fifth & Sixth Aves.)

Subway:	57 St
Phone:	212-371-7777
Fax:	212-371-9362
e-mail:	mocnyoffice@swrg.com
Web:	www.manhattanoceanclub.com
Prices:	$$$

Monday - Thursday noon - 4pm
& 5pm - 10pm
Friday noon - 4pm & 5pm - 11pm
Saturday 5pm - 11pm
Sunday 5pm - 10pm
Closed Thanksgiving Day & Christmas

XXX This 20-year veteran of the Midtown restaurant scene was treated to a facelift by Adam Tihany in 2004. New furnishings, dark woods and a cream-colored coat of paint rejuvenated the two-tiered dining room, which is highlighted by a collection of Picasso ceramic plates displayed in framed shadowboxes. In spring 2005, the Manhattan Ocean Club launched a new menu, emphasizing fish grilled «a la plancha» with a choice of sauces, from five-herb aioli to basic extra virgin olive oil and balsamic vinegar. There are other entrées, too, ranging from spicy shrimp salad, to the Ocean Club lobster roll and crispy crab cakes with shaved fennel.

Michael's

Contemporary

019

24 W. 55th St. (bet. Fifth & Sixth Aves.)

Subway:	57 St	Monday - Friday noon - 2:30pm
Phone:	212-767-0555	& 5:30pm - 10:30pm
Fax:	212-581-6778	Saturday 11:30am - 2pm
e-mail:	N/A	& 5:30pm - 10:30pm
Web:	www.michaelsnewyork.com	Sunday 11:30am - 2pm
Prices:	**$$$**	Closed major holidays

East Coast expense accounts meet West Coast cooking at this busy Midtown institution. California style infuses the interesting array of American dishes here. And it's no wonder, since chef/owner Michael McCarty, who founded the original Michael's near the beach in Santa Monica in 1979, developed his market-driven menu way before using fresh, seasonal fare was fashionable. In the airy dining room, light pours in from a wall of windows, illuminating the artwork on the peach-tone walls. Favored by media moguls, Michael's gets mobbed at lunchtime, and the waitstaff has to run at a big-city pace. The fact that everyone seems to be a regular here is proof enough that they're up to the task.

Petrossian

French

020

182 W. 58th St. (at Seventh Ave.)

Subway:	57 St	Monday - Friday 11:30am - 3pm
Phone:	212-245-2214	& 5:30pm - 11:30pm
Fax:	212-245-2214	Saturday 11:30am - 4pm
e-mail:	info@petrossian.com	& 5:30pm - 11:30pm
Web:	www.petrossian.com	Sunday 5:30pm - 10:30pm
Prices:	**$$$**	

You'll want to linger on the sidewalk to marvel at the ornate Renaissance-style 1907 Alwyn Court Building that frames the entrance to Petrossian. Opened in the 1980s, this is the New York sister to Petrossian Paris, which has been delighting French diners since the 1920s. It was then that the two Petrossian brothers from Armenia made caviar the toast of the town in Paris, and founded the company that now ranks as the premier importer of Russian caviar—the restaurant's specialty. Located a block from Carnegie Hall, Petrossian showcases ingredients that are as luxurious as its surroundings, which are decked out with Lalique crystal wall sconces, etched Erté mirrors, and Limoges china.

Remi

021

Italian

145 W. 53rd St. (bet. Sixth & Seventh Aves.)

Subway:	7 Av
Phone:	212-581-4242
Fax:	212-581-5948
e-mail:	N/A
Web:	www.reminyc.com
Prices:	$$

Monday - Friday noon - 2:30pm
& 5pm - 11pm
Saturday 5pm - 11:30pm
Sunday 5pm - 10pm

XXX
&
⌂

Dreams of Venice come to mind when you enter this perennially busy Italian restaurant. Between the Venetian-glass chandelier, the fresco-like 120-foot-long mural of Venice that covers one wall, and the bright sunlight streaming in through the large front windows, there's much to suggest that lovely city. Indeed, remi means "oars" in Italian, a reference to the famous canals of Venice. In keeping with this theme, the food here derives much of its influence from the Veneto. The homemade pastas are particularly good, but be sure to leave room for dessert. Managers keep a watchful eye over the dining room, ensuring that the whole establishment operates like a well-oiled machine.

San Domenico NY

022

Italian

240 Central Park South (Broadway & Seventh Ave.)

Subway:	59 St - Columbus Cir
Phone:	212-265-5959
Fax:	212-397-0844
e-mail:	sandomny@aol.com
Web:	www.sandomenicony.com
Prices:	$$$

Monday - Friday noon - 2:30pm
& 5:30pm - 11pm
Saturday 5pm - 11:30pm
Sunday 11:30am - 3pm & 5pm - 10pm

XXX
⌐

There's no denying that San Domenico has a lot going for it: it's enviable location across from Central Park; its sumptuous ambience, recently given a facelift by designer Adam Tihany; its memorable Italian cuisine. Opened by restaurateur Tony May (formerly of the Rainbow Room) in 1988, San Domenico shows off a style that is matched by its well-heeled patrons as well as by the team of waiters in ties and waistcoats. Tihany's redesign shows off leather-wrapped columns, fabric-covered light "boxes" and furnishings imported from Italy. House-made pastas shine here, with a delicacy and a lightness all their own. If you're watching your wallet, go for the set-price lunch.

Shaan of India

023

57 W. 48th St. (bet. Fifth & Sixth Aves.)

Subway:	47-50 Sts - Rockefeller Ctr	Monday - Sunday noon - 3pm
Phone:	212-977-8400	& 5pm - 11pm
Fax:	212-977-3069	
e-mail:	N/A	
Web:	www.shaanofindia.com	
Prices:	$$	

A large red awning with "Shaan" emblazoned on it, and a doorman wearing a traditional tunic mark the Midtown location of this stylish Indian restaurant, whose name means "pride." Marble, wood carvings and intricate, framed Indian tapestries decorate the high-ceilinged dining space, where immaculately set tables are well spaced for private conversations. The extensive menu travels across the Indian continent with its list of dishes. Presented in copper pots, the creamy, coconut-infused Goan curries especially stand out. Indian breads, such as naan and pappadam, are fresh and tasty. The lunch buffet attracts hordes of office workers, while in the evening, live Indian music entertains diners.

Town

024

15 W. 56th St. (bet. Fifth & Sixth Aves.)

Subway:	57 St	Monday - Thursday noon - 2:30pm
Phone:	212-582-4445	& 5:30pm - 10:30pm
Fax:	212-582-5535	Friday noon - 2:30pm & 5:30pm - 11pm
e-mail:	N/A	Saturday 5:30pm - 11pm
Web:	www.townnyc.com	Sunday 11am - 2:30pm
Prices:	$$$	& 5:30pm - 10pm

At the Chambers Hotel, "a night on the town" translates as a meal at the property's stylish restaurant, located downstairs from the lobby bar. The discreetly understated yet hip décor, designed by David Rockwell in blond woods and cascades of beads, appeals to Gotham fashionistas and well-heeled tourists. First independent venture by chef Goeffrey Zakarian, Town opened in 2001. Zakarian prides himself on the quality of his ingredients, and the menu changes frequently to include the freshest market produce. At Town, innovative dishes—risotto of escargots, Basque-style veal tongue, chocolate beignets—are presented to catch your eye. To top it off, service is well-timed and courteous.

V Steakhouse

025

10 Columbus Circle (in the Time Warner Center)

Subway:	59 St - Columbus Cir
Phone:	212-823-9500
Fax:	212-823-9470
e-mail:	N/A
Web:	www.jean-georges.com
Prices:	$$$$

Monday - Sunday noon - 3pm
& 5:30pm - 11:30pm

Enjoying a sweeping view of Central Park, V Steakhouse is couched on the fourth floor of the Time Warner Center, headquarters for some of the best new restaurants in the city. All of these places boast a unique sense of identity, but none more so than Jean-Georges Vongerichten's striking baroque steakhouse, all done up in gold leaf and rich reds. After all, who needs park views when you can immerse yourself in French designer Jacques Garcia's fairytale fantasy of handcrafted brass trees lit by sparkling chandeliers? The menu centers on grass-fed steaks from Niman Ranch, with a large choice of sides as well as fresh fish. As you'd expect, service here is seamless and well organized.

Abboccato

026

136 W. 55th St. (bet. Sixth & Seventh Aves.)

Subway:	57 St
Phone:	212-265-4000
Fax:	212-265-4007
e-mail:	N/A
Web:	www.abboccato.com
Prices:	$$$

Monday - Saturday noon - 3pm
& 5:30pm - 11pm
Sunday noon - 10pm

Bought to you by the Livanos family, whose stable includes Molyvos and Oceana, this stylish Italian restaurant bears the hallmarks of these experienced restaurateurs. The menu eschews the ubiquitous offerings found in many Italian eateries and instead provides more unusual fare such as half-moon pasta filled with beets and Gorgonzola Dolce, suckling pig cooked in milk and hazelnuts, and Vaniglia e Cioccolato, vanilla-scented braised veal cheeks, served with soft polenta and chunks of wild boar braised in red wine accented with spices and bitter chocolate. The dining room has a certain understated elegance, and the staff seems genuinely interested in their guests' well-being.

Acqua Pazza

Italian

36 W. 52nd St. (bet. Fifth & Sixth Aves.)

Subway:	5 Av - 53 St	Monday - Friday 11am - 3pm
Phone:	212-582-6900	& 5:30pm - 10:30pm
Fax:	212-765-5419	Saturday 5:30pm - 10:30pm
e-mail:	info@acquapazzanyc.com	Closed Sunday
Web:	www.acquapazzanyc.com	
Prices:	$$$	

The name Acqua Pazza (Italian for "crazy water") recalls a practice of fishermen in southern Italy, who simply doused their catch of the day with a little olive oil and baked the fish whole in seawater. Indeed, the kitchen at this stylish Midtown establishment takes much of its epicurean inspiration from the coastline of Italy (meat and pasta lovers will find selections aplenty to satisfy them, too). Surroundings here are crisp and sophisticated without any undue pomp and circumstance, which is why the atmosphere remains so convivial (walk past this place in the rain and you can't help but be drawn in). The staff, smartly attired in blue shirts, provides prompt and efficient service.

Bar Americain

American

152 W. 52nd St. (bet. Sixth & Seventh Aves.)

Subway:	7 Av	Monday - Friday noon - 2:30pm
Phone:	212-265-9700	& 5pm - 11:30pm
Fax:	212-265-9025	Saturday - Sunday 5pm - 11:30pm
e-mail:	N/A	
Web:	www.baramericain.com	
Prices:	$$$	

Bobby Flay opened this spacious new restaurant in May 2005, and judging by the crowds that are already flocking here, the place is an instant hit. Bar Americain's name brings to mind the classic brasserie, which, in this case, David Rockwell has painted in warm orange hues, with cheese-wheel-shaped lanterns hanging from the barrel-vaulted ceiling. The cooking sets its heart in the U.S., yet the dishes challenge your expectations with some far-reaching (in a geographical sense) interpretations; rotisserie poussin, for example, is paired with red chiles and fry bread salad. Cocktails, such as the Hemingway Dacquiri or the Bronx Cocktail, have their own American flavor.

Beacon

029

25 W. 56th St. (bet. Fifth & Sixth Aves.)

Subway:	57 St	Monday - Thursday noon - 2:30pm
Phone:	212-332-0500	& 5:30pm - 10pm
Fax:	212-262-4787	Friday - Saturday noon - 2:30pm
e-mail:	N/A	& 5pm - 10:30pm
Web:	www.beaconnyc.com	Sunday 11:30am - 2:30pm & 4pm - 8pm
Prices:	$$	

XX
&
A

Open-fire cooking is the theme at Beacon, where a wood-burning oven, rotisserie and grill are the preferred means of cooking. The reason it works so well is that chef and co-owner Waldy Malouf uses the best-quality raw ingredients he can get his hands on. Whether it's a spit-roasted suckling pig or a wood-roasted Catskill trout, there's something on the menu to appeal to most any appetite—and bringing your appetite is de rigueur, since the portions here are generous. The best tables are on the mezzanine for those who want to enjoy the view of the bustling dining room below; diners who consider cooking to be a spectator sport should grab one of the ringside seats by the open kitchen.

Becco

030

355 W. 46th St. (bet. Eighth & Ninth Aves.)

Subway:	50 St	Monday - Friday noon - 3pm
Phone:	212-397-7597	& 5pm - midnight
Fax:	N/A	Saturday 11:30am - 2:30pm
e-mail:	N/A	& 4pm - midnight
Web:	www.becconyc.com	Sunday 5pm - 10pm
Prices:	$$	

XX

If you're seeking a quick bite before a show, this Restaurant Row town house in the Theater District can get you in and out with time to spare before the curtain rises. If you have a free evening, come later to appreciate hearty Italian cooking in less frenetic surroundings. Hanging copper pots, Italian landscapes and shelves full of country knick knacks dress the three separate dining spaces here. Owned by Lidia Bastianich and her son, Joseph, Becco features a varied menu augmented by a list of specials. For those with big appetites, the *Sinfonia di pasta* offers an abbondanza of unlimited portions of the chef's three daily pasta creations—just make sure your pants have an elastic waist.

Manhattan Midtown West

Ben Benson's

Steakhouse

031

123 W. 52nd St. (bet. Sixth & Seventh Aves.)

Subway:	5 Av - 53 St
Phone:	212-581-8888
Fax:	212-581-1170
e-mail:	N/A
Web:	www.benbensons.com
Prices:	$$$$

Monday - Thursday noon - 11pm
Friday noon - midnight
Saturday 5pm - midnight
Sunday 5pm - 10pm

If you grimace at the mere thought of fusion cooking, then this is the place for you. Since 1982, Ben Benson has been serving Prime cuts of USDA meats and other classic American fare to its contented macho clientele of corporate power brokers and politicians. (It's easy to tell the regulars—their names are emblazoned on brass plaques set in the wainscoting.) The bright, high-ceiling dining room is airier than many of the wood-paneled steakhouses in town. Refreshingly, this New York steakhouse remains stubbornly independent from chain ownership. For those who favor al fresco dining, the spacious sidewalk terrace provides a pleasant setting in nice weather.

Blue Fin

Seafood

032

1567 Broadway (at 47th St.)

Subway:	49 St
Phone:	212-918-1400
Fax:	212-918-1462
e-mail:	N/A
Web:	www.brguestrestaurants.com
Prices:	$$$

Sunday - Thursday 11:30am - 4pm
& 5pm - midnight
Friday - Saturday 11:30am - 4pm
& 5pm - 1am

You'd think it would be easy to spot this two-tier 400-seat restaurant on Times Square, but Blue Fin seductively conceals itself behind its glass-front bar. Connected with the W Hotel Times Square, the restaurant adds another notch to Steve Hanson's belt. Downstairs, the dazzling design incorporates ocean-blue walls, polished mirrors reflecting glittering light, and a fanciful mobile of fish that seem to swim above the diners. Follow the floating staircase upstairs, where the mood turns sultry in the live-jazz club. The extensive menu celebrates all creatures from the sea, from black bass to big-eye tuna—including a selection of fresh oysters and clams from the raw bar.

Bricco

033

304 W. 56th St. (bet. Eighth & Ninth Aves.)

Subway:	Midtown - 57 St - 7 Av	Monday - Thursday noon - 11pm
Phone:	212-245-7160	Friday noon - midnight
Fax:	212-245-6085	Saturday 4pm - midnight
e-mail:	info@bricconyc.com	Sunday 4pm - 11pm
Web:	www.bricconyc.com	Closed major holidays
Prices:	$$	

⅄⅄

Amore comes to mind when you see the rose-red walls and autographed lipstick kisses that cover the ceiling in this romantic Italian place. The dining space spreads over two floors, with the upstairs room being the sunnier and more tranquil of the two. If it's action you want, stick to the first floor, where chefs fire pizzas in the wood-burning oven and waiters scurry around the perpetually busy room. Despite the hectic pace, the waitstaff skillfully manages to keep the dishes coming without rushing diners. The strength of the menu lies in its wide choice of savory homemade pasta dishes, which are particularly light and flavorful.

Bryant Park Grill

034

25 W. 40th St. (bet. Fifth & Sixth Aves.)

Subway:	42 St - Bryant Pk	Monday - Wednesday 11:30am - 3:30pm
Phone:	212-840-6500	& 5pm - 10pm
Fax:	212-840-8122	Thursday - Saturday 5pm - 11pm
e-mail:	bryantpark@arkrestaurants.com	Sunday 11:30am - 3:30pm
Web:	www.arkrestaurants.com	& 5pm - 10:30pm
Prices:	$$$	

⅄⅄
&
♨
☕

Bryant Park Grill enjoys an enviable location overlooking Midtown's only green oasis and adjacent to the stately, Beaux-Arts New York Public Library. The restaurant takes its design cues from the park, with abundant natural light and a colorful, wall-length bird mural. Lunch and dinner menus are similar, with pasta dishes and grilled meat and fish entrées; a few extra salad selections are available at midday. A new feature, the children's fixed-price brunch menu (for ages 12 and under), includes favorites like scrambled eggs, blueberry pancakes and grilled cheese sandwiches. Ask for a window table for the best park views, or dine on the pleasant terrace in summer.

China Grill

A s i a n

60 W. 53rd St. (bet. Fifth & Sixth Aves.)

Subway:	7 Av	Monday - Wednesday 11:45am - 11pm
Phone:	212-333-7788	Thursday - Friday 11:45am - midnight
Fax:	212-581-9299	Saturday 5:30pm - midnight
e-mail:	N/A	Sunday 5:30pm - 10pm
Web:	www.chinagrillmgt.com	
Prices:	$$$	

If ever a restaurant represented Midtown and all its corporate machismo, it's China Grill. Set within the CBS Building, the cavernous space, with its 30-foot ceilings, acres of black marble, and open kitchen, can get awfully noisy, but that doesn't seem to dissuade the large numbers of corporate diners who crowd the place every day for lunch. The restaurant bills their food as "world cuisine," which, in this case, means the appetizers and entrées take their influences from across Asia, while the desserts bear assorted European accents. Enormous portions of dishes, such as barbecued salmon with Chinese mustard sauce or grilled Szechuan beef with sake and soy, are perfect for sharing.

DB Bistro Moderne

C o n t e m p o r a r y

55 W. 44th St. (bet. Fifth & Sixth Aves.)

Subway:	5 Av	Monday - Saturday noon - 2:30pm
Phone:	212-391-2400	& 5:45pm - 11pm
Fax:	212-391-1188	Sunday 5pm - 10pm
e-mail:	info@danielnyc.com	Closed major holidays
Web:	www.danielnyc.com	
Prices:	$$$	

More moderne than bistro, Daniel Boulud's classy Midtown restaurant blends the freshest American ingredients with French recipes in a way that would make the UN proud. A glass bar divides the space into two dining rooms; the more informal front room boasts deep-red, rubbed-plaster walls hung with large, lustrous floral photographs that are reflected in mirrors on the opposite wall. Arranged by category (shellfish, asparagus, red meat, tuna), the impressive menu singles out the house specialties—Boulud's smoked salmon, tomato tarte Tatin, Baeckeoffe of escargots—as well as the dishes of the day. Effortlessly efficient service adds to the dining experience here.

Etcetera Etcetera

352 W. 44th St. (bet. Eighth & Ninth Aves.)

Subway: 42 St - Port Authority Bus Terminal
Phone: 212-399-4141
Fax: 212-399-4899
e-mail: etcrest@aol.com
Web: www.etcrestaurant.com
Prices: $$

Tuesday - Saturday 5pm - 11:15pm
Sunday 5pm - 10pm
Closed Monday & major holidays

ViceVersa's little sister opened in 2005, and shares the same combination of stylish surroundings and confident, affable service. Like its older sibling, Etcetera Etcetera's menu is Italian, but here they add Mediterranean accents such as feta cheese, preserved lemons and Serrano ham. Philippe Starck designed the molded plastic chairs in pastel colors to complement the ebony woodwork and the gray ceramic-tile wall in the dining room; modern artwork and aluminum sculptures complete the picture. Located just two blocks from The Great White Way, Etcetera Etcetera makes a convenient and pleasant place for a pre- or post-theater meal. The large room upstairs is perfect for private parties.

Manhattan Midtown West

Frankie & Johnnie's
S t e a k h o u s e

039

32 W. 37th St. (bet. Fifth & Sixth Aves.)

Subway:	34 St - Penn Station	Monday - Thursday noon - 2:30pm
Phone:	212-947-8940	& 4pm - 10:30pm
Fax:	212-629-5952	Friday noon - 2:30pm & 4pm - 11pm
e-mail:	N/A	Saturday 4pm - 11pm
Web:	www.frankieandjohnnies.com	Closed Sunday
Prices:	$$$	

The fourth and newest location of Frankie & Johnnie's Steakhouse empire (the first was established in 1926 on W. 45th Street) offers diners a little bit of history in the heart of the Garment District. The renovated town house in which it is set was once the home of acting legend John Drew Barrymore. In fact, Barrymore's library, with its coffered ceiling and original fireplace, forms part of the masculine, wood-panelled main dining room on the second floor. Diners with booming baritone voices feel no need to tone down their bonhomie while chowing down on some serious cuts of Prime dry-aged beef here. No one seems to mind, though; the all-male brigade of waiters has seen it all before.

Gallagher's
S t e a k h o u s e

040

228 W. 52nd St. (bet. Broadway & Eighth Ave.)

Subway:	50 St	Monday - Sunday noon - midnight
Phone:	212-245-5336	
Fax:	212-245-5426	
e-mail:	info@gallagherssteak.com	
Web:	www.gallaghersnysteakhouse.com	
Prices:	$$$	

A taste of old New York is what you'll get at Gallagher's. Established in 1927 next door to what is now the Neil Simon Theater, Gallagher's satisfies carnivores with beef, beef and more beef. From the outside, you'd think you were in front of a butcher's shop; all you see in the window are rows of assorted cuts of beef hanging in the meat locker. Past that, you enter a wood-paneled dining room where the waiters wear gold-trimmed blazers, and the walls are lined with photographs of Broadway stars, politicians, and athletes of both the human and equine varieties. While it doesn't come cheap, the beef shows a quality that really shines. Gallagher's is, as they say, "New York City to the bone."

Giovanni

041

47 W. 55th St. (bet. Fifth & Sixth Aves.)

Subway:	57 St	Monday - Saturday 11:30am - 11:30pm
Phone:	212-262-2828	Sunday noon - 10:30pm
Fax:	N/A	
e-mail:	info@giovanni-ristorante.com	
Web:	www.giovanni-ristorante.com	
Prices:	$$	

✗✗

Coincidentally, both the chef and the owner here are named Giovanni, although they're two different people. Either way, you know you're going to be well looked after, since both men are duly invested in this establishment. You'll find genuine warmth at Giovanni's, not only in the affable service, but in the sunny interior design, which looks to the colors and textures of the Italian countryside for inspiration. In addition to the main room, there are a number of different dining areas, each of which has its own personality (the Pavilion Room is cloaked beneath a Palio-style striped tent). The menu travels from the Dolomites to the Adriatic Sea in northeast Italy for its regional cuisine.

Ida Mae

042

111 W. 38th St. (bet. Broadway & Sixth Ave.)

Subway:	Times Sq - 42 St	Monday - Friday noon - 3pm
Phone:	212-704-0038	& 6pm - 10pm
Fax:	212-704-0501	Saturday 6pm - 10pm
e-mail:	N/A	Closed Sunday
Web:	www.idamae.com	
Prices:	$$$	

✗✗
&

Shining like a beacon on an otherwise drab Garment District street is the glamorous "kitchen-n-lounge" called Ida Mae. In a city where all culinary bases seem covered, Ida Mae adds down-home Southern to the mix. Here, though, the traditional fare of the South receives a thoroughly modern makeover with the addition of both Caribbean influences and classic French twists. You'll find Louisiana crab cakes and barbecue shrimp on the menu, but also kicked-up combinations like lobster with grits and crayfish butter, and Cajun tuna with curried plantain. The exuberantly decorated room divides its space with the chic lounge/bar, where DJ's and live jazz music entertain diners on a regular basis.

Josephs Citarella

Mediterranean

043

1240 Sixth Ave. (at 49th St.)

Subway:	47-50 Sts - Rockefeller Ctr
Phone:	212-332-1515
Fax:	212-332-1590
e-mail:	N/A
Web:	www.josephscitarella.com
Prices:	$$$

Monday - Friday 11:30am - 2:30pm
& 5:30pm - 11pm
Saturday 5:30pm - 11pm
Closed Sunday

This pretty 19th-century house may hunker below the towers of busy Rockefeller Center, but as the hostess whisks you, via elevator, to the upstairs dining room, you'll find yourself transported to a tranquil Midtown sanctuary. The dining room sports light woods and lots of large windows, but its most striking features are the little portholes filled with color-changing displays of shells and coral. This seaside theme continues in the Mediterranean menu, where dishes range from bouillabaisse to scallops ceviche to lobster risotto. Best to order fish here; after all, the restaurant is owned by its namesake, Joe Gurrera, who runs the local chain of Citarella seafood shops.

Koi

Japanese

044

40 W. 40th St. (bet. Fifth & Sixth Aves.)

Subway:	42 St - Bryant Pk
Phone:	212-921-3330
Fax:	212-921-3360
e-mail:	mail@koirestaurant.com
Web:	www.koirestaurant.com
Prices:	$$$

Monday - Friday noon - 2:30pm
& 5:30pm - 11pm
Saturday 5:30pm - 11pm
Sunday 6pm - 10pm

This New York offshoot of the über-trendy flagship in West Hollywood opened in March 2005 in the Bryant Park Hotel, and already it's packed with the young, the restless, and the affluent. The first thing you'll notice is the enormous white lattice canopy that dominates the dining room; underneath it, many of the elements of feng shui have been incorporated into the eye-popping design (excepting the pulsating music at night). The menu is equally à la mode: an extensive choice of sushi and sashimi, as well as fusion fare with some creative combinations. Dinnertime is when this place really starts jumping, so if you want to have a conversation without sign language, you'd better go for lunch.

La Masseria

045

235 W. 48th St. (bet. Broadway & Eighth Ave.)

Subway:	50 St	Monday - Saturday noon - 3pm
Phone:	212-582-2111	& 5pm - midnight
Fax:	212-582-2420	Sunday noon - 10pm
e-mail:	masserianyc@aol.com	
Web:	N/A	
Prices:	$$	

With its wrought-iron chandeliers, beamed ceiling, and walls plastered with an array of antique farming implements, La Masseria's décor takes its cue from the ancient fortified farmhouses of Puglia. The overall effect creates a warm country feel in the dining room, which retains a hint of intimacy despite its large size—especially the space at the back, with its own mezzanine level. The cooking adds another delightfully rustic note with dishes such as rabbit slowly roasted and served in an earthenware pot, and homemade stuffed fresh mozzarella—a house speciality. If you're looking for a relaxed meal, La Masseria operates at a less frenetic pace than many places in this neighborhood.

Marseille

046

630 Ninth Ave. (at 44th St.)

Subway:	42 St - Port Authority Bus Terminal	Monday - Sunday noon - 3pm
Phone:	212-333-2323	& 5:30pm - midnight
Fax:	212-333-4488	
e-mail:	marseillerestaurant@hotmail.com	
Web:	www.marseillenyc.com	
Prices:	$$	

As vibrant and bustling as the southern French city for which it's named, Marseille boasts a Casablanca feel with its handmade Art Deco floor tiles, stained glass, green-trimmed arches and zinc bar. The menu is basically French but it includes overtones from Morocco, with dishes ranging from bouillabaisse to lamb tagine. Owing to Marseille's proximity to theaters (the restaurant is two blocks west of Times Square), it's busy almost constantly; the waitstaff handles the crowds with visible ease, though. Downstairs, the dimly lit lounge hints at something both secretive and alluring; while you're down there, check out the wine cellar—it's housed in a former bank vault.

Manhattan *Midtown West*

Molyvos

Greek

047

871 Seventh Ave. (bet. 55th & 56th Sts.)

Subway:	Midtown 57 St - 7 Av	Monday - Thursday noon - 3pm
Phone:	212-582-7500	& 5:30pm - 11:30pm
Fax:	212-582-7502	Friday noon - 3pm & 5:30pm - midnight
e-mail:	N/A	Saturday noon - 3pm & 5pm - midnight
Web:	www.molyvos.com	Sunday noon - 3pm & 5pm - 11pm
Prices:	$$	

XX

An attractive Greek storefront façade beckons diners to Molyvos, named for the Greek village on the island of Lesvos, where owner John Livanos grew up. Inside, Greek artifacts, ceramics, and vintage family photographs create a warm, homey ambience in the roomy dining space; mirrors and glass partitions lend a brasserie feel. Chef/partner James Botsacos designed the menu based on Greek home-style dishes, which he reproduces with contemporary flair. Many of the dishes are cooked in a wood-fired oven, and everything, including the phyllo dough, is made on the premises. Begin your meal with a round of shared mezes (small plates), washed down with a glass of Greek ouzo.

Nick & Stef's

Steakhouse

048

9 Penn Plaza (bet. Seventh & Eighth Aves.)

Subway:	34 St - Penn Station	Monday - Friday 11:30am - 3pm
Phone:	212-563-4444	& 5pm - 10pm
Fax:	212-563-9184	Saturday 5pm - 10pm
e-mail:	N/A	Closed Sunday
Web:	www.nickandstefs.com	
Prices:	$$$	

XX
&

Sports fans going to Madison Square Garden to catch a Knicks or a Rangers game will no doubt appreciate the succulent cuts of Prime beef served at Nick & Stef's. Portions are hefty, and you can choose sides from macaroni and cheddar to asparagus to go with your steak (of course, they also offer the requisite baked potatoes and creamed spinach). You'll find fresh seafood on the menu, too, in the form of Maine lobster, meaty crab cakes, shrimp scampi and more. What sets this steakhouse apart is its contemporary feel; with its large windows, angled pine ceiling, and warm tones, Joachim Splichal's version of a steakhouse—named for his twin sons—is less masculine than many others in the city.

Orso

049

322 W. 46th St. (bet. Eighth & Ninth Aves.)

Subway:	49 St	Sunday - Tuesday noon - 11:45pm
Phone:	212-489-7212	Wednesday 11:30am - 11:45pm
Fax:	212-265-3383	Friday noon - 11:45pm
e-mail:	N/A	Saturday 11:30am - 11:45pm
Web:	www.orsorestaurant.com	
Prices:	$$	

XX

A respected member of the Restaurant Row dining fraternity, Orso concentrates on what it does well, and does it with aplomb. As at its two other branches, in Los Angeles and London, the restaurant offers diners a wide choice of Italian fare, running the gamut from risotto to pizza, calf's liver to monkfish. The dining room, done in warm pastel shades, accommodates those who come in for a quick meal before the theatre, as well as diners who are making an evening of it. Star gazers will be interested to know that the later you dine, the more likely you are to see an actor from one of the neighboring theaters catching a post-performance bite to eat.

Osteria Del Circo

050

120 W. 55th St. (bet. Sixth & Seventh Aves.)

Subway:	57 St	Monday - Friday 11:30am - 2:30pm
Phone:	212-265-3636	& 5:30pm - 11:30pm
Fax:	212-265-9283	Saturday - Sunday 5:30pm - 11:30pm
e-mail:	N/A	
Web:	www.osteriadelcirco.com	
Prices:	$$$	

XX

From the Maccioni family, who brought you the famous Le Cirque, comes this less formal but exuberantly decorated Italian restaurant. Here the circus motif dominates, from the big-top tent billowing from the ceiling to the trapeze that swings down over the bar. Clown and monkey figurines abound, and a sculptural acrobat overlooks diners from his lofty platform. With such a spirited décor, it's little wonder that the atmosphere is always lively, too. The menu offers a wide choice of attractively presented Northern Italian fare, along with daily changing specials (come Monday for tripe, Thursday for osso buco). As you leave, you can purchase a copy of the *Maccioni Family Cookbook*.

René Pujol

051

French

321 W. 51st St. (bet. Eighth & Ninth Aves.)

Subway:	50 St	Tuesday - Sunday noon - 2:30pm
Phone:	212-246-3023	& 5pm - 11pm
Fax:	212-245-5206	Closed Monday
e-mail:	N/A	& August 21 - September 7
Web:	www.renepujol.com	
Prices:	$$$	

ⅩⅩ

In a city where the trendy establishments du jour seems to eclipse other eateries, René Pujol stands out as a 30-year veteran in the Theater District. A loyal clientele often bring their offspring with them to ensure the restaurant's continued success with the next generation. What's the draw? They all come for the classic French cuisine, which remains true to its roots here by respecting Gallic culinary tradition. And they come for the calm atmosphere created in the carpeted dining room, with its lace curtains and working brick fireplace. The pre-theater rush can be a little overwhelming for newcomers, but the mature waitstaff handles it all with quiet proficiency.

Sardi's

052

American

234 W. 44th St. (bet. Broadway & Eighth Ave.)

Subway:	42 St - Port Authority Bus Terminal	Tuesday - Satuday 11:30am - 11:30pm
Phone:	212-221-8440	Sunday 11:30am - 8pm
Fax:	212-302-0865	Closed Monday
e-mail:	info@sardis.com	
Web:	www.sardis.com	
Prices:	$$$	

ⅩⅩ
&

Grande dame of New York's theater-district restaurants, Sardi's has been serving patrons of the Great White Way since the 1920s. Stage-curtain red is the color scheme in the dining room, from the walls to the leather banquettes, to the jackets worn by the mature brigade of waiters. And, of course, no self-respecting show-biz star can claim to have made it until they see their caricature on Sardi's walls. Exemplified by signature dishes like cannelloni au gratin and shrimp Sardi (sautéed in garlic sauce), the American fare here provides ample sustenance to get you through a show. (Portions tend toward the large size, so don't eat too much or you'll be snoozing through the second act.)

The Sea Grill

053

19 W. 49 St. (bet. Fifth & Sixth Aves.)

Subway:	47-50 Sts - Rockefeller Ctr	Monday - Friday 11:30am - 2:30pm
Phone:	212-332-7610	& 5pm - 10pm
Fax:	212-332-7677	Saturday 5pm - 10pm
e-mail:	N/A	Closed Sunday
Web:	www.seagrillnyc.com	
Prices:	$$$	

You'll descend in an elevator like a deep-sea diver down to this Rockefeller Center seafood emporium, where the blues and beiges of the stylish décor capture the colors of the sand and sea. As the bartender pours your aperitif, you can watch the skaters glide on the ice rink just outside the window. Offerings include everything from shellfish from the seafood bar to sushi and sashimi to roasted whole Greek daurade. There's a decidedly Iberian flair to the menu, from the fixed-price menu of Spanish dishes to the fish selections prepared à la plancha (on a traditional cast-iron griddle). Whatever your choice, you'll savor a daily changing selection of fish and shellfish, fresh off the boat.

Siam Inn

054

854 Eighth Ave. (bet. 51st & 52nd Sts.)

Subway:	50 St	Monday - Thursday 11:45am - 11pm
Phone:	212-757-4006	Friday - Saturday noon - 11:30pm
Fax:	N/A	Sunday noon - 10:30pm
e-mail:	siaminn@hotmail.com	
Web:	www.siaminn.com	
Prices:	⊜	

Harmony of tastes, colors and textures characterizes Thai cuisine, and this unpretentious restaurant successfully blends all these elements. Don't walk by the dark, windowed façade, or you'll miss out on fragrant and consistent Thai cooking. Set menus at lunch or dinner offer copious quantities of food for a reasonable price; dishes such as chicken green curry in silky coconut sauce, or shrimp Massaman are perfect for sharing. Sweet-natured service further elevates this place above the norm. The only incongruous note to the plain dining room, embellished with flowers and pictures of the Thai royal family, is the contemporary music that plays in the background.

Manhattan *Midtown West*

Sushi Zen

055

108 W. 44th St. (bet. Broadway & Sixth Ave.)

Subway:	42 St - Bryant Pk	Monday - Friday Noon - 2:45pm
Phone:	212-302-0707	& 5:30pm - 10pm
Fax:	212-944-7710	Saturday 5pm - 10pm
e-mail:	N/A	Closed Sunday
Web:	www.sushizen-ny.com	
Prices:	$$$	

Chef/owner Toshio Suzuki creates delicately textured sushi and sashimi, which, while it certainly tastes good, is also good for you (that's the Zen part). There's a wealth of different menus here. If you're new to raw fish, try the «Introduction to Sushi» from the sushi bar. Teriyaki, hand rolls, sashimi and more are all available à la carte, but you can also choose among three fixed-price tasting menus. The latter provide a good way of experiencing the kitchen's expertise, while you sample the impressive sake selection to accompany your meal. As the restaurant's name implies, decoration is minimal, but still bright and comfy. The helpful staff will happily guide you through the menu.

Thalia

056

828 Eighth Ave. (at 50th St.)

Subway:	50 St	Monday - Friday noon - 2:30pm
Phone:	212-399-4444	& 5:30pm - midnight
Fax:	212-399-3268	Saturday - Sunday 11:30am - 3pm
e-mail:	thaliamanager@restaurant.com	& 5:30pm - midnight
Web:	www.restaurantthalia.com	Closed Christmas Day
Prices:	$$	

Thalia couldn't be more convenient to the subway; its corner location is right next to the 50th Street exit. The setting is Theater District dramatic, from the elliptical bar to the soaring ceilings to the red walls decorated with vintage theater posters. At night, the volume turns up and the lights turn down with wall sconces holding lit votive candles, and individual alcoves at the rear of the room displaying backlit blown-glass bottles. Salads and sandwiches take center stage at lunchtime, while dinner brings more sophisticated fare (mushroom duxelle ravioli, sesame-crusted Altantic salmon) along with an elevated noise level. There's also a three-course, prix-fixe option at dinner.

Trattoria Dell' Arte

Italian

057

900 Seventh Ave. (bet. 56th & 57th Sts.)

Subway:	57 St
Phone:	212-245-9800
Fax:	212-265-3296
e-mail:	info@trattoriadellarte.com
Web:	www.trattoriadellarte.com
Prices:	$$

Monday - Saturday 11:45am - 3pm
& 5pm - 11:30pm
Sunday 11am - 3pm & 5pm - 10:30pm

The nose knows. Take your cue from the much-larger-than-life nose sculpture that tops the entrance to Trattoria dell Arte. Designed as an idiosyncratic artist's studio, the interior exhibits unfinished paintings, sculptural body parts, and a gallery of works depicting Italian noses. The trattoria, which is bigger than it first appears, sits opposite Carnegie Hall, and its location assures that the restaurant is constantly busy. A vast antipasto bar teems with assorted seafood, cured meats and cheeses, while the menu offers a substantial selection of Italian favorites from pappardelle to pannetone. Confident service adds to the contagiously exuberant air of the place.

Triomphe

Contemporary

058

49 W. 44th St. (bet. Fifth & Sixth Aves.)

Subway:	42 St - Bryant Pk
Phone:	212-453-4233
Fax:	N/A
e-mail:	N/A
Web:	www.triomphe-newyork.com
Prices:	$$$

Monday - Friday 11:45am - 2:30pm
& 5:30pm - 11:30pm
Saturday 5:30pm - 11:30pm
Closed Sunday

Triomphe may be tied to the Iroquois Hotel, but the restaurant is very much its own entity, with a separate entrance from the street. Opened in 2002, this discreet little place focuses on New American cooking with some original touches, always underscored by a resolutely classical base and a sound understanding of the ingredients used. The tiny dining room is not much bigger than the bar that adjoins it, but a wall of mirrors creates an illusion of space that would make a magician proud. With its pristine white color scheme, illuminated alcoves, and cheery staff, Triomphe as a whole has a freshness and an intimacy that you won't find in many places in this part of Midtown.

Manhattan Midtown West

Tuscan Square

Italian

059

16 W. 51st St. (at Fifth Ave.)

Subway:	47-50 Sts - Rockefeller Ctr	Monday - Friday 11:30am - 3:30pm
Phone:	212-977-7777	& 5pm - 10pm
Fax:	212-977-3144	Saturday noon - 10pm
e-mail:	N/A	Sunday noon - 8pm
Web:	www.tuscansquare.citysearch.com	
Prices:	$$	

All things Tuscan infuse this restaurant with the ambience of the Italian countryside. Start with the warm yellow and green walls in the 200-seat dining room. Next, turn your attention to the bright plates, the tile floors, and the sideboards set with dried flowers and bottles of olive oil. And then there's the food. From osso buco to lobster Fra Diavolo, the menu offers authentic Italian staples; be sure to sample a bottle of robust Tuscan red wine. Downstairs, you'll find the espresso bar, bakery and market, all showcasing the best products Tuscany has to offer. This restaurant deserves to be sponsored by the tourist board of Tuscany; after a meal here, you'll be booking a flight to Italy.

21 Club

American

060

21 W. 52nd St. (bet. Fifth & Sixth Aves.)

Subway:	5 Av - 53 St	Monday - Friday noon - 2:30pm
Phone:	212-582-7200	& 5:30pm - 9:30pm
Fax:	N/A	Saturday 5:30pm - 11pm
e-mail:	N/A	Closed Sunday, and Saturday in summer
Web:	www.21club.com	
Prices:	$$$	

A dowager among New York City restaurants, the 21 Club started as a speakeasy during the Prohibition era. In the 1950s, the club debuted in its first film, *All About Eve*. Since then, the restaurant has starred in a host of movies and TV shows, as well as playing host to a galaxy of movie stars, including Humphrey Bogart, Frank Sinatra, Sammy Davis Jr. and Helen Hayes. With its dim lighting and once-secret wine cellar (located in a vault in the basement of the building next door), this place still has a clandestine air about it. Cuisine here sticks to the tried and true; "21 classics," including the burger favored by Aristole Onassis, are indicated in red on the menu.

ViceVersa

061

325 W. 51st St. (bet. Eighth & Ninth Aves.)

Subway:	50 St	Monday - Friday noon - 2:30pm
Phone:	212-399-9291	& 5pm - 11pm
Fax:	212-399-9327	Saturday 5pm - 11pm
e-mail:	vicerest@aol.com	Closed Sunday & major holidays
Web:	www.viceversarestaurant.com	
Prices:	$$	

Run by an experienced Italian team of three men who cut their teeth at San Domenico in New York, ViceVersa (pronounced VEE-cha versa) celebrates *la dolce vita*. The restaurant fashions an urbane ambience in its earth-toned dining space, highlighted by a zinc bar and softly lit wall alcoves displaying antique classical urns. Approachable fixed-price menus complement extensive à la carte offerings, all of which come to the table in artful presentations. Be sure to leave room for the irresistible desserts like the rich, dark chocolate cake, served warm beside a scoop of vanilla gelato. The enclosed terrace at the back is a wonderful spot for summer dining.

Bar Masa

062

10 Columbus Circle (at the Time Warner Center)

Subway:	59 St - Columbus Cir	Monday - Saturday 11:30am - midnight
Phone:	212-823-9800	Closed Sunday
Fax:	212-823-9809	
e-mail:	info@masanyc.com	
Web:	www.masanyc.com	
Prices:	$$$	

If you want killer sushi, but don't feel like blowing your budget for the next six months, head to Bar Masa. Adjacent to its pricey sister, Masa, Bar Masa features a long, thin dining room, with a bar on one side and a line of tables on the other. Topped by a single plank of African wood, the bar offers an intriguing list of cocktails and sake. A gauzy burgundy curtain separates the tables from the bar, and Japanese limestone tiles and dark woods lend an earthy element to the room. The structured seasonal menu provides a wide choice of appetizers, rolls, sushi, noodles and other entrées. Dessert choices range from refreshing grapefruit granité to rich chocolate rainbow cake.

Bistro Du Vent

063

411 W. 42nd St. (bet. Ninth & Tenth Aves.)

Subway:	42 St - Port Authority Bus Terminal	Monday 11:45am - 2:30pm
Phone:	212-239-3060	& 5pm - 10:30pm
Fax:	212-239-3062	Tuesday - Saturday 11:45am - 2:30pm
e-mail:	N/A	& 5pm - midnight
Web:	www.bistroduvent.com	Sunday 11:45am - 10:30pm
Prices:	$$	

Opened in early 2005 and under the same stewardship as Esca (run by chef David Pasternak and partners), Bistro du Vent appeals to both locals and theatergoers with its authentic menu of hearty bistro fare. As soon as the warm baguette and the bowl of olives arrive at your table, you'll find yourself practicing your French and humming along to the Edith Piaf tunes playing in the background. From onion soup to steak frites and spit-roasted organic chicken, all meals come in man-size portions. Wine, from the exclusively French list, is served by the bottle, or by the pichet (about a third of a bottle) instead of by the glass.

Cho Dang Gol

064

55 W. 35th St. (bet. Fifth & Sixth Aves.)

Subway:	34 St - Herald Sq	Monday - Sunday 11:30am - 10pm
Phone:	212-695-8222	
Fax:	N/A	
e-mail:	N/A	
Web:	N/A	
Prices:		

Named after a village in South Korea that's famed for its tofu, this unassuming eatery in Korea Town offers something different from the host of surrounding places that all seem to serve Korean barbecue. Tofu, or soybean curd (doo boo in Korean) is the house specialty at Cho Dang Gol. Made fresh here each day, tofu forms the basis of many of the dishes; it absorbs the flavors of the spices or sauces it is cooked in, and is said to have many health benefits. Dishes are big—many of the appetizers are entrée-size—so be prepared to share. The friendly staff caters to a largely Korean clientele in the modest dining room, decorated with musical instruments and comfortable, high-backed chairs.

44 & X Hell's Kitchen
Contemporary

622 Tenth Ave. (at 44th St.)

Subway:	42 St - Port Authority Bus Terminal	Monday - Friday 5:30pm - midnight
Phone:	212-977-1170	Saturday - Sunday 11:30am - 1am
Fax:	212-977-1169	
e-mail:	N/A	
Web:	www.44andx.com	
Prices:	$$	

This restaurant's striped awning and crisp, white flower boxes brighten up the intersection at Tenth Avenue and 44th Street. (The "X" in the title refers to Tenth Avenue.) Inside, white and cream tones, molded chairs and leather banquettes create a cool, contemporary vibe. In keeping with their motto that this place is "a little bit of heaven in Hell's Kitchen," the young staff sports T-shirts emblazoned with "Heaven" on the front, and "in Hell" on the back. American classics take on a 21st-century twist here (for example, buttermilk fried chicken comes with a chive waffle). A mix of theatergoers and neighbors from the 'hood makes for a lively atmosphere.

Hell's Kitchen
Contemporary Mexican

679 Ninth Ave. (bet. 46th & 47th Sts.)

Subway:	50 St	Sunday - Monday 5pm - 11pm
Phone:	212-977-1588	Tuesday 11:30am - 3pm & 5pm - 11pm
Fax:	212-871-0927	Wednesday - Friday 11:30am - 3pm
e-mail:	info@hellskitchen-nyc.com	& 5pm - midnight
Web:	www.hellskitchen-nyc.com	Saturday 5pm - midnight
Prices:	$$	

As any New Yorker can tell you, this restaurant's name speaks to the 19th-century moniker for the surrounding neighborhood (the area between 34th and 59th streets, west of Eighth Avenue). At this hip Mexican eatery, the only thing devilish can be the wait you sometimes have to endure to snag a table. The "progressive Mexican" menu eschews the bland and the predictable in favor of dishes that are robust, yet possess a delicacy of execution and a real understanding of textures and flavors. Bolstered by the unflappable staff, a convivial atmosphere prevails in the narrow room, where tables line one side, and a bar lines the other. Check out the cool chandeliers made from glass bottles.

Manhattan *Midtown West*

Joe Allen

American

326 W. 46th St. (bet. Eighth & Ninth Aves.)

Subway:	50 St	Monday - Friday noon - midnight
Phone:	212-581-6464	Saturday - Sunday 11:30am - midnight
Fax:	212-265-3383	
e-mail:	N/A	
Web:	www.joeallenrestaurant.com	
Prices:	$$	

This chain sensibly applies the principle "if it ain't broke, don't fix it" to their New York City operation on Midtown West's restaurant row. Opened in 1965 and named for its owner, the 46th Street location is the original; since then, branches have sprouted up in Florida, Maine, and as far away as Europe. As is typical of many eateries in this neighborhood near the Theater District, Joe Allen papers its walls with old playbills. But wait, look closer: these aren't Broadway hits—these are the shows that bombed! Luckily the menu of tried-and-true American dishes is successful, and, for late risers, Joe Allen even offers omelets and frittatas until 4pm every day.

Osteria Al Doge

Italian

142 W. 44th St. (bet. Broadway & Sixth Ave.)

Subway:	Times Sq - 42 St	Monday - Friday 11:30am - 12:30am
Phone:	212-944-3643	Saturday - Sunday 4pm - midnight
Fax:	212-944-5754	
e-mail:	info@osteria-doge.com	
Web:	www.osteria-doge.com	
Prices:	$$	

Set amid the hustle and bustle of Times Square, Osteria Al Doge presents an inviting, Mediterranean-style ambience enhanced by wrought-iron chandeliers, Italian ceramics and fresh flowers. Homemade green pappardelle with lamb ragu, and tortellini filled with Atlantic salmon and goat cheese exemplify the authentic pasta dishes here. These are complimented by a good selection of fish and meat entrées—all served by a smiling and efficient staff of waiters. There's even a list of pizzas if you don't feel like bothering with multiple courses. Staying in the Times Square area? Call in your order and the restaurant will deliver it.

Sarabeth's

069

40 Central Park South (bet. Fifth & Sixth Aves.)

Subway: 5 Av - 59 St
Phone: 212-826-5959
Fax: 212-826-0140
e-mail: sarabethscps@verizon.net
Web: www.sarabethscps.com
Prices: $$

Monday - Sunday 8am - 11pm

Scattered across the city, Sarabeth's homey restaurants offer a winning formula of relaxed dining and American comfort food. This location, set opposite the park, amid the expensive hotels and at the starting line for serious shoppers, is perhaps the most convenient for visitors. Although Sarabeth's serves breakfast, lunch and dinner, it is most popular in the morning hours or at midday brunch on weekends—little wonder, since Sarabeth Levine made her name selling her celebrated homemade jams and cakes. Pumpkin waffles, fresh-made granola and farmer's omelets are just a few of the tempting breakfast dishes. At dinner, calves liver, chicken pot pie and butcher's spaghetti figure on the menu.

Sugiyama

070

251 W. 55th St. (bet. Broadway & Eighth Ave.)

Subway: Midtown - 57 St - 7 Av
Phone: 212-956-0670
Fax: 212-956-0671
e-mail: N/A
Web: www.sugiyama-nyc.com
Prices: $$$

Tuesday - Saturday 5:30pm - 11:45pm
Closed Sunday & Monday

When you walk into Sugiyama, your first thought may be that this place is defying New York City's smoking ban. Fear not, the cloud of smoke you see here rises from the red-hot stones on the tabletops, where beef or seafood are cooking. Welcome to the world of Kaiseki, a multicourse dining experience that teases your taste buds with a variety of small dishes of differing colors, textures and flavors. Helpful waiters will explain the dishes and the concept; all you have to do is decide how many courses your appetite or wallet can accommodate (with advance notice, the restaurant will arrange an all-vegetarian version). Sugiyama's popularity and limited space mean you'd best make reservations.

Manhattan Midtown West

Sushiya

Japanese

28 W. 56th St. (bet. Fifth & Sixth Aves.)

Subway:	57 St	Monday - Friday 11:30am - 2:30pm
Phone:	212-247-5756	& 5pm - 10:30pm
Fax:	212-247-5752	Saturday noon - 3pm & 5pm - 10:30pm
e-mail:	N/A	Sunday 4:30pm - 10pm
Web:	www.sushiyaonline.com	
Prices:	$$	

On a street where a gaggle of restaurants all clamor for your attention, Sushiya makes an effective pitch by offering very reasonably priced Japanese food with a strong selection of sushi and sashimi. The restaurant spreads over two floors, offering a quiet upstairs room for those who prefer to avoid the livelier atmosphere of the ground-floor space, where the sushi counter resides. Don't be overwhelmed by the three-page menu; if you're having trouble narrowing down your choices, the best bet is to try one of the Bento boxes or deluxe sushi selections. The T-shirt-clad staff provides friendly and helpful service, whether you're in for a quick bite or a lengthy meal.

Wondee Siam II

Thai

813 Ninth Ave. (bet. 53rd & 54th Sts.)

Subway:	50 St	Monday - Sunday 11am - 11pm
Phone:	917-286-1726	
Fax:	917-286-1728	
e-mail:	N/A	
Web:	N/A	
Prices:		

Regulars don't care that Wondee Siam II will never win any awards for its plain interior design. They don't come for the décor—they come for well-prepared, fragrant Thai dishes at very reasonable prices, and the busy take-out service testifies to the restaurant's popularity. If you do eat here (as opposed to getting food to go), stick with the traditional dishes and you won't go wrong (you can recognize some of the newer menu items by their kitschy names). Just look around at the contented cadre of regulars: they wear the smug look of people who know they have a good thing going in their neighborhood. (The original Wondee Siam is a block away at 792 Ninth Avenue.)

Xing

073

785 Ninth Ave. (bet. 52nd & 53rd Sts.)

Subway:	50 st	Monday - Tuesday 11:30am - 11pm
Phone:	212-289-3010	Wed - Thurs 11:30am - midnight
Fax:	212-289-3014	Friday 11:30am - 1am
e-mail:	N/A	Saturday 5pm - 1am
Web:	www.xingrestaurant.com	Sunday 5pm - 11pm
Prices:	SS	

True to its name, which means «star» in Chinese, Xing has been shining bright in this developing West Side neighborhood since the restaurant opened in early 2005. The front space sports a cool, cafe style, done in blond woods and bright bamboo green. If you continue through to the back room, you'll find the mood turns sultry with deep-red velvet-covered walls and banquettes, sobered by black furnishings. Xing (say «shing») is run by John Dempsey, who owns Hell's Kitchen; here he gives his favorite Chinese fare a modern tweak, illustrated by dishes such as smoked tofu spring roll, lobster in black-bean sauce, and Sichuan grilled hangar steak.

Yangpyung Seoul

074

43 W. 33rd St. (bet. Fifth Ave. & Broadway)

Subway:	34 St - Herald Sq	Monday - Sunday 24 hours
Phone:	212-629-5599	
Fax:	N/A	
e-mail:	N/A	
Web:	N/A	
Prices:		

Hard by the Empire State Building in the area known as Little Korea, Yang Pyung Seoul brings an authentic slice of Korea to this section of Midtown. What draws many people from New York's Korean community to this nondescript little place, which is open 24 hours a day, is the quality and authenticity of its cuisine. Don't worry if your Korean is a little rusty; the menu includes helpful photographs of the various dishes. Banchan, complimentary offerings that are served before your meal, are tasty as well as generous in size. Specialties of the house here include the rich and robust broths, particularly the hae jang gook, which is reputed to stave off winter colds and even cure hangovers.

About **Murray Hill**

One of the last laid-back neighborhoods in Manhattan, Murray Hill is a residential enclave of opulent mansions, elegant brownstones and converted carriage houses dating back to the 19th century. Adjacent to Midtown, the quarter covers the ten blocks between 40th Street and 30th Street, and extends from Fifth Avenue to the East River. Quiet Murray Hill may lack the cachet of other areas of the city, but foodies will find it worth a detour to sample a variety of cuisines from sophisticated sushi to good, old-fashioned steak.

A Bit of History – Known as Inclenburg in the Dutch colonial days, Murray Hill takes its name from early settlers Robert and Mary Murray, who moved here from Pennsylvania in 1753. The Murrays first set up housekeeping on the corner of present-day Pearl and Wall streets, so that merchant Robert could be close to his business, based out of one of the wharfs in Lower Manhattan. Deciding they needed a "country estate," the Murrays purchased a tract of wilderness in the Common Lands of Inclenburg. Originally called Belmont, the estate soon became known as Murray Hill.

When Robert died in 1786, his younger brother purchased the land. The Murray family left a lasting legacy to the neighborhood in the form of a covenant that allowed only "brick or stone dwellings" to be built on their land. Churches, private stables, and carriage houses were the only

© Martha Cooper

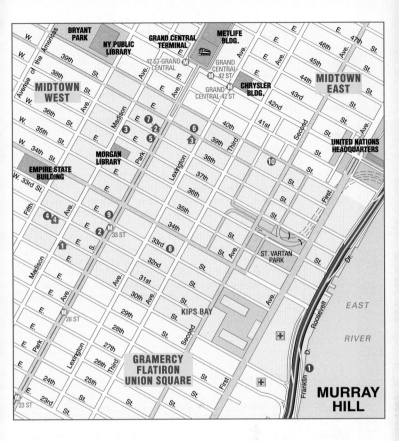

exceptions to this rule, which plagued real-estate developers for decades to follow. A boon to those who came to live there, the Murray's covenant prevented the area from being riddled with railroad tracks in the mid-19th century, and, later, with high-rise office towers.

Murray Hill Arrives – Murray Hill became a neighborhood of note in the late 1800s, when financier William Astor and his wife, Caroline, took residence in a mansion on the corner of Fifth Avenue and East 33rd Street. Reigning queen of New York society in the decades before World War I, Mrs. Astor outfitted her stately digs with a ballroom that only held 400 people—"the only 400 who counted," as she put it.

By the end of the 19th century, Murray Hill had taken on the character that you see here today. For a trip back to that gentler time, stroll the blocks between Fifth and Park avenues, and Park and Lexington avenues, and check out the converted carriage houses at Sniffen Court *(E. 36th St. between Lexington and Third Aves.)*.

The Water Club

001

E. 30th St. at the East River (enter on 34th St.)

Subway:	33 St
Phone:	212-683-3333
Fax:	212-545-1155
e-mail:	waterclub@aol.com
Web:	www.thewaterclub.com
Prices:	$$

Monday - Saturday noon - 3pm
& 5pm - 11pm
Sunday 11:30am - 3pm & 5pm - 11pm

Set on an elegant barge on the East River, the Water Club boasts the perfect ambience for a romantic night out in Murray Hill. With floor-to-ceiling windows overlooking the river, and water views from every table, the restaurant provides a respite from the crowded city streets. Marine signal flags hanging from the ceiling and a waitstaff dressed as a ship's crew complete the nautical theme. The specialty is, of course, fish and shellfish, with a few meat dishes added to please those pesky landlubbers. Water Club features live piano music nightly, and in summer (May to October), the Crow's Nest on the restaurant's upper deck offers outdoor dining and a casual menu.

Artisanal

002

2 Park Ave. (enter on 32nd St. bet. Park & Madison Aves.)

Subway:	33 St
Phone:	212-725-8585
Fax:	212-481-5455
e-mail:	fbismuth@artisanalcheese.com
Web:	www.artisanalcheese.com
Prices:	$$

Monday - Sunday 11:45am - 11pm

Say cheese. That's the focus of Terrance Brennan's Artisanal restaurant, which celebrates cheese from around the world. Opened in 2001, Brennan's Murray Hill brasserie, with its high ceilings, mirrored walls, and velour banquettes, serves cheese in many forms: fondue, macaroni and cheese, puffy gougères and cheese ravioli, to name a few. In fact, there's even a separate cheese menu, offering tastings of some 250 types of artisanal cheese. To wash it down, choose from the equally dizzying list of more than 150 wines by the glass. Don't like cheese? Never fear, Artisanal offers a wide selection of classic French fare, such as escargots, trout amandine, lamb cassoulet, and mussels marinières).

Asia de Cuba

003

237 Madison Ave. (bet. 37th & 38th Sts.)

Subway:	42 St - Grand Central
Phone:	212-726-7755
Fax:	212-726-7575
e-mail:	kelli.cresham@morganshotelgroup.com
Web:	www.chinagrillmanagement.com
Prices:	$$$

Monday - Wednesday noon - 11pm
Thursday - Friday noon - midnight
Saturday 5:30pm - midnight
Sunday 5:30pm - 11pm

A trendy venue in staid, residential Murray Hill, Asia de Cuba still packs in a chic crowd, despite the fact that it's not new (the restaurant opened in the Morgans Hotel in 1997). Designer Philippe Starck fitted the interior of the bi-level dining room with gauzy drapes lining the soaring walls, a 25-foot-high hologram of a flowing waterfall, and a 50-foot-long, alabaster communal table running the length of the downstairs room. Dishes here, which are sized for sharing, marry elements of Asian and Latin cuisines in entrées such as grilled barbecue salmon with Asian rellenos and avocado-wasabi cream. Round up a few friends who like to share, and sample the three-course, prix-fixe lunch.

HanGawi

004

12 E. 32nd St. (bet. Madison & Fifth Aves.)

Subway:	33 St
Phone:	212-213-0077
Fax:	121-689-0780
e-mail:	info@hangawirestaurant.com
Web:	www.hangawirestaurant.com
Prices:	$$

Monday - Friday noon - 3pm
& 5pm - 10:30pm
Saturday - Sunday noon - 10:30pm

Don't worry about wearing your best shoes to HanGawi, you'll have to take them off at the door before settling in at one of the restaurant's low tables. In the serene space, decorated with Korean artifacts and soothed by meditative music, it's easy to forget you're in Manhattan. The menu is completely vegetarian (many of the dishes conform to vegan diets), in keeping with the restaurant's philosophy of healthy cooking to balance the yin and yang—or *um* and *yang* in Korean. Of course, all good things must end, and eventually you'll have to rejoin the rat race outside. Still, it's nice to get away from the pulsing vibe of the city . . . now and Zen.

Nadaman Hakubai

Japanese

005

66 Park Ave. (at 38th St., in the Kitano Hotel)

Subway:	42 St - Grand Central
Phone:	212-885-7111
Fax:	212-885-7095
e-mail:	hakubai@kitano.com
Web:	www.kitano.com
Prices:	$$$

Monday - Sunday 11:45am - 2:30pm
& 6pm - 10pm

Dinner at Hakubai will set you back a pretty penny (plan to spend as much as $150 a person), but for that amount you'll be assured of having an authentic Japanese dining experience. It is worth it? You decide. Go for broke by savoring a kaiseki meal (available at dinner only) in one of the restaurant's three private tatami rooms. Associated with the light meal traditionally served during a Japanese tea ceremony, kaiseki consists of artfully presented dishes served in a series of small courses by kimono-clad waitresses; fresh ingredients symbolize the season. Courses include an appetizer, soup, and sushi, followed by steamed, fried and vinegar dishes, and finally a light fruit dessert.

Shaburi

Japanese

006

125 E. 39th St. (bet. Lexington & Park Aves.)

Subway:	Grand Central - 42 St
Phone:	212-867-6999
Fax:	212-867-7435
e-mail:	shaburi@shaburi.com
Web:	www.shaburi.com
Prices:	$$

Monday - Thursday 11:30am - 10:30pm
Friday 11:30am - 11:30pm
Saturday 1pm - 11:30pm
Sunday 1pm - 10:30pm

In an age when everything is interactive, Shaburi fits right in with hands-on dining. Both the communal bar and the individual tables here are equipped with electric burners for making shabu shabu. Just order the ingredients that appeal (Matsuzaka beef, Kurobuta pork, seafood, assorted veggies) and simmer them in hot broth at the table. It's lots of fun for a group of friends—or a great ice-breaker for that awkward first date. And while you're at it, you can also use those tabletop burners to stir-fry bite-size pieces of meat or tofu marinated in sugar and soy, for sukiyaki (served over rice or udon). The first American outpost of a Taiwanese restaurant chain, Shaburi opened in late 2004.

Silverleaf Tavern

007

43 E. 38th St. (at Park Ave., in the 70 Park Avenue Hotel)

Subway:	42 St	Monday - Wednesday 11:30am - 3pm
Phone:	212-973-2550	& 5:30pm - 10:30pm
Fax:	212-973-2551	Thursday - Friday 11:30am - 3pm
e-mail:	joel.steiger@silverleaftavern.com	& 5:30pm - 11:30pm
Web:	www.silverleaftavern.com	Saturday 5:30pm - 11:30pm
Prices:	$$	Sunday 5:30pm - 10:30pm

You're sure to go for baroque at the Silverleaf Tavern in 70 Park Avenue Hotel *(see hotel listings)*, decorated as it is with black-lacquered wood columns, tufted leather banquettes, illuminated amethyst bar, and 17th-century-style still-life paintings couched in ornate gold frames. The tavern's most eye-catching element, though, is the custom-designed chandelier, a modern fantasy of sculpted metal branches finished in silver leaf and beset with glittering crystal foliage. Luckily the food here is more subtle than the décor. The menu looks to Europe for some dishes (pork Schnitzel, duck confit), and returns to the streets of New York for others (grilled hanger steak with short rib horseradish knish).

Trio

008

167 E. 33rd St. (bet. Lexington & Third Aves.)

Subway:	33 St	Monday - Saturday 11:45pm - 11pm
Phone:	212-685-1001	Closed Sunday
Fax:	212-685-1017	
e-mail:	triornb@aol.com	
Web:	www.triorestaurant.com	
Prices:	$$	

Inside this Murray Hill brownstone you'll find an attractive neighborhood restaurant highlighting the cuisine of the Dalmatian Coast of Croatia in a dining room adorned with art prints on the walls and fresh flowers on the tables. In case you're not familiar with the diverse foodways of that part of the world, the dishes at Trio borrow from the cooking of Italy, France, Spain and Austria. A good way to introduce yourself to the food here is to start with the "Dalma" antipasto, a plate of cured meats and cheeses imported from the private Dalmatian Coast estate of the Ivanac family, who own the restaurant. Then move on to an authentic dish like seafood Buzara, a Croatian seafood stew.

Manhattan Murray Hill

Wolfgang's Steakhouse

S t e a k h o u s e

009

4 Park Ave. (at 33rd St.)

Subway:	33 St
Phone:	212-889-3369
Fax:	N/A
e-mail:	N/A
Web:	www.wolfgangssteakhouse.com
Prices:	$$$

Monday - Thursday noon - 10pm
Friday noon - 11pm
Saturday 5pm - 11pm
Sunday 5pm - 10pm

Wolfgang Zweiner worked for 41 years as a headwaiter at Brooklyn's Peter Luger steakhouse. Just as he was planning his retirement to the coast of Florida, he got sidetracked into starting his own restaurant in Manhattan in partnership with his son and several other former waiters at Luger's. Opened in 2004, Wolfgang's occupies the former main dining room of the 1912 Vanderbilt Hotel. What sets this space apart is its gorgeous vaulted, tiled ceiling, crafted by Rafael Guastavino. It's all about meat here—strapping portions of porterhouse served on the bone (for fish fans, there's a three-pound lobster). Side dishes are à la carte, so expect to pay more to add spinach or German potatoes.

Phoenix Garden

C h i n e s e

010

242 E. 40th St. (bet. Second & Third Aves.)

Subway:	Grand Central - 42 St
Phone:	212-983-6666
Fax:	212-490-6666
e-mail:	N/A
Web:	N/A
Prices:	

Monday - Sunday noon - 9:45pm

You will find this gem of a Chinese place not in Chinatown, but tucked into a modest brick building in residential Murray Hill. Inside, there's nothing remarkable about the décor, but the savory, aromatic Cantonese specialities—and reasonable prices, to boot—keep locals coming back for more. The generous menu cites some 200 different choices, ranging from steamed flounder in black bean sauce and the much-acclaimed pepper and salty shrimp to crispy roasted duck and shredded pork, and a variety of noodle dishes including rice noodles (mai fun), pan-fried noodles and lo mein. Don't forget to bring your own wine or beer, since Phoenix Garden doesn't serve alcohol.

Show the locals around.

Michelin® Green Guides will introduce you to a world of information on the history, culture, art, and architecture of a destination. You'll be so well informed, they'll never suspect you're a tourist. To learn more, visit michelintravel.com.

A better way forward

About
SoHo & Nolita

The heart of Manhattan's downtown fashion scene, SoHo—short for South of Houston—is New York at its trendiest and most colorful. Visitors throng the district (bounded by West, W. Houston, Lafayette and Canal streets) on weekends, making even walking down the sidewalk difficult—especially given the proliferation of sidewalk tables full of purses and jewelry, sunglasses and scarves, and "outsider" art. The restaurant scene is a lively one here, as eclectic as SoHo itself. Here you'll find everything from designer-decorated, high-end restaurants to tiny, decidedly untrendy eateries.

Nolita (for North of Little Italy), Little Italy's über-fashionable sister, actually sits within that district's former boundaries; four blocks long and three blocks wide, it stretches from Kenmare to Houston streets on Mulberry, Mott and Elizabeth streets. The moniker Nolita came courtesy of real-estate developers, who in the 1990s wanted to distinguish it from the red-sauce joints of the old neighborhood. Today Nolita is chock-a-block with chic cafes that are ideal for people watching.

A Bit of History – Site of the first free black community in Manhattan, SoHo was settled in 1644 by former slaves of the Dutch West India Company, who were granted land for farms. In the early 19th century, Broadway was paved and a number of prominent citizens, including *Last of the Mohicans* author James Fenimore Cooper, moved in, bringing cachet to the district. In the late 1850s, large stores such as Tiffany & Co. and Lord & Taylor were joined

© Martha Cooper

Manhattan SoHo & Nolita

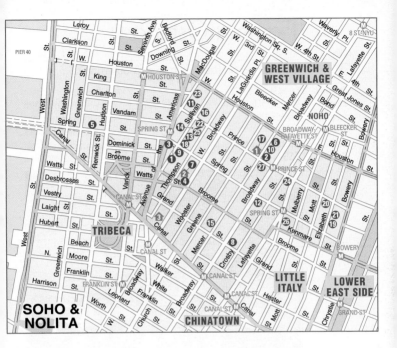

on Broadway by grand hotels. Theaters, casinos and brothels entertained visitors—and drove respectable middle-class families uptown. The exodus made room in the late 1800s for a slew of new warehouses and factories, many built with ornamented cast-iron façades, which looked like carved stone. The area thrived as a commercial center until the 1890s, when fashionable businesses began relocating to Fifth Avenue.

Art Brings a New Start – By the late 1950s the neighborhood was a slum known as "Hell's Hundred Acres," and city planners slated it for demolition to make room for an expressway until residents objected. Often in violation of building codes, painters and sculptors converted vacant warehouses into studios, galleries and living quarters. An underground art scene took root and thrived until the early 1980s, when uptown galleries, boutiques and affluent professionals began to push out the very artists who'd made the neighborhood so desirable in the first place.

Today few artists can afford to live or work in Soho, and the migration of galleries northward to Chelsea continues. Locally owned boutiques have been largely supplanted by international couturiers, making SoHo a Mecca for moneyed fashionistas. Overflowing with traffic, pedestrians and sidewalk vendors, **Broadway** is SoHo at its most commercial. The west end of Broadway ranks as the neighborhood's premier corridor for fashion and art as well as dining.

Fiamma Osteria ❀

001

206 Spring St. (bet. Sixth Ave. & Sullivan St.)

Subway:	Spring St	Monday - Thursday noon - 2:30pm
Phone:	212-653-0100	& 5:30pm - 11pm
Fax:	212-653-0101	Friday noon - 2:30pm
e-mail:	N/A	& 5:30pm - midnight
Web:	www.brguestrestaurants.com	Saturday 5:30pm - midnight
Prices:	**$$$**	Sunday 5:30pm - 10pm

Fiamma Osteria/Eric Laignel

The jewel in SoHo's culinary crown, Fiamma Osteria resulted from a partnership between renowned chef Michael White and Steven Hanson, head of the B.R. Guest Restaurant Group. A glass elevator whisks guests—who have included a veritable Who's Who of Hollywood stars—to the upper two of three distinct dining levels (the third is reserved for private dining). Rich brown and fawn hues, warm ambient lighting from large, hanging lanterns, and elegantly laid tables set a seductive tone.

In keeping with the restaurant's name, which is Italian for "flame," tantalizing and artfully presented dishes will spark your taste buds using premium regional Italian ingredients such as aged prosciutto di Parma, lentils from Castellucio, truffled pecorino cheese, and fragrant Tuscan olive oil. A seeming army of waiters show a reassuring pride in their restaurant as well as a knowledge of its menu.

Framma Osteria/Eric Laignel

Garganelli with Proscuitto San Daniele and Spring Peas

Serves 4

1 lb. garganelli
1 ½ cups heavy cream
4 oz. truffle butter
4 oz. proscuitto di San Daniele, julienned
4 oz. fresh peas, shelled and blanched
2 oz. Parmigiano Reggiano, grated
Salt to taste

Method

Boil pasta in a big pot of salted water. While pasta is boiling, in a separate saucepan, heat the heavy cream and proscuitto over medium heat. Allow to simmer until the cream is reduced by half. Once the cream is reduced, whisk in the truffle butter.

Next, toss in the blanched peas. Drain pasta and add to pan with sauce and toss with Parmigiano Reggiano. Divide among 4 shallow bowls or plates and serve immediately.

Lure Fishbar

Seafood

002

142 Mercer St. (bet. Houston & Prince Sts.)

Subway: Prince St
Phone: 212-431-7676
Fax: 212-925-4018
e-mail: info@lurefishbar.com
Web: www.lurefishbar.com
Prices: $$$

Monday - Sunday noon - 11pm

Ahoy matey! If your credit card's not maxed out from visiting the Prada shop above it, Lure Fishbar makes a great place to drop anchor. The seafaring-themed restaurant opened in 2004, decked out with porthole windows, teak paneling, and a navy blue and white-leather décor reminiscent of a luxury ocean liner. Nautical photographs add to the maritime motif—the only thing missing is the sound of seagulls. Have a seat at the fishbar, where the high quality of the raw ingredients speaks for itself, and order the fishbar tasting to share. Or grab a table in the main dining room and choose among the fresh catches listed on the Fish Board. Just one visit and you'll be hooked.

Aquagrill

Seafood

003

210 Spring St. (at Sixth Ave.)

Subway: Spring St
Phone: 212-274-0505
Fax: 212-274-0587
e-mail: N/A
Web: N/A
Prices: $$

Tuesday - Thursday noon - 3pm
& 6pm - 10:30pm
Friday - Saturday noon - 3pm
& 6pm - 11:30pm
Sunday noon - 3pm & 6pm - 10:15pm
Closed Monday & major holidays

From the staggering selection of oysters at the raw bar to simple grilled fish, Jeremy and Jennifer Marshall's establishment aims to please all seafood lovers. The husband-and-wife team divides up the work here: Culinary Institute of America-trained chef Jeremy keeps watch over the kitchen and Jennifer oversees the dining room, set about by lamps and pictures made from sea shells. The chef treats his fresh supplies with due deference, adding subtle Asian accents to enhance the preparations. Lunch is always busy, but it's at dinner that the kitchen staff really struts their stuff. Service is smoothly choreographed, and an air of professionalism pervades the whole operation.

Downtown Cipriani

Italian

376 W. Broadway (bet. Broome & Spring Sts.)

Subway:	Spring St
Phone:	212-343-0999
Fax:	212-925-3610
e-mail:	N/A
Web:	www.cipriani.com
Prices:	**$$$**

Monday - Sunday noon - midnight

Part of the Cipriani restaurant group, which has four restaurants in Manhattan, the Downtown satellite enjoys a spot in SoHo, where it seems right at home in its oh-so-chic surroundings. The interior is decked out like a high-style bistro, with soaring ceilings, oversize framed posters and leather chairs. With its laid-back atmosphere, Downtown Cipriani features a fittingly casual menu of hearty Italian fare. Don't be surprised if you recognize some faces among the well-heeled regulars here; this place attracts a high-profile clientele. Tables on the sidewalk terrace, shaded by market umbrellas, afford good people-watching along bustling Broadway.

Giorgione

Italian

307 Spring St. (bet. Hudson & Greenwich Sts.)

Subway:	Spring St
Phone:	212-352-2269
Fax:	212-352-8734
e-mail:	giorgionerest@aol.com
Web:	N/A
Prices:	**$$**

Sunday - Thursday noon - 3pm
& 5pm - 11pm
Friday noon - 3pm & 5pm - midnight
Saturday 5pm - midnight

All the buzz is found inside rather than outside Giorgione, situated as it is in a relatively isolated spot in SoHo. Giorgio DeLuca, one of Dean & DeLuca's founders, owns this lively Italian place, which you enter via the sleek bar. Follow the narrow space toward the back, and the room widens into the main dining room, where chrome-topped tables, boxy light fixtures, white-leather seating, and ice-blue walls contribute to the cool vibe. A party-hearty crowd drops in for a select menu of oven-fired pizzas, pastas, risottos and the fresh catch from the oyster bar. After dinner, you'll doubtless find it difficult to resist the charms of the dessert trolley as your waiter rolls it to your table.

Manhattan SoHo & Nolita

Honmura An

006

170 Mercer St. (bet. W. Houston & Prince Sts.)

Subway:	Broadway - Lafayette St	(Closed Mon.) Tuesday 6pm - 10pm
Phone:	212-334-5253	Wednesday - Thursday noon - 2:30pm
Fax:	212-334-6162	& 6pm - 10pm
e-mail:	N/A	Friday - Saturday noon - 2:30pm
Web:	N/A	& 6pm - 10:30pm
Prices:	**$$$**	Sunday 6pm - 9:30pm

Buckwheat noodles, called soba, are the speciality at this second-floor Japanese restaurant, whose flagship is in Tokyo. Chefs learn the art of preparing delicate soba noodles in practically the same time it takes to become an architect, so when you see the chefs at work behind the glass wall of the kitchen, you should appreciate their skill. While you can order handmade noodles cold or hot, it's the latter, swathed in salty broth, that really stand out—slurping from your bowl is expected. Small tasting plates are designed for sharing any time of day, and the set menu at lunchtime gives newcomers the soba experience without breaking the bank.

Kittichai

007

60 Thompson St. (bet. Broome & Spring Sts.)

Subway:	Spring St	Monday - Thursday noon - 2:30pm
Phone:	212-219-2000	& 5:30pm - 11pm
Fax:	212-925-2991	Friday - Saturday noon - 2:45pm
e-mail:	thomsixty@aol.com	& 5:30pm - midnight
Web:	www.kittichairestaurant.com	Sunday noon - 2:45pm
Prices:	**$$$**	& 5:30pm - 10pm

Located in the Sixty Thompson Hotel *(see hotel listings)*, this sensual SoHo newcomer offers subtly spiced Thai cooking, thanks to chef Ian Chalermkittichai, who comes to New York from the Four Seasons Hotel in Bangkok. The food is as appealing as the exotic setting here, where orchids float in bottles on lighted shelves, lush silk fabrics and Thai artifacts adorn the walls, and a reflecting pool forms the centrepiece of the dining room. Why, with all this opulence, it's amazing that the menu is so sensibly priced. Waiters in black tunics offer sound advice about the dishes, and sticklers for authenticity will seem churlish for questioning why chopsticks have replaced the more usual Thai fork and spoon.

L'Ecole

008

462 Broadway (at Grand St.)

Subway:	Canal St
Phone:	212-219-3300
Fax:	212-334-4866
e-mail:	info@frenchculinary.com
Web:	www.frenchculinary.com
Prices:	$$

Monday - Wednesday 12:30pm - 2:30pm
& 6pm - 9:30pm
Thursday - Friday 12:30pm - 2:30pm
& 5:30pm - 9:30pm
Saturday 5:30pm - 9:30pm
Closed Sunday

If you've got to be a guinea pig, this is the place to do it. The restaurant of New York's French Culinary Institute provides the opportunity for its students to show off what they've learned—and that's a lot! They've certainly mastered the first rule of good cooking: use the best-quality ingredients you can find and don't mess around too much with a good thing. The prix-fixe lunch menu is a great—and inexpensive—way to sample the menu of flavorful regional French fare, which changes every six weeks (be sure to make reservations). A conscientious student waitstaff caters to customers in a soothing yellow room decorated with photographs depicting the frenetic world of a restaurant kitchen.

Savore

009

200 Spring St. (at Sullivan St.)

Subway:	Spring St
Phone:	212-431-1212
Fax:	212-343-2605
e-mail:	N/A
Web:	N/A
Prices:	$$

Monday - Sunday noon - midnight
Closed December 25 - 26

SoHo certainly claims its fair share of jam-packed eateries where the dictates of fashion override any serious thought of the cuisine. Fortunately for those who put food first, there's Savore. Bang in the middle of SoHo, this restaurant with its sunny atmosphere provides a comforting haven for those seeking refuge from the terminally hip. Warm yellow hues and architectural drawings provide a soothing backdrop for savoring solid Northern Italian cooking, complemented by a good selection of Tuscan wines. Service is courteous and attentive, and you'll find yourself wanting to linger a while before braving the bustling neighborhood outside.

Woo Lae Oak

Korean

010

148 Mercer St. (bet. W. Houston & Prince Sts.)

Subway:	Prince St
Phone:	212-925-8200
Fax:	212-925-8232
e-mail:	woolaeoak@aol.com
Web:	www.woolaeoaksoho.com
Prices:	$$

Monday - Thursday noon - 11pm
Friday - Saturday noon - 11:30pm
Sunday noon - 11pm

Want to go out to cook tonight? Each of the marble-topped tables in stylish Woo Lae Oak contains a built-in griddle for customers to barbecue anything from tuna loin and tiger prawns to shiitake mushrooms and free-range chicken breast. If this sounds gimmicky, it actually works well, due in large part to the good quality of the ingredients. For those whose idea of cooking is making reservations, the restaurant also offers Korean specialties, created with a flair for depth of flavor. It's not just the cooking that sets this place apart from more traditional eateries in Korea Town; it's the attractive dining space, too, with its roomy, open floor plan.

Ama

Italian

011

48 MacDougal St. (bet. W. Houston & Prince Sts.)

Subway:	Spring St
Phone:	212-358-1707
Fax:	212-358-1238
e-mail:	rsvp@amanyc.com
Web:	www.amanyc.com
Prices:	$$

Monday - Sunday 5pm - 11pm

How appropriate that a restaurant whose name derives from the Italian word for love should open on Valentine's Day (2005). Passers-by are drawn here by the warm glow coming from within. Once inside, they find a narrow room balanced by mirrors and an impressionistic painting on the ceiling; tables cluster close together, adding to the intimate feel. The menu avoids run-of-the-mill Italian fare in favor of cooking that takes its influences from Puglia. Ingredients, in dishes like quail filled with pancetta and served on polenta with cardoncelli mushrooms, are first-rate. After a meal here, being attended to by the charming waitstaff, you're bound to leave feeling a little better about the world.

Balthazar

012

80 Spring St. (bet. Broadway & Crosby St.)

Subway:	Spring St	Monday - Friday 7:30am - 1am
Phone:	212-965-1414	Saturday 8am - 4pm & 5:45pm - 2am
Fax:	212-966-2502	Sunday 8am - 4pm & 5:30pm - midnight
e-mail:	N/A	
Web:	www.balthazarny.com	
Prices:	$$$	

What sets this establishment apart is its authentic ambience, constantly animated by lively conversation. Sure, all the requisite décor elements are here (red leatherette banquettes, mosaic tile floor, mirrors bearing extracts of the menu), conjuring up late-19th-century Paris. There's nothing surprising about the menu, either, but the products are fresh and the dishes are well-prepared. Specials correspond to the day of the week (come Friday for bouillabaisse), and the restaurant gets its baguettes and pastries from its own bakery. Like any self-respecting brasserie, Balthazar offers a late-night supper menu, which runs from salade niçoise to poached eggs and boudin noir.

Blue Ribbon

Contemporary

013

97 Sullivan St. (bet. Spring & Prince Sts.)

Subway:	Spring St	Monday - Sunday 4pm - 4am
Phone:	212-274-0404	
Fax:	N/A	
e-mail:	N/A	
Web:	www.blueribbonrestaurants.com	
Prices:	$$$	

Anyone who has ever waited tables will testify to the importance of wearing comfortable shoes, but when a restaurant serves dinner until 4am, infinite reserves of stamina are required. Simple comforts here create an convivial atmosphere that makes you feel like a Soho insider, although the closeness of the tables means that conversation is rarely private. The kitchen turns out an eclectic array of American fare; be adventurous and order the duck or pigeon. Since this Blue Ribbon was so successful, they opened another one in Brooklyn *(280 Fifth Ave., in Park Slope)*. Neither location takes reservations for parties of less than five people.

Manhattan SoHo & Nolita

Blue Ribbon Sushi

Japanese

014

119 Sullivan St. (bet. Spring & Prince Sts.)

Subway:	Spring St	Monday - Sunday noon - 2am
Phone:	212-343-0404	
Fax:	N/A	
e-mail:	N/A	
Web:	www.blueribbonrestaurants.com	
Prices:	$$	

A few doors down from its sister restaurant Blue Ribbon, the equally popular Blue Ribbon Sushi bears a sign so discreet that you'd think they were trying to keep the place a secret. Inside the cozy, compact room, you'll find wooden booths and a sushi counter behind which the chefs jostle for space to prepare their specialties. Divided into sections by ocean (Atlantic and Pacific), the extensive menu of sushi can appear bewildering at first glance, but what sets it apart are unusual offerings such as jellyfish, and spicy lobster with egg wrapper. If you're going for dinner, be sure to get there early; the no-reservations policy means the restaurant fills up quickly in the evening.

Cendrillon

Asian

015

45 Mercer St. (bet. Broome & Grand Sts.)

Subway:	Canal St	Tuesday - Sunday 11am - 4:30pm
Phone:	212-343-9012	& 6pm - 11pm
Fax:	212-343-9670	Closed Monday
e-mail:	N/A	
Web:	www.cendrillon.com	
Prices:	$$	

All too often, fusion cuisine merely reflects where the chef took his last vacation, but at this roomy SoHo restaurant, a real understanding of Asian culinary culture underscores the cooking. With Filipino cuisine at its core, Cendrillon surprises diners with zesty and vivacious flavors, guaranteed to cheer the most sullen taste buds. The place is typical SoHo, incorporating the requisite exposed brickwork and vent shafts, with the brightest spot at the back, past the open kitchen. Although portion size is on the generous side, you'll definitely want to leave room for dessert. Check out the impressive selection of exotic Asian teas to complement your meal.

Jean Claude

016

137 Sullivan St.

Subway:	Spring St	Monday - Sunday 6pm - 11pm
Phone:	212-475-9232	
Fax:	N/A	
e-mail:	N/A	
Web:	N/A	
Prices:	SS	

Just add a plume of Gauloise smoke, and this little French bistro could be on the Left Bank in Paris instead of planted in the heart of SoHo. Simply decorated with bottles and assorted Gallic-themed posters, the dining room sports a lively atmosphere. Brown-paper-covered tables here snuggle so close together that if you like the looks of your neighbor, it wouldn't be difficult to start up a conversation about the tasty, classic French fare. Newcomers may be deterred by the fact that Jean Claude doesn't take credit cards, but if you don't mind coming early, you won't need oodles of cash to afford the inexpensive fixed-price menu, offered from 6pm to 7:30pm.

Mercer Kitchen

017

99 Prince St. (at Mercer St., in the Mercer Hotel)

Subway:	Prince St	Monday - Sunday noon - 3pm
Phone:	212-966-5454	& 6pm - midnight
Fax:	212-965-3855	
e-mail:	N/A	
Web:	www.jean-georges.com	
Prices:	SS	

When it opened in the basement of SoHo's Mercer Hotel (see hotel listing) in 1998, Mercer Kitchen took a position at the vanguard of the culinary new wave. Today the restaurant, which owes its existence to wunderkind Jean-Georges Vongerichten, remains fiercely fashionable. This is the quintessential SoHo experience: a Prada-clad crowd, eccentric décor (think hanging umbrellas), and a staff all dressed in—you guessed it—black. In the subterranean dining room, with its arched brick entryways and open kitchen, you'll be treated to cooking that has roots in France but travels to other faraway locales for inspiration. If you want to make a new friend, sit at one of the communal tables overlooking the kitchen.

Manhattan SoHo & Nolita

Mezzogiorno

018

Italian

195 Spring St. (at Sullivan St.)

Subway:	Spring St	Monday - Friday noon - 3:30pm
Phone:	212-334-2112	& 5pm - 11:30pm
Fax:	212-941-6294	Saturday - Sunday noon - 11:30pm
e-mail:	mezzogiorno@aol.com	
Web:	www.mezzogiorno.com	
Prices:	$$	

A SoHo veteran established more than 12 years ago by Vittorio and Nicola Ansuini, Mezzogiorno (the name means "high noon") re-creates the warm, vibrant ambience of the owners' native Florence. More than 100 Italian artists were asked to interpret the restaurant's logo, a smiling sun; their collection of collages, paintings and small objets d'art fill boxes at one end of the room. The Florentine theme continues in the menu of seasonal dishes, which include a host of fresh products imported from Italy. Outside, the attractive, raised terrace provides a great vantage point for people-watching, weather permitting.

Peasant

019

Italian

194 Elizabeth St. (bet. Prince & Spring Sts.)

Subway:	Spring St	Tuesday - Saturday 6pm - 11pm
Phone:	212-965-9511	Sunday 6pm - 10pm
Fax:	212-965-8471	Closed Monday & December 24 - 28
e-mail:	N/A	
Web:	www.peasantnyc.com	
Prices:	$$	

Chef Frank DeCarlo named his restaurant for his cooking style. Opened in 2000, Peasant emphasizes honest, Italian country fare, much of which is cooked in the wood-burning brick oven at the back of the room and served in terra-cotta pots. Comforts are simple here, too, with church-pew seating, exposed brick walls, and tabletop candles providing the main source of light. (Sure, the restaurant is dark, but then again, who doesn't look good in dim, romantic candlelight? Besides, the menu is entirely in Italian, so you can always use the lack of light as an excuse to ask for a translation.) Rustic entrées include lamb with polenta, gnocchi with meaty wild mushrooms, and steak Florentine.

Porcupine

Contemporary

20 Prince St. (bet. Mott & Elizabeth Sts.)

Subway:	Prince St	Monday 5:30pm - 11pm
Phone:	212-966-8886	Tuesday - Friday noon - 3pm
Fax:	212-966-8966	& 5:30pm - 11pm
e-mail:	N/A	Saturday - Sunday 11:30am - 4pm
Web:	www.jacquesnyc.com/porcupine	& 5:30pm - 11:30pm
Prices:	$$	

Strolling eastward down Prince Street, you just begin to think you've past all the restaurant choices when suddenly you stumble across Porcupine. It may have just opened in late 2004, but Porcupine already feels like an established part of the local fabric. The simple, unpretentious room lets the customers, not the décor, create the atmosphere (okay, the noise level can get high at times, but you never feel as if you're fighting against it). The kitchen intelligently pairs roast suckling pig with apples, grilled chicken with marjoram, and black bass with anise, tomatoes and black olives. As for service, the chatty waitstaff aims to please.

Public

Fusion

210 Elizabeth St. (bet. Prince & Spring Sts.)

Subway:	Spring St	Monday - Sunday 6pm - 2am
Phone:	212-343-7011	
Fax:	212-343-0918	
e-mail:	info@public-nyc.com	
Web:	www.public-nyc.com	
Prices:	$$$	

Here's your chance to sample Tasmanian sea trout, grilled kangaroo or New Zealand venison, complemented by a good selection of antipodean boutique wines. Public's kitchen takes it cue from London restaurant The Providores (owned by the same pair of chefs who founded Public) in creating a unique style of cooking that fuses Australian and New Zealand ingredients with influences that span the globe. Designed by AvroKO, this bright, airy Nolita spot incorporates salvaged pieces of public buildings into the erstwhile muffin factory it occupies, adding whimsical touches like shelves of library books and vintage card catalogs, and bronze post office boxes in which regulars can stash wine.

Manhattan SoHo & Nolita

Raoul's

022

180 Prince St. (bet. Sullivan & Thompson Sts.)

Subway:	Spring St	Monday - Sunday 5:30pm - 1am
Phone:	212-966-3518	Closed Thanksgiving Day
Fax:	212-966-0205	& Christmas Day
e-mail:	raoul@raouls.com	
Web:	www.raouls.com	
Prices:	$$$	

For any restaurant to survive for thirty years in this fickle business, they must be doing something right—and Raoul's does a lot of things right. The restaurant boasts authentic bistro charm, its walls covered with an assortment of pictures, many of whose subjects are in various stages of undress. Waiters here have mastered the stereotypic Gallic insouciance, and the kitchen turns out good classic French food, from escargot to frogs' legs; the menu is presented on small, individual blackboards. You can't help but be caught up in the lively atmosphere in the dimly lit main dining room, but if you're seeking something quieter, try the bright upstairs space or the tiny garden room.

Salt

023

58 MacDougal St. (bet. W. Houston & Prince Sts.)

Subway:	Spring St	Monday - Thursday 11:30am - 4pm
Phone:	212-674-4968	& 6pm - 11pm
Fax:	212-529-9111	Friday - Saturday 11:30am - 4pm
e-mail:	N/A	& 6pm - midnight
Web:	www.saltnyc.com	Closed Sunday & major holidays
Prices:	$$	

The term "neighborhood restaurant" is bandied about on a fairly casual basis these days, but Salt genuinely deserves this moniker. Here diners are encouraged to sit at one of three communal tables in the middle of the room, where you can rub elbows with the locals—and maybe even eavesdrop on some juicy SoHo gossip. The short but interesting menu contains a section called "Protein + 2," which is perfect for South Beach dieters, since it allows you to chose your entrée and pair it with any two side items (most of which are vegetables). You'd do equally well to trust the kitchen, though; the chef's selections are always fresh and seasonal.

Savoy

024

70 Prince St. (at Crosby St.)

Subway:	Prince St	Monday - Thursday noon - 10:30pm
Phone:	212-219-8570	Friday - Saturday noon - 11pm
Fax:	N/A	Sunday 4pm - 10pm
e-mail:	ph@savoynyc.com	
Web:	www.savoynyc.com	
Prices:	$$	

✗ If this restaurant wasn't so successful, locals would gladly keep Savoy as their own little secret. The little place is as unpretentious as it is relaxed, and it makes an ideal respite from the stresses of the day. Peter Hoffman and his wife, Susan Rosenfeld, opened Savoy in 1990 with the idea of creating memorable meals from the best local ingredients. To that end, they have developed relationships with local growers and producers so that the food you eat here quite literally has roots in the community. Items like sausage and bread are made in-house. The restaurant takes up two floors of an 1830s Federal-style town house, where wood-burning fireplaces add charm to each floor.

Snack

025

105 Thompson St. (bet. Prince & Spring Sts.)

Subway:	Spring St	Monday - Saturday noon - 11pm
Phone:	212-925-1040	Sunday noon - 9pm
Fax:	212-925-0696	Closed major holidays
e-mail:	N/A	
Web:	N/A	
Prices:	$$	

✗ Don't blink, or you're liable to walk right past Snack. Seating just ten people at five lime-green tables, this sweet little Greek place offers a refreshing antidote to SoHo's über-trendy temples of gastronomy. Enveloped by sepia-toned photographs of Hellenic landmarks and shelves of Mediterranean grocery items, you'll feel transported to sunnier climes. Indeed, when you taste the fresh, unpretentious and authentic Greek cuisine, you'll half-expect to feel sand between your toes. The friendly staff is more than willing to offer guidance to diners unfamiliar with the dishes here, which are reassuringly scrawled on a blackboard. Makes you wish your grandma was Greek.

Manhattan *SoHo & Nolita*

Va Tutto!

Italian

026

23 Cleveland Pl. (bet. Spring & Kenmare Sts.)

Subway:	Spring St	Monday - Sunday noon - 11pm
Phone:	212-941-0286	
Fax:	N/A	
e-mail:	N/A	
Web:	www.vatutto.com	
Prices:	SS	

Any restaurant whose name means "anything goes" has to be worth at least a look, and Va Tutto is worth much more. From the kitchen here comes rustic fare redolent with the flavors of Tuscany. Mozzarella is made in-house and served on wooden chopping boards; chicken is roasted and served with goat-cheese polenta and oyster mushrooms. Like the cooking, the décor echoes the Tuscan countryside with wine bottles lining shelves in the dining room, and bunches of garlic cloves hanging here and there. This is one of the relatively few places in SoHo that's open at midday; in warm weather, the outdoor garden is a relaxing spot to lunch, shaded by a vine-covered pergola and white market umbrellas.

Zoë

Contemporary

027

90 Prince St. (bet. Broadway & Mercer St.)

Subway:	Spring St	Monday noon - 3pm
Phone:	212-966-6722	Tuesday - Friday noon - 3pm
Fax:	212-966-6718	& 6pm - 10:30pm
e-mail:	zoerest@aol.com	Saturday 11:30am - 3pm
Web:	www.zoerestaurant.com	& 5:30pm - 11:30pm
Prices:	SS	Sunday 11:30am - 3pm & 5:30pm - 10pm

With its terra-cotta columns, rich colors and mosaic tiles, Zoë's bold surroundings have been packing 'em into this 19th-century SoHo landmark since 1992. The cuisine is American at heart, but it roams from the Far East to the Mediterranean for its inspiration. Fish is a popular menu staple here, and Zoë offers more than 35 wines by the glass as accompaniment. Just be sure to leave room for such goodies as caramelized banana tart and cappuccino cheesecake. Clad in matching blue shirts, the waitstaff boasts the courteous and unflustered manner that comes from being proficient at working a busy room. As a whole, the operation possesses the confidence of a well-oiled machine.

EVERYTHING YOU GET FROM MICHELIN TIRES NOW IN A NEW RANGE OF AUTOMOTIVE ACCESSORIES.

TAKE THEM FOR A TEST DRIVE TODAY.

or over a hundred years, Michelin has developed products and services to make fe on the road safer, more efficient and more enjoyable. And now Michelin offers n innovative collection of automotive accessories which epitomize its long-standing alues of performance, dependability and safety. The collection includes flation and pressure monitoring products, air compressors and air tools, mergency/breakdown assistance products, wiper blades, wheel and tire change quipment, wheel and tire care products, pressure washers, floor mats and air esheners. **The Michelin Automotive Accessories Collection is on the road right now.**

MICHELIN

A better way forward

About
TriBeCa

An intriguing wedge of warehouses, loft residences, art galleries and oh-so-chic restaurants, TriBeCa was named in the 1970s by a real-estate agent hoping to create a hip identity for the area. The acronym—which stands for Triangle Below Canal—stuck, and true to expectations, TriBeCa has become a trendy place. So far, it has not been commercialized nearly to the extent that SoHo has, despite being home to dozens of celebrities, most notably actor Robert DeNiro. For paparazzi-dodging starlets, that is precisely its appeal.

Technically, TriBeCa is not a triangle but a trapezoid. Its boundaries are *(clockwise from north)* Canal Street, Broadway, Murray Street, and the Hudson River. Greenwich and Hudson Streets are the main thoroughfares for dining and nightlife; art and interior-design stores are scattered throughout the district.

A Bit of History – Once used as farmland by Dutch settlers, the area now known as TriBeCa was included in a large tract granted to Trinity Church in 1705. In the ensuing century, wealthy families built elegant residences around Hudson Square (now the Hudson River Tunnel traffic rotary). A fruit and produce market opened in 1813 at the western edge of the neighborhood, but the quarter remained primarily residential until the mid-19th century, when the shipping and warehousing industries formerly located at the South Street Seaport moved to deepwater piers on the Hudson River. Five- and six-story "store and loft" buildings were built around the district to accommodate the new trade. By 1939, Washington Market, as the area along Greenwich Street came to be known, boasted a greater volume of business than all the other markets in the city combined.

© Martha Cooper

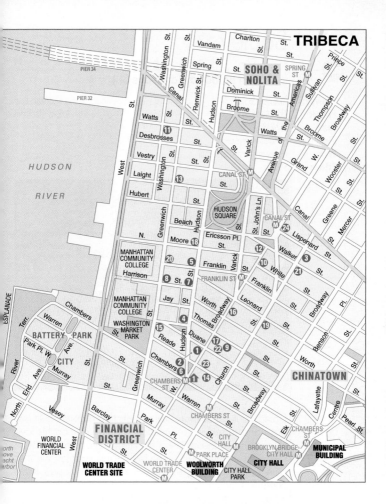

In the 1960s, city planners approved urban-renewal projects that called for the demolition of many old buildings along the waterfront. Luckily, enough of the old commercial warehouses remained to attract artists pushed out of SoHo and others seeking cavernous industrial living space. Today, those same artists would be hard-pressed to afford such a space in TriBeCa; loft-apartment prices now start at around $1 million.

Trendy TriBeCa – Catering as they do to a local clientele of creative types, TriBeCa is a cool place to eat. You can splurge on a meal here in expensive restaurants whose reputations precede them, or go for more modest fare. If it's a sunny day, snag an umbrella-shaded table outside—TriBeCa's wide sidewalks accommodate lots of them.

Bouley ✿✿

Contemporary French

120 West Broadway (at Duane St.)

001

Subway:	Chambers St	Monday - Sunday 11:30am - 3pm
Phone:	212-964-2525	& 5pm - 11:30pm
Fax:	212-219-3443	
e-mail:	info@bouleynyc.com	
Web:	www.bouleyrestaurants.com	
Prices:	$$$$	

Bouley/Tobias Everke

David Bouley's culinary skill reflects two different cultures. Born and raised in Connecticut, Bouley gained his love of cooking at the stove of his French grandmother. Afte r stints in a number of U.S. restaurants, Bouley went to France, where he worked with some of Europe's finest chefs.

At Bouley, diners have the choice of eating in one of two different vaulted-ceilinged rooms: the intimate red room, with its claret-colored Venetian-stucco walls; or the airy white room, with its antique French fireplace. The menu reflects Bouley's travels to Japan, along with his strong grounding in French technique. Innovatively prepared and presented, the food exhibits a festival of flavors (think Texas Kobe beef with Asian celery purée, and Japanese yellowtail with Cavaillon melon and Hon-Shimeji mushrooms). You can even take home a souvenir from the new Bouley Market and Bakery across the street.

Ocean Herbal Broth with Shrimp

Ingredients

- 4 large diver scallops, deeply scored on one side
- 3 oz. squid bodies, scored
- 1 oz. squid heads and tentacles
- 12 sweet baby shrimp, shelled
- 4 (20- to 25-count) tiger shrimp, peeled and deveined
- 2 oz. jumbo lump crabmeat
- 1 tsp. freshly ground pepper
- ½ oz. grated coconut
- 1 tsp. salt
- 1 cup Wondra flour
- ½ cup canola oil
- 2 Tbsp. butter
- 1 oz. phyllo dough

Ocean Herbal Broth Ingredients

1.7 oz. tomato water	.5 oz. garlic purée
.4 oz. fennel purée	.3 oz. onion purée
.5 oz. celery purée	.4 oz. basil oil
.4 oz. chive oil	3.4 oz. clam juice
.4 oz dill oil	

Slice phyllo dough into thin strips, 3 inches long. Coat shrimp with coconut. Press each side of shrimp into phyllo. Shrimp should be evenly coated on both sides with both ingredients.

Combine flour, salt and pepper. Dredge squid and scallops in seasoned flour. Heat two sauté pans over high heat and add 2 Tbsp. oil to each. Add scallops to one pan, scored side down. Push gently with a spatula to flare out the scoring. Sauté at medium-high heat for a minute, then add 1 Tbsp. of butter. Baste scallops with melting butter. Cook until underside is brown, then flip and cook on the other side for a few seconds. Remove and set aside. Add 2 Tbsp. of oil to same pan with baby shrimp and sauté a few minutes, until just translucent.

Meanwhile, add squid to other pan. Sauté on high heat until the flat pieces curl and tentacles are cooked through, 1-2 minutes. Remove from pan and add 2 Tbsp. of canola oil and tiger shrimp and sauté on each side until phyllo is golden and the shrimp curl slightly. Remove and set aside. In same pan, melt 1 Tbsp. of butter and add crabmeat. Season with salt and pepper to taste. Remove and set aside.

In sauté pan, combine clam juice, tomato water, garlic, fennel, onion and celery purées. Bring to a simmer and season with salt and pepper. Remove from heat and whisk in oils slowly.

Place a small mound of crabmeat in four shallow bowls. Spoon hot ocean herbal broth around it. Place a scallop on top of crabmeat. Prop tiger shrimp next to it. Arrange squid and baby shrimp around the plate.

Danube ✿✿

30 Hudson St. (bet. Duane & Reade Sts.)

Subway:	Chambers St	Monday - Saturday 5pm - 11:30pm
Phone:	212-791-3771	Closed Sunday
Fax:	212-219-3443	
e-mail:	info@bouleyrestaurants.com	
Web:	www.thedanube.net	
Prices:	$$$	

Manhattan *TriBeCa*

Danube/Tobias Everke

Named for the river that flows through Vienna, Danube represents chef David Bouley's Austrian fantasy, as realized by designer Jacques Garcia and architect Kevin White. Have a seat in the stately dining room, and you'll be cosseted in the luxury of late-19th-century Vienna. Plush sofas stand in for banquettes here; ceilings are covered in Venetian stucco, and dark drapes dress tall, arched windows. Stunning paintings, inspired by the work of Austrian artist Gustav Klimt, line the walls.

Menu selections here include the chef's weekly market choices, an Austrian menu, a "modern eclectic" menu, and the chef's five-course tasting menu. Whatever you decide, you'll relish excellent creations like high-altitude Austrian cheese ravioli with harvest corn sauce, and seared wild sturgeon with Austrian crescent potato and Oscetra caviar. The interesting wine list spans Austria, France and the U.S.

Danube/Thomas Schauer

Yellowtail Tuna with Caviar and Vodka Sauce

Serves 4

Spinach Purée

3 Tbsp. unsalted butter 3 shallots, diced
1 tsp. sea salt   ½ cup heavy cream
1 sprig thyme   ¼ tsp. white pepper
¼ tsp. cayenne pepper
¼ tsp. grated nutmeg
¾ cup vegetable stock
1 bunch flat-leaf spinach, cleaned, stems removed 2 large garlic cloves, minced

Melt butter in a saucepan over medium-high heat. Cook until milk solids fall to the bottom and turn brown. Add shallots and ½ tsp. of salt. Cook, stirring, until shallots soften. Add garlic and cook until soft. Add cream and thyme, bringing liquid to a boil. Simmer until reduced by one-third. Add vegetable stock and let liquid return to boil. Add spinach and cook gently, tossing until wilted and tender. Remove thyme. With a slotted spoon, transfer spinach and shallots to a blender, reserving ½ cup of liquid. Purée spinach and season with salt, cayenne, white pepper and nutmeg. Keep warm.

Yellowtail Tuna

4 cups canola oil   8 garlic cloves
1 sprig thyme   1 bay leaf
1 pound yellowtail tuna, cut crosswise into 8 equal slices

Pour oil into a saucepan to fill halfway. Place a deep-frying thermometer in pan. Add garlic, thyme, and bay leaf to the oil and heat gently to 145°F. Lay fish in a single layer on top of garlic and herbs so each piece is submerged but does not touch the bottom of pan. Maintaining 145°F, cook fish until medium (8-10 minutes). Drain and lay on a paper-towel-lined plate.

Vodka-Caviar Sauce

½ cup crème fraîche   2 Tbsp. vodka
2 ½ tsp. minced shallots 1 ¼ tsp. orange zest
1 tsp. each minced chervil, parsley, tarragon and chives
½ tsp. lemon juice   2 tsp. CK caviar

Bring crème fraîche to boil in saucepan over medium heat. Simmer rapidly until reduced by half. Reduce heat, add vodka, shallots, orange zest, herbs and lemon juice. Season with salt and white pepper to taste. Keep warm. Before serving, stir in 2 tsp. caviar.

To Serve

1 cup potato salad, finely chopped
Spoon a wide round of spinach on each plate. Lay 2 thin lines of potato salad across spinach. Arrange 2 fish filets on each plate. Spoon vodka sauce over fish and garnish with caviar.

Lo Scalco ✿

Italian

003

313 Church St. (bet. Lispenard & Walker Sts.)

Subway:	Canal St	Monday - Thursday 6:30pm - 11:30pm
Phone:	212-343-2900	Friday noon - 3pm & 6:30pm - midnight
Fax:	212-343-2904	Saturday 6:30pm - midnight
e-mail:	N/A	Closed Sunday
Web:	N/A	
Prices:	$$$	

XXX

Lo Scalco/David Joseph

This isn't your mama's red-sauce joint, so don't expect run-of-the-mill Italian fare here. It's the love child of chef/owner Mauro Mafrici and his wife, Kimberly, who designed the dining space. Every dish that comes out of the kitchen bears the innovative signature of chef Mafrici, whose résumé includes stints at Felidia and I Trulli. He fashions his menu around different ingredients (artichokes, tomato, asparagus, tuna, veal, lamb, duck, etc.) and offers three preparations of each (appetizer, pasta and entrée). Of course, the list changes constantly to reflect what's freshest at the market.

Italian vintages form the core of the wine collection, and the knowledgeable sommelier will happily help you make a selection. This is the place for a relaxing meal; you can feel free to linger in the restful, beige-toned dining room, knowing that the staff won't rush you out to seat other guests.

Standup Cannelloni with Sheep Ricotta

Serves 4

Filling

- 2 lbs. sheep ricotta (fresh ricotta Calabro can be substituted)
- ¼ lb. artichokes, cleaned, julienned and sautéed
- 2 Tbsp. Parmigiano Reggiano
- 1 tsp. parsley, chopped
- 2 Tbsp. roasted tomato (see technique below)
- 4 eight-inch-square dried lasagna sheets

Sauce

- 1 cup chicken stock
- 4 Tbsp. veal demi-glace
- ¼ lb. grated Parmigiano Reggiano
- ¼ lb. butter
- 1 tsp. parsley chopped
- salt and pepper to taste

Method

Roast tomatoes on a sheet pan in the oven at 220°F until they are semi-dry. Allow tomatoes to cool and chop coarsely.

Mix roast tomatoes with sheep ricotta, artichokes, Parmigiano Reggiano and parsley. Season with salt and pepper to taste.

Boil pasta for 3-4 minutes and cool in ice-water bath. Drain pasta, dry carefully and lie the sheets out on a table. Spread pasta evenly with filling and roll into tubes.

Preheat oven to 375°F. Place cannelloni in the freezer for 30 minutes until solid (this makes pasta easier to cut). Remove and cut into three 2½-inch slices. Place cannelloni slices on a buttered sheet pan, sprinkle with Parmigiano Reggiano and bake until golden.

While cannelloni are baking, combine in a sauté pan over medium heat, chicken stock, butter, parsley, salt and pepper. Stir constantly until the sauce turns creamy. Bring the demi-glace to a boil in a separate sauté pan. Place 3 cannelloni on each plate and spoon parsley sauce over top of each piece. Drizzle demi-glace over the top and sprinkle Parmigiano Reggiano on plate to finish.

Scalini Fedeli ✿

004

165 Duane St. (bet. Greenwich & Hudson Sts.)

Subway:	Chambers St	Monday 5:30pm - 10pm
Phone:	212-528-0400	Tuesday - Thursday noon - 2:30pm
Fax:	212-587-8773	& 5:30pm - 10pm
e-mail:	N/A	Friday noon - 2:30pm & 5:30pm - 11pm
Web:	www.scalinifedeli.com	Saturday 5:30pm - 11pm
Prices:	$$$	Closed Sunday

XXX

Scalini Fedeli

Manhattan *TriBeCa*

After training in several big-name restaurants in Italy and Monaco, young chef Michael Cetrulo decided to take a bite out of the Big Apple in 2000. It was then that he added Scalini Fedeli («steps of faith» in Italian) to TriBeCa's restaurant roster. In the space formerly occupied by Bouley, Cetrulo fashioned a seductive Tuscan ambience embellished with graceful vaulted ceilings and light-yellow hues. Diners here have a choice of three different fixed-price menus, all showcasing recipes from northern Italy. If the sound of wild striped bass with spicy white bean and rosemary stew, or pappardelle with a game sauce made with venison and hare, finished with Barolo wine and bitter chocolate makes your mouth water, make tracks for Scalini Fedeli. For chocoholics, there's a separate dessert menu that just lists chocolate sweets. (Hint: If you're on a budget, go for lunch.)

Scalini Fedeli

Risotto with Mushrooms and Crispy Zucchini

Serves 4

Risotto

2 cups chicken broth
1 cup + 1/3 cup white wine
5 Tbsp. Arborio rice
4 oz. heavy cream
¼ cup dried porcini mushrooms
¼ cup sliced shitaki mushrooms
¼ cup sliced portobello mushrooms
¼ cup sliced crimini mushrooms
¼ cup sliced champanian mushrooms
2 Tbsp. butter
2 Tbsp. black truffle juice
2 Tbsp. grated Parmagiano Reggiano
1 Tbsp. Spanish onions, finely chopped
1 clove garlic
1 tsp. olive oil
1 tsp. finely chopped black winter truffle
1 tsp. chopped fresh thyme

Soak dry porcini mushrooms in 1 cup of white wine for at least 45 minutes. Whip heavy cream to until it forms soft peaks. Put olive oil, butter, onion and garlic in a heavy-bottomed pot over medium-high heat and sauté for 2 minutes. Add all sliced fresh mushrooms. Cook for 10 minutes or until mushrooms are soft, stirring occasionally. Add rice and cook for 2 more minutes. Add white wine and cook until wine is reduced. Then add truffle juice, fresh thyme, dried porcini mushrooms and their strained soaking liquid. Lower flame and let liquid reduce. Stirring constantly, add chicken broth, one ounce at a time. Once the liquid has almost evaporated, and the risotto is creamy (about 15 minutes), check for tenderness. If risotto is not tender enough, add more chicken broth and cook until reduced.

Off the flame, stir in Parmagiano Reggiano, and season to taste with salt and fresh ground black pepper. Slowly fold whipped cream and serve in four bowls. Top with fried zucchini batons (recipe follows).

Garnish

1 medium-size zucchini 3 Tbsp. flour
3 cups vegetable oil for frying

Cut zucchini in batons, about 2 inches long and ¼-inch wide. Rinse in cold water and drain. Heat oil to 375°F. Dust zucchini in flour, lightly fry until golden brown, about 4-5 minutes. Dry on paper towels. Season to taste with salt and fresh ground black pepper.

Nobu ✿

Contemporary Japanese

005

105 Hudson St. (at Franklin St.)

Subway:	Franklin St	Monday - Sunday 11:45am - 2:15pm
Phone:	212-219-0500	& 5:45pm - 10:15pm
Fax:	212-219-1441	
e-mail:	N/A	
Web:	www.myriadrestaurantgroup.com	
Prices:	$$	

Nobu/Steven Freeman

Nobu Matsuhisa started his epicurean empire in 1987, when he opened Matsuhisa sushi bar in Beverly Hills, California. From there, the renowned Japanese-born chef expanded his holdings to cities in Europe and across the U.S. In 1994 Matsuhisa's New York City Nobu was born in TriBeCa, in partnership with Drew Nieporent and actor Robert DeNiro. Architect David Rockwell imagined the Japanese countryside in Nobu's dining room, replete with stylized birch trees and a wall of black river stones (although the décor looks a bit tired these days).

Once you taste the seductive sushi and sashimi, you'll understand Nobu's appeal. But don't pass up Matsuhisa's signature miso-glazed black cod, or monkfish pâté with caviar. Next Door Nobu offers similar food in a simpler ambience *(reservations not accepted)*. In Midtown, try Nobu Fifty Seven *(40 W. 57th St.)*, which opened in summer 2005.

Manhattan *TriBeCa*

White Fish Tiradito, Nobu Style

Serves 4

18 oz. (500g) red snapper fillet

2 Tbsp. rocoto chile paste (or other hot chile sauce with thick consistency)

40 cilantro leaves

1 Tbsp. plus 1 tsp. yuzu juice

3 Tbsp. lemon juice

sea salt

Method

Chill 4 plates in refrigerator for at least one hour. Cut the fish into paper-thin slices using a very sharp knife and arrange evenly on 4 plates. Place a cilantro leaf and a small dollop of rocoto chile paste on each slice of fish.

Drizzle the sliced fish with yuzu and lemon juice and season generously with sea salt. The flavor of this dish depends on the salt—if too little is used, the dish will taste bland.

Acappella

Italian

006

1 Hudson St. (at Chambers St.)

Subway:	Chambers St	Monday - Friday noon - 3pm
Phone:	212-240-0163	& 5pm - 10:30pm
Fax:	212-267-8641	Saturday 5pm - 11pm
e-mail:	N/A	Closed Sunday
Web:	www.acappella-restaurant.com	
Prices:	$$$	

XXX

If this restaurant looks familiar, it may be because you saw it in the first episode of the popular HBO series *The Sopranos*, part of which was filmed here. A large reproduction of the imposing portrait of Frederico da Montefeltro, erstwhile duke of Urbino, dominates the brick wall of the dining room (the original, painted by Piero della Francesca in 1645, is on display in Florence). The rest of the lovely room boasts stately columns, antique tapestries, and large, curtained windows in front. Overseen by chef/owner Sergio Acappella, the kitchen turns out carefully prepared Northern Italian dishes, including homemade pastas. At the end of your meal, enjoy a complimentary glass of grappa.

Chanterelle

Contemporary French

007

2 Harrison St. (at Hudson St.)

Subway:	Franklin St	Monday 5:30pm - 11pm
Phone:	212-966-6960	Tuesday - Saturday noon - 2:30pm
Fax:	212-966-6143	& 5:30pm - 11pm
e-mail:	info@chanterellenyc.com	Closed Sunday & major holidays
Web:	www.chanterellenyc.com	
Prices:	$$$$	

XXX
&

It's not easy to keep a restaurant going for more than 20 years, but owners Karen and David Waltuck have managed to do it, and do it well. Set within the 19th-century New York Mercantile Exchange, the Art Nouveau-style dining room reflects Karen's feminine touch in its peach tones, lace curtains, fresh flowers, and the menu's sprawling handwritten script. The monthly changing menu offers David's take on French cuisine with a light contemporary touch. Be sure to check out Chanterelle's collection of menu covers near the reception desk; Robert Mapplethorpe, Roy Lichtenstein and Louise Nevelson number among the artists who have designed covers for the restaurant.

The Harrison

008

355 Greenwich St. (at Harrison St.)

Subway:	Franklin St	Monday - Thursday 5:30pm - 11pm
Phone:	212-274-9310	Friday - Saturday 5:30pm - 11:30pm
Fax:	212-274-9376	Sunday 5pm - 10pm
e-mail:	N/A	
Web:	www.theharrison.com	
Prices:	$$	

XXX

Chef-restaurateur team Jimmy Bradley and Danny Abrams have another hit on their hands with The Harrison, the second of their four restaurants (The Red Cat in Chelsea was first; Mermaid Inn and Pace followed The Harrison). Located at the corner of Greenwich and Harrison streets, the restaurant opened in 2001. The professional team is always ready to help; the staff keeps a constant lookout around the rustic-chic dining room to make sure their customers have everything they want. From the kitchen here come serious contemporary American cuisine and delectable desserts. To accompany your meal, wines by the glass and half-bottles from the 200-bottle wine list are yours for the choosing.

Megu

009

62 Thomas St. (bet. West Broadway & Church St.)

Subway:	Franklin St	Monday - Friday 11:30am - 2:30pm
Phone:	212-964-7777	& 5:30pm - 11:30pm
Fax:	212-964-7776	Saturday - Sunday 5:30pm - 11:30pm
e-mail:	info@megunyc.com	
Web:	www.megunyc.com	
Prices:	$$$	

XXX

For an awe-inspiring experience, follow the kimono-clad hostess downstairs to the 13,000-square-foot, two-story space Megu reserves for diners. Ultra-sleek design meets traditional Japanese elements in this spacious room, which centers on an ice carving of Buddha floating over a rose-petal-strewn pool. Above the Buddha hangs a huge bonsho, an exact replica of Japan's largest temple bell. White porcelain columns, fashioned from rice bowls and sake vases, line the upper tier of the room. The progression of courses in Megu's different tasting menus may include skewered meat or fish grilled over rare Bincho-tan charcoal, as well as meat seared on hot river stones imported from Japan.

Manhattan TriBeCa

Montrachet

Contemporary French

010

239 West Broadway (bet. Walker & White Sts.)

Subway:	Canal St	Monday - Thursday 5:30pm - 10:30pm
Phone:	212-219-2777	Friday noon - 2:30pm & 5:30pm - 11pm
Fax:	N/A	Saturday 5:30pm - 11pm
e-mail:	N/A	Closed Sunday
Web:	www.myriadrestaurantgroup.com	
Prices:	$$	

If you're looking for a great restaurant for wine in New York City, look no farther. Named for the much-celebrated white Burgundy wine, Montrachet offers a superb wine list from its 16,000-bottle cellar. The roster includes, of course, a huge selection of Burgundies. Part of Drew Nieporent's Myriad Restaurant Group, Montrachet has been around since 1985, a fact that qualifies it as one of TriBeCa's first fine-dining restaurants. Customers here can choose from the à la carte menu or several different chef's tasting menus. Monday is BYOB night, when patrons are welcome to bring a bottle of their own choosing, and the restaurant will waive their usual corkage fee.

Capsouto Frères

French

011

451 Washington St. (at Watts St.)

Subway:	Canal St	Monday 6pm - 11pm
Phone:	212-966-4900	Tuesday - Sunday noon - 3:30pm
Fax:	212-925-5296	& 6pm - 11pm
e-mail:	anyfrere@capsoutofreres.com	
Web:	www.capsoutofreres.com	
Prices:	$$	

Before you enter Capsouto Frères, be sure to stop and take a gander at the striking 1891 landmark structure in which the restaurant is housed. A handsome mix of Romanesque and Flemish Revival style, this brick and stone building on the corner of Watts Street once held a shoe factory. Although you won't find a trendy interior inside the ground-floor restaurant, you will discover old-fashioned charm in the dining room. Since 1980, Capsouto Frères has been pleasing diners with the likes of sole meunière, duck confit and cassoulet. The yummy soufflés, a specialty here, are the best choice if your sweet tooth is crying for dessert.

Della Rovere

012

250 West Broadway (at Beach St.)

Subway:	Canal St	Monday - Wednesday noon - 3pm
Phone:	212-334-3470	& 6pm - 11pm
Fax:	N/A	Thursday - Friday noon - 3pm
e-mail:	N/A	& 6pm - midnight
Web:	N/A	Saturday 6pm - midnight
Prices:	$$	Closed Sunday & major holidays

Della Rovere honors the name of the owner's ancestors, who count two popes—Sixtus IV and Julius II—in their family tree. But don't worry; the restaurant's casual atmosphere belies this lofty lineage. Painted in hues of yellow and red, the warm and rustic dining room overlooks the raw bar and the open kitchen. From the former, you can order an assortment of meat and cheeses, as well as a selection of raw oysters. In the latter, a professional team plates up hearty pastas and delightful Italian entrées such as roasted cod with toasted bread salad. Check out the balcony where the wines are stored on dark wood shelves; most of the labels can be ordered by the glass.

Dylan Prime

013

62 Laight St. (at Greenwich St.)

Subway:	Canal St	Monday - Wednesday noon - 2:30pm
Phone:	212-334-4783	& 5:30pm - 11pm
Fax:	N/A	Thursday - Friday noon - 2:30pm
e-mail:	info@dylanprime.com	& 5:30pm - midnight
Web:	www.dylanprime.com	Saturday - Sunday 5:30pm - midnight
Prices:	$$$	

Dylan Prime lies a bit off the beaten track from the heart of TriBeCa's action, but you won't regret the detour. The menu here is contemporary American with an emphasis on meat: Prime cuts of filet mignon, aged prime rib, and a man-sized 32-ounce Porterhouse are all served with your choice of sauces (from herb Béarnaise to foie gras butter). Then there's the Carpetbagger steak, the chef's creation of an 11-ounce filet mignon stuffed with Blue Point oysters. You'll also find a few seafood entrées, but the meat's the thing here. Low, moody lighting provides an intimate vibe, and a window wall affords diners a look at the impressive wine selection, which consists mainly of California vintages.

Manhattan *TriBeCa*

Fresh

Seafood

014

105 Reade St. (bet. Church St. & West Broadway)

Subway:	Chambers St	Monday - Friday 11:30am - 2:30pm
Phone:	212-406-1900	& 5pm - 11pm
Fax:	212-406-4814	Saturday 5pm - 11pm
e-mail:	freshshorecoast@gmail.com	Closed Sunday
Web:	www.freshshorecoast.com	
Prices:	$$	

It's easy to ensure that your restaurant serves the freshest seafood possible when you own your own seafood company. That's the case with Eric Tevrow, owner of Fresh. His seafood company supplies products to some of the best-known chefs in New York, as well as being the sole provider of fish to Tevrow's three Manhattan restaurants (the other two are Coast and Shore). As you'd expect, the menu at Fresh changes every day to feature the daily catch, which might include choices from Maine peekytoe crab to Nantucket strawberry bass and Florida Keys grouper. The restaurant, with its affable waitstaff and sea-themed dining room, nets a steady stream of loyal fish lovers.

Gigino Trattoria

Italian

015

323 Greenwich St. (bet. Duane & Reade Sts.)

Subway:	Chambers St	Monday - Thursday 11:30am - 11pm
Phone:	212-431-1112	Friday - Sunday 11:30am - midnight
Fax:	212-431-1294	
e-mail:	N/A	
Web:	www.gigino-trattoria.com	
Prices:	$$	

Picture a trattoria in a little town in Italy. When you walk in, you receive a warm greeting by the kind staff; the décor is unpretentious, but cheery, with a wood-beamed ceiling, glowing yellow walls, and a wood-burning oven. You'll find this same ambience at Gigino, hidden away in lower TriBeCa. With an extensive list of reasonably priced dishes ranging from oven-fired pizzas to hearty entrées to the signature pasta, spaghetti del Padrino (made with beets, escarole, garlic and anchovy-flavored olive oil), Gigino works at satisfying the appetites of every member of the family. In the Financial District, Gigino at Wagner Park (20 Battery Pl.) boasts an outdoor terrace with harbor views.

Landmarc

French

179 West Broadway (bet. Leonard & Worth Sts.)

Subway:	Franklin St	Monday - Friday noon - 5pm
Phone:	212-343-3883	& 5:30pm - 2am
Fax:	N/A	Saturday - Sunday 11am - 5pm
e-mail:	info@landmarc-restaurant.com	& 5:30pm - 2am
Web:	www.landmarc-restaurant.com	
Prices:	$$	

Established by chef Marc Murphy and his wife, Pamela, in spring 2004, Landmarc brings innovative bistro-style fare to TriBeCa. As the son of a diplomat, Murphy grew up traveling in France and Italy, a heritage that is reflected in the restaurant's menu and well-priced wine list. With its exposed brick walls, sleek booths and contemporary artwork, the bi-level dining room blends well with the neighborhood's trendy ambience. Be sure to try dessert here; for one low set price you can sample every sweet on the menu. For families, Landmarc offers a seasonal kids' menu. At the end of the meal, little ones are treated to cotton candy in unconventional flavors. *Reservations not accepted, except for parties of 6 or more.*

The Odeon

American

145 West Broadway (at Thomas St.)

Subway:	Chambers St	Monday - Sunday noon - 2am
Phone:	212-233-0507	
Fax:	212-406-1962	
e-mail:	theodeonpr@mac.com	
Web:	www.theodeonrestaurant.com	
Prices:	$$	

A red neon marquee above the door marks The Odeon, a TriBeCa hot spot since the early 1980s. Now as then, you can still catch a glimpse of big-name entertainers and artists here, but regular folks are welcome, too. The Art Deco space uses Formica-topped tables, wood paneling and 1930s light fixtures to suggest a casual Parisian bistro, and the kitchen interprets American dishes with a discreet French flair. Check out the weekday fixed-price menu for lunch; it's the perfect way to snag unpretentious, refined cuisine at reasonable prices. If you're out partying late, drop by for the brasserie menu of light fare, served every night from midnight until 2am.

Manhattan TriBeCa

Pace

Italian

018

121 Hudson St. (at N. Moore St.)

Subway:	Franklin St	Monday - Saturday 5:30pm - 11:30pm
Phone:	212-965-9500	Sunday 5pm - 10pm
Fax:	212-965-4753	
e-mail:	N/A	
Web:	www.pacetribeca.com	
Prices:	$$	

Pace (say PAH-chay; it's Italian for "peace") is the most recent venture of the dynamic restaurant duo Jimmy Bradley and Danny Abrams. Opened in 2004, the restaurant fills the first floor of a post-Industrial redbrick building and is designed to look like it has been a neighborhood fixture for years. This is a place where you feel immediately at ease—whether you sit at the animated bar; in the welcoming dining room, with its mural of ancient Rome and its distinctive wrought-iron chandelier with green and yellow blown-glass globes; or at one of the outdoor terrace tables. Refined Italian regional fare keeps 'em coming back for more.

66

Chinese

019

241 Church St. (at Leonard St.)

Subway:	Franklin St	Monday - Wednesday noon - 3pm
Phone:	212-925-0202	& 5:30pm - 11pm
Fax:	212-925-5440	Thursday - Saturday noon - 3pm
e-mail:	N/A	& 5:30pm - midnight
Web:	www.jean-georges.com	Sunday noon - 3pm
Prices:	$$	& 5:30pm - 10:30pm

Celebrated chef-cum-entrepreneur Jean-Georges Vongerichten has long been fascinated with the Orient, based on his many years of work and travel in that part of the world. Contemporary is the key word here, from the sleek décor to the modern interpretations of traditional Chinese dishes. At 66, red cloth festooned with Chinese characters drapes like flags in a line above the communal table, and curving frosted-glass panels divide the dining space. One of the areas even has a view of the kitchen through an aquarium stocked with exotic fish. Entrées run from steamed cod with caramelized onions, ginger and scallions to stir-fried Niman Ranch pork.

Tribeca Grill

020

375 Greenwich St. (at Franklin St.)

Subway:	Franklin St	Monday - Thursday 11:30am - 11pm
Phone:	212-941-3900	Friday 11:30am - 11:30pm
Fax:	212-941-3915	Saturday 5:30pm - 11:30pm
e-mail:	N/A	Sunday 11:30am - 3pm
Web:	www.myriadrestaurantgroup.com	& 5:30pm - 10pm
Prices:	$$$	

Another venture by Drew Nieporent and actor Robert DeNiro, Tribeca Grill burst on the scene in 1990. The building that now serves as the headquarters for DeNiro's TriBeCa film company housed the Martinson Coffee factory in the early 1900s. Today the first two floors pay homage to another beverage: wine. More like a tome, the wine list cites 1,700 labels at prices starting as low as $30; selections include more than 250 vintages of Châteauneuf-du-Pape. The kitchen treats regional ingredients (peekytoe crab, Hudson Valley foie gras) with a light hand to showcase their natural flavors. Recalling the building's industrial origins, pipes and brickwork are left exposed in the dining room.

Bread Tribeca

021

301 Church St. (at Walker St.)

Subway:	Canal St	Sunday - Thursday 11:30am - 11pm
Phone:	212-334-8282	Friday - Saturday 11am - midnight
Fax:	212-334-3272	
e-mail:	N/A	
Web:	www.breadtribeca.com	
Prices:	$$	

Inside this windowed façade on the corner of Church and Walker streets, you'll find a simple, contemporary décor upstaged by good Italian cuisine that's easy to eat any time of day. As you'd guess from the name, Bread Tribeca specializes in a variety of tasty sandwiches, with fillings such as Sicilian sardines, handmade mozzarella, and prosciutto di Parma stuffed between crusty ciabatta bread or baguettes. But wait, there's more. Don't overlook the fresh salads, pastas, seafood entrées, and thin-crust pizzas cooked in the wood-burning oven. And be sure to leave room for the yummy caramelized banana tart, served with vanilla ice cream.

Manhattan TriBeCa

Le Zinc

022

139 Duane St. (bet. Church St. & West Broadway)

Subway:	Chambers St	Monday 11:30am - 11pm
Phone:	212-513-0001	Tuesday - Wednesday 11:30am
Fax:	212-513-7269	- midnight
e-mail:	info@lezincnyc.com	Thursday - Friday 11:30am - 1am
Web:	www.lezincnyc.com	Saturday 10am - 4pm & 5pm - 1am
Prices:	**$$**	Sunday 10am - 4pm & 5pm - 11pm

Karen and David Waltuck, the couple behind Chanterelle, brought this little TriBeCa bistro to life. For the décor, they papered the walls with art posters, and added red banquettes, bistro chairs and a long zinc bar. All this makes a pleasant atmosphere (despite the loud rock music) in which to dine on the likes of crispy skate, balsamic-braised short ribs, and herb ricotta gnocchi. At lunchtime, there's also a list of sandwiches, but not your normal deli fare (think duck leg confit wrap or albacore tuna on a brioche with pickled ginger and pea shoots). The friendly waitstaff takes pains to make sure that everything is satisfactory.

Nam

023

110 Reade St. (bet. West Broadway & Church St.)

Subway:	Chambers St	Monday - Thursday noon - 2pm
Phone:	212-267-1777	& 5:30pm - 10pm
Fax:	212-267-3781	Friday noon - 2pm & 5:30pm - 11pm
e-mail:	N/A	Saturday 5:30pm - 11pm
Web:	N/A	Sunday 5:30pm - 10pm
Prices:		

It was a brave move to open a new restaurant in Lower Manhattan in the fall of 2001, when the area was still digging out following the terrorist attacks that brought down the World Trade Center towers. Located about six blocks north of the WTC site, Nam attracts eager crowds of diners who come for generous, tasty and inexpensive Vietnamese cooking, flavored by the likes of chile-lime sauce, coconut, curry and peanut satay. Efficient service by a young staff, and a simple but pleasant atmosphere, filled with bamboo trees, circular light fixtures and black-and-white photographs of Vietnam, are just a few more reasons to like this place.

Pepolino

Italian

281 West Broadway (bet. Canal & Lispenard Sts.)

Subway: Canal St
Phone: 212-966-9983
Fax: 212-966-3858
e-mail: N/A
Web: www.pepolino.com
Prices: $$

Monday - Thursday noon - 4pm
& 5:30pm - 11pm
Friday - Saturday noon - midnight
Sunday noon - 11pm

A variety of thyme that grows wild in the hills of Tuscany, pepolino makes a fitting namesake for this rustic Italian eatery on TriBeCa's northern edge. Indeed, herbs play a big part in the cooking here, and pepolino is the favorite herb of owner Patrizio Siddu, who shares the kitchen with partner Enzo Pezone. Both chefs grew up in Italy, where they mastered the nuances of regional Italian cuisine before opening Pepolino in 1999. Charming country décor complements reasonably priced Tuscan recipes enhanced by extra-virgin olive oil, aged balsamic vinegar, and fresh ricotta and mozzarella. American Express is the only credit card accepted here, so if you don't have one, be sure to bring cash.

Manhattan *TriBeCa*

About the
Upper East Side

An enclave for the wealthy and fashionable, the Upper East Side represents a broad cross section of New York neighborhoods and contains an impressive concentration of restaurants. In the area that stretches from Fifth Avenue to the East River, and from 60th Street to 97th Street, you'll find food to please every palate, from Austrian cuisine to vegetarian fare.

Rimming the east edge of the park, the Metropolitan Museum of Art, the Guggenheim Museum, the Jewish Museum, the Whitney Museum of American Art, the Frick Collection, the Neue Galerie, and the Cooper-Hewitt National Design Museum are collectively known as **Museum Mile**. An impressive concentration of galleries, along with elegant shops, upscale restaurants, clubs, exclusive private schools and fabulous residences grace this area as well. East of Lexington Avenue, where there's a significant population of single people, the atmosphere becomes more casual. Here, modern high-rise apartment buildings dominate, sharing space with a variety of pubs, sports bars and pizza joints.

A Bit of History – In the late 19th century, rich industrialists including Andrew Carnegie and Henry Clay Frick began building mansions on the large lots along Fifth Avenue, abutting Central Park. One of the first sections to be developed was around East 86th Street, where several prominent families of German descent, including the Schermerhorns, the Astors and the Rhinelanders, built country estates. Yorkville, as it was known, soon moved east past Lexington

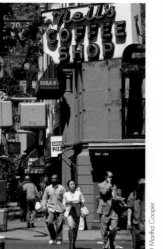
© Martha Cooper

Avenue and became a suburb of middle-class Germans, many of whom worked in nearby piano factories and breweries—although hardly a rathskeller survives today. In the 1950s, waves of immigrants from Hungary and Eastern Europe established their own communities, only to disappear as gentrification set in a couple of decades ago.

Over the years, the posh East Side has been a magnet for celebrities— Greta Garbo, Andy Warhol, Richard Nixon and Woody Allen among them. Today, **Fifth Avenue** remains the neighborhood's most impressive thoroughfare, **Madison Avenue** is chock-a-block with chi-chi shops and art galleries; and **Park Avenue** is an elegant residential boulevard.

Manhattan Upper East Side

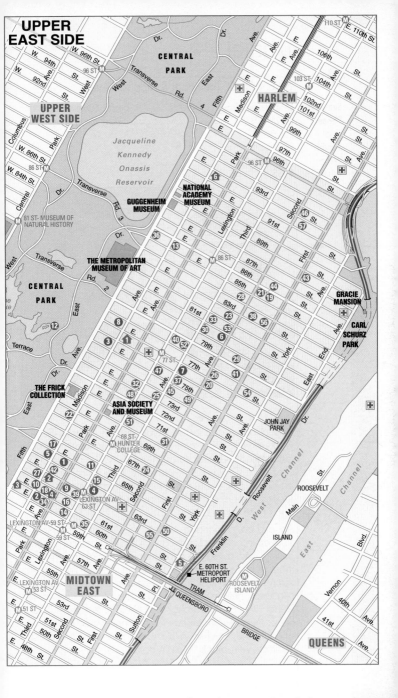

About the Upper East Side **317**

Daniel ❀❀

001

60 E. 65th St. (bet. Park & Madison Aves.)

Subway:	68 St - Hunter College
Phone:	212-288-0033
Fax:	212-396-9014
e-mail:	info@danielnyc.com
Web:	www.danielnyc.com
Prices:	$$$$

Monday - Saturday 5:45pm - 11pm
Closed Sunday & major holidays

ⵝⵝⵝⵝⵝ
&
88
👤

Daniel/P. Medilek

Manhattan Upper East Side

Raised on a farm outside Lyon, France, Daniel Boulud worked with some of the best chefs in France before landing in the United States. Here, he worked as executive chef of Le Cirque for seven years, and launched Daniel in 1993. His eponymous restaurant now occupies the ground floor of the former Mayfair Hotel and the space once filled by Le Cirque.

An arched colonnade defines the Italian Renaissance-style dining room, designed with an 18-foot-high coffered ceiling and a bronze chandelier with alabaster globes that seem to float above the room. It is in this palatial setting that Boulud turns the best domestic and imported seasonal products into artful dishes prepared in the French tradition. The chef and his talented team add a soupçon of American flair to such entrées as cassoulette of Louisiana crayfish with chanterelles, and Maine sea scallops with black truffle in golden pastry.

Daniel/H. Amiard

Peekytoe Crab Salad in Carrot Coulis

Serves 4

Carrot Coulis

2 tsp. extra-virgin olive oil
2 large carrots, peeled and sliced
1/4 cup sliced onions
1/3 stalk celery, sliced
1/4 medium leek, white part only, sliced
1 spice sachet (1/4 tsp. each: fennel, coriander, and cumin seeds, peppercorns, parsley leaves and pinch of crushed red pepper, tied in cheesecloth)
3 cups chicken stock   3/4 cup carrot juice
Juice of 1 lime
1 to 3 dashes of Tabasco
salt and freshly ground pepper

Warm olive oil in a large skillet over medium heat. Add vegetables and cook, stirring, about 15-20 minutes. Add chicken stock and spice sachet and bring to a boil. Lower heat and simmer, until almost all liquid has evaporated, about 30 minutes. Discard spice sachet and allow mixture to cool.

Process vegetables in a blender until smooth. Add an equal amount of carrot juice to the purée and blend. Purée should coat the back of a spoon; if it's too thick, add more juice. Season to taste with lime juice, salt, pepper and Tabasco.

Cumin-Coriander Mousseline

2 tsp. coriander seeds   1 tsp. cumin seeds
1 egg yolk   2 tsp. lemon juice
1 tsp. Dijon mustard
1/2 tsp. sherry vinegar
salt and freshly ground white pepper to taste
1/2 cup vegetable oil   2 cups heavy cream
1/2 small clove garlic, peeled and finely chopped

Toast coriander and cumin in a small skillet over high heat until fragrant, 3-5 minutes; remove from heat and grind finely. Whisk together egg yolk, lemon juice, mustard and vinegar. Whisking constantly, drizzle in the oil. Fold in garlic and heavy cream. If mousseline is too thick, add a splash of water. Season to taste.

Crab Salad

1 pound Maine peekytoe crab meat
3 Tbsp. Extra virgin olive oil
1 Tbsp. lemon juice
1 small head frisée
salt and freshly ground pepper

Toss crabmeat gently with olive oil and ½ of lemon juice; season with salt and pepper. Repeat with frisée. Spoon 3 Tbsp. of coulis in center of each shallow soup plate and spread the coulis into a circle. Place a ring mold in center of coulis. Divide crab meat among the molds and top each with a small spoonful of mousseline. Carefully remove the ring. Top with frisée.

From *Chef Daniel Boulud: Cooking in New York City*, Daniel Boulud and Peter Kaminsky, Assouline 2002

Aureole ❀

34 E. 61st St. (bet. Park & Madison Aves.)

Subway:	5 Av - 59 St
Phone:	212-319-1660
Fax:	212-750-8613
e-mail:	info@charliepalmer.com
Web:	www.aureolerestaurant.com
Prices:	$$$$

Monday - Friday noon - 2:30pm
& 5:30pm - 11pm
Saturday 5pm - 11pm
Closed Sunday

XXXX
❀
👤

Aureole/Vitaly Agibalov

Manhattan Upper East Side

Housed in a 1920s brownstone, this Upper East Side beauty belongs to Charlie Palmer's restaurant kingdom (there's a second Aureole in the Mandalay Bay Resort and Casino in Las Vegas). The refined atmosphere of the bi-level dining room goes hand in hand with the prestigious neighborhood. Fronted by a two-story window wall, the restaurant is filled with hanging ferns, honey-colored woodwork, and burgundy-leather banquettes. If you were admiring the contemporary artwork on the walls, you're in luck—it's for sale through the nearby Pace Prints gallery.

Artisanal food items and products from small local farms form the basis of the "progressive American" cuisine. Atlantic salmon "three ways" (margarita gravlax, tartare, smoked salmon egg), and rosemary-roasted milk-fed veal mignon are just a sampling of the tempting tasting menus. The computerized wine list cites more than 800 global selections.

Port-Glazed Foie Gras and Tuna Terrine

Serves 4

1 quart plus ½ cup Port
1 lobe of A-grade foie gras
½ cup olive oil
3 shallots, minced
¼ cup red wine
¼ cup red-wine vinegar
2 six-ounce blocks of tuna
¼ cup spicy greens
salt and freshly ground pepper

Place 1 quart of Port in saucepan over medium-low heat. Bring to a simmer and slowly reduce port to a thick syrup.

Allow foie gras to come to room temperature before handling. Once soft, separate the pieces and remove all membranes and veins. Push pieces back together and lay on a sheet tray lined with parchment paper. Pour remaining Port over foie gras and sprinkle with salt and pepper. Wrap tray in plastic wrap and refrigerate overnight. Remove from refrigerator and allow to sit at room temperature until soft. Make an indentation in the center with your thumb and pour in half of the Port reduction. Gently roll the foie gras until it is 2 inches in diameter and wrap tightly in plastic. Place

a saucepan filled with water over medium-low heat and bring to a low simmer. Place an ice bath nearby. Cook the wrapped foie gras in the simmering water for 3 minutes and then place in ice bath for 2 minutes, or until cool to the touch.

In a sauté pan, heat 2 Tbsps. of the olive oil. Reduce heat and add shallots. Once shallots are soft, add red wine and vinegar and raise heat to medium-high. Allow mixture to reduce by two-thirds. Remove from heat, whisk in remaining oil and season to taste.

Cut each piece of tuna into two 2-inch-thick square blocks and season. Use a ring cutter, about 1" in diameter, to punch out a hole in the center of each block. Remove plastic from the foie gras and cut into four segments close to the size of the hole punched in the tuna. Insert one segment into the center of each block of tuna. Place a sauté pan over medium high heat and add the remainder of the olive oil. Sear tuna on all four outside edges. Plate tuna, top with greens and drizzle with remaining reduced Port and vinaigrette.

Café Boulud ❀

003

20 E. 76th St. (bet. Fifth & Madison Aves.)

Subway:	77 St	Sunday - Monday 5:45pm - 11pm
Phone:	212-772-2600	Tuesday - Saturday noon - 2:30pm
Fax:	212-772-7755	& 5:45pm - 11pm
e-mail:	info@danielnyc.com	Closed major holidays
Web:	www.danielnyc.com	
Prices:	$$$	

Daniel/P. Manville

Café Boulud brings a taste of the Old Country to New York's East Side. Operated by famed French chef Daniel Boulud, this restaurant pays homage to the cafe that Boulud's family owned just outside Lyon in France.

Four different menus here appeal to different moods. If you're feeling old-fashioned, choose La Tradition, made up of French country classics (frisée salad with lardons, smoke-roasted duck). If you want to dine according to the season, try La Saison. For vegetarians, there's Le Potager, which follows what's fresh at the market. Armchair travelers will favor Le Voyage, a menu inspired by world cuisines (such as a meal based on chiles from around the world). Boulud's food exhibits a controlled creativity and an intelligent marriage of ingredients. Recalling 1930s Paris, the dining room is done in earth tones, with custom-designed mahogany chairs.

Daniel/C.T. O'Shea

Oven-Roasted Vegetable Casserole

Serves 4

1/3 cup extra-virgin olive oil, plus more for serving

8 small turnips, peeled and trimmed

8 small to medium fingerling potatoes, washed

8 small carrots, peeled and trimmed

8 cipollini onions, peeled and trimmed

8 medium white mushrooms, stemmed and cleaned

8 medium pink radishes, washed, dried and trimmed

2 to 3 stalks celery, peeled and cut into eight 3-inch pieces

2 large cloves garlic, peeled

bouquet garni (1 bay leaf, 1 thyme sprig, and the reserved basil stems from below, tied together with kitchen twine)

1 tsp. crushed coriander seeds, tied in cheesecloth

salt and freshly ground white pepper

½ cup Niçoise olives

½ bunch basil, washed, dried, and stems and leaves separated (use stems for the bouquet garni)

1 lemon, cut into 4 wedges

fleur de sel or coarse sea salt

grated Pecorino, Romano or Parmesan cheese (optional)

Preheat oven to 350°F. Warm 3 Tbsp. of olive oil in a shallow casserole or an ovenproof sauté pan over medium heat. Add turnips, potatoes and carrots, and cook, turning frequently, for 8 to 10 minutes—or until vegetables take on a little color. Add the remaining oil, the onions, mushrooms, radishes, celery, garlic, bouquet garni, and coriander sachet. Season well with salt and pepper and cook, stirring, for another 8-10 minutes, until the newly added vegetables are also lightly and evenly browned.

Transfer the pan to the oven and roast for about 30 minutes, stirring two or three times during this period, until the vegetables are tender when pierced with a knife. Remove the pan from the oven, discard the garlic, bouquet garni, and coriander sachet, and stir in the olives and half the basil leaves.

Scatter the remaining basil leaves over the vegetables and bring the casserole to the table. Serve the oven-roasted vegetables and their cooking juices directly from the pan. Offer the lemon, fleur de sel or coarse salt, pepper, and olive oil at the table. If desired, top each serving with some grated cheese.

From Daniel Boulud's Café Boulud Cookbook, Daniel Boulud and Dorie Greenspan, Scribner, November 1999

JoJo ❀

004

160 E. 64th St. (bet. Third & Lexington Aves.)

Subway:	Lexington Av - 63 St	Monday - Thursday noon - 2:30pm
Phone:	212-223-5656	& 5:30pm - 10:30pm
Fax:	212-755-9038	Friday - Saturday noon - 2:30pm
e-mail:	N/A	& 5:30pm - 11pm
Web:	www.jean-georges.com	Sunday noon - 2:30pm
Prices:	$$	& 5:30pm - 10pm

Jean-Georges Management

JoJo will always be special to its "father," award-winning chef Jean-Georges Vongerichten. After all, this bistro was his first restaurant in New York, launched in 1991. Given the nickname that Vongerichten knew as a boy, JoJo got a major overhaul for its tenth birthday. Now the two-story town house drips with plush velvets, rich tapestries and fine silks. Low lighting from crystal chandeliers plays on the room's deep hues of green and eggplant, creating sultry surroundings that many have likened to a French bordello.

In this sexy lair, the chef presents his modern version of French cuisine, in dishes like roasted cod with marinated vegetables in a fragrant sauce of olive oil and basil, or roast chicken with ginger, green olives and coriander. Top it all off with accommodating and polished service, and you'll know why this teenager can anticipate a bright future.

Black Bass in Carrot Confit

Serves 6

Carrot Confit

2.2 lbs. organic carrots, peeled
4 ¼ cups orange juice
¼ cup cumin seed
4 oz. olive oil
3 cloves garlic, thinly sliced
zest of 1 large orange

Preheat over to 275°F. Toss all ingredients together in a bowl. Once carrots are evenly coated, transfer to a sheet pan and bake for 3 hours. Remove from oven and set aside.

Baked Lemon

1 lemon   ½ cup coarse salt
½ cup sugar

Preheat oven to 350°. On a sheet pan, spread the coarse salt in the center. Cut lemon in half and press both halves, cut side down, on the salt. Top lemons with sugar and place in the oven to bake for 20-30 minutes or until tender. Remove from oven and set aside. Once cool, cut halves into thick slices.

To Serve

six 4-oz. filets of black bass, skin on
1 ½ cups water   1 cup couscous
½ cup currants   2 Tbsp. olive oil
2 Tbsp. lemon juice 2 Tbsp. unsalted butter
¼ tsp. salt
¼ tsp. cayenne pepper
¼ cup cilantro, roughly chopped

Fill a bowl with warm water and soak currants until tender, at least one hour. Bring salted water, lemon juice and olive oil to a boil in a saucepan. Add couscous to liquid, remove from heat, cover and set aside. After liquid has been absorbed, fluff with a fork and cover.

Set up a steamer and bring water to a boil. Cut slits in skin of fish and sprinkle filets with salt and cayenne pepper. Place in steamer, reduce heat and cook until tender.

While fish is cooking, melt butter in sauté pan over medium-low heat. Add couscous and season to taste with salt and pepper. Toss in currants.

Arrange carrots on six plates with roasting juices drizzled over top. Place a piece of fish on top of carrots and add a spoonful of couscous on the side. Garnish with baked lemon and chopped cilantro.

La Goulue ✿

La Goulue

746 Madison Ave. (bet. 64th & 65th Sts.)

Subway:	Lexington Av - 63 St
Phone:	212-988-8169
Fax:	212-396-2552
e-mail:	N/A
Web:	www.lagoulerestaurant.com
Prices:	$$$

Monday - Saturday noon - 4pm
& 6pm - 11:30pm
Sunday noon - 4pm & 6pm - 10:30pm

Few places in Gotham say "Paris" more than this venerable bistro, opened in 1972. Named for the shameless 19th-century Moulin Rouge dancer immortalized in paintings by Henri de Toulouse-Lautrec, La Goulue re-creates La Belle Epoque with framed vintage posters, lace cafe curtains, brass railings, and a light fixture signed by Art Nouveau furniture designer Louis Marjorelle.

The menu, too, respects the time-honored bistro tradition with well-rendered classics. Succulent skate wing is seared golden and sauced with lemon butter and capers; profiteroles are filled with vanilla ice cream and drizzled with chocolate sauce perfumed with orange zest. While you're enjoying your meal, indulge in a bit of star-gazing; celebrities like Pierce Brosnan, Rod Stewart and Uma Thurman have been known to dine here. From spring to fall, the few tables on the sidewalk terrace afford great people watching.

Manhattan Upper East Side

![La Goulue]

Cheese Soufflé

Serves 4

1 ½ quarts whole milk
10 egg yolks
20 egg whites
1 Tbsp. butter
1 cup grated Parmesan
1 cup grated Gruyère
¼ tsp. corn starch
¼ tsp. salt
¼ tsp. baking powder
¼ tsp. white pepper
1 medium onion studded with 3 cloves
1 Tbsp. + 1 tsp. white truffle oil
¼ tsp. freshly grated nutmeg
¼ tsp. cayenne pepper
1 thin slice of Parmesan, cut into a diamond
   shape
flour, as needed
¾ cup roux (recipe follows)

Method

Preheat oven to 350°F. Bring milk to a boil with clove-studded onion, cayenne pepper, nutmeg, salt and white pepper. Reduce heat and simmer 10-15 minutes, being careful not to let the milk reduce. Remove onion and, using a whisk, start adding the roux, a small amount at a time, whisking constantly and making sure that the milk comes back to a boil before adding the next amount. Make sure that there are no lumps. The mixture needs to be at a thickness where the whisk will almost stand upright on its own in the mixture.

Cook the mixture 10 minutes more on low, being careful not to burn the bottom. Add half the egg yolks while the mixture is still on the heat; remove from heat and add the rest. Next add 2 Tbsp. of the truffle oil, and the Parmesan and Gruyère. Combine well. Transfer the mixture to a large mixing bowl and leave to cool. In another bowl, whisk the egg whites with cornstarch and baking powder until the mixture forms soft peaks. Gently fold egg whites into the cooled egg and cheese mixture with a rubber spatula.

Grease a 16-ounce soufflé dish with the butter and dust it with flour on all sides. Pour soufflé mixture into the dish, leaving about a half-inch at the top to allow mixture to rise. Top with Parmesan diamond and remaining truffle oil. Bake in oven for 25 minutes.

Roux

½ lb. butter (2 sticks)   16 Tbsp. Flour

Melt butter in a thick-bottomed pan; then slowly add flour, mixing well with a wooden spoon. Cook until there is no color and the mixture starts to leave the sides of the pan. Cool the roux; work small pieces in your hand before adding.

Etats-Unis ✿

006

242 E. 81st St. (bet. Second & Third Aves.)

Subway: 77 St
Phone: 212-517-8826
Fax: 212-517-8742
e-mail: etats-unis@verizon.net
Web: N/A
Prices: $$$

Monday - Sunday 6pm - 11pm
Closed major holidays

Etats-Unis

Manhattan Upper East Side

If you've ever felt that a restaurant's décor upstaged its food, you'll appreciate Etats-Unis. Delightful food here comes without luxurious surroundings. The little shoebox of a dining room is done in Moderne style with bare light bulbs hanging from the ceiling, molded plastic chairs and uncovered varnished-wood tables. Never mind the style. The atmosphere is warm, made more so in this family-run place by the staff's philosophy that eating here should be like having an intimate dinner party in your home, only without the work.

Designed by owner Tom Rapp, the short menu changes daily to reflect the market. Vermont-raised veal scallops braised in white wine with chanterelles, onions and herbs, and handmade gnocchi with slow-roasted organic duck exemplify the type of fare you'll be treated to. Can't get a table? The Bar across the street offers a simpler, but no less tasty, menu.

Shropshire Blue Cheese Souffleed Pudding

Serves 8

- ½ cup + 1 Tbsp. butter
- ½ cup all-purpose flour
- 2 cups half-and-half
- 4 oz. Shropshire blue cheese or other top-quality blue cheese, crumbled
- ¼ cup freshly grated Parmesan, plus shavings for garnish
- 8 large egg yolks at room temperature
- salt and freshly ground black pepper, to taste
- 10 large egg whites, at room temperature
- ¼ tsp. cream of tartar
- ½ cup of heavy cream
- 2 Tbsp. chopped chives

Method

Butter four 2 ½ -inch ramekins and set aside.

Preheat oven to 350°F. Melt butter in a medium saucepan over low heat. Add the flour, stirring constantly until completely incorporated. Slowly stir in the half-and-half. Cook, stirring with a wire whisk, for about 2 minutes, until thickened and smooth. Add the blue cheese and Parmesan and stir until melted. Remove from the heat and beat in the egg yolks one at a time. Transfer to a large bowl and season

with salt and black pepper. The mixture should be slightly over-seasoned.

With an electric mixer, beat the egg whites and cream of tartar until the mixture forms soft peaks. Carefully fold the egg whites into the cheese mixture. Divide the mixture among the buttered ramekins, filling them to about a quarter-inch from the top. Carefully, place the filled ramekins in a shallow roasting pan. Pour enough hot water into the pan to come three-quarters of an inch up the sides of the ramekins. Bake for 40-45 minutes, until the tops are set and brown. Remove from the water bath and cool to room temperature. (At this point the puddings can be kept at room temperature for several hours or covered in plastic wrap and refrigerated for up to 2 days.)

To serve, preheat the oven to 400°F. Run a knife around the edges of the puddings. Gently unmold each one into the palm of your hand and place right side up on an oven-proof dish. Drizzle one tablespoon of cream over the top of each soufflé. Bake for 15-20 minutes, or until the cream is slightly brown and bubbly. Garnish with Parmesan shavings and chives.

Atlantic Grill

Seafood

007

1341 Third Ave. (bet. 76th & 77th Sts.)

Subway:	77 St	Monday - Friday 11:30am - 4pm
Phone:	212-988-9200	& 5pm - midnight (Friday 12:30am)
Fax:	212-988-9200	Saturday 11:30am - 4pm
e-mail:	N/A	& 4:30pm - 12:30am
Web:	www.brguestrestaurants.com	Sunday 10:30am - 4pm
Prices:	$$	& 4:30pm - 11pm

Atlantic Grill is another drop in the bucket of the B.R. Guest Restaurant Group, whose finny empire also includes Blue Water Grill on Union Square and Ocean Grill on the Upper West Side. The 200-seat restaurant, which sports different color schemes in different sections, hooks a sophisticated East Side clientele. One room is done in crisp, nautical blue and white; the other has a sunny aspect with cream-colored walls and potted palms. Despite the restaurant's name, seafood selections here come from both the Atlantic and the Pacific. For dinner, go with one of the chef's entrées or try the fresh catch (anything from wild King salmon to Alaskan halibut, depending on the day), simply grilled.

Mark's

Contemporary

008

25 E. 77th St. (bet. Fifth & Madison Aves.)

Subway:	77 St	Monday - Sunday 11:30am - 2:30pm
Phone:	212-879-1864	& 6pm - 10pm
Fax:	212-744-2749	
e-mail:	N/A	
Web:	www.themarkhotel.com	
Prices:	$$$	

A half-block east of Central Park and three blocks south of the Metropolitan Museum of Art, The Mark claims a truly enviable location. Set off the lobby inside this elegant Upper East Side hostelry, you'll find Mark's to be a fitting culinary complement to the hotel. The restaurant, done up with stylish furnishings, fine linens, and deep-gray walls, features a bi-level dining room where breakfast, lunch, dinner, and afternoon tea are served. New American dishes, like sautéed wild striped bass with braised fennel and shallot confit, are prepared with a light French touch. The 10,000-bottle wine list really hits the mark with its combination of New and Old World selections.

Park Avenue Cafe

009

100 E. 63rd St. (at Park Ave.)

Subway:	Lexington Av - 63 St
Phone:	212-644-1900
Fax:	212-688-0373
e-mail:	N/A
Web:	www.parkavenuecafe.com
Prices:	$$$

Monday - Friday 11:30am - 3pm
& 5:30pm - 10pm (Friday 11pm)
Saturday 11am - 2:30pm & 5:30pm - 11pm
Sunday 11am - 2:30pm
& 5:30pm - 10pm
Closed Christmas Day

Set on a tree-lined block at the intersection of prestigious Park Avenue, this comfortable neighborhood cafe gives off an Upper East Side vibe with its attractive crowd of locals. Opened in 1992, the restaurant was refurbished in 2004 with cheery red-and-white-striped banquettes and crimson Venetian plaster walls. The kitchen turns a creative hand to dishes like braised short rib ditalini, and French fries with truffle mayonnaise. Pasta, smoked meat and fish, and bread are all made fresh in-house. The cafe's new wine program lets diners make their selections from displays of bottles set around the dining room; prices and characteristics of the wines are explained on tags around each bottle.

Post House

010

28 E. 63rd St. (bet. Park & Madison Aves.)

Subway:	Lexington Av - 63 St
Phone:	212-935-2888
Fax:	212-371-9264
e-mail:	N/A
Web:	www.theposthouse.com
Prices:	$$$

Monday - Friday noon - 11pm
Saturday - Sunday 5:30pm - 11pm

There's no need to wonder "Where's the beef?" at this Upper East Side steakhouse. Part of the Smith & Wollensky Restaurant Group, Post House raises the steaks in its classic filet mignon, Prime rib and sirloin, while daily specials provide an alternative to the usual fare. Tufted leather banquettes and tilework give an upscale feel to the dining room, where the noise quotient ratchets up at night. A natural haven for the male business set, Post House has inaugurated a fixed-price "Ladies' Lunch" menu, to attract some feminine energy to the place. Of course, men are also welcome to take advantage of this offer, which comes with a choice of appetizer, entrée, and either a glass of wine or dessert.

Manhattan Upper East Side

Barbalùc

011

135 E. 65th St. (bet. Park & Lexington Aves.)

Subway:	Lexington Av - 63 St
Phone:	212-774-1999
Fax:	212-772-3046
e-mail:	N/A
Web:	www.barbaluc.com
Prices:	$$

Monday - Saturday noon - 3pm
& 5pm - 11pm
Closed Sunday & major holidays

✗✗

Is that an elf in your wine glass? Don't panic, it's just Barbalùc, the elfin spirit of wine (as the story on the menu explains) for whom the restaurant is named. Just ignore him and get on with the real business at hand: savoring fine northern Italian fare crafted by chef/owner Emanuele Simeoni, a native of the Friuli region. "Sleek" best describes the streamlined décor, with its white-marble floor and furniture custom-made for the restaurant by designer Luca Botto. Shelves near the bar showcase a nice selection of Italian wines, including some boutique wines from Friulian vintners. And perhaps best of all, a meal at Barbalùc won't break the bank.

Boathouse Central Park

012

The Lake at Central Park (72nd St. & Park Dr. North)

Subway:	77 St
Phone:	212-517-2233
Fax:	212-744-3947
e-mail:	N/A
Web:	www.thecentralparkboathouse.com
Prices:	$$

Monday - Friday noon - 4pm
& 5:30pm - 9pm
Saturday - Sunday 9:30am - 4pm
& 6pm - 9:30pm

✗✗
&
🍴
🛶

You couldn't dream up a more romantic setting for a first date or a special occasion. Nestled on the shore of the lake in the middle of Central Park, the Boathouse features peaceful water views through its floor-to-ceiling windows. Built in the 1950s, Loeb Boathouse replaced the original two-story Victorian structure designed by architect Calvert Vaux in the 1870s. Today it's the only place in Manhattan for a lakeside meal. And the food (jumbo lump crab cake, house-made cavatelli, mushroom-encrusted wild salmon) is good, too. On sunny days, sit out on the deck and watch the boats float by (be sure to make a reservation). After lunch, why not rent a rowboat and take a spin on the water?

Centolire

013

1167 Madison Ave. (bet. 85th & 86th Sts.)

Subway:	86 St
Phone:	212-734-7711
Fax:	212-794-5001
e-mail:	N/A
Web:	www.centolire.citysearch.com
Prices:	$$

Sunday - Thursday noon - 3:30pm
& 5:30pm - 10:30pm
Friday - Saturday noon - 3:30pm
& 5:30pm - 11pm

With 100 (cento) lire, you can go to America, or so an old Italian song goes. Accordingly, prolific Tuscan-born restaurateur Pino Luongo (also of Tuscan Square) opened Centolire in 2001 to honor those Italians who, like himself, came to America to start a new life. The dining room mixes designer fabrics with antique coffeepots, knives, and other kitchen tools and artifacts used by the early immigrants. At lunch, Centolire proposes a three-course menu at a price you just can't refuse. Dinner brings a range of well-prepared entrées from osso buco to Tuscan fish stew. Before you leave, check out the cookbooks by Pino, which are on display on a table near the entrance.

Circus

014

132 E. 61st St. (bet. Park & Lexington Aves.)

Subway:	59 St
Phone:	212-223-2965
Fax:	212-223-6410
e-mail:	N/A
Web:	www.circusrestaurante.com
Prices:	$$

Monday - Saturday noon - 11:30pm
Sunday 5pm - 10:30pm

Don't confuse this zesty Brazilian restaurant with The Greatest Show on Earth. The only show you'll see here has to do with happy diners devouring South American cuisine. Naturally, the décor reflects the owner's love of the circus; everywhere you look there are colorful drawings of clowns, trapeze artists, acrobats and lion tamers. Even the bathrooms are papered with old programs advertising the circus. Potent cachaca (a Brazilian liquor made from sugarcane) shows up in everything from kickin' capirinhas to miso- and cachaca-glazed black cod. Coconut milk, yucca, chorizo and plantains are just a few of the other ingredients that spice up Circus' Brazilian-inspired fare.

Da Giacomo

Italian

015

156 E. 64th St. (bet. Third & Lexington Aves.)

Subway:	Lexington Av - 63 St	Monday - Thursday noon - 2:30pm
Phone:	212-308-1300	& 5:30pm - 10:30pm
Fax:	N/A	Friday - Saturday noon - 2:30pm
e-mail:	N/A	& 5:30pm - 11:30pm
Web:	N/A	Sunday noon - 2:30pm
Prices:	$$	& 5:30pm - 10pm

A renowned trattoria that has served diners in Milan for nearly half a century, Da Giacomo now has a satellite on the Upper East Side. An elegantly refurbished town house just off Lexington Avenue forms the setting for the restaurant's New York branch. Those lucky enough to have eaten in the Milan flagship will note that Da Giacomo New York displays a similar décor (celadon and butter-colored walls, antique tiles, varnished wood floor) as well as the same delicate balance between casual attitude and sophisticated atmosphere. The menu draws heavily from the sea, and also offers a good choice of pasta dishes, all prepared with a delightful Italian flair.

Davidburke & Donatella

Contemporary

016

133 E. 61st St. (bet. Park & Lexington Aves.)

Subway:	Lexington Av - 59 St	Monday - Friday noon - 2:30pm
Phone:	212-813-2121	& 5pm - 10:30pm
Fax:	212-486-2322	Saturday 5pm - 10:30pm
e-mail:	info@dbdrestaurant.com	Sunday 11am - 2:30pm & 4:30pm - 9pm
Web:	www.dbdrestaurant.com	
Prices:	$$$	

Opened in December 2003 by chef David Burke and manager Donatella Arpaia, this restaurant refigures a restored town house with sleek lines, geometric patterns and a color palette that runs from chocolate brown to lipstick red. Since it opened, the place has been mobbed with a chic crowd of diners, all clamoring for a spot to see and be seen. Burke, who oversees the kitchen, describes his cooking style as "David Burke unplugged." You'll know better what this means when you taste dishes such as day boat sea scallops "Benedict," a take on the popular egg dish. In Burke's version, scallops replace the eggs, chorizo stands in for the ham, and a potato pancake masquerades as an English muffin.

Frederick's Madison

017

768 Madison Ave. (bet. 65th & 66th Sts.)

Subway:	Lexington Av - 63 St
Phone:	212-737-7300
Fax:	212-737-7337
e-mail:	info@fredericksnyc.com
Web:	www.fredericksnyc.com
Prices:	$$$

Monday - Saturday 11:30am - 11pm
Sunday noon - 11pm

Brothers Frederick and Laurent Lesort, known for Frederick's Bar & Lounge *(8 W. 58th St.)*, expanded their restaurant holdings in May 2005 with the opening of Frederick's Madison. The menu has expanded, too, from Asian-inspired small plates to contemporary Mediterranean fare. Signature dishes include foie gras chaud-foid, which comes seared, and in a cold terrine served with kumquat jam; open ravioli of braised rabbit; and slow-baked cod with clam nage. In the dining room, blond woods, brass wall sconces and claret-colored velour chairs add to the elegant feel. If you plan to get an early start on Madison Avenue shopping, you'll be glad to know that Frederick's is open for breakfast at 8am.

Geisha

018

33 E. 61st St. (bet. Park & Madison Aves.)

Subway:	59 St
Phone:	212-813-1112
Fax:	N/A
e-mail:	N/A
Web:	www.geisharestaurant.com
Prices:	$$$

Monday - Friday noon - 3:30pm
& 5:30pm - 11:30pm
Saturday 5:30pm - 11:30pm
Closed Sunday

The world of the geisha is a sensual one. Likewise this restaurant, owned by the same guys—Vittorio Assaf and Favio Granato—who introduced Serafina to the New York dining scene. Four individually decorated dining spaces on two floors incorporate elements of Japanese costumes (silver beads like those used in geisha headdresses), Oriental flowers (cherry blossom light fixtures), and origami (a "3-D" wall of stacked, fabric-covered cubes). The result is a cool, seductive space in which to savor the menu of French-accented Asian fare conceived by Eric Ripert of Le Bernardin. Sure, there's sushi galore, but why not try something different, like grilled shrimp lollipops on sugarcane skewers?

Ian

019

322 E. 86th St. (bet. First & Second Aves.)

Subway:	86 St	Sunday - Thursday 5pm - 11pm
Phone:	212-861-1993	Friday - Saturday 5pm - midnight
Fax:	212-861-7255	
e-mail:	N/A	
Web:	www.ianrestaurant.com	
Prices:	$$$	

🍴🍴
&

Born and bred in Brooklyn, Ian Russo left home for France at the age of 20 with a backback and a Michelin Guide in hand. His dream? To learn to cook. And learn he did, from renowned chefs including Michel Guérard, André Daguin and David Bouley. Now with his own restaurant in New York, Russo describes his culinary style as "nouveau New York cuisine." To the chef, this means a fusion of flavors from around the world, which reflects his travels abroad as well as the spirit of New York City. With signature dishes such as dancing shrimp (wrapped in kataifi—a type of phyllo dough—fried and served with yucca), Malaysia ribs, and truffle chicken, you can see how global the chef's influences are.

Il Monello

020

1460 Second Ave. (bet. 76th & 77th Sts.)

Subway:	77 St	Monday - Thursday noon - 3pm
Phone:	212-535-9310	& 5pm - 11pm
Fax:	N/A	Friday - Saturday noon - 3pm
e-mail:	N/A	& 5pm - midnight
Web:	www.ilmonellonyc.com	Sunday noon - 3pm & 5pm - 10pm
Prices:	$$	Closed major holidays

🍴🍴
&
🍸

There's something to be said for maturity, and, in fact, the old-fashioned décor of this little place lends it a certain charm. Set in a residential area close to Upper East Side shopping, Il Monello was established in 1974. It's a quiet spot to stop for a meal; here you'll feel far removed from the bustle of the city outside. The menu of Northern Italian fare cites a generous selection of courses, well balanced between pasta, meat and fish. Several of the dishes, like the risotto and ravioli del giorno, change daily depending on what's fresh at the market, and they're priced accordingly. Friendly service brings back regulars from the neighborhood.

Ithaka

Greek

308 E. 86th St. (bet. First & Second Aves.)

Subway:	86 St
Phone:	212-628-9100
Fax:	212-734-6619
e-mail:	ithaka@ithakarestaurant.com
Web:	www.ithakarestaurant.com
Prices:	$$

Monday - Sunday noon - 11:30pm

A Mediterranean-blue awning welcomes visitors to Ithaka, the way the sea would welcome them to Greece. In this cozy place, with its beamed ceiling, brick walls and stone floors, you'll discover an authentic Old World cuisine. Greek favorites like moussaka and pasticio share menu space with kalamari scharas (grilled calamari) and arni youvetsi (baby lamb baked in a clay pot with orzo, tomato sauce and feta cheese). And perhaps best of all, the prices won't break the bank. If you still have room for dessert after a hearty meal here, the creamy house-made yogurt *(yiaourti sakoulas)* is as good as any you'll get in Greece; here, it's drizzled with perfumed honey and topped with crunchy hazelnuts.

Kai

Japanese

822 Madison Ave. (bet. 68th & 69th Sts.)

Subway:	68 St - Hunter College
Phone:	212-988-7277
Fax:	212-570-4500
e-mail:	kairestaurant@itoen.com
Web:	www.itoen.com
Prices:	$$$

Monday - Saturday noon - 3pm
& 5:30pm - 9:30pm
Closed Sunday

You'll find Kai hidden away on the second floor of the Upper East Side tea shop owned by Ito En, one of the best-known tea companies in Japan. A serene setting marked by clean lines and soothing tones creates just the right vibe in which to experience Kaiseki cuisine. Centuries ago, Kaiseki originated in the temples of Kyoto as small dishes served during a traditional Japanese tea ceremony. Kai revives this tradition with a Kaiseki menu that balances its offerings between land and sea. You can enjoy these dishes at lunch or dinner in the form of multicourse menus that change with the season (or there's always the selection of sushi and sashimi). Zen tea is served daily from noon to 4pm.

Manhattan Upper East Side

Kings' Carriage House

Contemporary

023

251 E. 82nd St. (bet. Second & Third Aves.)

Subway:	86 St	Monday - Saturday noon - 5pm
Phone:	212-734-5490	& 6pm - 10:30pm
Fax:	212-717-2352	Closed Sunday
e-mail:	lillibetking@aol.com	
Web:	www.kingscarriagehouse.com	
Prices:	$$	

XX

This restored carriage house now holds an elegant restaurant and tearoom for diners seeking a romantic getaway in the heart of the Upper East Side. Run by Elizabeth King and her husband, Paul Farell (who hails from Dublin), Kings' Carriage House resembles an Irish country manor, set about with Chinese porcelains, antique furnishings and taxidermed hunting trophies on the walls. There's nothing Old World about the food, though. American dishes are given a contemporary twist (think roasted loin of lamb with blackberry-mint compote) on the daily changing fixed-price menu. The lunch menu is especially inexpensive, but if you can't make it for a meal, do drop 'round for afternoon tea.

L'Absinthe

French

024

227 E. 67th St. (bet. Second & Third Aves.)

Subway:	68 St - Hunter College	Monday - Saturday noon - 3pm
Phone:	212-794-4950	& 5:30pm - 11pm
Fax:	212-794-1589	Sunday noon - 3pm & 5:30pm - 10pm
e-mail:	labsinthe@covad.net	
Web:	www.labsinthe.com	
Prices:	$$$	

XX
&
≈
88

Remember the good old days, when you sat around cafes all day, railing on the political system and sipping the mind-blowing liquor, absinthe, until you could no longer see? Of course you don't—unless you happened to grow up in late-19th-century Paris. Though absinthe has long since been replaced by the gentler aperitif Pernod, the Art Nouveau age lives on at Jean-Michel Bergougnoux's brasserie. Chandeliers with tulip-shaped fixtures, walls of large framed mirrors, and sprays of bright flowers bring to mind Belle Epoque Paris. Meanwhile, the kitchen interprets timeless French dishes like cold paté of quail and foie gras, coq au vin, choucroute Alsacienne, for 21st-century patrons.

Lenox Room

Contemporary

1278 Third Ave. (bet. 73rd & 74th Sts.)

Subway:	77 St
Phone:	212-772-0404
Fax:	212-772-3229
e-mail:	lennoxroom@aol.com
Web:	www.lenoxroom.com
Prices:	$$

Monday - Sunday noon - 2:30pm
& 5:30pm - 10:30pm

Looking for good food in a cocoon-like ambience? You've come to the right place. Opened in 1995 by maitre d' Tony Fortuna, hotelier Edward Bianchini and partner Charlie Palmer, the Lenox Room wraps diners in cozy comfort with its claret-red walls, cushy banquettes, and warm, wood-paneled walls. The updated American cuisine fits right in with this relaxed environment, and the service is pleasant and professional. Lunch brings salads, sandwiches and a short list of entrées; at dinner, there's a nice balance of choices, including "Tiers of Taste," a combination of three small plates for a set price. For lunch, the three-course, I Love New York menu is such a deal.

Lusardi's

Italian

1494 Second Ave. (bet. 77th & 78th Sts.)

Subway:	77 St
Phone:	212-249-2020
Fax:	212-585-2941
e-mail:	N/A
Web:	www.lusardis.com
Prices:	$$

Monday - Friday noon - 3pm
& 5pm - midnight
Saturday - Sunday 5pm - midnight

Both the décor and the service are warm at Lusardi's, an Upper East Side staple since Luigi and Mauro Lusardi founded the restaurant in 1982. Decorated with vintage Italian posters, the well-kept yellow dining room tends to be quiet at lunch; it comes alive in the evening, though, with a loyal following of diners who pack the place in the evenings. An ample choice of classic Northern Italian fare attracts customers year-round, while special menus designed around white truffles or wild game are tuned to the season. Lusardi's fans will be glad to know that they can purchase bottles of the family's own marinara sauce and extra virgin olive oil at the restaurant.

Manhattan Upper East Side

Nello

Italian

027

696 Madison Ave. (bet. 62nd & 63rd Sts.)

Subway:	Lexington Av - 63 St	Monday - Sunday 11:30am - midnight
Phone:	212-980-9099	
Fax:	N/A	
e-mail:	N/A	
Web:	N/A	
Prices:	**$$$$**	

It's all about the Beautiful People at Nello. This place appeals to a dress-to-impress, moneyed clientele, who don't flinch at the restaurant's uptown prices. (After all, Nello needs to keep pace with neighbors Givenchy, Christofle, Hermès and Lalique.) Inside, black-and-white photographs of an African safari adorn the walls and little crystal vases of fresh flowers brighten the tabletops. It's worth the splurge, not only for the delectable Italian cuisine and the charming waitstaff, but for the opportunity to see how the "other half" lives. Before you leave, pause inside the entrance to check out photographs of the rich and famous patrons who have dined here in the past.

Paola's

Italian

028

245 E. 84th St. (bet. Second & Third Aves.)

Subway:	86 St	Monday - Sunday 1pm - 11pm
Phone:	212-794-1890	
Fax:	212-517-6633	
e-mail:	bottero1@aol.com	
Web:	www.paolasrestaurant.com	
Prices:	**$$**	

You won't mind forfeiting trendy design in this delightful little Upper East Side Italian place. Attentive service, a quiet atmosphere (where you won't need to yell above the din to converse with your dining partners), and a good location a few blocks' walk from the Met will be more than enough to keep you happy at Paola's. Then there's the regional Italian cuisine. Short but appealing, the menu changes with the seasons. Fennel-cured salmon carpaccio brightened with sections of orange and grapefruit; and ravioli stuffed with asparagus and napped with morel sauce are just a couple of examples of the palate-pleasing entrées. The freshly made torta di ricotta is available any time of year.

Quatorze Bis

French

029

323 E. 79th St. (bet. First & Second Aves.)

Subway:	77 St
Phone:	212-535-1414
Fax:	N/A
e-mail:	N/A
Web:	N/A
Prices:	$$

Tuesday - Friday noon - 2:30pm
& 5:30pm - 11pm
Saturday - Sunday noon - 3pm
& 5:30pm - 11pm
Closed Monday

XX

This French bistro has changed its location, but not its name—which refers to its former address on 14th Street ("quatorze" in French). The word "bis" was added to the title when the restaurant moved in 1989 (bis is French for "once again"). Regulars hope Quatorze Bis is on the Upper East Side to stay, so they can keep enjoying the likes of homemade pork terrine, boeuf Bourguignon, cassoulet, and cream-filled profiteroles right in their own neighborhood. The zinc bar, old French posters and cozy banquettes make for an inviting and oh-so-Parisian atmosphere. Be sure to check out the two caricatures of King Louis XIV of France that grace the wall.

Taste

Contemporary

030

1411 Third Ave. (at 80th St.)

Subway:	77 St
Phone:	212-717-9798
Fax:	212-717-2600
e-mail:	info@elizabar.com
Web:	www.elizabar.com
Prices:	$$

Monday - Sunday 6pm - 11pm

XX

Youngest son of the founders of Zabar's, New York's landmark West Side delicatessen, Eli Zabar launched his own fresh-food market in 1998. A recent adjunct to that market is Taste, a restaurant devised to pair a menu of small plates with Eli's favorite regional wines. Drop in after work, take a seat at the gleaming bar and sample affordable wines by the glass. Of course, you'll need something to nosh on, and small plates such as roasted eggplant and tomato tart, and baby burgers on brioche should do the trick. Dinner is full-service (at lunch it's cafeteria-style), and the list of entrées changes daily, as you'd expect from a proprietor who supplies fresh products from his market next door.

Manhattan Upper East Side

Restaurants **341**

Trata Estiatorio

Greek

031

1331 Second Ave. (bet. 70th & 71st Sts.)

Subway:	68 St - Hunter College	Monday - Sunday noon - 3:30pm
Phone:	212-535-3800	& 5pm - 11:30pm
Fax:	N/A	
e-mail:	tratanyc@aol.com	
Web:	www.trata.com	
Prices:	$$	

✗✗ Everything about this bright trattoria will remind you of the sea, from the crisp blue and white façade to the stone-washed white walls and the colorful mosaics of sea life above the bar. And with the Greek islands for a theme and fresh seafood displayed on ice by the open kitchen, what else would you expect on the menu but a daily changing list of fish and shellfish? Whole fish are the house specialty; fresh catches like Arctic char, American snapper, and barbouni from the Mediterranean Sea are charcoal-grilled and priced per pound. Don't overlook the wine list here; there are numerous Greek vintages cited, along with descriptions of their characters. Go for lunch if you want a bargain.

Vivolo

Italian

032

140 E. 74th St. (bet. Park & Lexington Aves.)

Subway:	77 St	Monday - Sunday noon - 3pm
Phone:	212-737-3533	& 5pm - 11pm
Fax:	212-717-4828	
e-mail:	N/A	
Web:	www.vivolonyc.com	
Prices:	$$	

✗✗ Inside this 1878 town house, you'll find good, moderately priced Italian food cooked by a family with a long history in the business—the restaurant business, that is. It all started in Brooklyn in the 1930s, where Carmine Vivolo opened his first restaurant; his grandson launched Vivolo in 1977. With its fireplace and dark wood paneling, the dining room furnishes a charming Old World atmosphere to match the building's vintage, while the Vivolo family recipes offer diners a taste of traditional Italian fare. For a quick, light meal in a contemporary setting or for gourmet fare to go, stop by Cucina Vivolo, right next door.

Beyoglu

033

1431 Third Ave. (at 81st St.)

Subway:	77 St	Monday - Thursday noon - 11pm
Phone:	212-650-0850	Friday - Sunday noon - midnight
Fax:	212-650-0849	
e-mail:	comments@rosamexicano.com	
Web:	www.beyoglunyc.com	
Prices:	⊜⊜	

Small plates star at this Mediterranean mezze house, where low prices and a casual atmosphere add to the appeal. The simple dining room with its bright walls and inlaid-tile tables sets the scene for sharing mezzes from homemade yogurt with cucumber and garlic to stuffed grape leaves to pan-fired cubes of calves liver. Most of the recipes come from Turkey, but there are Greek and Lebanese accents in items like char-grilled octopus and hummus. If you're particularly hungry, there's also a short list of daily specials, including meat kebabs and grilled fish. Your waiter will fill you in on the delightful desserts, such as baklava, and kadayif filled with almonds, pistachios and honey.

Bistro 60

French

034

37 E. 60th St. (bet. Park & Madison Aves.)

Subway:	5 Av - 59 St	Monday - Sunday 11am - 11pm
Phone:	212-230-1350	
Fax:	212-230-1363	
e-mail:	info@bistro60.com	
Web:	www.bistro60.com	
Prices:	$$	

A block and a half from Central Park, Bistro 60 enjoys its location in this chic part of town. The moment you enter this place, you'll be immersed in a Gallic ambience, from the manager who greets guests in French, to the smiling, well-organized French (mostly) waitstaff. The dining room screams French brasserie, complete with all the requisite elements: a wall of red banquettes, 1950s-style posters, tulip-shaped wall sconces. Written in French, the menu lists all the classics: trout Amandine, grilled lamb chops, mussels marinière, steak tartare prepared at the table. End your meal with a dessert such as tarte tatin or crème brûlée, and you're likely to leave humming "La Marseillaise."

Manhattan Upper East Side

Cabana

Cuban

035

1022 Third Ave. (bet. 60th & 61st Sts.)

Subway:	Lexington Av - 59 St	Monday - Sunday 11:30am - midnight
Phone:	212-980-5678	Closed major holidays
Fax:	212-750-6470	
e-mail:	N/A	
Web:	www.cabanarestaurant.com	
Prices:	$$	

In a vibrant room swathed in bright yellows and blues, Cabana celebrates what it calls "Nuevo Latino" cuisine. As far as the food is concerned, this can mean anything from Cuba to the Caribbean islands, with a dash of Spanish flavor thrown in for good measure. From paella to chicharrónes de pollo, the kitchen honors dishes with a Latin soul; a daily trip to the fish market ensures that the day's catch will be the freshest possible. The restaurant, which cultivates a carnival atmosphere with its lively (and loud) Latin music, is part of a chain. Cabana has two other locations: one in the Financial District at South Street Seaport (Pier 17), and one in Forest Hills, Queens.

Café Sabarsky

Austrian

036

1048 Fifth Ave. (at 86th St., in Neue Galerie)

Subway:	86 St	Monday & Wednesday 9am - 6pm
Phone:	212-288-0665	Thursday - Sunday 9am - 9pm
Fax:	212-645-7127	Closed Tuesday
e-mail:	N/A	
Web:	www.wallse.com	
Prices:	$$	

Art alone is reason enough to visit the Neue Galerie, founded in 2001 by cosmetics mogul Ronald Lauder to display his collection of early 20th-century Austrian and German art, as well as the collection of his friend, art dealer Serge Sabarsky. Besides fine art, you'll find a real gem in this 1914 Beaux-Arts mansion, in the form of Café Sabarsky. Old World charm oozes from this cafe, modeled on a late-19th-century Viennese kaffeehaus. In the superb dining room, adorned with reproductions of Josef Hoffmann sconces, Otto Wagner fabrics, and a Bösendorfer piano, chef Kurt Gunterbrunner (of Wallsé in Greenwich Village) offers fine Austrian cuisine. Whatever you do, don't pass up the pastries!

Candle Cafe

Vegetarian

037

1307 Third Ave. (bet. 74th & 75th Sts.)

Subway:	77 St
Phone:	212-472-0970
Fax:	212-472-7169
e-mail:	candle_cafe@msn.com
Web:	www.candlecafe.com
Prices:	෧෧

Monday - Saturday 11:30am - 10:30pm
Sunday 11:30am - 9:30pm

ꭕ

ᕦ

"Food from farm to table" is the mantra of Candle Cafe. In keeping with that philosophy, the restaurant zeroes in on seasonal organic ingredients for its original vegetarian dishes. As you might expect, the cafe is a no-frills kind of place, but they're serious about healthy food (Southwestern chili layered with three types of beans with corn, spices and smoked chiles over brown rice). Got the sniffles? Try a "flu and cold fighter," an elixir made with ginger, orange, carrot, lemon and grapefruit juices. In 2003 the cafe opened a second branch, Candle 79 *(154 E. 79th St. near Lexington Ave.)*, boasting a larger menu and a sophisticated bi-level space.

Donguri

Japanese

038

309 E. 83rd St. (bet. First & Second Aves.)

Subway:	86 St
Phone:	212-737-5656
Fax:	N/A
e-mail:	N/A
Web:	www.itoen.com
Prices:	$$

Tuesday - Sunday 5:30pm - 10pm
Closed Monday

ꭕ

With only 24 seats, this little place fills up quick with regulars who were smart to make a reservation. Its minimal décor, with exposed-brick walls and a line of simply set tables, lets you focus on the food. Try one of the tasting menus, which might start with miso soup and a delightful plate of assorted appetizers, followed by sashimi, then tender, broiled Chilean sea bass scented with ginger. All products are ultra-fresh and selections change regularly. In May 2005, Ito En, a well-known Japanese tea company, acquired Donguri after its chef retired. Ito En, which also owns Kai restaurant, has no immediate plans to change Donguri's cozy dining space or its menu.

Fig & Olive

Mediterranean

039

808 Lexington Ave. (bet. 62nd & 63rd Sts.)

Subway:	Lexington Av - 63 St
Phone:	212-207-4555
Fax:	212-207-4477
e-mail:	N/A
Web:	www.fig-and-olive.com
Prices:	ᐸᐳ

Monday - Sunday 10am - midnight

If you like olive oil, this Mediterranean restaurant and olive oil shop is a great place to have a big, crisp salad topped with dressing made from wonderful extra virgin olive oil. Of course, your choices aren't limited to salads. Settle into the pleasant dining room, with its white and olive stucco walls and zinc tables, and order tartines, carpaccio, crostini, a sampling of cheeses, and charcuterie plates piled with prosciutto, bresaola, jamon Iberico and saucisson sec. (Hot entrées are served only after 6:30pm.) You'll find different flavors of oil from France, Italy and Spain here. If one particularly tickles your fancy, be sure to pick up a bottle of it before you leave the restaurant.

Il Riccio

Italian

040

152 E. 79th St. (bet. Third & Lexington Aves.)

Subway:	77 St
Phone:	212-639-9111
Fax:	212-639-9528
e-mail:	N/A
Web:	N/A
Prices:	$$

Sunday - Thursday noon - 2:45pm
& 5pm - 11pm
Friday - Saturday noon - 2:45pm
& 5pm - 11:30pm
Closed major holidays

Located four blocks from the Metropolitan Museum of Art, Il Riccio makes a great lunch spot when you simply can't take in any more fine art. A shiny brass door beckons you into the restaurant, which sits on a busy street, surrounded by boutiques and eateries. Two different dining rooms here offer diners a comfortable respite from trekking through museum galleries. Although the menu is not extensive, it does offer a nice choice of dishes—the emphasis here is on pasta, from spaghetti with crab meat and tomato to gnocchi with Taleggio cheese and radicchio—along with a roster of daily specials. The short wine list includes several fine venerable vintages of Italian wine.

Iron Sushi

041

355 E. 78th St. (bet. First & Second Aves.)

Subway:	77 St	Monday - Sunday 11:30am - 3:30pm
Phone:	212-772-7680	& 5pm - 11pm
Fax:	212-772-7690	
e-mail:	N/A	
Web:	N/A	
Prices:	&cap;	

This Upper East Side newcomer is an offshoot of the Murray Hill sushi restaurant of the same name. An intriguing balance between Asian inspiration (bamboo elements and traditional sushi bar) and Modernist minimalism (purple-gray walls and exposed brick) marks the simple décor of the small dining space. The menu sticks to authentic Japanese fare, with a wide range of choices. Entrées run the gamut from teriyaki to tempura and noodles to Nabemono, and the sushi bar offers a copious list of combinations. Iron Sushi also offers several good specials at midday, including Bento boxes, sushi bar lunches, and Maki meals.

Le Bilboquet

042

25 E. 63rd St. (bet. Park & Madison Aves.)

Subway:	Lexington Av - 63 St	Monday - Sunday noon - midnight
Phone:	212-751-3036	Closed major holidays
Fax:	212-684-1659	
e-mail:	N/A	
Web:	N/A	
Prices:	**$$**	

Le Bilboquet is a clubby kind of place. Clubby, in the sense of "insider." First of all, there's no sign on the door announcing this bistro, so you have to know it's there. Once inside, you'll observe that most of the patrons (many of them are French) seem to know each other. And while the French cuisine here is fragrant and well prepared (filet of sea bass is complemented by fennel; veal scallop is fragrant with lemon), an insouciant attitude pervades the service. Nonetheless, if you're looking for a lively place to enjoy a meal to the tune of loud music and a party atmosphere, you won't be disappointed at Le Bilboquet.

Manhattan Upper East Side

Luca

Italian

043

1712 First Ave. (bet. 88th & 89th Sts.)

Subway:	86 St	Monday - Saturday noon - 3pm
Phone:	212-987-9260	& 5pm - 11pm
Fax:	N/A	Sunday 5pm - 11pm
e-mail:	lucarestaurant@verizon.net	
Web:	www.lucatogo.com	
Prices:	$$	

Here's a good reason to take a trip up to the Yorkville neighborhood in the upper 80s. An unpretentious little Italian bistro, Luca provides a welcome alternative to the expensive and often snooty eateries elsewhere in the Upper East Side. Owned by Luca Marcato and his wife, the restaurant delivers—literally and figuratively—the likes of bigoli with lamb ragu, ravioli with spinach and ricotta, and tagliatelle with shrimp, all with pastas made on the premises. Check out the wine list for a good selection of Italian labels. While you're in the neighborhood, consider a tour of Gracie Mansion *(East End Ave. & 89th St.)*, the official residence of the mayor of New York City since 1942.

Maz Mezcal

Mexican

044

316 E. 86th St. (bet. First & Second Aves.)

Subway:	86 St	Monday - Friday 5pm - 11pm
Phone:	212-472-1599	Saturday 5pm - midnight
Fax:	N/A	Sunday 4pm - 11pm
e-mail:	mazmezcal@nyc.rr.com	Closed major holidays
Web:	www.mazmezcal.com	
Prices:	$$	

Simple Mexican food—and lots of it—leaves customers eager to return to Maz Mezcal, located on a busy commercial street. Edouardo Silva now runs his family's longtime Upper East Side restaurant (formerly El Sombrero); after he took the reins, he renamed the place Maz Mexcal and expanded it several years ago. From arroz con pollo to paella, dishes are tailored to mild palates, but if you prefer your food picante, the kitchen will be happy to spice things up. With more than 50 different types of tequila, and its cousin, mescal, available from the bar, you can count on a party atmosphere almost every night in the bright, terra-cotta-colored dining room.

Mezzaluna

Italian

1295 Third Ave. (bet. 74th & 75th Sts.)

Subway:	77 St	Monday - Sunday noon - 3:30pm
Phone:	212-535-9600	& 6pm - 11:30pm
Fax:	212-517-8045	
e-mail:	N/A	
Web:	www.mezzalunany.com	
Prices:	$$	

Mezzaluna is a restaurant that takes its name seriously. So much so, that they offered 20 meals to any artist (many of them Italian) who would agree to render his or her version of the restaurant's namesake crescent-shaped chopping knife. As you'll see, the 77 different artworks that paper the walls here each depict a unique take on this design and provide an eye-catching backdrop for well-prepared seasonal Italian dishes. Founded by Aldo Bozzi (who previously headed Alfa Romeo in North America), the restaurant has been around since 1984. Antiques imported from Italy and tables nesting close together add to the simple comfort and convivial atmosphere here.

Nick's

Italian

1814 Second Ave. (at 94th St.)

Subway:	96 St	Monday - Thursday 10am - 11pm
Phone:	212-987-5700	Friday - Sunday 10am - midnight
Fax:	212-987-7777	
e-mail:	info@nicksny.com	
Web:	www.nicksny.com	
Prices:		

New York has long been known for its pizzerias, and this one takes the cake—or, rather, the pie. The Manhattan satellite of the Forest Hills (Queens) original, Nick's is everything you want a pizza place to be. The tin-ceilinged dining room is pleasant and cozy; the service is jovial and efficient; and you can watch the cooks hand-tossing the dough and firing your pizza in the wood-burning oven. Pizzas here turn out thin and crispy, spread with a good balance of tomato sauce, herbs, and your choice of toppings. On the list of pasta (properly called "macaroni" in the traditional Italian-American lexicon) and meat entrées, half portions accommodate those with less hearty appetites.

Orsay

047

1057 Lexington Ave. (at 75th St.)

Subway:	77 St	Monday - Saturday 11:30am - 11pm
Phone:	212-517-6400	Sunday 11am - 10pm
Fax:	212-517-3896	Closed Christmas Eve Day
e-mail:	info@orsayrestaurant.com	& Christmas Day
Web:	www.orsayrestaurant.com	
Prices:	$$	

In true Parisian fashion, this large brasserie at the corner of 75th Street overflows onto the sidewalk terrace through its large French doors. Inside, the Paris of the 1950s comes alive through the zinc bar, the fan-patterned mosaic-tile floor, and the mahogany paneling. Arched walls and frosted-glass partitions add to the Art Nouveau stylings. Unlike the décor, the food here is more American than strictly French. Lamb navarin, escargot and steak tartare share the menu with a preponderance of items like diver sea scallops, grilled sesame tuna, burgers and other American fare. Adapted to the local palate, many of the French dishes, while good, lack the classic preparation.

Payard

048

1032 Lexington Ave. (bet. 73rd & 74th Sts.)

Subway:	77 St	Monday - Thursday noon - 3pm
Phone:	212-717-5252	& 5:45pm - 10:30pm
Fax:	212-717-0986	Friday - Saturday noon - 3pm
e-mail:	N/A	& 5:45pm - 11pm
Web:	www.payard.com	Closed Sunday & major holidays
Prices:	$$$	

Famous for its handmade chocolates and its mouth-watering French pastries, Payard is also a restaurant. Since you have to walk past the cases of tempting sweets to reach the dining room, there's always the danger that you'll decide to bag lunch or dinner and go straight for dessert. If you do resist (until the end of the meal, that is), you can expect classic French cuisine made with products such as farm-raised chicken, New York Black Angus sirloin, and homemade gravlax. Oh, and don't even think of leaving without a souvenir—perhaps a box of macarons, some champagne truffles, or a selection of pâtes de fruits—to tide you over until breakfast.

Persepolis

049

1423 Second Ave. (bet. 74th & 75th Sts.)

Subway:	77 St	Monday - Sunday noon - 11pm
Phone:	212-535-1100	
Fax:	212-737-1155	
e-mail:	contact@persepolisnyc.com	
Web:	www.persepolisnyc.com	
Prices:	**$$**	

In 1990, Persian cuisine became accessible to New Yorkers, thanks to founder Kaz Bayati. His eatery bears the name of one of the ancient capitals of Persia, established by Darius I in the late-6th century BC. It also happens to be the name of the city where Bayati made a name for himself on the local soccer team in the 1970s. Accordingly, a couple of large photographs of the Persepolis soccer squad decorate the orange walls of the dining room, which is filled with rows of closely spaced tables, globe-shaped light fixtures, and tapestry-print banquettes. Olive oil, lemon, garlic, saffron, cinnamon—and even a few secret ingredients—flavor tasty kebabs and vegetarian dishes here.

Pongal

050

1154 First Ave. (bet. 63rd & 64th Sts.)

Subway:	Lexington Av - 63 St	Tuesday - Friday noon - 3pm
Phone:	212-355-4600	& 5:30pm - 10pm
Fax:	N/A	Saturday - Sunday noon - 10pm
e-mail:	pongal@worldnet.att.net	Closed Monday
Web:	www.pongal.org	
Prices:		

For four days in mid-January (autumn in India), people celebrate the bounty of the harvest in a festival called Pongal (the word means "boiling over"). Located an ocean away, Pongal restaurant celebrates the harvest every day with its freshly prepared South Indian cuisine. Here, you'll discover reasonably priced vegetarian fare, which is Kosher as well. The menu offers a wide variety of dishes—around 100 of them—with a large choice of utthappam and dosai, pancakes and crêpes made of rice and lentil flour. These can be filled—or not, depending on your taste—with combinations ranging from onions and potatoes to coconut and cilantro. (The original Pongal is at 110 Lexington Avenue.)

Sette Mezzo

Italian

051

969 Lexington Ave. (bet. 70th & 71st Sts.)

Subway:	68 St - Hunter College
Phone:	212-472-0400
Fax:	212-427-0986
e-mail:	N/A
Web:	N/A
Prices:	$$

Monday - Sunday noon - 2:30pm
& 5pm - 11:30pm

Celebrity appeal has always been a hallmark of this little trattoria. In fact, Oprah even declared the place, whose name refers to an Italian card game, to be her favorite restaurant in New York City. Whether they're known or not, diners of all stripes crowd the long, narrow dining room here; they seem to be infatuated with the convivial atmosphere and the considerate waitstaff. Not to mention the honest Italian cuisine, which respects its roots, even if it is a bit on the pricey side. Sette Mezzo's popularity means that the tables turn over quickly. When the bill comes, don't be gauche enough to offer your credit card, though; Sette Mezzo only accepts cash.

Shanghai Pavilion

Chinese

052

1378 Third Ave. (bet. 78th & 79th Sts.)

Subway:	77 St
Phone:	212-585-3388
Fax:	212-288-9325
e-mail:	N/A
Web:	N/A
Prices:	

Monday - Friday 11:30am - 11pm
Saturday - Sunday noon - 11pm

While so many of the Upper East Side's restaurants seem to tailor their prices to their upscale clientele, Shanghai Pavilion is a real gem if you're watching your wallet. For less than $25, you can dine well here on Eastern Chinese cuisine in a pleasing, contemporary setting. Served with two appetizers, a choice of soup and entrée, the lunch special is an incredible deal. For dinner, the generous menu covers all the bases, from vegetarian meals to the intriguing-sounding lion's head casserole (made with pork dumplings and vegetables). If it's a Shanghai-style banquet you crave, call the day before to arrange it with the restaurant, then round up a group of friends for a multicourse feast.

Spigolo

Italian

1561 Second Ave. (at 81st St.)

Subway:	86 St
Phone:	212-744-1100
Fax:	212-744-1204
e-mail:	N/A
Web:	N/A
Prices:	$$

Sunday - Thursday 5:30pm - 11pm
Friday - Saturday 5:30pm - 2am

Even at the beginning of the week, this shoe-box-size dining room is packed. The draw? They want to be among the lucky few (the restaurant only seats 26 people) to relish the inspired Italian cooking at Spigolo. Husband-and-wife team Scott and Heather Fratangelo met at Union Square Cafe, where they both used to work. In their present venture, Scott turns out dishes like hake fish in "crazy water" (a tomato-and-fish-based broth made with garlic and hot chiles), and a marinated roasted portobello mushroom appetizer, served with herbed goat cheese mousse. Heather plays the charming hostess when she's not whipping up delectable pastries.

Sushi of Gari

Japanese

402 E. 78th St. (bet. First & York Aves.)

Subway:	77 St
Phone:	212-517-5340
Fax:	212-288-9235
e-mail:	N/A
Web:	N/A
Prices:	$$

Tuesday - Saturday 5pm - 10:45pm
Sunday 5pm - 9:45pm
Closed Monday
& December 31 - January 7

Nestled on a quiet street near First Avenue, Gari is named for its owner, Masatoshi "Gari" Sugio, who also operates a branch in Tokyo. Gari's reputation is so good that its clientele is not limited to the neighborhood; diners make a special trip to come here. Sushi connoisseurs, including many Asian regulars, think that the wide choice of creative Japanese fare is well worth the detour. For a piece of the action, belly up to the sushi bar (there are tables, too) to sample the likes of Gari's special eight-piece tuna assortment or the chef's selection of the day's fresh catch. The two small dining rooms are sparely furnished with blond wood tables.

Manhattan Upper East Side

Sushi Seki

Japanese

055

1143 First Ave. (bet. 62nd & 63rd Sts.)

Subway:	Lexington Av - 59 St	Monday - Saturday 5:30pm - 3am
Phone:	212-371-0238	Closed Sunday
Fax:	N/A	
e-mail:	N/A	
Web:	N/A	
Prices:	🍪	

Sushi Seki offers very good quality for the price, making it a sure bet if you're a raw-fish fan looking for a good reason to go out for dinner. It's a several-block walk from the subway, but it's worth the trek to sample the creations of the namesake chef, whose former gig at Sushi of Gari prepped him well to open his own place. In the modest, dimly lit dining room, the waitstaff keeps up a steady tempo, clearing plates and bringing more dishes with equal finesse. Meanwhile, at the sushi bar, chefs craft fresh-from-the-boat products into tasty morsels. If you opt for Seki's omakase, you'll get the chef's choice of seafood air-shipped from the market in Tokyo.

Triangolo

Italian

056

345 E. 83rd St. (bet. First & Second Aves.)

Subway:	86 St	Monday - Saturday 5pm - midnight
Phone:	212-472-4488	Sunday 3pm - 10:30pm
Fax:	212-517-3256	
e-mail:	Triangolo@verizon.net	
Web:	www.triangolorestaurant.com	
Prices:	$$	

Although it's tucked away in an Upper East Side neighborhood off the beaten track of upscale shops and world-class museums, Triangolo nonetheless keeps customers lining up outside the door. Why? Attentive service might be one reason. The warm décor in the simple dining room, another. Probably the greatest draw is the generous menu of pastas, cooked correctly and topped with hearty homemade sauces from bolognese to creamy vodka sauce. Of course, you won't want to dive into the pastas without first sampling the long list of antipasti. For dessert, go for the tasty tiramisu. Be sure to stop by the ATM before you come, though; Triangolo doesn't accept credit cards.

Zebú Grill

Brazilian

305 E. 92nd St. (bet. First & Second Aves.)

Subway:	86 St
Phone:	212-426-7500
Fax:	212-426-7930
e-mail:	N/A
Web:	www.zebugrill.com
Prices:	$$

Sunday - Tuesday 5pm - 11pm
Wednesday - Saturday 5pm - 11:30pm

Set on a quiet side street way up on the Upper East Side, closer to the East River than to Central Park, this little Brazilian place takes its name from a breed of humped cattle raised in Brazil. Zebú charms guests with its warm ambience and rustic décor. Latin rhythms play in the background, while patrons dig into copious portions of churrasco (the house specialty combination of steak, chicken and sausage), and feijoada, a meaty stew that is the Brazilian national dish. While sides include baked potatoes and creamed spinach, try something out of the ordinary and order a side of yucca fries. This is a place you'll be glad to come back to.

Manhattan Upper East Side

Great cultural institutions and good food are what you can expect from the Upper West Side, along with tidy rows of restored brownstones and stunning apartment buildings bordering Central Park. Reaching from Central Park West to the Hudson River between 59th Street and 125th Street, the Upper West Side is home to the **Lincoln Center for the Performing Arts**, the **American Museum of Natural History**, and the campus of **Columbia University**. This neighborhood is also where you'll run into some of the city's favorite food markets, such as Zabars (*80th St. & Broadway*), a family-run New York institution for more than 75 years.

A Bit of History – Development has been relatively recent in this neighborhood. In the late 19th century, shantytowns, saloons and stray goats populated the area now considered the Upper West Side. This all changed in 1884 when Henry Hardenbergh built New York's first luxury apartment house—the celebrated **Dakota**—at 1 West 72nd Street. With its eclectic turrets, Gothic gables and ornate finials, the Dakota made a fitting setting for the 1968 film *Rosemary's Baby*. Over the years, the Dakota housed many celebrities, including Leonard Bernstein, Lauren Bacall and John Lennon, who was shot outside the 72nd Street entrance by a crazed fan in 1980.

After the Dakota came the ornate **Ansonia Hotel** (*2101-2119 Broadway*) in 1904, the first to have a drive-in courtyard, and the elegant **San Remo** (*145 Central Park West*), with its stunning Central Park views. These sumptuous digs appealed to many bankers, lawyers and other well-to-do professionals, who were followed in the 1930s by prosperous Jewish families relocating from the Lower East Side. Gentrification of the older row houses in recent years has made the cross streets quite desirable, particularly among young professionals and college students. Today the Upper West Side's tree-lined residential blocks provide a quiet contrast to the bustle of Broadway, the area's commercial spine.

© Martha Cooper

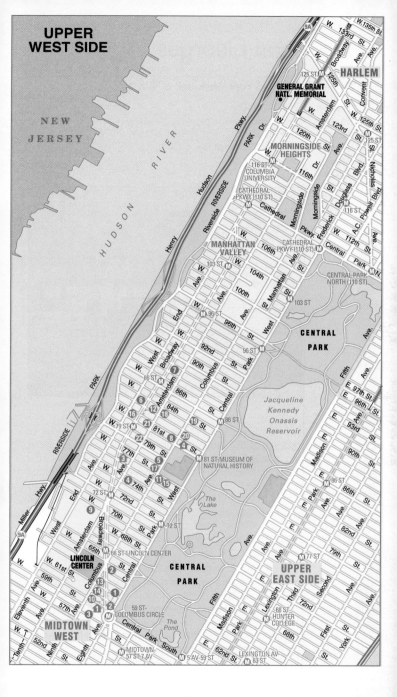

Jean Georges ✿✿✿

C o n t e m p o r a r y

1 Central Park West (bet. 60th & 61st Sts.)

Subway:	59 St - Columbus Cir
Phone:	212-299-3900
Fax:	212-299-3914
e-mail:	jean-georges@jean-georges.com
Web:	www.jean-georges.com
Prices:	$$$$

Monday - Friday noon - 2:30pm
& 5:30pm - 11pm
Saturday 5:30pm - 11pm
Closed Sunday

Jean-Georges Management

Jean-Georges Vongerichten owns a veritable galaxy of restaurants in New York City, but this one shines above the others. Premiering in 1997 on the ground floor of the Trump International Hotel, Jean-Georges wraps its space with huge window walls looking out on Columbus Circle. Adam Tihany sculpted the minimalist geometric motif, orchestrating the interior lighting to mimic natural light at different times of the day. But the décor serves as a mere stage set for the main attraction here: the extraordinary cuisine.

Unexpected combinations of flavors and textures characterize the perfectly timed courses; meltingly tender morsels of duck might be topped with crunchy, caramelized almonds, or foie gras brûlée sparked by kumquat marmalade and pink peppercorns. No matter the menu, you can expect sublime ingredients transformed by the delicate hand of a master.

Egg Caviar

Serves 4

Cream

½ cup whipping cream
1 tsp. vodka
1 tsp. lemon juice
¼ tsp. salt
¼ tsp. cayenne pepper

Whip cream until it forms stiff peaks. Season with salt and pepper. Stir in vodka and lemon juice. Scoop cream into a pastry bag and set aside in a cool place.

Egg

4 eggs
¼ tsp. salt
pinch cayenne pepper
2 Tbsp. butter
¼ Tsp. salt and freshly ground pepper

Carefully cut top off of egg shells. Pour egg whites and yolks into a bowl and set aside. In a small saucepan, bring water to a boil. Place emptied eggshells in water for 15 seconds, remove and drain. When cool to the touch, gently remove skin and any other debris from inside of shell. Over a medium flame, melt butter in an 8-inch sauté pan. Beat eggs with salt, cayenne and pepper. Add to sauté pan and whisk constantly until egg is lightly curdled. Season with salt and cayenne.
Stand eggshells upright in egg cups and carefully divide scrambled eggs evenly in shells. Pipe whipped cream around the top of eggshell filled with the scrambled egg. Top with a teaspoon of caviar. Serve with an espresso spoon. To eat, combine the hot eggs, cold cream and salty caviar in one bite.

Picholine ✿

35 W. 64th St. (bet. Broadway & Central Park West)

Subway:	66 St-Lincoln Center	Monday - Wednesday 5pm - 11pm
Phone:	212-724-8585	Thursday - Friday 5pm - 11:45pm
Fax:	212-875-8979	Saturday 11:45am - 2pm
e-mail:	N/A	& 5pm - 11:45pm
Web:	N/A	Sunday 5pm - 9pm
Prices:	$$$	

Picholine

Elegant old sister to Artisanal—chef/proprietor Terrance Brennan's Murray Hill brasserie—Picholine pulls in a cadre of smartly dressed regulars who come for Brennan's sophisticated French-inspired cuisine. Regulars here seem to have their preferred spot, in either the main dining room, adorned with tapestries and crystal chandeliers; or in the smaller, intimate room behind it. The menu changes eight times a year to feature the best products (squab, pea shoots, blood oranges, Maine lobster) that each season has to offer. Don't pass up Picholine's cheese course—it's one of the best in the city.

In 2003 Brennan opened his Artisanal Cheese Center, custom-designed with 5 caves for aging 300 types of cheese. The restaurant's location close to Lincoln Center means that early evenings here can be frantic; if you're not rushing to catch a show, go later for a quiet dinner.

Manhattan Upper West Side

Saddle of Lamb

Serves 4

Lamb

4 pieces (8 oz. each) Niman Ranch (or other high quality) lamb loin, trimmed of fat and sinew
½ cup olive oil

Basquaise Chutney

4 roasted peppers (2 red, 2 yellow), peeled and diced
1 small yellow onion, diced
6 pitted Moroccan olives, chopped
1 oz. Serrano ham, small dice
1 clove of garlic, minced
pinch of cayenne pepper
1 tsp. salt   1 Tbsp. olive oil
6 capers, chopped 2 tsp. sherry vinegar
To make the chutney, preheat oven to 300°F. Place an ovenproof pan over medium heat on the stove and add olive oil. Sweat onions and garlic until soft, about five minutes. Combine all other ingredients in pan and place in oven for 2 hours.

Romesco Mousse

½ cup heavy cream   ½ roasted red pepper
dash of sherry vinegar pinch of saffron
1 Tbsp. toasted sliced almonds

1 tsp. powdered gelatin
Combine all the ingredients except the gelatin and bring to a boil. Simmer 10 minutes and then purée. Dissolve gelatin in 1 Tbsp. cold water in a small bowl and add to the cream mixture. Pass mixture through a fine strainer and allow to cool completely. Whip the mixture until soft peaks form.

Olive Crust

1 cup pitted Niçoise olives
½ cup Panko (Japanese breadcrumbs)
Dry the pitted olives in the oven at 200°F, until crisp and dry (about two hours). Allow the olives to cool. Put olives and breadcrumbs in a food processor and process until they are ground to a fine texture.

To Serve
Add a ½ cup of olive oil to a sauté pan over medium heat. Dredge the lamb in the olive-breadcrumb mixture. Gently place the dredged loins of lamb in the pan and cook 4 to 6 minutes. Turn over and cook for another 4-6 minutes. Remove lamb and set aside to rest. Divide the Basquaise chutney evenly in four parts and place it in a circle in the middle of the plate. Cut the lamb loins into 5 slices and arrange on top of the chutney. Place a scoop of the Romesco mousse next to the lamb and serve.

Asiate

Contemporary Asian

80 Columbus Circle (at 60th St.)

Subway:	59 St - Columbus Cir	Monday - Friday noon - 2pm
Phone:	212-805-8881	& 5:30pm - 10pm
Fax:	212-805-8842	Saturday 11:30am - 2:30pm
e-mail:	N/A	& 5:30pm - 10:30pm
Web:	www.mandarinoriental.com	Sunday 5:30pm - 8:30pm
Prices:	$$$$	

From its 35th-floor aerie in the Mandarin Oriental hotel *(see hotel listings)*, Asiate gazes out over the city through wraparound window walls. It's in this contemplative atmosphere, fashioned by Tony Chi with stylized tree branches sprawling across the ceiling, that chef Noriyuki Sugie creates Asiate's sought-after cuisine. Sugie, a native of Japan who's cooked in kitchens all over the world, plates up courses such as black sea bass in broth infused with ginger and Thai basil, and muscovy duck with red wine plum and black bean purée. As for wine, you noticed the wall of wine near the entrance? Stocked with 1,300 bottles, it will no doubt provide the correct vintage to complement your meal.

'Cesca

Italian

164 W. 75th St. (at Amsterdam Ave.)

Subway:	72 St	Monday - Thursday 5pm - 11pm
Phone:	212-787-6300	Friday - Saturday 5pm - 11:30pm
Fax:	212-787-1081	Sunday 5pm - 10pm
e-mail:	cesca@cescanyc.com	Closed major holidays
Web:	www.cescanyc.com	
Prices:	$$$	

Bright and bold, 'Cesca is the newest venture by Godfrey Polistina and chef Tom Valenti, who enlivened the Upper West Side dining scene with 'Cesca's French sister, Ouest. ('Cesca is short for Francesca, Godfrey Polistina's daughter.) Brown velvet covers the chairs and banquettes in the castle-rustic dining room, with its custom-made iron chandeliers and granite-topped bar. A list of set daily specials complements the menu; on Sunday, it's what else but "Sunday Sauce," just like your nonna used to make. Although the wine list does include a few American bottles, the focus is on Italian vintages, with all Italy's major wine-producing regions represented.

Ocean Grill

005

384 Columbus Ave. (bet. 78th & 79th Sts.)

Subway:	79 St	Monday - Thursday 11:30am - 4pm
Phone:	212-579-2300	& 5pm - 11pm
Fax:	212-579-0409	Friday 11:30am - 4pm & 5pm - midnight
e-mail:	N/A	Saturday 11:30am - midnight
Web:	www.brguestrestaurants.com	Sunday 10:30am - 11:30pm
Prices:	$$	

Set sail for a culinary adventure. Right across the street from the Museum of Natural History, Ocean Grill is one of the restaurants owned by the B.R. Guest group. You'll think you've just boarded an elegant ocean liner when you set foot inside the elegant room, bedecked with black-and-white photographs of the seashore, and porthole windows peeking in on the kitchen. You'll find something for every fish-lover here, whether it's a plate of oysters from the raw bar, simply grilled fish, Maine lobster, or the house maki rolls. And be sure to sample one of the scrumptious desserts. The "sunset menu" of light fare is served weekdays from 4pm to 5pm.

Ouest

006

2315 West Broadway (bet. 83rd & 84th Sts.)

Subway:	86 St	Monday - Thursday 5pm - 11pm
Phone:	212-580-8700	Friday - Saturday 5pm - midnight
Fax:	212-580-1360	Sunday 11am - 2pm & 5pm - 10pm
e-mail:	info@ouestny.com	
Web:	www.ouestny.com	
Prices:	$$$	

If you find yourself Uptown, head Ouest ("west") to discover this polished restaurant from chef Tom Valenti. Keep going past the perennially busy bar until you reach the large room at the back, with views on the open kitchen. Bring a group of friends so you'll be more likely to snag one of the terrific circular booths covered in deep-red tufted leather. Behind the stoves, a veritable army of chefs riffs on American classics, resulting in dishes, such as skate with Yukon potato purée, celery and caperberries, which are high on originality and strong on presentation. Many bottles on the ample, well-balanced wine list are attractively priced.

Manhattan Upper West Side

Aix

007

2398 Broadway (at 88th St.)

Subway:	86 St	Monday - Thursday 5:30pm - 10:30pm
Phone:	212-874-7400	Friday - Saturday 5:30pm - 11pm
Fax:	N/A	Sunday 11:30am - 2:30pm
e-mail:	info@aixnyc.com	& 5:30pm - 10:30pm
Web:	www.aixnyc.com	Closed major holidays
Prices:	$$$	

To describe the cooking at Aix as Provencal would send any French culinary traditionalist crying into their copies of Larousse Gastronomique. Provencal cuisine is merely the jumping-off point for chef/owner Didier Virot's original, elaborate and playful takes on the dishes of southern France. Virot's plates become a canvas on which he paints intricate patterns using unusual combinations (cured baked chicken with star anise and honey, apple tart with rosemary), always using the best quality ingredients. His food will surely challenge your palate as well as your expectations. Ranging over two levels, the dining space reflects perfectly the warm orange, red, green and azure hues of Provence.

Calle Ocho

008

446 Columbus Ave. (bet. 81st & 82nd Sts.)

Subway:	81 St - Museum of Natural History	Monday - Thursday 6pm - 11pm
Phone:	212-873-5025	Friday 6pm - midnight
Fax:	212-873-0216	Saturday 5pm - midnight
e-mail:	calleocho@msrpgroup.com	Sunday 11:30am - 3pm & 5pm - 10pm
Web:	www.calleochonyc.com	
Prices:	$$	

Looking for good food *and* fun? You've come to the right place. Calle Ocho pulls in the partyers with its winning mix of pulsating salsa music, potent caipirinhas and mojitos, and zesty food—all taking their influences from Argentina to Puerto Rico and Cuba to Peru. Named for the bustling main drag in Miami's Little Havana neighborhood, Calle Ocho (Spanish for "Eighth Street") is always jumping, no matter which night you go. The 200-seat dining room sets the tone for a good time with the vivid Cuban-themed mural that lines one wall, and the bold cuisine follows suit by balancing such ingredients as chipotle chiles, calabaza, yucca and plantains.

Compass

009

208 W. 70th St. (bet. Amsterdam & West End Aves.)

Subway:	72 St	Monday - Thursday 5pm - 11pm
Phone:	212-875-8600	Friday - Saturday 5pm - midnight
Fax:	212-875-8400	Sunday 11:30am - 2:30pm
e-mail:	N/A	& 5pm - 10pm
Web:	www.compassrestaurant.com	
Prices:	$$	

Head north-northwest from Midtown and point yourself in the direction of the Upper West Side and the sophisticated surroundings of Compass and its popular bar. Slate-covered square pillars, marble floors, bright-red high-backed banquettes, and vibrant, modern artwork combine with subtle, recessed lighting to create a décor that is at once confident and cool. You can choose one of the chef's "Compositions" (intricate preparations interpreted in a modern American idiom) or order from the list of "Simply Roasted" entrées and pick your own side dish. The impressive wine collection, stored behind frosted glass, is well worth investigating.

Gabriel's

Italian

010

11 W. 60th St. (bet. Broadway & Columbus Ave.)

Subway:	59 St - Columbus Cir	Monday - Thursday noon - 3pm
Phone:	212-956-4600	& 5pm - 11pm
Fax:	212-956-2309	Friday noon - 3pm & 5pm - midnight
e-mail:	N/A	Saturday 5pm - midnight
Web:	www.gabrielsbarandrest.com	Closed Sunday
Prices:	$$	

Despite this restaurant's enviable location opposite the Time Warner Center and near Lincoln Center, Gabriel's is much more than just a convenient place to catch a bite before the opera or after a day of shopping. Gabriel Aiello founded his eponymous eatery in 1991, and since then he has overseen every aspect of its management. Soft yellow and terra-cotta tones warm the dining-room walls, which are brightened by vibrant paintings. Against this sunny background, a crowd of locals, media moguls and celebrities enjoy everything from tagliatelle to wood-grilled trout to slow-roasted baby goat. A number of different wines are available by the glass.

Manhattan Upper West Side

Isabella's

Mediterranean

011

359 Columbus Ave. (at 77th St.)

Subway:	79 St	Monday - Thursday 11:30am - 4pm
Phone:	212-724-2100	& 5:30pm - midnight
Fax:	212-724-1156	Friday - Saturday 11:30am - 4pm
e-mail:	N/A	& 5:30pm - 1am
Web:	www.brguestrestaurants.com	Sunday 10am - 4:30pm
Prices:	$$	& 5:30pm - midnight

A member of the B.R. Guest restaurant group (another one, Ocean Grill sits across the street), Isabella's boasts a genuine neighborhood feel. In fact, the restaurant has been attracting a loyal following on the West Side for more than fifteen years. One of the few places that's open for lunch in this part of town, Isabella's makes a great spot to take a break if you're touring the nearby American Museum of Natural History. In summer, the airy bi-level dining space with its wicker chairs and French doors adds a pleasant outdoor terrace. The menu is Mediterranean in tone, offering dishes like skewered chicken, pastas and assorted fish. Drop by Sunday for the popular, and delicious, brunch.

Nëo Sushi

Japanese

012

2298 Broadway (at 83rd St.)

Subway:	86 St	Monday - Thursday 5pm - 11:30pm
Phone:	212-769-1003	Friday - Saturday 5pm - 12:30am
Fax:	212-769-1005	Sunday 4pm - 10:30pm
e-mail:	N/A	Closed Thanksgiving Day
Web:	www.neosushi.com	& Christmas Day
Prices:	$$$	

When you've finished checking out the photos of various celebrities who have dined here (which are displayed along with the menu on the outside of the restaurant's windows), step inside this minimally decorated space lit by teardrop-shaped lanterns and discover Japanese food for the New Age. Modern takes on Japanese cuisine are organized according to "Nëo Fusion" sushi, and dishes "From the Kitchen." Whatever you order, don't expect to find soy sauce on the table; delicate and subtly flavored fare comes fully seasoned and garnished with an assortment of sauces and condiments. Can't decide? Leave it up to Nëo, and choose from the multicourse tasting menus.

Rosa Mexicano

Mexican

013

61 Columbus Ave. (at 62nd St.)

Subway:	59 St - Columbus Cir	Monday - Friday noon - 3pm
Phone:	212-977-7700	& 5pm - 11pm
Fax:	212-977-7575	Saturday 11:30am - 2:30pm
e-mail:	comments@rosamexicano.com	& 5pm - 11:30pm
Web:	www.rosamexicano.com	Sunday 11:30am - 2:30pm
Prices:	$$$	& 4pm - 10pm

It's hard to tell whether it's the exuberant atmosphere, the flamboyant décor, the wicked Margaritas, or the location near Lincoln Center that makes Rosa Mexicano so wildly popular, but you can be sure that without reservations you'll wait for a table here. Give in to the party atmosphere in the bi-level dining room, with its vivid colors and tiled fountain wall flanking the staircase. Guacamole Molcajete is made fresh at your table in a lava-rock mortar, and dishes such as chile ancho relleno and tablones (grilled boneless short ribs in a piquant tomatillo-chipotle sauce) come in "supersize-me" proportions. The original Rosa Mexicano is in Midtown East at 1063 First Avenue (at 58th St.).

Sapphire

Indian

014

1845 Broadway (bet. 60th & 61st Sts.)

Subway:	59 St - Columbus Cir	Monday - Thursday noon - 2:45pm
Phone:	212-245-4444	& 5pm - 10:30pm
Fax:	212-245-9145	Friday - Saturday noon - 2:45pm
e-mail:	N/A	& 5pm - 10:45pm
Web:	www.sapphireny.com	Sunday 5pm - 10:30pm
Prices:	$$	

Sapphire's location near Lincoln Center and the Time-Warner Building assures it considerable walk-in traffic from this busy neighborhood. Location aside, Sapphire serves eminently satisfying Indian food in a room adorned with elaborately carved wood panels and embroidered silk panels draped like small flags from the ceiling. Recalling dishes from different regions of India, the food ranges from curries and kebabs to Tandoori specialties. Don't miss the unusual appetizers, like delicately spiced chutney *Idli* (steamed lentil cakes topped with coconut curry). Even when they're busy, the helpful waiters are willing to take time to guide novices through the extensive menu.

Scaletta

015

50 W. 77th St. (bet. Columbus Ave. & Central Park West)

Subway:	81 St - Museum of Natural History	Monday - Saturday 5pm - 11pm
Phone:	212-769-9191	Sunday 4pm - 10pm
Fax:	212-769-1501	
e-mail:	N/A	
Web:	www.scalettaristorante.com	
Prices:	$$	

This basement-level Italian eatery opposite the American Museum of Natural History is just the place if you're looking for a good, traditional Italian meal. The columned dining room, with its low ceiling, carpets to muffle the noise, and tables draped in pink linen, provides a tranquil ambience, while the efficient waitstaff greets all their regulars by name. This isn't fancy food; it's traditional Italian fare done right, and accompanied by a wine list that's weighted towards Italian and California varietals. Just make sure you don't fill up on the first two courses; after all, who can resist all those sweets when the dessert trolley comes rolling over to tempt you?

Artie's Deli

016

2290 Broadway (bet. 82nd & 83rd Sts.)

Subway:	79 St	Monday - Sunday 9am - 11pm
Phone:	212-579-5959	
Fax:	212-579-5958	
e-mail:	info@arties.com	
Web:	www.arties.com	
Prices:		

Opened in 1999, Artie's may not have many years behind it, but it still manages to re-create the authentic feel of a 1930s Jewish deli. What the place lacks in history, it more than makes up for in its bright, shiny décor and its helpful service. All the deli classics are here—house-cured corned beef, handmade hot dogs, pastrami, chicken soup, chopped liver. And if you missed having turkey at grandma's house, Thanksgiving dinner is available here every day. So stop by for a sandwich piled high with deli meats and served, of course, with Kosher pickles. If you're hankering for a taste of old New York, Artie's will have you purring with nostalgic contentment.

Gari

017

Japanese

370 Columbus Ave. (bet. 77th & 78th Sts.)

Subway:	81 St	Monday - Thursday 5pm - 11pm
Phone:	212-362-4816	Friday - Saturday 5pm - 11:30pm
Fax:	212-288-9235	Sunday 5pm - 10pm
e-mail:	N/A	
Web:	N/A	
Prices:	$$$	

As of January 2005, Upper West Side residents no longer need to travel to the other side of the park to enjoy Masatoshi Sugio's trademark omakase. Gari, little sister of Sushi of Gari (*402 E. 78th St.*) features a number of unique combinations from the sushi bar. At the chef's whim, raw salmon might be topped by grilled tomato, or fatty tuna served with creamy tofu sauce. From the kitchen come innovative hot dishes like pan-roasted beef short ribs with yucca fries, or sea bass with sake-infused black beans. The plain room has a convivial atmosphere, complemented by communal seating alongside, rather than facing, the sushi bar, so diners aren't all looking in the same direction.

Good Enough to Eat

018

American

483 Amsterdam Ave. (bet. 83rd & 84th Sts.)

Subway:	81 St - Museum of Natural History	Monday - Thursday 8am - 10pm
Phone:	212-496-0163	Friday 8am - 11pm
Fax:	212-496-7340	Saturday - Sunday 9am - 11pm
e-mail:	N/A	
Web:	www.goodenoughtoeat.com	
Prices:	$$	

Comfort food, home cooking: call it what you want, it still spells food like mom used to make. During the day, this cute little place is known for its bountiful breakfasts (they serve light lunches, too); at night it morphs into a cozy, full-service restaurant dishing up ample portions of perennial favorites— meatloaf, pumpkin pie, and turkey dinner with all the trimmings. Sweet-natured servers deliver your order in a scene out of a Norman Rockwell painting, complete with folk art, quilts and antiques; there's even a white-picket fence outside. The case of homemade cakes may remind you so much of home that, after a meal here, you'll be tempted to ask chef/owner Carrie Levin to adopt you.

Jean-Luc

019

507 Columbus Ave. (bet. 84th & 85th Sts.)

Subway:	86 St	Monday 5:30pm - 10:30pm
Phone:	212-712-1700	Tuesday - Friday 5:30pm - 11:30pm
Fax:	212-712-2700	Saturday - Sunday 11:30am - 4pm
e-mail:	N/A	& 5:30pm - midnight
Web:	www.jeanlucrestaurant.com	
Prices:	$$	

Jean-Luc provides Westerners with a stylish French bistro, done up in while tiles, red-velvet banquettes and Art Deco-inspired mirrors. For those who require a little more in the way of creature comforts, the raised dining section at the back of the restaurant is more formal and subdued. Wherever you sit, you'll have access to the same menu, and it's one that showcases bistro staples as well as dishes of less Gallic persuasion (lobster and vegetable spring roll, pumpkin gnocchi)—all of which share the same degree of careful preparation. If you're headed to the Hamptons for the weekend, stop by one of Jean-Luc's two outposts—called JLX—on Long Island.

Kitchen82

020

461 Columbus Ave. (at 82nd St.)

Subway:	81 St - Museum of Natural History	Tuesday - Thursday 5:30pm - 10:30pm
Phone:	212-875-1619	Friday - Saturday 5pm - 11:30pm
Fax:	212-875-0780	Sunday noon - 4pm & 5pm - 8:30pm
e-mail:	info@charliepalmer.com	Closed Monday
Web:	www.charliepalmer.com	
Prices:	⊜	

A sequel to restaurateur Charlie Palmer's Kitchen22 *(36 E. 22nd St.)* in the Flatiron District, Kitchen82 proves that if you want good food in Manhattan, you don't have to take out a bank loan first. What's the winning formula? They provide an inexpensive fixed-price menu; you put up with the lines—the restaurant doesn't take reservations. So take a seat at the bar and chill out; the quality of the cooking here makes the wait worthwhile. The room, in muted fawn colors, is warm and inviting, and the charming staff contributes to the convivial atmosphere. You'll have ample choices on the three-course menu, and best of all, the kitchen lets the fresh ingredients speak for themselves.

Land Thai Kitchen

021

450 Amsterdam Ave. (bet. 81st & 82nd Sts.)

Subway:	79 St	Monday - Sunday noon - 10:45pm
Phone:	212-501-8121	
Fax:	212-501-8123	
e-mail:	N/A	
Web:	www.landthaikitchen.com	
Prices:	🍜	

Upper West Siders appear to have taken quickly to this newcomer, which opened in early 2005. With seats for just thirty people, Land Thai Kitchen makes the most of its limited space, decorated with exposed brick on one wall, and on the other, a colorful fabric panel that diffuses the light behind it. Executive chef and owner David Bank, who was born in Bangkok, creates high-quality Thai dishes that are marked by an appropriate degree of spice. If you prefer your food with even more of a kick, try one of the dishes indicated with an asterisk on the menu. The chef's specials include pan-seared duck breast and crispy boneless whole red snapper, both served with fragrant jasmine rice.

Nice Matin

022

201 W. 79th St. (at Amsterdam Ave.)

Subway:	79 St	Monday - Saturday 11:30am - 3:30pm
Phone:	212-873-6423	& 5:30pm - midnight
Fax:	212-873-1832	Sunday 11:30am - 3:30pm
e-mail:	N/A	& 5pm - 11pm
Web:	www.nicematinnyc.com	
Prices:	$$	

Named after the daily newspaper published in the major city on France's Côte d'Azur, Nice Matin transports diners to the sun-drenched Mediterranean coast. Niçoise dishes here exhibit as many vibrant colors as appear in the room's luminous décor. Done up as a French cafe, the place asserts its unique personality by avoiding all the decorative clichés you find in many faux-Gallic restaurants; lights dangle from the tops of high pillars that spread, umbrella-like, against the ceiling, and tables sport Formica tops. The menu, like a tanned French Lothario, is not just confined to the Riviera, but wanders the wider Mediterranean area for its inspiration.

Manhattan Upper West Side

About Washington Heights

Manhattan's northernmost neighborhood, Washington Heights reaches from West 145th Street to West 218th Street. This narrow neck of land is rimmed by water, the Hudson River on the west and the Harlem River on the east.

Attracted by the comparatively low rents and spacious apartments, young urban professionals are slowly adding to the ethnic mix in this neighborhood, thanks to a recent real-estate boom. The northwestern section of Washington Heights is dominated by the green spaces of Fort Tryon and Inwood Hill parks. Fort Tryon, the highest natural point in Manhattan, is home to the **Cloisters**. The main draw for visitors to this area, this re-created 12th-century monastery belongs to the Metropolitan Museum of Art and is fabled for its collection of medieval artifacts, including the 16th-century Unicorn tapestries.

Although you wouldn't necessarily think of Washington Heights as a dining destination, while you're visiting the Cloisters there are a few good restaurants to sample in this pleasant quarter.

A Bit of History – Wealthy New Yorkers sought rural sanctuaries near the water here in the late 18th and 19th centuries. One of these, the 130-acre estate where George Washington planned the battle of Harlem Heights in 1776, welcomes the public as the **Morris-Jumel Mansion** *(160th St. & Edgecombe Ave.)*. Lining the mansion's original cobblestone carriage drive, now called **Sylvan Terrace**, you can see some of the city's few remaining wood-frame houses.

By the turn of the 20th century, the neighborhood was populated primarily by working-class Greek and Irish immigrants, followed by German Jews fleeing Nazi persecution in the late 1930s and 40s. Cubans and Puerto Ricans began to move to the neighborhood in the 50s, and a large influx of residents immigrated from the Dominican Republic in the late 70s. African-American luminaries such as jazz great Duke Ellington, Supreme Court Justice Thurgood Marshall, and historian W.E.B. Dubois, co-founder of the NAACP, all lived in this area at one time.

© Martha Cooper

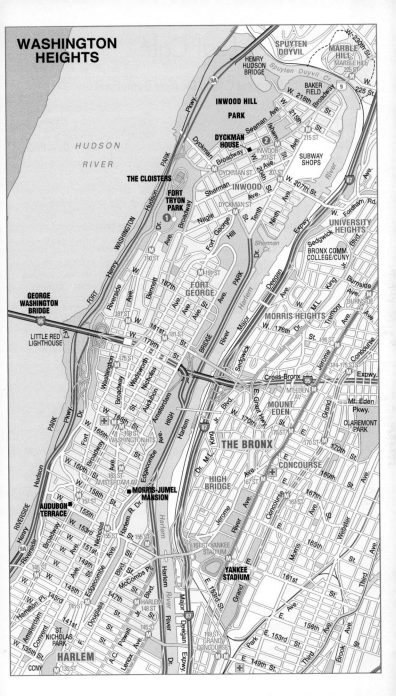

WASHINGTON HEIGHTS

HUDSON RIVER

INWOOD HILL PARK

SPUYTEN DUYVIL

HENRY HUDSON BRIDGE

MARBLE HILL

BAKER FIELD

DYCKMAN HOUSE

THE CLOISTERS

FORT TRYON PARK

INWOOD

SUBWAY SHOPS

UNIVERSITY HEIGHTS

BRONX COMM. COLLEGE/CUNY

FORT GEORGE

GEORGE WASHINGTON BRIDGE

LITTLE RED LIGHTHOUSE

MORRIS HEIGHTS

BURNSIDE

Cross-Bronx Expwy.

MOUNT EDEN

CLAREMONT PARK

THE BRONX

WASHINGTON HTS.

CONCOURSE

MORRIS-JUMEL MANSION

HIGH BRIDGE

AUDUBON TERRACE

YANKEE STADIUM

HARLEM

CCNY

New Leaf Café

American

001

1 Margaret Corbin Dr. (Fort Tryon Park)

Subway:	190 St	Tuesday - Saturday noon - 3pm
Phone:	212-568-5323	& 6pm - 10pm
Fax:	212-923-3222	Sunday 11am - 3pm & 5:30pm - 9:30pm
e-mail:	newleaf@nyrp.org	Closed Monday
Web:	www.nyrp.org/newleaf	
Prices:	**$$**	

There are few better places to be on a summer's day than on the sunny terrace of this adorable little place in Fort Tryon Park. Housed in a 1930s-era stone building a few minutes walk from the Cloisters, the cafe offers a cozy getaway with arched windows overlooking the park; live jazz entertains diners on Thursdays. If the sun is shining, this place fills up fast at lunch, so be sure to make reservations. Otherwise, go for dinner and enjoy the luxury of on-site parking. At lunch the menu offers salads and sandwiches, while at dinner the kitchen shows off its more creative instincts. Order freely, as all proceeds from the cafe go towards the upkeep of the historic park.

Park Terrace Bistro

Moroccan

002

4959 Broadway (bet. 207th & Isham Sts.)

Subway:	Inwood - 207 St	Monday - Friday 5pm - 11pm
Phone:	212-567-2828	Saturday - Sunday 11:30am - 3:30pm
Fax:	212-567-0099	& 5pm - 11pm
e-mail:	parkterracebistro@hotmail.com	
Web:	www.parkterracebistro.com	
Prices:	**$$**	

A slice of Morocco in Washington Heights, this sweet bistro sits just a couple of blocks east of Inwood Hill Park. Inside they've captured the essence of the Casbah with red and terra-cotta washed walls, paintings depicting life in Morroco, and an assortment of colorful glass lamps. France meets North Africa on the menu here; frisée salad with duck leg confit shares space with shrimp cigars (spiced shrimp rolled in layers of phyllo), and traditional tagines (some served with mashed potatoes instead of couscous) vie with steak au poivre for your attention. The Casablanca-born owner Karim Bouskou and his wife, Natalie Weiss, promote a convivial atmosphere, aided by the delightful waitstaff.

The Elevated Train, Washington Heights

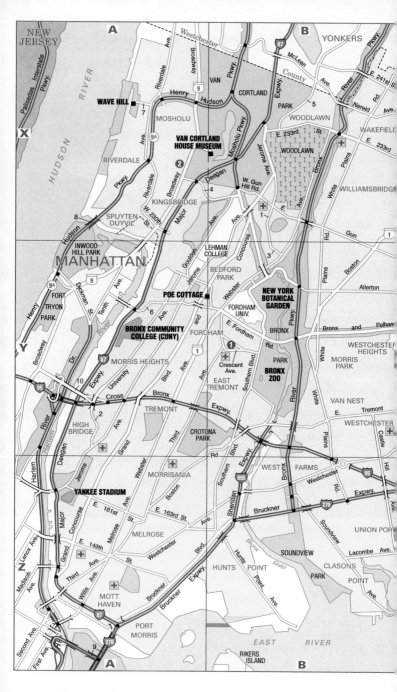

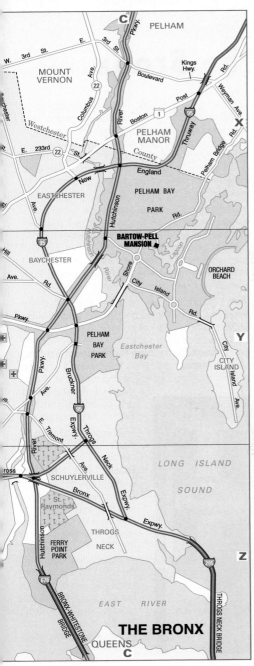

About The Bronx

The only borough attached to the mainland, the Bronx is marked by contrasts. Run-down apartment buildings and massive housing projects characterize the southern part of the borough, although, in recent years, funds have been allocated to make the area more livable. To the north, grand mansions and lush gardens fill prosperous sections such as Riverdale and Fieldston. Thanks to journalist John Mullaly, who led a movement in the late 1800s to buy inexpensive parcels of land and preserve them as parks, 25 percent of the Bronx today consists of parkland.

A Bit of History – Named after Jonas Bronck, a Swede who settled here in 1639, the borough developed in the late 1800s. In 1904, the first subway line connecting the Bronx to the island of Manhattan opened, causing significant migration to this outlying borough. Grand Art Deco apartment buildings sprang up along the wide tree-lined thoroughfare called the **Grand Concourse**, attracting Jews from Eastern and Central Europe; many of their descendents remain here to this day.

A Modern Melting Pot – Hispanics make up more than half of the population of the Bronx today. African-Americans, Irish-Americans, West Indies immigrants and others round out the cultural stew. A host of Italians settled in the Belmont area, though now they share their streets with Albanian immigrants. Located near the **Bronx Zoo** and **New York Botanical Gardens**, Belmont's main street, **Arthur Avenue**, lures diners from all over town, who come to eat authentic Italian fare, shop for salami and provolone at their favorite food shops, and pick up fresh produce in the mid-avenue arcade.

© Martha Cooper

The biggest food news in the Bronx today is the fact that New York's venerable **Fulton Fish Market**, where most of the city's restaurateurs purchase their finny fare, has moved from Lower Manhattan (where it's been since 1869) to new Bronx digs in Hunts Point. Spanning the length of four football fields, the market facility boasts a state-of-the-art climate-control system, which maintains the indoor temperature at a constant 41°F.

Roberto's

001

603 Crescent Ave. (at Hughes Ave.)

Subway:	Fordham Rd	Tuesday - Thursday noon - 2:30pm
Phone:	718-733-9503	& 5pm - 10pm
Fax:	N/A	Friday noon - 2:30pm & 5pm - 11pm
e-mail:	cpac61@aol.com	Saturday 4pm - 11pm
Web:	www.robertobronx.com	Sunday 4pm - 10pm
Prices:	$$	Closed Monday

There are no American accents in the southern Italian cuisine at Roberto Paciullo's restaurant near Arthur Avenue, the epicenter for Italian food in the Bronx. This is traditional Italian fare, simply the best you can find in this borough. Many of the excellent house-made pastas, like the tubetini with porcini, are best eaten with a spoon—as the helpful staff will explain—in order to fully appreciate the aroma of the dish and scoop up the rich sauce. The dining room mixes blocky farmhouse tables with elegant chandeliers and a wine wall on one side of the room. And speaking of wine, the list proffers more than 550 labels, most of them ranging over the different regions of Italy.

Riverdale Garden

002

4576 Manhattan College Pkwy. (at 242 St.)

Subway:	Van Cortlandt Park - 242 St	Monday 5pm - 11pm
Phone:	718-884-5232	Tuesday - Friday 11:30am - 2:30pm
Fax:	718-884-5232	& 5pm - 11pm
e-mail:	info@theriverdalegarden.com	Saturday - Sunday 10:30am - 2:30pm
Web:	www.theriverdalegarden.com	& 5pm - 11pm
Prices:	$$	

Close to Van Cortlandt Park in the Riverdale neighborhood, this town house sits on a quiet street adjacent to the subway station. Go on a warm, sunny day, when you can enjoy the lovely garden, filled with greenery, flowers and tile-inlaid tables. Chef/owner Michael Sherman updates his menu daily, but favors game dishes in season (venison, quail, wild boar); his wife, Lisa, creates the luscious desserts. On weekends, the restaurant features "Blunch," the best of breakfast (homemade granola, apple-cranberry-ricotta pancakes, egg-white fritatta) along with typical lunch entrées. And if you just can't be without your laptop, Riverdale Garden offers wireless Internet access.

The Bronx

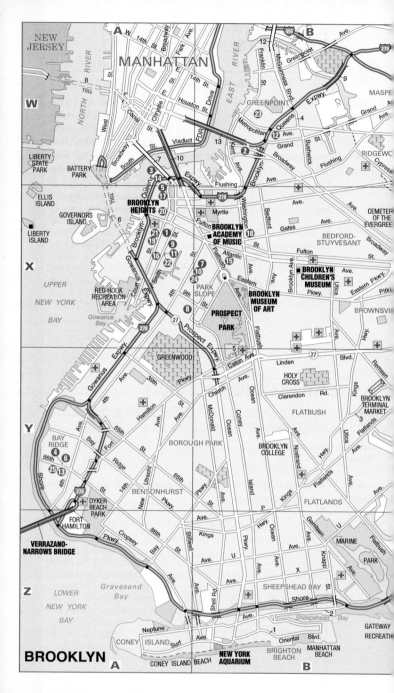

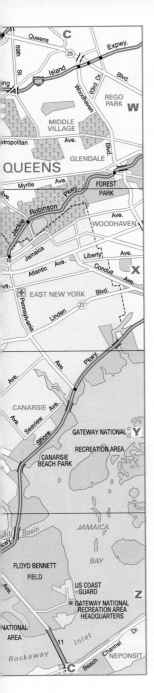

About Brooklyn

New York's most populous borough, with 2.5 million residents, Brooklyn sits on the western tip of Long Island. Its landmass extends from the East River to Coney Island and from the Narrows to Jamaica Bay. Although almost half a million Brooklynites commute to Manhattan, the borough retains a distinctive, country-village atmosphere in its eclectic mix of neighborhoods.

A Bit of History – Founded by the Dutch in 1636, the area now called Brooklyn was first christened Breuckelen ("broken land" in Dutch) after a small town near Utrecht. By the time it became part of New York City in 1898, Brooklyn was flourishing as a center of industry and commerce. Its first direct link to Manhattan came in 1883 in the form of the **Brooklyn Bridge**. Then came the Williamsburg Bridge (1903), the Manhattan Bridge (1909), and the first subway, in 1905. The 13,700-foot-long **Verrazano-Narrows Bridge**, completed in 1964, further facilitated travel between Brooklyn and the other boroughs.

A Taste of the Neighborhoods – A close look at Brooklyn reveals a patchwork of neighborhoods. Verdant **Park Slope**, a choice residential community, is the most recent haven for the diaper-and-stroller crowd. Staid **Brooklyn Heights** reigns as a wealthy enclave of narrow, tree-lined streets bordered by historic brownstones. Don't miss a walk along the riverside **Esplanade**, which affords stunning views of Lower Manhattan.

Traditionally an Italian, Hispanic and Hasidic Jewish neighborhood, hipster **Williamsburg** now welcomes an influx of young artists, who have

© Martha Cooper

© Martha Cooper

created their own community called DUMBO (District Under Manhattan Bridge Overpass). Bedford Avenue is where you'll find hip art galleries, boutiques and cafes. Brooklyn's Little Italy, **Bensonhurst** boasts a proliferation of pizza joints and pasta restaurants.

You can't ignore **Coney Island**. A bit faded since its mid-20th-century heyday, this place still brings crowds to its boardwalk for Coney Island hot dogs—not to mention the wide expanse of beach. Less than a mile east of Coney Island, **Brighton Beach** is a thriving Russian neighborhood; this is where you want to go for authentic blinis and borscht.

Saul ✿

001

140 Smith St. (bet. Bergen & Dean Sts.)

Subway:	Bergen St
Phone:	718-935-9844
Fax:	718-532-1399
e-mail:	restsaul@earthlink.net
Web:	www.saulrestaurant.com
Prices:	$$

Monday - Sunday 5:30pm - 10:30pm

✕✕

♿

Brooklyn

Saul/Ellen Wallop

Saul Bolton named his restaurant after himself, and in this case the vanity is well deserved. The chef honed his skills in the kitchens of no less than Eric Ripert and David Bouley before setting out on his own in Boerum Hill, one of Brooklyn's prettiest neighborhoods. In the 35-seat dining room, with its exposed brick walls and tin ceiling tiles, Bolton offers top-quality seasonal ingredients sourced from local markets and New England farms.

Dishes such as seared day boat scallops with Anson Mills organic polenta, and pan-roasted Vermont-raised veal with spring garlic and fava beans, and the signature baked Alaska for dessert illustrate his considerable prowess in the kitchen. Ordering à la carte is the way to go here, although the blackboard does list a less ambitious prix-fixe menu. The sizable wine list is well-balanced between European, North American and South American labels.

Saul/Astrid Stawiarz

Baked Alaska

Serves 8

Parfait

1 cup heavy cream	4 egg yolks
1/2 cup sugar	1 Tbsp. water
1½ tsp. vanilla extract	2 egg whites
2 Tbsp. of strong coffee	
1 vanilla bean, split and scraped	

Whip heavy cream until it forms soft peaks, then set aside in refrigerator. Put egg yolks, sugar, water, vanilla seeds, and vanilla extract in a double boiler over medium-high heat and mix continuously until a candy thermometer reads 140°F. Scrape mixture into bowl of an electric mixer and whip at medium speed until doubled in volume. Let cool, then fold in whipped cream. Divide contents evenly between two bowls. Add coffee to one bowl. Whip egg whites until they form soft peaks, then fold half of egg whites into each bowl.

Butter eight muffin tins, and fill the bottom half of each with the non-coffee mixture, and the top half with the one containing coffee. Place in freezer until firmly set, about two hours.

Cookie Base

7 Oreo cookies	1/3 cup almond flour
3 egg yolks	

Finely grind Oreos in a food processor. Add them to bowl with the almond flour and egg yolks, and mix thoroughly. Place mixture between two pieces of plastic wrap and roll out with a rolling pin until base is 1/8-inch thick. Remove top sheet of plastic wrap and flip mixture on a cookie sheet lined with parchment paper. Bake at 350°F for 5 minutes. Remove from oven and, using a round cookie cutter slightly larger than the top of your muffin tins, cut out eight circles.

When cookies have cooled and parfait is frozen, gently run a warm knife around the perimeter of each parfait and invert it onto a cool surface. Place each parfait on the center of a cookie base, arrange on a baking sheet, and place in freezer.

Meringue

6 egg whites	3/4 cup of sugar
pinch of salt	

Put eggs whites, sugar and salt into a bowl of an electric mixer and whip at a medium-high speed until firm glossy peaks form. Place meringue in a pastry bag with a half-inch round tip.

To Serve

Remove parfaits from the freezer. Starting at bottom, and working in a circular motion toward the top, pipe meringue kisses until all of parfait is covered. Bake at 400°F until top is golden brown.

Peter Luger ✥

Steakhouse

178 Broadway (at Driggs Ave.)

Subway:	Marcy Av
Phone:	718-387-7400
Fax:	718-387-3523
e-mail:	N/A
Web:	N/A
Prices:	$$$

Sunday - Friday 11:45am - 9:45pm
Saturday 11:45am - 10:45pm

Brooklyn

Peter Luger

Don't be fooled by the beer-hall ambience; Peter Luger serves some of the best steaks in the country. Famed for its velvety USDA Prime beef, dry-aged on the premises, this Williamsburg institution has been catering to carnivores since 1887. Brooklyn factory-owner Sol Forman purchased the restaurant in the 1940s, after namesake Peter Luger passed away; today the Forman family hand-selects every cut of meat, and they only buy the best quality beef short loins.

The service can be brusque, but but who cares, when you can have steak this good? Sharing is de rigueur here, where the menu offers porterhouse steak for 2, 3 or 4 people (don't worry, there's a steak for one if you're dining alone), accompanied by crusty golden fries and the restaurant's signature steak sauce. Can't live without Peter Luger's steaks? Order some online for overnight delivery to your door.

Luger's German Fried Potatoes

Serves 4 - 5

5 large Idaho potatoes

1 large Spanish onion, diced

3 cups + 1/3 cup vegetable oil

6 Tbsp. butter

½ tsp. paprika

1 tsp. salt

¼ tsp. white pepper

Method

Preheat oven to 400°F. Peel the potatoes and cut into half-inch strips. In a frying pan or deep fryer, heat 3 cups of vegetable oil until very hot. Blanch the potato strips in the oil until light brown. Set the potatoes aside to cool on a paper towel. Heat the remaining vegetable oil in a frying pan. Add onion, season with salt and paprika to taste, and sauté until golden brown. Chop the cooled potatoes into quarter-inch cubes. In a heavy pan, melt the butter. Add the potatoes and cook until they brown a bit more.

Then add the sautéed onions and season the mixture to taste with the salt and white pepper. Continue to toss until the potatoes are thoroughly browned. Transfer the potato mixture to a baking dish and place it in the oven for about 10 minutes, or until sufficiently crisp.

River Café

Contemporary

1 Water St. (bet. Furman & Old Fulton Sts.)

Subway:	High St
Phone:	718-522-5200
Fax:	718-875-0037
e-mail:	N/A
Web:	www.rivercafe.com
Prices:	$$$

Monday - Saturday noon - 3pm
& 5:30pm - 11pm
Sunday 11:30am - 3pm
& 5:30pm - 11pm

Location, location, location: these are the three best reasons to eat at the River Café. Housed in a barge on the East River, the cafe has been around since 1977. The restaurant's spectacular view stretches across the river to the towers of the Financial District. At lunch you can order à la carte, while at dinner you must choose between three- or six-course tasting menus that spotlight products like wild King salmon, Maine lobster, and Hudson Valley foie gras. For dessert, take your cue from your surroundings and order the chocolate marquise Brooklyn Bridge; it's topped with a chocolate model of the span that looms nearby. When you make your reservation, ask for a table by the window.

Areo

Italian

8424 Third Ave. (bet. 84th & 85th Sts.)

Subway:	86 St
Phone:	718-238-0079
Fax:	718-238-1189
e-mail:	N/A
Web:	N/A
Prices:	$$$

Tuesday - Sunday 11:45am - 11:45pm
Closed Monday

With its large windows and attractive façade, this Bay Ridge Italian eatery packs in diners in the evening, while lunch is a more subdued affair. The bar divides the two dining rooms, which come decorated with dried flowers and Roman-themed wall stencils. Although the tables are well separated, the din at dinnertime rules out any hope of whispered conversation. Prices seem more Manhattan than Brooklyn, but that doesn't seem to deter the crowds that flock here for their favorite Italian dishes. So settle back and enjoy the complementary plate of bruschetta, olives and salami while you consider the list of daily specials, which best show off the kitchen staff's abilities.

Brooklyn

Noodle Pudding

Italian

38 Henry Street (bet. Cranberry & Middagh Sts.)

Subway:	High St	Tuesday - Thursday 5:30pm - 10:30pm
Phone:	718-625-3737	Friday - Saturday 5:30pm - 11pm
Fax:	N/A	Sunday 5pm - 10pm
e-mail:	N/A	Closed Monday
Web:	N/A	
Prices:	$$	

Expect a warm greeting and friendly service once you find this restaurant, but don't look for a sign on the door—there isn't one. Brooklyn Heights residents know where to come for good conversation and generous portions of rustic Italian fare, including hearty pastas and grilled meats. The restaurant takes its name from a baked pasta dish that resembles Jewish kugel, a savory pudding baked with noodles and traditionally served on the Sabbath. Diners have a great view of the Henry Street scene through the restaurant's large picture window, from well-spaced bistro tables covered with white tablecloths. You can savor the scene while you sip a cup of strong, aromatic espresso after your meal.

The Pearl Room

Seafood

8201 Third Ave. (at 82nd St.)

Subway:	86 St	Monday - Saturday noon - 10:30pm
Phone:	718-833-6666	Sunday 11:30am - 10:30pm
Fax:	718-680-4172	
e-mail:	info@thepearlroom.com	
Web:	www.thepearlroom.com	
Prices:	$$	

The wave-shaped awning is your first clue to the type of cuisine you'll enjoy at this Bay Ridge fish emporium. Fresh from the sea comes an array of well-prepared dishes, from pan-seared sea bass to jumbo Panama shrimp. And speaking of jumbo, the portions here are nothing to sneeze at; rest assured you won't go away hungry. Large windows add to the luminous feel of the room, with its shell-pink luster and fish-themed cubist-style paintings on the walls. This is a place that is as inviting in winter, with its open fireplace, as it is in the summer, with its spacious garden terrace. Expect the service to be good-natured and attentive any time of year.

Brooklyn

Al Di Lá

Italian

007

248 Fifth Ave. (at Carroll St.)

Subway:	Union St
Phone:	718-783-4565
Fax:	718-783-4555
e-mail:	N/A
Web:	www.aldilatrattoria.com
Prices:	$$

Monday, Wednesday -
Thursday 6pm - 10:30pm
Friday - Saturday 6pm - 11pm
Sunday 6pm - 10pm
Closed Tuesday

In a world of laminated menus, it's always a joy to find a daily changing menu that actually bears the day's date. At this perennially busy Park Slope trattoria, husband-and-wife team Emiliano Coppa and Anna Klinger offer diners a balanced selection of fresh and seasonal Italian dishes that are both robust in flavor and generous in size. The high-ceilinged room boasts a certain faded chic, with its church-pew seats and eccentric touches, such as the coffee pots hanging from the walls. If you have questions about the menu, the knowledgeable staff is happy to offer sound advice. Plan to get here early, though, since Al Di Lá's no-reservations policy means it fills up quickly.

Applewood

Contemporary

008

501 11th St. (bet. Seventh & Eighth Aves.)

Subway:	7 Av
Phone:	718-768-2044
Fax:	718-768-2032
e-mail:	info@applewoodny.com
Web:	www.applewoodny.com
Prices:	$$

Tuesday - Saturday 5pm - 11pm
Sunday 10am - 3pm
Closed Monday & December 24 - 30

Park Slope real-estate agents hoping to convince Manhattanites to make the big move across the river should bring them to Applewood. Set within a turn-of-the-century house, this place is a real neighborhood jewel, where everyone seems to know each other. Experienced husband-and-wife team David and Laura Shea run the restaurant along with help from family and friends. The pretty dining room is done in shades of lime green, with a bar at one end and a fireplace to warm diners in winter. The kitchen proudly uses the best local organic produce, hormone-free meats and wild fish in dishes like sautéed East Coast halibut and roasted Pennsylvania lamb that are well-balanced and full of flavor.

Banania Cafe

009

241 Smith St. (bet. Butler & Douglass Sts.)

Subway:	Bergen St	Monday - Thursday 5:30pm - 11pm
Phone:	718-237-9100	Friday 5:30pm - 11:30pm
Fax:	N/A	Saturday 10am - 4pm
e-mail:	N/A	& 5:30pm - 11:30pm
Web:	N/A	Sunday 10am - 4pm
Prices:	$$	& 5:30pm - 10:30pm

Named for a French brand of cocoa powder made with banana flour, Banania Cafe occupies a busy corner of Cobble Hill. You'll recognize this lively eatery by its yellow facade; inside it has all the trappings of a contemporary French bistro, with red leatherette banquettes, wood floors, a tin celing and copper sheeting on the walls. But, wait, is that Latin music playing softly in the background? When you open the menu, you'll notice more Latin influences, such as the tasty house-made guacamole that accompanies the tuna tartar, in the dishes listed. Locals pack the small white-paper-covered tables at lunch and dinner, and on weekends for the popular brunch.

Blue Ribbon Sushi

Japanese

010

278 Fifth Ave. (bet. 1st St. & Garfield Pl.)

Subway:	Union St	Sunday - Thursday 5pm - midnight
Phone:	718-840-0408	Friday - Saturday 5pm - 2am
Fax:	718-840-0071	
e-mail:	N/A	
Web:	www.blueribbonrestaurants.com	
Prices:	$$	

It's a good indication of how Japanese food has become an established part of the culinary fabric that Blue Ribbon Sushi features a kid's menu of assorted yakimono and maki (there's even fried chicken and catfish fingers). This Park Slope neighborhood favorite is the Brooklyn sister of the original location in SoHo. As you'd expect, it provides equally delicate fare with their own original touches—but in larger surroundings and at a slightly less frenetic pace. The square room is bright and airy, the service helpful and obliging. To help you narrow down your choices, the comprehensive menu of sushi and sashimi is classified as to whether each item comes from the Atlantic or Pacific Ocean.

Brooklyn

Chestnut

Contemporary

011

271 Smith St. (bet. DeGraw & Sackett Sts.)

Subway:	Carroll St	Tuesday - Saturday 5:30pm - 11pm
Phone:	718-243-0049	Sunday 11am - 3pm & 5:30pm - 11pm
Fax:	N/A	Closed Monday
e-mail:	info@chestnutonsmith.com	
Web:	www.chestnutonsmith.com	
Prices:	$$	

Some restaurants name their establishments with bad puns and some use their street address, but the owners of Chestnut christened their Carroll Gardens eatery with a moniker that perfectly sums up their philosophy; the name, like the restaurant, is comforting, seasonal and reminds diners that the best supermarket is nature itself. It's clear that time has been well spent here sourcing the best ingredients, whose natural flavors are allowed to come to the fore. Down-home style characterizes the dining room, and the young team provides personable and chatty service. Come on Tuesday or Wednesday night to take advantage of Chestnut's prix-fixe value menus.

DuMont

American

012

432 Union Ave. (bet. Metropolitan Ave. & Devoe St.)

Subway:	Lorimer St	Monday - Sunday 11am - 3pm
Phone:	718-486-7717	& 6pm - 11pm
Fax:	718-486-9084	Closed December 25 - 26
e-mail:	dumont11@verizon.net	
Web:	N/A	
Prices:	$$	

DuMont may look like just one more Williamsburg restaurant, but don't pass this one by. Inside, an antique sheen is reflected in the tile floor, and the weathered tin walls and ceiling. Rock music plays in the background, bringing the atmosphere up to the present. Chefs Cal Elliott and Polo Dobkin are DuMont's two hidden secrets. Formerly of Gramercy Tavern, they propose a list of seasonal specials along with a short menu of all-American fare such as barbecue ribs, the DuMont burger, and DuMac and cheese (their version is made with cheddar, Parmesan and Gruyère cheeses, tossed with radiatore pasta and studded with bits of bacon). The terrace out back makes a quiet, leafy hideaway.

Eliá

013

8611 Third Ave. (bet. 86th & 87th Sts.)

Subway:	86 St	Tuesday - Thursday 5pm - 10pm
Phone:	718-748-9891	Friday - Saturday 5pm - 11pm
Fax:	N/A	Sunday 4pm - 9pm
e-mail:	N/A	Closed Monday
Web:	N/A	
Prices:	$$	

You've spent the day on your scooter tooling around Santorini, the sun is starting to set, and now it's time for dinner . . . Okay, so you're in Brooklyn, and it's a cold Tuesday in February, but the sunny feel of this Bay Ridge taverna will nonetheless transport you to warmer climes. Whitewashed brick walls and marine blues in the modest dining room evoke sun-washed stucco buildings and the color of the Aegean Sea. Along with the usual Greek favorites, the menu lists items (like the fish of the day) that come simply prepared and well flavored—as they do in the Greek islands—with bounteous amounts of fragrant olive oil and lemon.

Five Front

014

5 Front St. (bet. Dock & Old Fulton Sts.)

Subway:	High St	Monday, Wednesday - Thursday
Phone:	718-625-5559	5:30pm - 11pm
Fax:	718-625-5523	Friday 5:30pm - midnight
e-mail:	plowry@fivefrontrestaurant.com	Saturday 11am - 4pm & 5:30pm - midnight
Web:	www.fivefrontrestaurant.com	Sunday 11am - 4pm & 5:30pm - 11pm
Prices:	$$	Closed Tuesday

Tucked into the up-and-coming new neighborhood dubbed DUMBO (for Down Under the Manhattan Bridge Overpass), Five Front takes its name from its address on busy Front Street. The restaurant is located just a block or so from the esplanade, with its fantastic views of Lower Manhattan. Weather permitting, the best dining space at Five Front is its spacious garden, which nestles under the span of the Brooklyn Bridge. Locals favor this pleasant space to savor sophisticated American fare, much of it interpreted with Italian accents. At dinner, the three-course, fixed-price meal adds another option to the already reasonably priced menu.

Brooklyn

Garden Café

Contemporary

015

620 Vanderbilt Ave. (at Prospect Pl.)

Subway:	7 Av	Tuesday - Saturday 6pm - 10pm
Phone:	718-857-8863	Closed Sunday & Monday
Fax:	N/A	
e-mail:	N/A	
Web:	N/A	
Prices:	**$$**	

This little unassuming gem of a restaurant has operated for 19 years in Prospect Heights, which is now in the process of being gentrified. Owner John Policastro does the cooking, using premium ingredients; his charming wife oversees the front of the house, seeing to the needs of her guests. Oddly, there's no garden here; the name comes from the ambience inside the restaurant, which is set about with lots of green plants, cane chairs, candlelight and soft music in the background. It may not be trendy, but this family-run cafe draws an epicurean crowd with its excellent cuisine. At night there's but one set menu, and it's a real bargain considering the high quality of the food here.

The Grocery

Contemporary

016

288 Smith St. (bet. Sackett & Union Sts.)

Subway:	Carroll St	Monday - Thursday 5:30pm - 10pm
Phone:	718-596-3335	Friday 5:30pm - 11pm
Fax:	N/A	Saturday 5pm - 11pm
e-mail:	N/A	Closed Sunday & 2 weeks in August
Web:	N/A	
Prices:	**$$**	

Can you tell a restaurant by its façade? In this case, you can. The inviting Grocery, its name etched on the glass window in front, beckons diners to experience the warm hospitality and charming ambience inside the avocado-green dining room. Co-owners Charlie Kiely and Sharon Pachter run this Carroll Gardens place with watchful eyes; she oversees the dining room, he presides over the kitchen. The chef lends his own flair to flavorful American dishes here, and the well-chosen wine list thoughtfully includes a few half-bottles. Since the tiny restaurant only seats 30 people, reservations are a must. In summer, though, the pleasant garden out back increases The Grocery's capacity.

Henry's End

017

44 Henry St. (bet. Middagh & Cranberry Sts.)

Subway:	High St	Monday - Sunday 5:30pm - 10pm
Phone:	718-834-1776	
Fax:	718-855-9036	
e-mail:	henrysend@verizon.net	
Web:	www.henrysend.com	
Prices:	**$$**	

Nearly under the bridge in Brooklyn Heights, two blocks from the esplanade with its fine views of Lower Manhattan, Henry's End serves up American dishes in a casual atmosphere. Bistro tables are tightly packed in the small dining room, where the décor is fading and the walls are lined with black and white photographs of Brooklyn through the years. Whether your tastes run to simple American classics (Southern fried chicken) or to more sophisticated preparations (wild Alaskan salmon), Henry's has something for you—and lots of it (portions are big here). Wash your meal down with a selection from the ever-changing list of American wines by the glass.

Locanda Vini & Olii

American

018

129 Gates Ave. (at Cambridge Pl.)

Subway:	Clinton - Washington Avs	Tuesday - Thursday 6pm - 10:30pm
Phone:	718-622-9202	Friday - Saturday 6pm - 11:30pm
Fax:	718-622-9227	Sunday 6pm - 10pm
e-mail:	vinieolii@yahoo.com	Closed Monday & major holidays
Web:	www.locandavinieolii.com	
Prices:	**$$**	

Gracious host François Louy and his wife, Catherine, are not strangers to the restaurant business. Both from northern Italy (he from Milan, she from Florence), the couple comes with good credentials. François worked for the Cipriani restaurant group, and Catherine was a manager for Balthazar before the pair opened their own place in Clinton Hill. Located in a restored 100-year-old pharmacy, Locanda uses the old apothecary shelves and drawers to hold wine bottles, antique crockery and other supplies. The menu changes daily, but the likes of house-made gnocchi in fresh tomato sauce, and branzino steamed *en papillote* in white wine and perfumed with fennel make a prescription for a good meal.

Brooklyn

Osaka

019

272 Court St. (bet. Kane & DeGraw Sts.)

Subway:	Bergen St	Monday - Friday noon - 2pm
Phone:	718-643-0044	& 5pm - 11pm
Fax:	N/A	Saturday - Sunday noon - 3pm
e-mail:	N/A	& 5pm - midnight
Web:	N/A	
Prices:	**$$**	

Osaka's plain brick façade fits in well with the village atmosphere of Cobble Hill. Inside the always crowded but small dining room, pistachio-colored walls, dark-blue linens and bamboo accents highlight the contemporary décor. The menu offers an extensive selection of maki and chef's special rolls (there's even a "Viagra roll," with eel, avocado and sea urchin, the latter prized by many as an aphrodisiac!) as well as raw seafood (sushi and sashimi are available as entrée plates or à la carte). Cooked entrées include tempura, teriyaki, broiled black cod, and grilled duck breast. If you're looking for a good deal, try the special combination boxes, available for both lunch and dinner.

Queen

020

84 Court St. (at Livingston St.)

Subway:	Borough Hall	Monday - Sunday 11:30am - 11pm
Phone:	718-596-5955	
Fax:	718-254-9247	
e-mail:	N/A	
Web:	www.queenrestaurant.com	
Prices:	**$$**	

What began in 1958 as a Brooklyn Heights pizza parlor has blossomed into a white-tablecloth restaurant offering fine regional Italian fare. The plain dining area, with its neat rows of tables marching down the room, may lack pizzazz, but the kitchen more than makes up for it with authentic dishes like homemade lasagna, chicken alla Cacciatora and veal saltimbocca Romana. Before you order, be sure to consider the long list of daily specials, which often overflow to a second page. Desserts range from simple biscotti and gelati to white-chocolate-Amaretto semifreddo and sweet ricotta cheesecake. If you're watching your pennies, go before 6pm for the bargain-priced prix-fixe menu.

Brooklyn

Quercy

021

242 Court St. (at Baltic St.)

Subway:	Bergen St	Tuesday - Friday 11am - 10:30pm
Phone:	718-243-2151	Saturday - Sunday 10:30am - 11pm
Fax:	N/A	Closed Monday
e-mail:	N/A	
Web:	N/A	
Prices:	$$	

The bistro décor in this attractive Cobble Hill eatery hearkens back to the 1950s with its Formica bar, warm, claret-colored walls, and posters of mid-20th-century French actors hanging here and there. The food is classic bistro, too—think boeuf bourguignon, coq au vin, and, for dessert, tarte Tatin made with tart apples or luscious golden carmelized pears. Chef/owner Jean-François Fraysse named his establishment after his hometown in southwest France; the menu pays homage to his native region with dishes such as cassoulet and foie gras. In French fashion, the day's specials are written on a blackboard.

Savoia

Italian

022

277 Smith St. (bet. DeGraw & Sackett Sts.)

Subway:	Carroll St	Monday - Sunday 11:30am - 11pm
Phone:	718-797-2727	
Fax:	718-797-3114	
e-mail:	N/A	
Web:	N/A	
Prices:	$$	

Multicolored hand-painted plates and cruets add color to the uncovered tables at this popular Carroll Gardens restaurant. Two compact rooms create an intimate feel to a space decorated with tile floors and black-and-white photographs of Italy. The big, family-size farmhouse table makes the perfect spot for large groups. Pizzas are a hot item here; they come fresh out of the wood-burning oven in the little, open kitchen, which is visible to diners. But there are plenty of other choices, too—most of them with a Southern Italian focus—from lasagna to Sicilian-style beef cutlet. Personable and relaxed service adds to Savoia's casual atmosphere.

Brooklyn

Sea

Thai

023

114 N. 6th St. (at Berry St.)

Subway:	Bedford Av
Phone:	718-384-8850
Fax:	N/A
e-mail:	N/A
Web:	www.searestaurant.com
Prices:	∞

Sunday - Thursday 11:30am - 1am
Friday - Saturday 11:30am - 2am

You could call Williamsburg's cool new Thai restaurant bubbly, since the bubble is Sea's logo. This shape appears on the menu and on the cutouts of the wooden partitions dividing the dining spaces, and it reflects from the disco ball that hangs from the ceiling. Check out the lifesize Buddha that overlooks a rectangular pool in the middle of the dining room, but be forewarned that all this Zen-like ambience dissolves at night into pulsing DJ music. Whatever time you go, the menu cites a wide selection of spicy Thai fare, from crispy basil spring rolls to noodle dishes and an array of curries and stir-frys. There's another location in the East Village (*75 Second Ave., between 4th & 5th Sts*).

Stone Park Cafe

Contemporary

024

324 Fifth Ave. (at 3rd St.)

Subway:	Union St
Phone:	718-369-0082
Fax:	718-369-6548
e-mail:	info@stoneparkcafe.com
Web:	www.stoneparkcafe.com
Prices:	$$

Tuesday - Thursday 5:30pm - 10pm
Friday 5:30pm - 11pm
Saturday 11am - 3pm & 5:30pm - 11pm
Sunday 11am - 3pm & 5:30pm - 9pm
Closed Monday

A run-down Park Slope bodega was given a facelift in the fall of 2004 and opened as this delightful, warm-hearted place that marks another example of Fifth Avenue's culinary coming of age. Named for the Old Stone House historical museum set in a little park across the street, Stone Park Cafe is casually decked out in earth tones and lime green, with brown paper covering the linen tablecloths. The service reflects the pride that the waitstaff clearly feels about the place, while the menu offers a selection of dishes well-balanced between simple food and more ambitious preparations. Best of all, the kitchen uses market-fresh ingredients and knows when to leave well enough alone.

Tuscany Grill

025

Italian

8620 Third Ave. (bet. 86th & 87th Sts.)

Subway:	86 St	Monday - Thursday 5pm - 10pm
Phone:	718-921-5633	Friday - Saturday 5pm - 10:45pm
Fax:	N/A	Sunday 4:30pm - 9:30pm
e-mail:	N/A	
Web:	N/A	
Prices:	$$	

Many restaurants lay claim to being romantic, but there's something about the combination of candlelight and a plate of pasta (remember that scene in Disney's *Lady and The Tramp*?) that just seems to naturally foster *amore*. For more than a decade, Tuscany Grill has been providing such an ambience for its customers, who come not only from the surrounding Bay Ridge area but from Manhattan as well. The room has a rustic appeal with its dried flowers, pine sideboards and yellow-hued walls, while the menu, as the restaurant's name suggests, celebrates the robust fare of Tuscany. Expect a wait—especially on weekends—if you don't have a reservation.

Brooklyn

Astoria Blvd.	BX		
Atlantic Ave.	BCYZ		
Braddock Ave.	DY		
Broadway	AXBY		
Brooklyn-Queens Expwy.	AYBX		
Clearview Expwy.	CXDY		
College Point Blvd.	**1** BX		
Conduit Ave.	BZ		
Cross Bay Blvd.	BZ		
Cross Island Pkwy.	CXDY		
Cypress Ave.	ABY		
Ditmars Blvd.	ABX		
Farmers Blvd.	CDZ		
Flushing Ave.	AY		
Francis Lewis Blvd.	CXDY		
Grand Ave.	AY		
Grand Central Pkwy.	BXY		
Greenpoint Ave.	AY		
Hempstead Ave.	DY		
Hillside Ave.	CDY		
Hollis Court Blvd.	CX		
Home Lawn St.	**2** CY	Shore Pkwy.	BZ
Jackie Robinson Pkwy.	CYBZ	Southern Pkwy.	CDZ
Jackson Ave.	AY	Springfield Blvd.	DXZ
Jamaica Ave.	BZDY	Sunrise Hwy.	DZ
Jericho Pkwy.	DY	Sutphin Blvd.	CYZ
Junction Blvd.	BXY	Union Turnpike	CYDX
Laurelton Pkwy.	DZ	Utopia Pkwy.	CXY
Lefferts Blvd.	CYZ	Van Wyck Expwy.	BXCZ
Liberty Ave.	BZCY	Vernon Blvd.	AX
Linden Blvd.	CDYZ	Whitestone Expwy.	BCX
Little Neck Pkwy.	DXY	Willets Point Blvd.	CX
Long Island Expwy.	AYDX	Woodhaven Blvd.	BY
Main St.	CXY	14th Ave.	BCX
Merrick Blvd.	CYDZ	21st St.	AX
Metropolitan Ave.	ACY	31st St.	AX
Myrtle Ave.	ABY	46th Ave.	CX
Nassau Expwy.	CZ	63rd Dr.	BY
Northern Blvd.	ADX	69th St.	BY
Parsons Blvd.	CX	94th St.	BX
Queens Blvd.	AXCY	147th Ave.	CDZ
Rockaway Blvd.	BYDZ	164th St.	CXY
Roosevelt Ave.	ABX	212th St.	DY

BRIDGES

Bronx-Whitestone Bridge	**3** CX
Kosciuszko Bridge	**4** AY
Pulaski Bridge	**5** AY
Queensboro Bridge	**6** AX
Queens-Midtown Tunnel	**7** AX
Throgs Neck Bridge	**8** CX
Triborough Bridge	AX

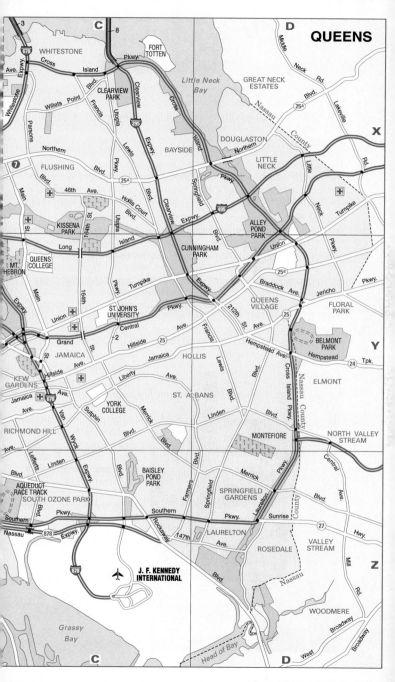

About Queens

Almost as large as Manhattan, the Bronx, and Staten Island combined, the borough of Queens covers 120 square miles on the western tip of Long Island. Thousands of immigrants come here each year, drawn by the borough's relatively affordable housing and its tight-knit ethnic communities. Restaurants in these neighborhoods reflect Queens' ethnic diversity as well. Take a stroll through Astoria to find Greek grilled octopus and baklava. Try Jackson Heights for eclectic foods ranging from Indian tandoori dishes to Bolivian arepas. Flushing reigns as Queens' most vibrant Asian neighborhood.

A Bit of History – Queens' first permanent settlement was established by the Dutch at present-day Flushing in 1645. Clashes between Dutch and English settlers marked its early years. When the English took over the colony of Nieuw Amsterdam in 1664, they named this county Queens, after Catherine of Braganza, wife of King Charles II of England. Until the mid-19th century, Queens remained a sparsely populated area of small villages and farms. As New York City grew, urbanization of Queens accelerated, attracting successive waves of German and Irish immigrants. In 1898, Queens was incorporated as a borough of New York City, and new transportation facilities made it easier for residents to commute to Manhattan. By the 1970's, nearly 30 percent of Queens' residents were foreign born; that number has nearly doubled today.

© Martha Cooper

For years, there wasn't much to attract tourists to Queens. That is slowly changing as film studios and art museums make use of abandoned factories in Long Island City Astoria. Sports thrive in **Flushing Meadows Corona Park** (between 111th St. & Van Wyck Expwy.), which encompasses **Shea Stadium**, home of the New York Mets, as well as the **National Tennis Center**, where the U.S. Open is held each summer. Of course, visitors traveling to New York by air come to Queens whether they want to or not: both LaGuardia and Kennedy airports are located here.

Water's Edge

001

44th Dr. (at the East River)

Subway:	23 St - Ely Av
Phone:	718-482-0033
Fax:	718-937-8817
e-mail:	watersedge11@netzero.com
Web:	www.watersedgenyc.com
Prices:	$$$

Monday - Saturday noon - 3pm
& 6pm - 11pm
Closed Sunday

Waterside dining with magnificent Manhattan views draws patrons to the Water's Edge. The entire back wall of the restaurant is made of windows, affording superb views of the East River and the skyscrapers of Midtown. Elegant table settings and Louis XV-style chairs mark the dining room, decked out with original artwork and Oriental rugs. Menus change seasonally here; spring, for instance, might bring veal loin with young spinach and baby fennel, or grilled halibut with mango relish. If you're coming from Manhattan, why not skip the cab ride and go in style? Make dinner reservations at Water's Edge, and you can take the complimentary boat shuttle to the restaurant from the 34th Street pier.

Piccola Venezia

002

42-01 28th Ave. (at 42nd St.)

Subway:	Steinway St
Phone:	718-721-8470
Fax:	718-721-2110
e-mail:	info@piccola-venezia.com
Web:	www.piccola-venezia.com
Prices:	$$

Monday - Friday noon - 11pm
Saturday 4pm - midnight
Sunday 2pm - 10pm

Even if Astoria is not threaded by canals, Piccolo Venezia will make you think of Venice—or at least of its cuisine. Since 1973 this restaurant has been pleasing diners with its ample menu, which emphasizes northern Italian fare. There's also a long list of daily specials to make your decision more challenging. And if you still can't find anything to suit your fancy, the kitchen honors special requests. Piccolo Venezia welcomes children, and will happily tailor meals to picky eaters (i.e., half-portions or pasta without sauce). The amiable manager greets guests as if they were eating in his home. You may arrive a stranger, but you'll leave feeling like part of a big Italian family.

Queens

Trattoria l'Incontro

003

21-76 31st St. (at Ditmars Blvd.)

Subway:	Astoria - Ditmars Blvd
Phone:	718-721-3532
Fax:	718-626-3375
e-mail:	N/A
Web:	www.trattorialincontro.com
Prices:	$$

Tuesday - Wednesday noon - 10pm
Thursday - Saturday noon - 11pm
Sunday 1pm - 10pm
Closed Monday

XX
&

From the warm welcome you'll receive at Trattoria l'Incontro, you'll know immediately how important the customers are to Abruzzi native Tina Sacramone and her son, Rocco, who rule the kitchen. Indeed, at this Astoria Italian restaurant the hospitality is as important as the food. The chef can be seen frequently in the dining area, greeting regulars and making sure everyone is happy with dishes such as Tina's homemade pastas. In the main dining room, beams punctuate the ceiling, and paintings of the Italian countryside fill the walls. The brick pizza oven, which is visible to diners, turns out a host of savory pies—including one stuffed with chocolate.

Bann Thai

004

69-12 Austin St. (bet. 69th Rd. & Yellowstone Blvd.)

Subway:	Forest Hills - 71 Av
Phone:	718-544-9999
Fax:	718-544-5928
e-mail:	info@bannthairestaurant.com
Web:	www.bannthairestaurant.com
Prices:	⊜⊜

Sunday - Friday 11:30am - 10pm
Saturday 11:30am - 11pm

X
&

Located on a Forest Hills street surrounded by shops, this charming Thai place entices diners with what it bills as «authentic Thai Cuisine.» There is no hype to their claim; Thai food connoisseurs will appreciate satay, spring rolls, Tom Yum Goong (Thai-style hot and sour soup made with shrimp, lemongrass, mushrooms, lime juice and hot chile) noodle dishes and fried rice. Vegetarian curries and seafood dishes, please non-meat eaters. Dining room décor also rings true to Thailand with brightly painted walls, silk tapestries, and Thai masks and other artifacts. And if you need more reasons to try Bann Thai, service is friendly and the prices are reasonable, especially at lunch.

Queens

Brick Cafe

Mediterranean

005

30-95 33rd St. (at 31st Ave.)

Subway:	Broadway	Monday - Friday 5pm - 11pm
Phone:	718-267-2735	Saturday - Sunday 11am - midnight
Fax:	516-467-4113	
e-mail:	adnan66@aol.com	
Web:	www.brickcafe.com	
Prices:	$$	

Resembling a European country inn, with its lace curtains, chunky wood tables, tin ceiling, and knick-knacks set around the room, the Brick Cafe wraps diners in a rustic, romantic atmosphere. This storefront eatery, set on a residential street in Astoria, is a good place to take a date. In the candlelit room, you can share plates that take their cues from the southern regions of France and Italy. Salads range from Caprese to Niçoise, while entrées include everything from penne alla vodka to striped bass oreganata. For dessert, tiramisu and crêpes Suzette represent the cafe's Franco-Italian tendencies. Locals favor the weekend brunch.

Jackson Diner

Indian

006

37-47 74th St. (bet. Roosevelt & 37th Aves.)

Subway:	Jackson Hts - Roosevelt Av	Sunday - Thursday 11:30am - 10pm
Phone:	718-672-1232	Friday - Saturday 11:30am - 10:30pm
Fax:	718-396-4164	
e-mail:	N/A	
Web:	www.jacksondiner.com	
Prices:		

You could call the décor in this Jackson Heights diner whimsical, or you could say it was gaudy, depending on your point of view. Either way, it's colorful and modern, from the 3-D leaves on the ceiling to the multi-hued chairs that are more functional than comfortable (you can excuse all this because diners are *supposed* to be basic). If you like curry, masala dosa and tandoori dishes, Jackson Diner won't disappoint. The inexpensive lunch buffet offers a wide variety of southern Indian dishes, including dessert, for one low price. After lunch, spend some time exploring the immediate neighborhood, which teems with jewelry stores, sari shops and groceries, all peddling Indian wares.

Queens

KumGangSan

007

138-28 Northern Blvd. (bet. Union & Bowne Sts.)

Subway:	Flushing Main St	Monday - Sunday 24 hours
Phone:	718-461-0909	
Fax:	718-321-2575	
e-mail:	N/A	
Web:	www.kumgangsan-nyc.com	
Prices:	⬤⬤	

Having hunger pangs in the middle of the night? If you happen to be near Flushing, Queens, make a beeline for KumGangSan; it's open 24/7. Named for a range of mountains (translated as the Diamond Mountains in English) in North Korea, the restaurant offers simple comforts, but that's of little matter to the lines of faithful customers who come here to dine on the large selection of authentic dishes (noodles, bowls of steaming broth, barbecued meats, casseroles) all made with seasonings imported from Korea. In summer, snag a table on the small terrace, with its burbling fountain. There's a second location in Midtown West *(49 W. 32nd St.)*, which is open all night, too.

Malagueta

008

25-35 36th Ave. (at 28th St.)

Subway:	36 Av	Tuesday - Sunday noon - 10pm
Phone:	718-937-4821	Closed Monday
Fax:	718-937-4821	
e-mail:	N/A	
Web:	www.malagueta.com	
Prices:	⬤⬤	

The neighborhood may be nondescript and the comfort may be basic here, but those aren't the reasons for coming to this tiny Brazilian restaurant. Authentic Brazilian food and reasonable prices are the reasons, and it would be a shame to visit Queens and miss this place. At Malagueta, chef/owner Herbert Gomes, who grew up in a little town in northern Brazil, dishes up the likes of acaraje (black-pea fritters), salpicao (traditional Brazilian salad), and moqueca de camarão (shrimp stew with palm oil, onions, peppers and coconut milk); feijoada, the national dish of Brazil, is offered only on Saturday. Just be sure to save room for the creamy-sweet passion fruit mousse.

Queens

Sapori d'Ischia

009

55-15 37th Ave. (at 56th St.)

Subway:	Northern Blvd
Phone:	718-446-1500
Fax:	718-446-0134
e-mail:	N/A
Web:	N/A
Prices:	$$

Tuesday - Saturday 11:30am - 3pm
& 5:30pm - 10pm
Sunday 5:30pm - 10pm
Closed Monday

Remember the movie *Big Night*? Like the Baltimore Italian restaurant that starred in that film, Sapori d'Ischia doesn't serve sides of spaghetti. In fact, their "house rules," posted at the bar, spell out a number of other things the restaurant doesn't do (for instance, they don't serve butter, grate cheese atop seafood, or put lemon peel in espresso). Set on an industrial block in Queens' Woodside neighborhood, Sapori d'Ischia started out as a wholesale Italian foods business. Over the years, owner Frank Galano (who runs the place with his son Antonio) added a market and then a small trattoria to the premises. Today, delectable pastas and low prices keep customers coming back for more.

718 - Seven One Eight

010

35-01 Ditmars Blvd. (at 35th St.)

Subway:	Astoria - Ditmars Blvd
Phone:	718-204-5553
Fax:	718-204-2507
e-mail:	info@718restaurant.com
Web:	www.718restaurant.com
Prices:	$$

Monday - Sunday noon - midnight

What's in a name? In this case, 718 refers to the Queens' area code, not the restaurant's street address. No matter. This cozy French bistro provides a welcome addition to the Greek and Italian places that pervade the Astoria dining scene. With its solid French base, the cuisine displays Spanish and American influences, all realized with fresh, seasonal products: shrimp meets mango in a salad, rack of lamb pairs with piquillo peppers, and thin-crust tartes flambées pay homage to that traditional Alsatian dish. Come Friday night to watch the belly dancer (shows at 9:30pm and 10:30pm) and listen to music from the Casbah. If you're out partying late, 718 offers a tapas menu every day until 2am.

Queens

Sripraphai

011

64-13 39th Ave. (bet. 64th & 65th Sts.)

Subway:	Woodside - 61 St
Phone:	718-899-9599
Fax:	718-457-4923
e-mail:	N/A
Web:	N/A
Prices:	

Thursday - Tuesday 11:30am - 10pm
Closed Wednesday & January 3 - 15

With so many restaurants in Manhattan, you'd likely never think to travel to Queens for Thai food. Think again, because little Sripraphai is well worth the 20-minute subway ride. Owner Sripraphai Tipmanee serves the real thing at her establishment, and she doesn't cop out by catering to American tastes. If you're not familiar with Thai cuisine, photographs on the menu will make your selection easier. The remarkable chicken soup makes a good starter; its subtle flavors are enhanced by coconut milk, lemongrass and tender mushrooms. The restaurant doesn't accept credit cards or reservations, and they don't have a liquor license, but feel free to bring your own beer or wine.

Taverna Kyclades

012

33-07 Ditmars Blvd. (bet. 33rd & 35th Sts.)

Subway:	Astoria - Ditmars Blvd
Phone:	718-545-8666
Fax:	718-726-4766
e-mail:	tavernakyclades@aol.com
Web:	www.tavernakyclades.com
Prices:	

Monday - Thursday noon - 11pm
Friday - Saturday noon - 11:30pm
Sunday noon - 10pm

Known for its large Greek population, Astoria doesn't lack for tavernas. This one, located on one of the commercial hubs of Greek Astoria, stands out for its seafood. A taxidermed trophy swordfish decorates the exposed-brick wall of the tiny dining room, where the waitstaff is clad appropriately in blue and white (the colors of the Greek flag). Lunch is simple here, with a short menu of fish entrées supplemented by burgers; pasta; and Greek spinach pie, layered with feta cheese and crispy phyllo. Desserts are only offered in the evening. Dinner presents a much wider choice of main dishes, with the emphasis on food from the sea, from calamari to shrimp stuffed with crabmeat.

Tournesol

French

50-12 Vernon Blvd. (bet. 50th & 51st Aves.)

Subway:	Vernon Blvd - Jackson Av	Tuesday - Sunday 11:30am - 11:30pm
Phone:	718-472-4355	Closed Monday
Fax:	N/A	
e-mail:	tournesol@verizon.net	
Web:	www.tournesolnyc.com	
Prices:	**$$**	

A sunflower grows in Long Island City, in the form of this petit *morceau* of a bistro, whose name means "sunflower" in French. With only 40 seats, Tournesol is a family affair, run by brother-and-sister-team Pascal and Patricia Escriout. In the simple, cheery dining room, you can feast on dishes from the South of France; the good news is that you only have to travel a single stop on the subway from Grand Central Station to get here. The changing menu lists the likes of sautéed snails with tarragon sauce, terrine of duck liver, braised beef cheeks and dark-chocolate marquise. If you're around on the weekend, try Tournesol's French-style brunch.

Queens

Restaurants **409**

About
Staten Island

New York City's "forgotten borough," Staten Island is primarily a bedroom community, culturally and economically related more to New Jersey than New York. The island, 14 miles long and 8 miles wide, boasts more wide-open green space than anywhere else is in the city.

Of course, to reach any of the restaurants here, you'll have to take the ferry. The borough's biggest attraction, the celebrated Staten Island Ferry carries over 3.5 million tourists and commuters a year between Manhattan's South Ferry and St. George terminals, passing the Statue of Liberty each way. Stunning views of the Manhattan skyline and New York Harbor, especially at night, are priceless. So is the fare—the ride is free!

A Bit of History – Staten Island got its name in the early 1600s from Dutch merchants, who dubbed it Staaten Eyelandt (Dutch for "State's Island"). The first permanent settlement was established at Oude Dorp by Dutch and French Huguenot families in 1661. Over the next two centuries, the island thrived on farming and agriculture, ferrying goods to nearby Manhattan and New Jersey.

Staten Island's economy grew considerably in 1898, after its citizens voted to incorporate as one of the five boroughs of Greater New York City. This move attracted hardworking immigrants, many of Italian and Irish descent, to its farms and factories and hard-playing society folks to its resort hotels. The boom went bust after World War I, when many residents left to make their fortunes on the mainland. The borough blossomed once again when the Verrazano-Narrows Bridge opened in 1964, linking the island with Brooklyn and bringing an influx of Manhattanites seeking refuge from the buzzing energy of New York.

© Martha Cooper

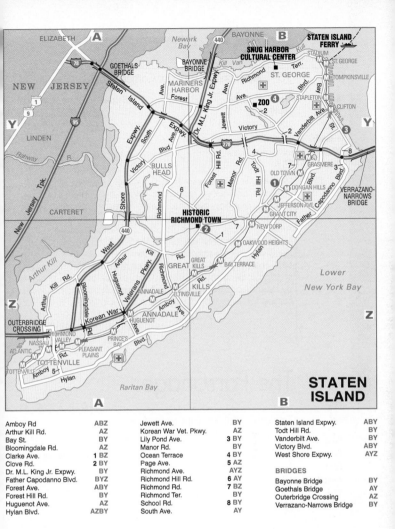

Amboy Rd	ABZ	Jewett Ave.	BY	Staten Island Expwy.	ABY
Arthur Kill Rd.	AZ	Korean War Vet. Pkwy.	AZ	Todt Hill Rd.	BY
Bay St.	BY	Lily Pond Ave.	3 BY	Vanderbilt Ave.	BY
Bloomingdale Rd.	AZ	Manor Rd.	BY	Victory Blvd.	ABY
Clarke Ave.	1 BZ	Ocean Terrace	4 BY	West Shore Expwy.	AYZ
Clove Rd.	2 BY	Page Ave.	5 AZ		
Dr. M.L. King Jr. Expwy.	BY	Richmond Ave.	AYZ	**BRIDGES**	
Father Capodanno Blvd.	BYZ	Richmond Hill Rd.	6 AY		
Forest Ave.	ABY	Richmond Rd.	7 BZ	Bayonne Bridge	BY
Forest Hill Rd.	BY	Richmond Ter.	BY	Goethals Bridge	AY
Huguenot Ave.	AZ	School Rd.	8 BY	Outerbridge Crossing	AZ
Hylan Blvd.	AZBY	South Ave.	AY	Verrazano-Narrows Bridge	BY

Staten Island Today – Though isolated, Staten Island is not without its attractions. Its sandy, relatively uncrowded **beaches**, especially South Beach, make for a lovely outing. **Historic Richmond Town**, a 25-acre village *(441 Clarke St.)*, marks the site of one of the earliest settlements on the island. History comes alive here, thanks to costumed guides who demonstrate crafts (printmaking, tinsmithing, weaving) and relate tales about 19th-century life in the former county seat. An unexpected treasure, the **Jacques Marchais Museum of Tibetan Art** houses rare objects from Tibet, Nepal, China, Mongolia and India in an enchanted setting atop Lighthouse Hill.

Carol's Cafe

American

1571 Richmond Rd. (at Four Corners Rd. & Seaview Ave.)

Bus:	X15, 74, 76, 84, 86
Phone:	718-979-5600
Fax:	718-987-4509
e-mail:	carolscuisine@aol.com
Web:	www.carolscafe.com
Prices:	$$

Wednesday - Saturday 6pm - 11pm
Closed Sunday - Tuesday

XX

Well-known on Staten Island for the cooking school she operates above her restaurant, owner and namesake Carol Frazetta presides over the kitchen here. Frazetta graduated from Le Cordon Bleu and studied at the Culinary Institute of America before opening Carol's Cuisine (the cooking school) in 1972. It was only natural that she would follow that act with her own cafe. Decorated with a feminine touch, evident in the pink linen napkins, fresh flowers on the tables and hanging plants that decorate the interior, Carol's Café only serves dinner by reservation. The seasonal menu travels through the U.S. and Europe for inspiration, fixing on the chef's favorite dishes.

The Parsonage

American

74 Arthur Kill Rd. (at Clarke Ave.)

Bus:	15, 54, 74, 84
Phone:	718-351-7879
Fax:	N/A
e-mail:	N/A
Web:	N/A
Prices:	$$

Sunday - Thursday 11:30am - 10pm
Friday - Saturday 11:30am - 11pm

XX

For good food in a place with fascinating history, head for The Parsonage. It's located in the heart of Historic Richmond Town, one of Staten Island's earliest settlements (established in the early 1700s), now a 25-acre living-history museum. Built in 1855 to house the minister of the Dutch Reformed Church, the Gothic Revival-style parsonage boasts rooms restored with vintage wallpapers and Belle Époque chandeliers—a perfect setting for a romantic meal. Choose from a prix-fixe seasonal menu at lunch, or an à la carte selection with Italian influences at dinner. If you're visiting in summertime, note that since it's set within an extended museum, this restaurant is popular with tourists.

Staten Island

Aesop's Tables

Contemporary

1233 Bay St. (bet. Maryland & Scarboro Aves.)

Bus:	51 & 81
Phone:	718-720-2005
Fax:	N/A
e-mail:	info@aesopstables.net
Web:	www.aesopstables.net
Prices:	$$

Tuesday - Saturday 5:30pm - 10:30pm
Closed Sunday & Monday

Aesop's Tables occupies a renovated storefront on the island's east shore. Since it opened in 1991, the restaurant has attracted a mixed crowd from the island as well as the other boroughs who have become fans of this charming place. The menu changes regularly, following fresh and seasonal ingredients, but American fare here can include anything from meatloaf to salmon roasted on a cedar plank. In the cozy dining room, where blue-and-white bistro chairs nuzzle up to little square tables, the specials are posted on a blackboard framed by silk flowers. Out back, the leafy garden, lit by candles at night, makes a great setting to eat on a balmy summer night.

American Grill

American

420 Forest Ave. (bet. Metropolitan & Sharon Aves.)

Bus:	48 & 98
Phone:	718-442-4742
Fax:	N/A
e-mail:	N/A
Web:	www.americangrill.org
Prices:	$$

Sunday - Monday 11:30am - 9pm
Tuesday - Thursday 11:30am - 10pm
Friday - Saturday 11:30am - 11pm
Closed major holidays

Red neon letters announce this West Brighton restaurant on busy Forest Avenue. Inside, the long, narrow dining room sports a rustic ambience, pleasantly embellished with wood wainscoting, a painting of the American flag and color caricatures of its famous patrons. The food is all-American, too, prepared with good products. Chicken breast is grilled with mushrooms, peppers, potatoes and whole roasted garlic; double-cut pork chops are napped with port-wine sauce; and a different whole roasted fish is featured daily. Weekly specials (veal stew, prime rib, Maine lobster) give diners yet another option. The young staff provides warm service.

Staten Island

Where to **stay**

Alphabetical list *of* **Hotels**

The Maritime

363 W. 16th St.

Subway:	14 St
Phone:	212-242-4300
Fax:	212-242-1188
e-mail:	N/A
Web:	www.themaritimehotel.com
Prices:	rooms: $295 suites: $650 - $1,400 Restaurant: **$$**

121 rooms
4 suites

The Maritime Hotel

Ocean liner or hotel? The Maritime, designed for the National Maritime Union in 1966, was meticulously renovated in 2003 to blend the atmospheres of both. Striking five-foot porthole windows, warm teak walls and built-ins, and details in deep blues and greens enhance the air of nautical nostalgia. The lobby, in elegant yet simple retro style, exudes a relaxed and cool ambience. Most of the cabinlike rooms, each with marble bath, face the Hudson River and all offer CD/DVD players, flat-screen TVs and wireless Internet access.

The hotel houses La Bottega, an Italian trattoria (where you can have breakfast), and chic Matsuri *(see restaurant listings)* for Japanese food. Relax with a drink at the Cabanas Rooftop Garden or visit trendy Hiro to test the hip Chelsea scene. The hotel is well situated for gallery hopping, as well as sampling Chelsea nightlife and upscale shopping.

Manhattan Chelsea

The Inn on 23rd

131 West 23rd St. (bet. Sixth & Seventh Aves.)

Subway:	23 St
Phone:	212-463-0330
Fax:	212-463-0303
e-mail:	innon23rd@aol.com
Web:	www.innon23rd.com
Prices:	rooms: $189 - $359

14 rooms

The Inn on 23rd Street/Mark Viker

Manhattan Chelsea

A warm and intimate atmosphere pervades this family-run bed-and-breakfast-style inn. Housed in a renovated 19th-century town house, it offers guest rooms on five floors, each tastefully decorated in a different style with antiques, heirlooms and art. All are spacious and comfortable with private, modern bathrooms; those on the top floor receive a nice dose of natural light. Care has been taken to minimize street noise with double-glazed windows and white-noise players. Business travelers will appreciate the two-line phones and complimentary high-speed Internet access.

A generous breakfast, served in the cozy second-floor library, includes goodies freshly baked by aspiring chefs from the New School Culinary Arts Program, which holds classes here. This is a rare find in Manhattan, reasonably priced for its comfort and setting, and apropos for both business and leisure travelers.

Ritz-Carlton Battery Park

001

2 West St. (at Battery Pl.)

Subway:	Rector St
Phone:	212-344-0800
Fax:	212-344-3804
e-mail:	N/A
Web:	www.ritzcarlton.com
Prices:	rooms: $395 - $645 suites: $850 - $1,300 Restaurant: **$$$**

255 rooms
43 suites

&

The Ritz-Carlton Hotel

Rising 39 stories above Battery Park in its glass and brick tower, the Ritz commands a stunning view of the Statue of Liberty and New York Harbor. Rooms with harbor views are equipped with high-power telescopes so you can better take in the dramatic waterscape. If your room doesn't have a harbor view, don't despair; you can enjoy the same striking panorama—and a cocktail—from the 14th-floor (the hotel's top floor) Rise Bar.

Guests here nestle in contemporary luxury amid soothing pale colors, lush fabrics, Frette linens and marble bathrooms; say the word and a butler will draw you a relaxing bath. After a workout at the hotel's 2,500-square-foot health club, you can justify a caloric splurge at 2 West restaurant, which prides itself on its prime Angus beef. While you're here, save time to walk through the hotel's Art Deco public areas to see the impressive collection of modern art.

Wall Street Inn

9 S. William St. (bet. William & Broad Sts.)

Subway: Wall St
Phone: 212-747-1500
Fax: 212-747-1900
e-mail: manager@thewallstreetinn.com
Web: www.thewallstreetinn.com
Prices: rooms: $159 - $449

46 rooms

The Wall Street Inn

Tucked into one of the narrow streets laid out by the Dutch in the 17th century, this hotel fills two landmark buildings (1895 and 1920), previously occupied by Lehman Brothers investment-banking firm. First-time guests soon become regulars here, drawn back time after time by the warm welcoming staff, well-appointed rooms, and the moderate prices for the location.

Cheery rooms are tastefully done in period reproductions, and accented with fresh flowers and plants. Larger rooms on the 7th floor boast Jacuzzi tubs. The location, right down the block from the New York Stock Exchange, is convenient for business travelers as well as families. Amenities such as in-room refrigerators, a small business center, a fitness facility equipped with a sauna and steam room, and a complimentary continental breakfast make the Wall Street Inn a good value for the price.

Manhattan Financial District

Best Western Seaport Inn

33 Peck Slip (at Front St.)

Subway:	Fulton St - Broadway - Nassau
Phone:	212-766-6600
Fax:	212-766-6615
e-mail:	info@seaportinn.com
Web:	www.seaportinn.com
Prices:	rooms: $169 - $259

72 rooms

Best Western Seaport Inn

Manhattan *Financial District*

Hard by the Brooklyn Bridge in Lower Manhattan, the Seaport Inn caters to both tourists and business travelers. The former enjoy its location in the popular South Street Seaport area, now known for its museums, shops and galleries. The latter find the hotel well situated for their business dealings in the Financial District. Both appreciate the inn's reasonable prices.

Inside this brick building you'll find clean, well-kept rooms sporting country-style furnishings, floral prints, and in-room safes. The business center offers free, high-speed Internet access. Continental breakfast and afternoon cookies come compliments of the house. Ask for a room on the 6th or 7th floor, where you'll have a private terrace overlooking the East River and the Financial District skyscrapers. And why not bring the family along? At the Seaport Inn, children 17 and under stay free in their parents' room.

W Union Square

201 Park Ave. South (at 17th St.)

Subway: 14 St - Union Sq
Phone: 212-253-9119
Fax: 212-253-9229
e-mail: N/A
Web: www.whotels.com
Prices: rooms: $349 - $569 suites: $599 - $699

250 rooms
20 suites

Manhattan Gramercy, Flatiron & Union Square

Starwood Hotels & Resorts

The granite and limestone Guardian Life Building (1911) has been reborn as a posh W hotel overlooking Union Square. Designed by David Rockwell, the interior sports a contemporary look, from the polished two-story lobby with its sweeping staircase to soundproofed rooms with sleek leather headboards. Comfort abounds in contemporary guest rooms, where you'll find goose-down comforters and pillows, cushy velvet armchairs, and terry-lined robes.

As for service, how can you argue with a hotel whose philosophy is "whatever you want, whenever you want it" (just press the button on your room phone)? There's even a Pet Package, where your four-legged friend will be walked, groomed and pampered with special meals. Add Olives' tasty Mediterranean cuisine (see restaurant listings) and the intimate Underbar, and it's no wonder that W Union Square attracts a brigade of Beautiful People.

Inn at Irving Place

56 Irving Pl. (bet 17th & 18th Sts.)

Subway: 14 St - Union Sq
Phone: 212-533-4600
Fax: 212-533-4611
e-mail: innatirving@aol.com
Web: www.innatirving.com
Prices: rooms: $325 - $495

12 rooms

The Inn at Irving Place/Roy Wright

Once you step inside the doors of this small, unmarked luxury hotel, you'll be immersed in a bygone day. Built in 1834, two single-family brownstones now house the Inn at Irving Place. The cozy, charming lobby welcomes guests to a world filled with 19th-century antiques and a quiet grace. Twelve individually decorated rooms are named for famous turn-of-the-20th-century New Yorkers, many of whom once lived in the neighborhood (actress Sarah Bernhardt, author Washington Irving; interior designer Elsie de Wolfe). Don't think, however, that you'll lack for 21st-century comforts; Sony CD players, VCRs, and wireless Internet connection come with each room.

In the morning, savor a continental breakfast in your room or in the parlor. Be sure to save time for afternoon tea (reservations required) in Lady Mendl's Victorian tea salon. Downstairs, Cibar lounge offers a menu of martinis and light appetizers.

Manhattan Gramercy, Flatiron & Union Square

The Gershwin

7 E. 27th St. (bet. Fifth & Madison Aves.)

Subway: 28 St
Phone: 212-545-8000
Fax: 212-684-5546
e-mail: reservations@gershwinhotel.com
Web: www.gershwinhotel.com
Prices: rooms: $99 - $239 suites: $179 - $309

128 rooms
4 suites

Gershwin Hotel

You can't miss the bold red façade and eye-catching, sculpted light fixtures that now hang from this 1905 building. Inside, the spirit of Andy Warhol lives on in the Pop Art lobby, which is embellished with one of Warhol's famous Campbell's Soup Cans, autographed by the artist himself. The Gershwin's free-wheeling soul and inexpensive prices appeal to young international travelers and struggling artists, while the hip vibe draws rockers, writers, models, artists and other creative types.

Each of the 13 floors are decorated with art by the likes of Warhol, Billy Name and Randy Bloom. Rooms are small and simple, but who cares when you're treated to stand-up comedy, theater performances and live music in the in-house cabaret as part of a stay here? To cater to fashion models, the hotel offers special "model floors," outfitted with extra closet space and message boards.

Washington Square

103 Waverly Pl. (at MacDougal St.)

Subway: Christopher St - Sheridan Sq
Phone: 212-777-9515
Fax: 212-979-8373
e-mail: reservations@wshotel.com
Web: www.washingtonsquarehotel.com
Prices: rooms: $141 - $205

160 rooms

Washington Square Hotel

At the heart of the heart of New York City for over a century, the Washington Square Hotel overlooks its namesake park, a Greenwich Village landmark since 1826 and crossroads for the city's bohemian world of jazz, literature, poetry and politics. Family ownership since 1973 accounts for the hotel's friendly and welcoming atmosphere. Its Art Deco décor, original artwork, and custom-designed furniture create a jazzy mood, especially in the Deco Room lobby bar.

New room renovations are underway, to be completed in late 2006. Jewel-tone walls establish a restful aura, while Deco details, such as faux ostrich-feather headboards, add a touch of playfulness. Rooms are equipped with complimentary high-speed Internet, with wireless access available in the bar and lobby areas. North Square restaurant *(see restaurant listings)* serves a topnotch breakfast and bistro fare at lunch and dinner.

Hotel on Rivington

107 Rivington St. (bet. Essex & Ludlow Sts.)

Subway:	Delancey St
Phone:	212-475-2600
Fax:	212-475-5959
e-mail:	info@hotelonrivington.com
Web:	www.hotelonrivington.com
Prices:	rooms: $265 - $325 suites: $450 - $600

90 rooms
20 suites

Hotel on Rivington/Flynn & Winner

The Hotel on Rivington has taken utmost advantage of its status as the first tall building in this swiftly gentrifying neighborhood. With floor-to-ceiling glass walls on at least two sides, rooms in its 21 stories offer stunning, unobstructed views of the surrounding cityscape. The remarkable result of a collaboration of cutting-edge architects, designers, decorators and artists from around the world, this hotel combines sleek minimalist décor with ultramodern amenities, and, yes, comfort.

If you notice anything but the view, you'll appreciate the Tempur-pedic mattresses, Frette linens, and wake-up calls synchronized with motorized curtains. The deluxe Italian-tile bathrooms are equipped with heated floors, steam showers and Japanese-style soaking tubs. You enter the lobby—accessible only to you and your invited guests—through the Eggtrance, designed as a deconstructed egg.

Manhattan Lower East Side

Gansevoort

18 Ninth Ave. (at W. 13th St.)

Subway:	8 Av - 14 St
Phone:	212-206-6700
Fax:	212-255-5858
e-mail:	contact@hotelgansevoort.com
Web:	www.hotelgansevoort.com
Prices:	rooms: $395 - $475 suites: $675 - $795

166 rooms
21 suites

Hotel Gansevoort/David Joseph

Slick, sleek, swank: the first new, upscale hotel in the Meatpacking District, the Gansevoort rises 14 stories above the burgeoning hip-dom of this once gritty area. Only the name, which belonged to the grandfather of Herman Melville, is historic. The lobby of this oh-so-cool property is outfitted in cherry-wood paneling and Matisse-inspired carpet. Eelskin-covered columns and mohair panels add texture, and special attention has been paid to lighting effects throughout.

Elegant rooms wear a dusky palette with touches of color, and huge windows overlook, from the high floors, the Hudson and surrounding city. Ono *(see restaurant listings)*, the hotel's Japanese restaurant, offers a robatayaki bar where cooks perform grilling feats, but the coup de grace is the hotel's rooftop, complete with gardens, a cosmopolitan lounge (Plunge) and a 45-foot-long heated pool with underwater music.

Four Seasons New York

57 E. 57th St. (bet. Park & Madison Aves.)

Subway: 59 St
Phone: 212-758-5700
Fax: 212-758-5711
e-mail: N/A
Web: www.fourseasons.com
Prices: rooms: $610 - $1,010   suites: $1,550 - $2,550   Restaurant: **$$$**

304 rooms
61 suites

Four Seasons Hotel

Noted architect I.M. Pei designed the monumentally elegant Four Seasons New York in 1993. Indeed, nothing is small about this property. The tallest hotel building in the city, the limestone-clad tower soars 52 stories in a Postmodern style that draws heavily on the 1920s. Inside the 57th Street entrance, you'll walk into a grand foyer decorated with temple-like pillars, marble floors and a 33-foot backlit onyx ceiling.

The hotel also boasts the city's largest rooms, which, at 600 square feet, are doubtless among the most luxurious as well. A recent refurbishment installed plasma-screen TVs in the opulent bathrooms, which also feature marble soaking tubs that fill in just 60 seconds. Top-drawer service includes a 24-hour concierge, perks for pets and children, and a fabulous spa. Fifty Seven Fifty Seven restaurant serves stylish American cuisine and even offers a special Japanese breakfast.

Manhattan *Midtown East*

The St. Regis

002

2 E. 55th St. (at Fifth Ave.)

Subway:	5 Av - 53 St
Phone:	212-753-4500
Fax:	212-787-3447
e-mail:	newyork@stregis.com
Web:	www.stregis.com/newyork
Prices:	rooms: $660 - $785 suites: $1,400 - $4,800 Restaurant: **$$$**

222 rooms
93 suites

The St. Regis Hotel

Stylish and elegant, and with service close to perfection, the St. Regis reigns among the city's finest hotels. Commissioned by John Jacob Astor in 1904, this Beaux-Arts confection at the corner of Fifth Avenue is located just blocks from Central Park, MOMA and other Midtown attractions. Its public spaces and lobby, from the painted ceilings to the marble staircase, are steeped in Gilded Age opulence. A redesign is underway to transform the guest rooms from their traditional Louis XVI style to a bright, more casual and cozy look.

Unparalleled service includes a butler you can call on 24 hours a day, an on-site florist, complimentary garment pressing when you arrive, and the newly opened Remede luxury spa. Be sure to stop into the King Cole Bar to peek at Maxfield Parrish's famous mural, and to sip a Bloody Mary, which was introduced here in the 1920s.

New York Palace

455 Madison Ave. (bet. 50th & 51st Sts.)

Subway: 51 St
Phone: 212-888-7000
Fax: 212-303-6000
e-mail: reservation@nypalace.com
Web: www.newyorkpalace.com
Prices: rooms: $595 - $1,750   suites: $900 - $1,850   Restaurant: **$$$**

817 rooms
88 suites

New York Palace

The opulent Palace joins the historic 1882 Villard town houses with a contemporary 55-story tower built in 1980. The hotel's public spaces occupy the lavishly restored town homes built in the Italian Renaissance style, which you can enter through the lovely carriage courtyard on Madison Avenue. Modern hotel rooms in the tower, including 88 suites, provide all the amenities.

The Palace houses a 7,000-square-foot spa and fitness club along with 22,000 square feet of excellent conference facilities. The sumptuous Villard Bar and Lounge makes the most of the building's Gilded Age pedigree, showing off its Tiffany windows on two levels, ornate fireplaces and rich wood paneling. The hotel is located an easy walk from Fifth Avenue shopping, Rockefeller Center and Midtown cultural attractions. West-facing rooms have a stunning view of St. Patrick's Cathedral just across Madison Avenue.

Manhattan Midtown East

The Waldorf-Astoria

301 Park Ave. (bet. 49th & 50th Sts.)

Subway:	51 St
Phone:	212-355-3000
Fax:	212-872-7272
e-mail:	reservations@hilton.com
Web:	www.waldorfastoria.com
Prices:	rooms: $420 - $638 suites: $706 - $1,479 Restaurant: **$$$**

1175 rooms
250 suites

The Waldorf-Astoria

Nothing says New York high society like the Waldorf-Astoria. Built in 1931, the hotel blends exquisite Art Deco ornamentation and lavish Second Empire furnishings. The original Waldorf, built in 1893, was demolished along with its companion, the Astoria, to make room for the Empire State Building. The huge "new" hotel (including its boutique counterpart with a private entrance, the Waldorf Towers) occupies the entire block between Park and Lexington avenues at 49th Street. Its lobby features a striking inlaid-tile mosaic and Deco chandelier.

A recent $400 million renovation refreshed the grand dame, and deluxe fabrics and classic furniture dress the richly appointed and beautifully maintained rooms and suites, with their marble baths. With 1,500 employees, a full-service spa, three restaurants—including Inagiku and Bull & Bear *(see restaurant listings)*—and four bars, you'll want for little here.

Manhattan Midtown East

The Alex

205 E. 45th St. (bet. Second & Third Aves.)

Subway: Grand Central - 42 St
Phone: 212-867-5100
Fax: 212-867-7878
e-mail: info@thealexhotel.com
Web: www.thealexhotel.com
Prices: rooms: $525 - $575   suites: $700 - $1,800

20 rooms
133 suites

The Alex Hotel

Opened in 2003, the Alex belongs to a new generation of sleekly understated hotels offering a Zen-inspired aesthetic, Scandinavian simplicity and space-age efficiency. A soothing, neutral palette dominates, punctuated with precious woods, bamboo, deluxe fabrics, Frette linens, and flat-screen liquid-crystal TVs in each room. Remarkable custom-designed furniture serves multiple purposes. Nightstands convert to writing tables and credenzas transform into flip-out desks, complete with T-1 Internet connections. Need a printer? Request an "office on wheels" that also includes a fax and scanner along with office supplies. In the suites, only Poggenpohl kitchens will do.

Restaurant Riingo *(see restaurant listings)* offers Japanese cuisine and a full room-service menu. The hotel is conveniently located along Third Avenue between the United Nations and Grand Central Terminal.

Manhattan Midtown East

Elysée

60 E. 54th St. (bet. Park & Madison Aves.)

Subway: 5 Av - 53 St
Phone: 212-753-1066
Fax: 212-980-9278
e-mail: contact@elyseehotel.com
Web: www.elyseehotel.com
Prices: rooms: $360 suites: $450 - $525

89 rooms
11 suites
&

Manhattan Midtown East

Elysée Hotel

Since the 1920s, the Elysée has earned a reputation as a discreetly private haven for writers, actors and musicians. Vladimir Horowitz once lived in the suite where his piano still stands; Tennessee Williams lived and died here (in the Sunset Suite); and Marlon Brando made this his New York home.

The period atmosphere lingers on in the Neoclassical-style furnishings, careful service and well-maintained rooms—some with terraces, kitchenettes or solariums. Lovely bathrooms are decorated in three tones of marble. Classic, yes, but modern conveniences like hotel-wide wireless Internet access and two-line phones are here, too. Complimentary breakfast, afternoon tea and cookies, and evening wine and cheese are served in the Club Room. The Elysée may be best known—and loved—for its Monkey Bar, where kitschy monkey murals, olive-shaped barstools and piano music set the mood.

Library

299 Madison Ave. (at 41st St.)

Subway:	42 St - Grand Central
Phone:	212-983-4500
Fax:	212-499-9099
e-mail:	reservation@libraryhotel.com
Web:	www.libraryhotel.com
Prices:	rooms: $325 - $395

60 rooms

Library Hotel

Nothing warms a room like books, and the Library Hotel proves the point. Steps from the New York Public and the Pierpont Morgan libraries, this boutique inn makes great use of its collection of 6,000 volumes. Each floor is numbered after a category in the Dewey Decimal system, and rooms contain books on a particular subject. History buff? Request the Biography room on the 9th floor. Literature your thing? Head to the 8th floor. Furnishings are simple, and, though small, rooms are comfortable and quiet.

Well equipped for business travelers, the hotel provides in-room Internet, and computer stations in its business center. Enjoy a continental breakfast daily, snacks throughout the day and a wine reception most evenings. The hotel's pleasant public spaces, including the Writer's Den with its fireplace and comfy chairs, and the terrace Poetry Garden, are perfect for—what else?—reading.

Manhattan Midtown East

Roger Smith

501 Lexington Ave. (at 47th St.)

Subway: 51 St
Phone: 212-755-1400
Fax: 212-758-4061
e-mail: reservations@rogersmith.com
Web: www.rogersmithhotel.com
Prices: rooms: $245 - $265   suites: $295 - $345

96 rooms
39 suites

Roger Smith Hotel

Full of playful character—and art—the Roger Smith offers a casual, warm ambience cultivated by an attentive and welcoming young staff. Spacious rooms in the bed-and-breakfast vein are decorated in crisp European and American country style, and the antique bathrooms (the building dates to 1929) remain in good condition. In the public spaces, you'll find rotating exhibits of original artwork, and the hotel even owns and operates its own gallery at the corner of 47th Street that features contemporary artists.

By special agreement, Roger Smith guests may use the New York Sports Club next door, and the hotel provides an iMac in the lobby for accessing your e-mail. Pets and children are welcome; kids 16 and under stay for free in their parents' room. The Roger Smith offers a good rate for its comfort, convenience and atmosphere.

Essex House

160 Central Park South (bet. Sixth & Seventh Aves.)

Subway: Midtown - 57 St - 7 Av
Phone: 212-247-0300
Fax: 212-315-1839
e-mail: essexhouse.sales@westin.com
Web: www.westin.com/essexhouse
Prices: rooms: $300 - $500 suites: $600 - $4,000 Restaurant: **$$$**

505 rooms
100 suites

Essex House

This well-known landmark was opened in 1931 in its commanding site at the very foot of Central Park. Its impressive marble and dark-wood lobby features a large lounge area, shops, and an atmosphere of discreet luxury. The rooms have a certain timeless quality, simply decorated in an Art Deco-inspired style (if you require it, request a room with Internet access, for an extra fee).

Have a cocktail at Journeys, the hotel's clubby bar, which offers a glimpse of old New York. Café Botanica brings the park indoors with lush plants and decorative wrought iron; stop in here for the popular express lunch. For a real treat, splurge on dinner at Alain Ducasse *(see restaurant listings)*. The Essex House has an on-site spa, steam room and fitness facility. You'll love the location on Central Park, especially if you're a runner; for shoppers, Fifth Avenue boutiques are nearby, too.

Manhattan *Midtown West*

The Peninsula

002

700 Fifth Ave. (at W. 55th St.)

Subway: 5 Av - 53 St
Phone: 212-956-2888
Fax: 212-903-3949
e-mail: pny@peninsula.com
Web: www.peninsula.com
Prices: rooms: $595 - $760   suites: $960 - $5,760

185 rooms
54 suites

The Peninsula, New York

Still sparkling from its $45 million restoration in 1998, this magnificent 1905 hotel serves beautifully as Peninsula's flagship U.S. property. When built as The Gotham, it was the city's tallest skyscraper, towering 23 stories. Plush rooms exude a timeless elegance, Art Nouveau accents complementing their rich colors and appointments. Ample in size and well conceived for business travelers, each guest room provides a silent fax machine, wireless Internet access, and a bottled-water bar. Service is a particularly strong suit at the Peninsula, and the smartly liveried staff effortlessly execute your every request.

You could spend hours in the 35,000-square-foot, three-story spa, complete with a luxurious indoor pool, but don't be late for afternoon tea or cocktails at the intimate Gotham Lounge. Ascend to the Pen-Top Bar and Terrace before dinner at Fives *(see restaurant listings)*.

Ritz-Carlton New York

50 Central Park South (at Sixth Ave.)

Subway:	5 Av - 59 St
Phone:	212-308-9100
Fax:	212-207-8831
e-mail:	N/A
Web:	www.ritzcarlton.com
Prices:	rooms: $750 suites: $1,495 Restaurant: **$$$**

217 rooms
44 suites

The Ritz-Carlton Hotel

Renovated as the city's newest Ritz-Carlton in 2002, this classic Central Park hotel was built in 1929 as the St. Moritz. The reception lobby remains intimate to invoke a small luxury property, but the lobby lounge opens into a grand two-story space. The facelift cut the number of guest rooms in half to create sumptuous accommodations of generous size. Steeped in Old World elegance, they offer the best in electronic amenities rivaled only by old-fashioned touches such as a bath butler, a telescope to explore Central Park, and, in the top-end suites, a choice of fine bed linens.

On the Club Level, guests may visit the hotel's exclusive Club Lounge, offering complimentary food and beverages daily. La Prairie provides the ultimate in spa treatments and pampering. At Atelier, the Ritz's formal dining room, the mood tends more toward the modern, and the cooking is contemporary French.

Manhattan Midtown West

Algonquin

59 W. 44th St. (bet. Fifth & Sixth Aves.)

Subway:	42 St - Bryant Pk
Phone:	212-840-6800
Fax:	212-944-1419
e-mail:	4reservations@algonquinhotel.com
Web:	www.algonquinhotel.com
Prices:	rooms: $249 - $509 suites: $399 - $699 Restaurant: **$$$**

150 rooms
24 suites

Algonquin Hotel

Manhattan Midtown West

New York's oldest operating hotel was fully renovated in 2004 but remains true to its classically elegant roots and timeless aura. Best known for the circle of literati, including Dorothy Parker and Robert Benchley, who lunched in the Round Table Room in the years after World War I, the Algonquin preserves the feel and look of a fine Edwardian club.

Rooms have been smartly renovated to include all modern amenities (tastefully hidden); top-quality fabrics and fittings lend brightness to the accommodations. You may not want to arise from your pillowtop mattress, 350-thread-count linen sheets, and the famous "Algonquin Bed." (Order one for home, if you like.)

For a taste of 1930s cafe society, step into the Oak Room, the legendary cabaret where famous audiences and performers made merry. The mood lingers, and shows still go on here, with such talent as Andrea Marcovicci and Jack Jones.

Le Parker Meridien

118 W. 57th St. (bet. Sixth & Seventh Aves.)

Subway: 57 St
Phone: 212-245-5000
Fax: 212-307-1776
e-mail: reservations@parkermeridien.com
Web: www.parkermeridien.com
Prices: rooms: $295 - $49   suites: $730 - $2,700   Restaurant: **$$**

691 rooms
40 suites

Le Parker Meridien/Andrew Rortwin

Manhattan Midtown West

The Parker Meridien underwent a complete refurbishment in 2002. Its grand Neoclassical lobby has been updated with modern touches in lighting, seating and carpeting. While the large lobby suits the hotel's size, the service is surprisingly personal. The ergonomic, well-planned accommodations bear the touch of a hotel-savvy designer. They are reasonable in size and uncluttered—streamlined, in fact—with Aeron desk chairs and Scandinavian-style cherry and cedar wood furniture. In the suites, televisions are cleverly mounted to swivel for viewing from any angle.

Get your work-out in at Gravity, the resident fitness club, offering spa services, group fitness classes and a penthouse pool. Fuel up with a good breakfast first at Norma's, which serves breakfast fare until mid-afternoon. For dinner try Seppi's, a French-style bistro, or, for a great burger, check out the rough-and-ready Burger Joint.

Sofitel

45 W. 44th St. (bet. Fifth & Sixth Aves.)

Subway:	47-50 Sts - Rockefeller Ctr
Phone:	212-354-8844
Fax:	212-354-2480
e-mail:	h2185@accor-hotels.com
Web:	www.sofitel.com
Prices:	rooms: $299 suites: $599 Restaurant: **$$$**

346 rooms
52 suites

Sofitel

Combining the best of French and American sensibilities, the Sofitel doesn't feel like a modern, 30-story tower hotel. Rich marble and leather greet guests in the spacious lobby filled with sofas and armchairs. Nicely sized guest rooms are attractively decorated with large windows (ask for a room on a higher floor for better views) and artwork that relates to both New York and Paris. Exceptional marble bathrooms include separate shower and tub.

For cocktails, try Gaby Bar, a stylish lounge in the Art Deco tradition, with plenty of tables and comfortable chairs. Its companion restaurant serves French cuisine with Asian accents. The Sofitel is ideally located for business and leisure travelers between Rockefeller Center and the Empire State Building, and just east of Times Square and the theater district.

Manhattan Midtown West

The Warwick

65 W. 54th St. (at Sixth Ave.)

Subway: 57 St
Phone: 212-247-2700
Fax: 212-247-2725
e-mail: res.ny@warwickhotels.com
Web: www.warwickhotelny.com
Prices: rooms: $245 - $425   suites: $525   Restaurant: **$$$**

359 rooms
67 suites

The Warwick Hotel

Newspaper magnate William Randolph Hearst built the Warwick in 1927 so that his lady friend, Marion Davies, could host their band of Hollywood and theatrical friends in style. The hotel underwent a major facelift in 2001, and the smart guest rooms haven't lost their traditional feeling. Larger than many city hotel rooms, rooms here incorporate slick modern touches such as temperature controls that sense your presence. Go for broke and book the Suite of the Stars, where Cary Grant lived for 12 years; it boasts 1,200 square feet of space and its own wrap-around terrace. For business travelers, high-speed Internet access is available in the business center. There's also an on-site fitness facility.

After working, or working out, dine at Murals under Dean Cornwall's historic paintings. Commissioned by Hearst in 1937, these paintings have now been restored to their original luster.

Manhattan Midtown West

Chambers

15 W. 56th St. (bet. Fifth & Sixth Aves.)

Subway:	57 St
Phone:	212-974-5656
Fax:	212-974-5657
e-mail:	N/A
Web:	www.chambersnyc.com
Prices:	rooms: $325 - $375 suites: $1,600

72 rooms
5 suites
&

Chambers Hotel

Behind its latticework door, the soaring lobby of this sophisticate sets the mood. It's all about art here: the hotel displays over 500 original pieces by young artists. Lobby furnishings and design details in various textures—warm wood floors, leather rugs, velvet sofas—complete the look of a swank town home. On the mezzanine, roving waiters provide refreshments all day, while books, art, and stylish seating create a comfortable atmosphere. Explore the hotel's 14 floors, as each hallway houses a site-specific work of art.

Guest rooms resemble urbane loft spaces with wide-plank hardwood floors and an eclectic but handsome blend of warm and cool materials—gray-washed oak furniture and details in blackened steel, chenille, leather, glass and artist's canvas. Make dinner reservations at Town *(see restaurant listings)* for sophisticated dining.

Manhattan Midtown West

Iroquois

49 W. 44th St. (bet. Fifth & Sixth Aves.)

Subway: 42 St - Bryant Pk
Phone: 212-840-3080
Fax: 212-398-1754
e-mail: reservations@iroquois.com
Web: www.iroquois.com
Prices: rooms: $385 - $485 suites: $610 - $1,090

105 rooms
9 suites

The Iroquois

Well-known, well-kept and comfortable, the historic Iroquois evokes the mood of a private mansion. Modern European furnishings added during a recent renovation suit its 1923 vintage. A cozy library offers a computer with high-speed Internet access as well as a selection of classic books. Rooms are subdued but rich in tone and color; Italian marble bathrooms sparkle in peach and cream. All rooms have both tub and shower, while the nine suites are equipped with Jacuzzis. If you're sleeping in, press the button on your doorknob for privacy. The hotel's 24-hour health club features a Finnish sauna for the ultimate in relaxation.

To dine at Triomphe *(see restaurant listings)*, be sure to make a reservation, as the room is tiny and popular with theatergoers. Given the hotel's queenly grace, it's ironic to remember that bad boy James Dean lived in suite 803 from 1951 to 1953.

Manhattan Midtown West

Casablanca

147 W. 43rd St. (bet. Sixth Ave. & Broadway)

Subway:	42 St - Times Sq
Phone:	212-869-1212
Fax:	212-391-7585
e-mail:	casahotel@aol.com
Web:	www.casablancahotel.com
Prices:	rooms: $199 - $265 suites: $375 Restaurant: **$$**

**37 rooms
5 suites**

Casablanca Hotel

No surprises here—except perhaps that the concept of designing a hotel after the famous Bogart movie works without being kitchsy or overdone. The illusion begins as you enter through the ornate doors into the small tiled lobby, and while there is no nightclub on the premises, up a flight of stairs you'll find a tamer version of the famous Rick's. Complimentary continental breakfast is served here, or you can relax by the fireplace later for tea or champagne. A pianist—not necessarily named Sam—entertains on Fridays. You'll find a computer here to surf or check your e-mail, and high-speed Internet access comes complimentary in each room.

The Casablanca ambience extends into the fair-sized rooms as well, which are furnished with Moroccan-inspired fabrics and carved headboards. Bathrooms are done up nicely in dark and light tile, just exotic enough to evoke a more remote setting than Midtown.

Manhattan Midtown West

City Club

55 W. 44th St. (bet. Fifth & Sixth Aves.)

Subway:	42 St - Bryant Pk
Phone:	212-921-5500
Fax:	212-944-5544
e-mail:	N/A
Web:	www.cityclubhotel.com
Prices:	rooms: $295 suites: $995

62 rooms
3 suites

What started life in 1904 as a gentleman's club is now an urbane and sophisticated hotel. The City Club prides itself on its small, private lobby, more like the entryway to an exclusive residence than to a hotel. On the mezzanine, Salontea seats 12 for a civilized spot of afternoon tea on Thursday through Saturday; the salon doubles as a cocktail lounge at other times.

The rooms are small but set about with pillows and other accessories that make them feel like guest rooms in a swank private home. Handsome black-marble bathrooms include spacious tubs or showers with bidets, a telephone and TV speakers. Truly spectacular are the hotel's three duplex suites, where circular stairways lead up to the sleeping room from a well-appointed sitting room below. For dining, try DB Bistro Moderne *(see restaurant listings)*, which connects to the lobby via a paneled wine bar.

Manhattan Midtown West

Hotels **445**

Metro

45 W. 35th St. (bet. Fifth & Sixth Aves.)

Subway: 34 St - Herald Sq
Phone: 212-947-2500
Fax: 212-279-1310
e-mail: info@hotelmetronyc.com
Web: www.hotelmetronyc.com
Prices: rooms: $165 - $265   Restaurant: **$$**

179 rooms

Hotel Metro/Linda Davis

Though not hip or stylish, the Hotel Metro is nonetheless a good stay for the money. Located in the heart of the Garment District, New York's fashion center, the building was constructed in 1901. An Art-Deco inspired lobby leads into a spacious breakfast room/lounge where complimentary breakfasts are served each morning, and tea and coffee are available during the day.

Guest rooms have been recently refurbished (the Metro opened its doors in 1995) and are equipped with refrigerators. Many of the marble bathrooms benefit from natural light, and the overall standard of housekeeping is good. The hotel now offers high-speed wireless Internet access, as well as a fully equipped business center. From the large rooftop terrace, you'll have stunning views of the Empire State Building and the surrounding neighborhood (which includes Macy's, for all you hard-core shoppers).

The Shoreham

33 W. 55th St. (bet. Fifth & Sixth Aves.)

Subway: 57 St
Phone: 212-247-6700
Fax: 212-765-9741
e-mail: N/A
Web: www.shorehamhotel.com
Prices: rooms: $189 - $399   suites: $499   Restaurant: **$$**

149 rooms
25 suites

The Shoreham

Manhattan *Midtown West*

Step beyond the nondescript façade of the Shoreham into an oasis of modernist chic. Strong, bold, but simple lines, smooth surfaces and carefully balanced décor lend an air of Asian serenity to the spaces, both public and private. While the guest rooms are quite small, they are immaculate and original in décor. Fabric covers the walls and headboards in a restful earth tone, and fresh flowers add dabs of color. You'll luxuriate in the fine Belgian linens that dress the beds, while plush towels, Frette robes and Aveda aromatherapy products await you in the bathroom. All rooms and public areas are equipped with wireless high-speed Internet access.

Located in the heart of Midtown between Fifth and Sixth avenues, the Shoreham is centrally located for shopping, theatergoing, sightseeing and business, and it offers a lot of style for the money.

Roger Williams

131 Madison Ave. (at E. 31st St.)

Subway: 33 St
Phone: 212-448-7000
Fax: 212-448-7007
e-mail: rw-info@hotelrogerwilliams.com
Web: www.hotelrogerwilliams.com
Prices: rooms: $280 - $420

190 rooms
♿
🛁

Manhattan Murray Hill

Hotel Roger Williams

Clean lines and pure color best describe the freshly renovated Roger Williams. In a departure from fashionable dark woods and minimalist palettes of gray and beige, colorful highlights accent light furnishings here. Simple interior design and furniture give "the Roger" a distinctly Scandinavian air. The rooms, 15 with terraces (nice for romantic alfresco dining), feature flat-screen TVs, wireless high-speed Internet access, and modern bathrooms, though some only have showers (no tubs). Most rooms have spectacular views of the nearby Empire State Building.

A "help-yourself" breakfast is available in the Breakfast Pantry, and jazz plays by candlelight several evenings a week in the lounge. Located at 31st Street, the Roger is convenient to Madison Square Garden, Macy's and the trendy nightlife and shopping of Chelsea.

70 Park Avenue

70 Park Ave. (at 38th St.)

Subway:	42 St - Grand Central
Phone:	212-973-2400
Fax:	212-973-2401
e-mail:	info@70parkave.com
Web:	www.70parkavenuehotel.com
Prices:	rooms: $460 - $1,500 suites: $1,100 - $5,000

202 rooms
3 suites

Kimpton New York / David Phelps

Manhattan Murray Hill

In elegance and style, this Kimpton hotel lives up to the fashionable residential neighborhood it occupies. Taking a cue from its historic façade, the interior color scheme, from lobby to guest rooms, ranges from limestone gray to shimmery bronze and light cocoa brown; a sandstone and limestone fireplace makes a notable centerpiece in the cushy lobby. Très chic, yes, but all set in a friendly and relaxing atmosphere; you can even mix and mingle at evening wine receptions.

The rooms, comfortably contemporary, brim with electronic amenities, including phones that feature a touch-screen, keyboards with Internet access, and 42-inch flat-screen TVs. There's wireless Internet access throughout the hotel as well. For dinner, Silverleaf Tavern *(see restaurant listings)*, serves seasonal delights from the Northeastern seaboard. Good news for pet owners: Fido is welcome here.

W - The Tuscany

003

120 E. 39th St. (bet. Lexington & Park Aves.)

Subway: 42 St - Grand Central
Phone: 212-686-1600
Fax: 212-779-7822
e-mail: N/A
Web: www.whotels.com
Prices: rooms: $300 - $480   suites: $450 - $500

111 rooms
11 suites

Starwood Hotels & Resorts

Tucked away on tree-lined 39th Street, not far from Grand Central Station, The Tuscany (not to be confused with its sister spot, W New York-The Court, located on the same block and designed for business travelers) cultivates a sensual, relaxed atmosphere. It begins in the cozy lobby (or "living room" in W speak) done up in luxuriant purples, greens and browns. Velvets and satins, rich woods and supple leather add to the lush feeling of the space, which beckons as a comfortable spot for a drink or a private conversation.

Spacious rooms, highlighted by bold, deep colors and textures, feature original contemporary furnishings. Bathrooms, however, are on the small side. In-room electronics include access to a CD/DVD library. W's signature "Whatever, Whenever" service is available 24/7 by pressing 0 on your cordless, dual-line phone.

The Avalon

16 E. 32nd St. (bet. Fifth & Madison Aves.)

Subway: 33 St
Phone: 212-299-7000
Fax: 212-299-7002
e-mail: rooms@theavalonny.com
Web: www.theavalonny.com
Prices: rooms: $240 - $450   suites: $450 - $750   Restaurant: **$$**

70 rooms
30 suites

The Avalon

A classic boutique property, the Avalon appeals especially to business travelers whose work takes them to the nearby Gramercy Park, lower Madison, Flatiron and Murray Hill areas. The lobby is elegant, if busy with pillars, patterns and paneling. Withdraw to the library/club room, complete with fireplace, for a bit more tranquility.

In addition to its Superior rooms, the hotel has 80 large suites boasting traditional comforts designed in a conventional European style. They are particularly well outfitted for professionals, with three two-line telephones and T1 lines for Internet access; many enjoy a view of the Empire State Building. Each room has two 27-inch television sets, as well. Jacuzzi tubs, bidets and double sinks furnish marble baths in the larger suites. A complimentary continental breakfast is available in the Avalon Bar and Grill, which also serves lunch and dinner.

Manhattan *Murray Hill*

The Mercer

147 Mercer St. (at Prince St.)

Subway: Prince St
Phone: 212-966-6060
Fax: 212-965-3838
e-mail: reservations@mercerhotel.com
Web: www.mercerhotel.com
Prices: rooms: $410 - $1,800

75 rooms

Mercer Hotel/ Thomas Loof

Even if your name isn't Leonardo DiCaprio, Cher or Calvin Klein, you'll be equally welcome at The Mercer. Housed in a striking Romanesque Revival-style building erected in 1890, the hotel caters to the glitterati with discreet, personalized service and intimate elegance. A Zen vibe pervades the guest rooms, fashioned by Parisian interior designer Christian Liaigre with high, loft-like ceilings, large windows that open, and soothing neutral palettes. Spacious baths with oversize marble tubs, 400-thread-count Egyptian cotton sheets, flat-screen TVs, and complimentary access to nearby fitness facilities number among the amenities.

Sure, the hotel offers 24-hour room service, but in this case the food comes from Jean-Georges Vongerichten's Mercer Kitchen *(see restaurant listings)*, located in the basement. Don't fret if you get a room facing the street; soundproofing filters out the noise.

Manhattan SoHo & Nolita

Sixty Thompson

60 Thompson St. (bet. Broome & Spring Sts.)

Subway:	Spring St
Phone:	212-431-0400
Fax:	212-431-0200
e-mail:	info@thompsonhotels.com
Web:	www.60thompson.com
Prices:	rooms: $325 - $505 suites: $525 - $650

87 rooms
11 suites
&

60 Thompson

Manhattan SoHo & Nolita

With its spare 1940s look inspired by French designer Jean-Michel Frank, Sixty Thompson absolutely oozes SoHo style. The lobby, decorated in gray, brown, and moss-green tones, is accented by bouquets of fresh flowers, and natural light floods in from floor-to-ceiling windows. Room sizes vary, but all sport a minimalist look, with crisp, white Frette linens standing out against a wall of dark, paneled leather. (Business travelers take note that Sixty Thompson has replaced the requisite in-room desk with a sitting area in its standard rooms.) Bathrooms are tiled with veined, chocolate-colored marble and stocked with Philosophy spa products.

Be sure to check out the rooftop bar on the 12th floor, where you can sip a cocktail while you drink in great views of the city. Downstairs, Kittichai restaurant *(see restaurant listings)* specializes in Thai cuisine.

Soho Grand

310 West Broadway (bet. Canal & Grand Sts.)

Subway:	Canal St
Phone:	212-965-3000
Fax:	212-965-3200
e-mail:	reservations@sohogrand.com
Web:	www.sohogrand.com
Prices:	rooms: $319 - $459 suites: $3,000 Restaurant: **$$**

365 rooms
2 suites

Soho Grand Hotel

Manhattan SoHo & Nolita

The architecture of this hip hotel (opened in 1996) recalls SoHo's industrial past, from the exposed-brick walls to the superb suspended steel staircase that connects the ground floor to the main lobby. Two metal dog statues stand near the elevator, reminding guests of the Soho Grand's pet-friendly policy—what else would you expect from the same guys who own Hartz Mountain Industries? There's even a fish bowl in every room; if you grow attached to your new fishy friend, you're welcome to take him home with you.

And speaking of rooms, they're done in tones of gray and gold, with large picture windows overlooking the neighborhood. You'll relax in state-of-the-art style with Bose Wave CD/radios, in-room fax machines and broadband Internet connections. If you can't get a reservation at the Soho Grand, the hotel's nearby sister, the Tribeca Grand Hotel, may be able to accommodate you.

Cosmopolitan

95 West Broadway (at Chambers St.)

Subway:	Chambers St
Phone:	212-566-1900
Fax:	212-566-6909
e-mail:	chnyc95@aol.com
Web:	www.cosmohotel.com
Prices:	rooms: $119 - $179

120 rooms

(Cosmopolitan)

Located in the heart of TriBeCa, the Cosmopolitan ranks as the longest continually operated hotel in New York City, dating back to 1853. It's just a five-minute walk from here to Wall Street, SoHo and Chinatown, and the Chambers Street subway station lies practically right outside the door. Newly renovated rooms may be small, simple and practical, but they are perfectly maintained. All guest chambers have private bathrooms and color TVs; ask for a room on the back side of the hotel, if you're worried about the street noise.

The Cosmopolitan doesn't have a restaurant, but for breakfast or a snack, there's a Starbucks coffee shop in the building. Don't expect fawning service or a multitude of amenities, and you won't be disappointed. The cleanliness, location and modest price are reasons enough to stay here.

Manhattan *TriBeCa*

The Carlyle

35 E. 76th St. (at Madison Ave.)

Subway:	77 St
Phone:	212-744-1600
Fax:	212-717-4682
e-mail:	thecarlyle@rosewoodhotels.com
Web:	www.thecarlyle.com
Prices:	rooms: $550 - $850 suites: $950 - $5,000

123 rooms
56 suites

The Carlyle

Since it opened across from Central Park in 1930, The Carlyle has hosted every American president since Truman, along with a roster of foreign dignitaries from Prime Minister Nehru to Princess Diana—how's that for an A-list? Named for British historian Thomas Carlyle, the hotel epitomizes luxury with its fine artwork, Baccarat crystal light fixtures, and nothing-is-too-much-to-ask service. Though small, individually decorated classic (Carlyle-speak for "standard") rooms are dressed with original Audubon prints, fine linens, plush carpets and lavish marble baths.

For entertainment, there's Café Carlyle, where Woody Allen plays on Monday nights, and Bemelmans Bar, decorated with whimsical mural of characters from Ludwig Bemelmans' *Madeline* series. Treat yourself to French fare at Dumonet, (whose title may change in the future, since the the namesake chef no longer mans the kitchen).

The Lowell

28 E. 63rd St. (bet. Madison & Park Aves.)

Subway: Lexington Av - 63 St
Phone: 212-838-1400
Fax: 212-319-4230
e-mail: reservations@lowellhotel.com
Web: www.lowellhotel.com
Prices: rooms: $495 - $825 suites: $1,025 - $5,000

23 rooms
47 suites

The Lowell Hotel

A block from Central Park and hard by Madison Avenue boutiques, The Lowell occupies a landmark 1928 building on a tree-lined Upper East Side street. The hotel's intimate size, discreet staff and sumptuous ambience are the reasons most fans give for coming back time after time. From the moment you step inside the silk-paneled lobby, you'll sense the European elegance that defines The Lowell. Guests here are cosseted in lavish suites, most of which have working fireplaces and private terraces (the Garden Suite has two terraces). A recent renovation added new marble-clad baths—complete with mini TVs—king size, half-canopy beds, new designer fabrics and upgraded kitchens to all accommodations.

Savor a steak in the hotel's clubby Post House restaurant, or drop by the aristocratic Pembroke Room, all swagged in English chintz, for breakfast, afternoon tea or weekend brunch.

Manhattan Upper East Side

The Pierre

2 E. 61st St. (at Fifth Ave.)

Subway: 5 Av - 59 St
Phone: 212-838-8000
Fax: 212-826-8109
e-mail: N/A
Web: www.fourseasons.com/pierre
Prices: rooms: $505 - $960   suites: $725 - $1,230   Restaurant: **$$$**

149 rooms
52 suites
&

The Pierre

Opened in 1930 by Charles Pierre Casalasco, The Pierre has pampered the crème de la crème of New York society for decades. The location of the Neoclassical-style building is unparalleled: overlooking lovely Central Park, The Pierre stands near the prestigious shops of Fifth Avenue—a big plus for hard-core shoppers.

Inside, handmade carpets, silk draperies, and ebullient bouquets of fresh flowers are just a sampling of the luxury that awaits you. Murals abound, from The Rotunda tea room/lounge to the 1,600-square-foot fitness center. Outfitted with wingback chairs, mahogany furnishings, and black and white marble baths, rooms have an old-fashioned elegance; many enjoy city or park views. Elevator operators wearing white gloves epitomize the quality of service at a hotel where the business center and the concierge are available 24 hours a day.

The Regency

540 Park Ave. (at 61st St.)

Subway:	Lexington Av - 63 St
Phone:	212-759-4100
Fax:	212-339-4099
e-mail:	reservations@loewshotels.com
Web:	www.loewshotels.com
Prices:	rooms: $329 - $659 suites: $879 - $3,500 Restaurant: $$$

244 rooms
87 suites

The Regency ▲ Loews Hotel

Manhattan Upper East Side

A recent multimillion-dollar renovation spiffed up this flagship of Loew's hotel properties, just two blocks east of Central Park. Lush fabrics, Frette linens, CD players, and double-paned windows are a few of the amenities you'll find in the contemporary-style rooms—the smallest of which is 225 square feet. Even Fido gets the royal treatment here with his own room-service menu.

Boasting a staff-to-guest ratio of 1 to 1, the hotel delights in serving its guests. Forget your reading glasses? Need a humidifier in your room? The Regency's staff is only too happy to oblige. Business travelers will appreciate rooms equipped with large writing desks, fax/printers, and high-speed Internet access. And for that power breakfast, you need not go any farther than the hotel's 540 Park restaurant. For night owls, Feinstein's at the Regency offers big-name cabaret acts six nights a week.

Bentley

500 E. 62nd St. (at York Ave.)

Subway: Lexington Av - 59 St
Phone: 212-644-6000
Fax: 212-207-4800
e-mail: N/A
Web: www.nychotels.com
Prices: rooms: $139 - $257   suites: $247 - $307   Restaurant: **$$**

161 rooms
36 suites

Manhattan Upper East Side

Bentley Hotel

Trendy it's not, but the Bentley nevertheless offers oversize rooms for a good price in an area that's within walking distance of the shops and restaurants of Midtown and the attractions of Central Park. The Art Deco lobby makes a sleek first impression, with its beige and brown furnishings, boxy lamps and geometric-print area rugs. Belgian linens, down comforters, and streamlined furnishings highlight the comfortable, contemporary-style rooms. In many of them, large windows—especially on the south side—take in views of the East River and the nearby Queensboro Bridge.

If you're not up for going out for dinner, the hotel's rooftop restaurant affords a glittering nighttime panorama of the City That Never Sleeps. Although the Bentley doesn't serve breakfast, guests do have complimentary access to the cappuccino bar (located off the lobby) 24 hours a day.

Wales

1295 Madison Ave. (bet. 92nd & 93rd Sts.)

Subway:	96 St
Phone:	212-876-6000
Fax:	212-860-7000
e-mail:	reservations@waleshotel.com
Web:	www.waleshotel.com
Prices:	rooms: $199 - $375 suites: $269 - $700

64 rooms
23 suites
Spa

Hotel Wales

Manhattan Upper East Side

Built in 1902, the Hotel Wales sits atop Carnegie Hill, on the same block with the mansion of steel magnate Andrew Carnegie. Close to Upper East Side museums (including the Metropolitan Museum of Art), the hotel exudes a countryside feel in its soothing lobby, complete with a fireplace, marble staircase, coffered ceiling and mosaic floor. All rooms profited from a 2000 renovation, which preserved the turn-of-the-20th-century spirit with period furnishings, Belgian linens and sepia-tone photographs of the neighborhood; bathrooms are on the small side.

Spend some time on the rooftop terrace taking in city views, or indulge in a treatment at M Spa. Continental breakfast is served each morning in the Pied Piper Room, decorated as a Victorian-era parlor. The hotel also includes Sarabeth's restaurant, loved by locals for its homemade breads and pastries, and weekend brunch.

Mandarin Oriental

80 Columbus Circle (at W. 60th St.)

Subway: 59 St - Columbus Cir
Phone: 212-805-8800
Fax: 212-805-8888
e-mail: monyc-reservations@mohg.com
Web: www.mandarinoriental.com
Prices: rooms: $625 - $935   suites: $1,600 - $12,595   Restaurant: **$$$**

203 rooms
48 suites

Mandarin Oriental Hotel/George Apostolidis

Occupying floors 35 to 54 in the north tower of the Time Warner Center, the Mandarin Oriental affords sweeping views of Central Park and the city, while bathing its guests in über-luxury. If the views from the floor-to-ceiling windows in your room don't do it for you, walk across the marble-floored lobby to the Lobby Lounge and take in the dramatic panorama while you sip—what else?—a Manhattan.

All of the 251 soundproofed guest rooms reflect subtle elegance with their Oriental color schemes and 1940s-style furnishings; most bathrooms are equipped with soaking tubs set by picture windows. And don't forget about the 14,500-square-foot, full-service spa and the fitness center with its indoor lap pool. Granted, the Time Warner Center contains some must-try restaurants, but why leave the hotel floors when you can enjoy excellent contemporary Asian cuisine at *(see restaurant listings)* Asiate?

Manhattan Upper West Side

Trump International Hotel & Tower

1 Central Park West (at Columbus Circle)

Subway: 59 St - Columbus Cir
Phone: 212-299-1000
Fax: 212-299-1150
e-mail: contactus@trumpintl.com
Web: www.trumpintl.com
Prices: rooms: $645 - $675   suites: $845 - $2,100

38 rooms
129 suites

Trump International Hotel & Tower

Don't let the diminutive lobby fool you; the accommodations here are oh-so-The Donald. Inhabiting the third through the 17th floors of this 52-story tower, the hotel offers luxurious guest rooms and suites that promise spectacular views of Manhattan through their floor-to-ceiling windows. Shades of cinnamon, paprika or sage define the décor, while marble bathrooms, complete with Jacuzzi tubs, invite you for a relaxing soak above the hustle and bustle of the Big Apple. Or, for an even more "at home in the city" feel, choose a suite with a posh European-style kitchen.

Over-the-top amenities include 42-inch plasma TVs, CD and DVD players, personalized business cards, a spa, and in-room catering from the hotel's restaurant Jean-Georges *(see restaurant listings)*. Appropriate for business or pleasure, lodgings at Trump International are that perfect mix of posh yet approachable.

Manhattan *Upper West Side*

On the Ave

2178 Broadway (at 77th St.)

Subway: 79 St
Phone: 212-362-1100
Fax: 212-787-9521
e-mail: reservations@stayinny.com
Web: www.ontheave.com
Prices: rooms: $225 - $395   suites: $425 - $795

259 rooms
7 suites
&

On the Ave Hotel

Only a short walk away from Lincoln Center and Central Park, this early 20th-century structure was recently renovated and updated with early 21st-century accommodations. Flat-screen plasma TVs and Italian black-marble bathrooms will appeal to the cool in you, while the Frette robes and the complimentary Belgian chocolates left on your pillow at turndown will leave you feeling appropriately pampered. Nightly piano music in the lobby makes a nice prelude to a refreshing sleep in feather beds adorned with 310-thread-count Italian cotton linens. Rooms on the top three floors boast balconies and afford views of the Hudson River or the trees of Central Park.

If your room doesn't have a view, take the elevator to the landscaped balcony on the 16th floor; this pleasant space is equipped with Adirondack chairs for relaxing. All this, and a 24-hour business center, too.

Excelsior

45 W. 81st St. (bet. Central Park West & Columbus Ave.)

Subway: 81 St - Museum of Natural History
Phone: 212-362-9200
Fax: 212-580-3972
e-mail: hotelexcel@aol.com
Web: www.excelsiorhotelny.com
Prices: rooms: $169 - $249 suites: $189 - $399

170 rooms
40 suites

Excelsior

Located within a dinosaur bone's throw from the American Museum of Natural History, the 16-story Excelsior sits in the center of the action of the Upper West Side touring scene. Parents can charge to their hearts' delight at the shops on nearby Columbus Avenue, then let the kids lead the charge through Central Park. A country-French motif characterizes the décor of the reasonably priced standard rooms and one- and two-bedroom suites, while newly renovated bathrooms, sporting sparkling white tiles, remind you of why you love to stay in hotels. Bear in mind that while the street-view bedrooms are brighter, the rooms on the back side of the hotel offer peace and quiet.

After a day of museum-hopping, why not retire to the Entertainment Room, where you can work out in the fitness center, peruse the books in the well-stocked library, or simply relax in front of the TV?

Manhattan Upper West Side

Coming soon

Known as "the City which never sleeps," New York is constantly on the move, especially in regard to its ever changing restaurant scene. Here are a few rumors heard by our inspectors while finalizing the selection for the 2006 edition.

After many years of success at Layla, Drew Neiporent has decided to convert the space on West Broadway. Working with Aarón Sanchez, son of New York Mexican legend Zarela Martinez, he has opened **Centrico**, a sunny space featuring various cuisines of Mexico. It is well known that the seats at Nobu and Nobu Next Door are constantly in high demand. Luckily the uptown crowd is about to have a shorter commute with the opening of **Nobu 57**, also from the Myriad family. In the architecturally spectacular but highly-criticized Richard Meier towers, Jean-Georges Vongerichten has struck again. His new restaurant there, aptly named **Perry Street**, home of the southernmost tower, is reportedly already booked for months. After a short hiatus, **Le Cirque** is planning to reopen in the smashing One Beacon Court Condominium, and whether its former home in the Palace Hotel will be filled by something of equal force, we'll have to wait and see. Fans of Hakkasan in London will be excited to know that Alan Yau is bringing his sexy Chinese spot to New York. Hopefully the outpost will also have a Ling Ling lounge, with equally sultry and sleek zen décor. In the Lower East Side Hotel on Rivington, Kurt Guntenbrunner from Wallsé and Café Sabarsky is opening **Thor**, sure to be an instant hot spot. Of course a few more big name chefs are coming to New York to try their toques. Gordon Ramsay is headed this way, though hopefully the cameras will be absent. Joël Robuchon is to open a restaurant, likely in the **Four Seasons Hotel**. One more big hitter is expected at the **Time Warner Center**, and if the stars align, Charlie Trotter will open in early 2006 next to Kunz, Keller and Company.

Of course, this is not a comprehensive list, only a sampling of what is expected to arrive over the next few months. We look forward to next year's edition as we continue our quest to discover new restaurants for the 2007 New York City Michelin Guide.

Notes

Notes

Notes

Notes

Notes

Notes

Notes